Inland Waterways of France

Volume 1 – North and Centre

David Edwards-May

Imray, Laurie, Norie & Wilson Ltd

Published by
Imray, Laurie, Norie & Wilson Ltd
Wych House, St Ives, Cambridgeshire PE27 5BT England
www.imray.com
2021

All rights reserved. No part of this publication may be reproduced, transmitted or used in any form by any means – graphic, electronic or mechanical, including photocopying, recording, taping or information storage and retrieval systems or otherwise – without the prior permission of the publishers.

First published 1956
5th edition 1984
6th edition 1991
7th edition 2002
8th edition 2010
9th edition 2021 (published in three volumes)

© David Edwards-May 2021

David Edwards-May has asserted his right to be identified as the author of this work, including all unattributed photographs, in accordance with the Copyright, Designs and Patents Act 1988.

ISBN 978 178679 304 1

British Library Cataloguing in Publication Data.
A catalogue record for this book is available from the British Library.

CAUTION
While every care has been taken to ensure accuracy, neither the Publishers nor the Author will hold themselves responsible for errors, omissions or alterations in this publication. They will at all times be grateful to receive information which tends to the improvement of the work.

Printed in Croatia by Denona

Contents

PREFACE 1

INTRODUCTION 3

Part I - PLANNING A CRUISE 9

Part II - ROUTE DESCRIPTIONS AND MAPS 23

CHAPTER I – NORTHERN FRANCE 25
1. Dunkirk port and canals (Furnes, Bergues and Bourbourg) 26
2. Liaison Dunkerque-Escaut 30
3. Calais port and Canal de Calais 37
4. Port of Gravelines and River Aa 40
5. River Lys 43
6. Canal de la Deûle 46
7. Canal de Roubaix 50
8. River Scarpe 54
9. Canal du Nord 58
10. Seine-Nord Europe Canal 62
11. Canal de Saint-Quentin 68
12. River Escaut 72
13. Canal de Pommerœul à Condé 75
14. River Sambre and Canal de la Sambre à l'Oise 76
15. Saint-Valery and Canal de la Somme 80

CHAPTER II – RIVER SEINE AND ROUTES EAST AND NORTH 85
16. Lower River Seine (Honfleur to Paris) 86
17. Le Havre port and Canal du Havre à Tancarville 97
18. Paris Canals 99
19. River Oise and Canal latéral à l'Oise 106
20. Canal de l'Oise à l'Aisne 111
21. River Aisne and Canal latéral à l'Aisne 113
22. Canal de l'Aisne à la Marne 116

CHAPTER III – CENTRAL FRANCE 121
23. Upper Seine 122
24. River Marne 128
25. Canal latéral à la Marne 135
26. Canal entre Champagne et Bourgogne 138
27. River Yonne 146
28. Canal de Bourgogne 150
29. Canal du Nivernais 158
30. Canal du Loing 166
31. Canal de Briare 169
32. Canal latéral à la Loire 174
33. Canal du Centre 182
34. Canal de Roanne à Digoin 187
35. Canal d'Orléans 190
36. River Cher and Canal du Berry 193

INDEX 196

Companion volumes
Inland Waterways of France – Volume 2: Northeast and Southeast
Inland Waterways of France – Volume 3: South and West

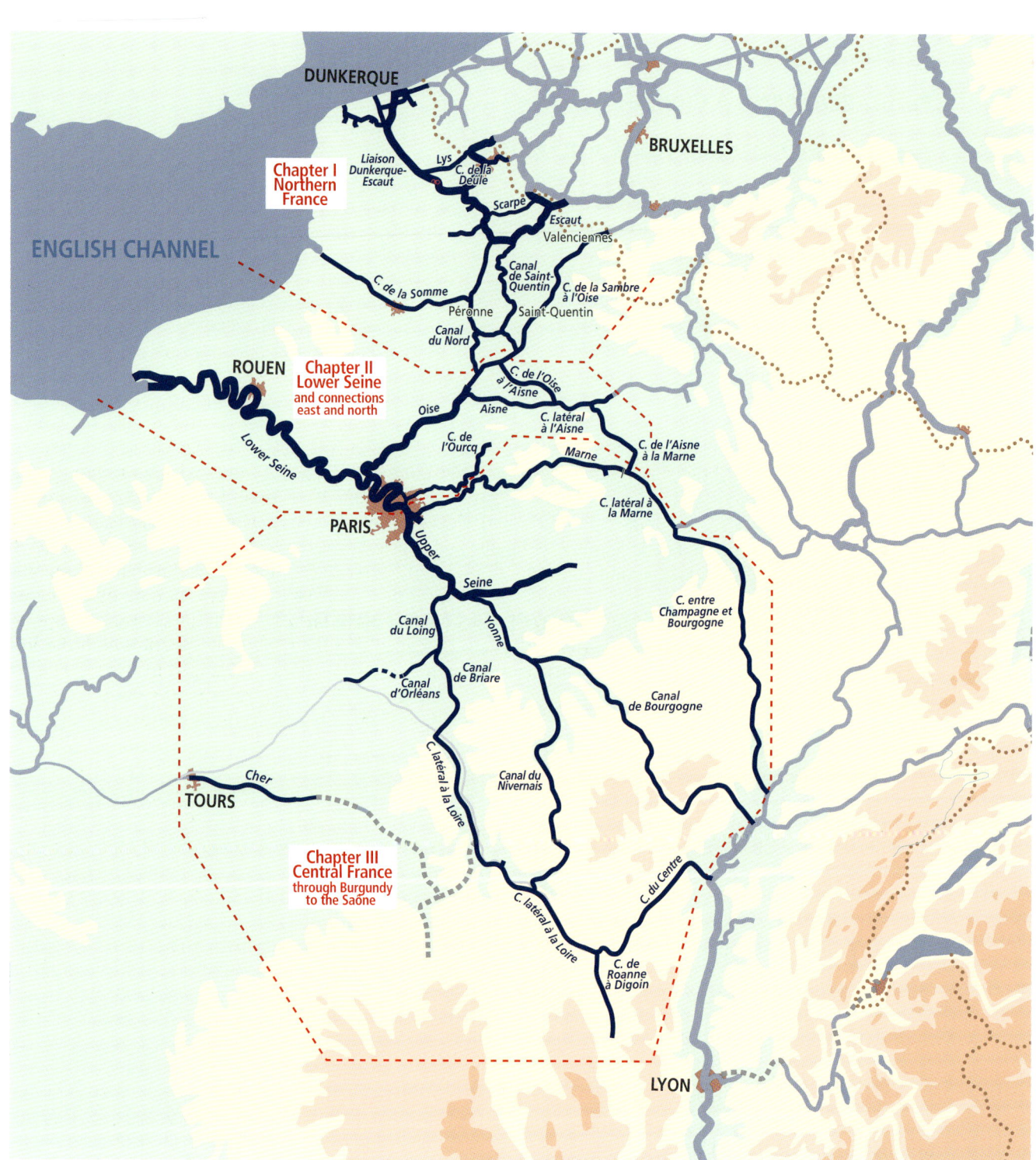

Preface

The ways of enjoying the uniquely diverse and appealing waterways of France are changing. In this digital age, we felt that it was important to publish products that would be of greatest practical use, not only to boaters but also to all the other waterway users who are increasingly attracted to the canal towpaths and river valleys. This work was first published two thirds of a century ago as a single volume presenting nearly 80 waterways in alphabetical order. However, boat ownership, cruising habits, leisure and lifestyle choices have changed significantly over the years, and the extent of useful information has expanded.

Consequently, the 9000 kilometres of navigable waterways in France are now covered by three volumes. This Volume 1 covers Northern France down to the capital region Île-de-France, central France and Burgundy. Volume 2 presents the waterways from the northeast to the southeast, hence the classic cruising itineraries from Northern Europe to the Mediterranean Sea via the Rivers Meuse, Moselle, Sarre or Rhine, converging on the 'common trunk' of the Saône and Rhône. Volume 3 brings together all the other navigable waterways, from Southern France (the 'Midi') via the rivers flowing into the Atlantic Coast, to the remarkable network of canals and canalised rivers in Brittany.

Among the reasons for expanding into three volumes is the insertion of descriptive texts – and more images – into the itineraries, to do better justice to the varied places encountered along the waterways. The new texts break up the former 'distance tables'. These texts do not pretend to replace tourist guides for the places visited, but give some context and tips, relating either to the mooring facility itself or to the corresponding town or village.

For convenience and reference, the sequence of eight chapters is continued through the three volumes. This volume 1 includes Chapter I, Northern France, Chapter II, River Seine and connections east and north, and Chapter III, Central France. Each volume has its separate index. We hope that all those who love exploring the French waterways, or who are planning future adventures, will find all three of the expanded, split publications both an inspiration to extend their own travels and practical to use while actually navigating on the system.

As author I am indebted to James Newcombe for his contributions and extensive feedback from users. His website, **french-waterways.com**, reproduces much of the contents of this work, and by agreement with Imray is the place to go for updates for any specific route or waterway.

Imray's editor Jane Russell was a forensic proof-reader whose corrections and suggestions have added significant value to the guide. Both Jane and Imray's managing director Lucy Wilson gave constant guidance and encouragement during the preparation of this work, and for that the author is truly grateful.

Voies Navigables de France has given the author meaningful support for this edition, as in the past, through its Development Department and the unit in charge of waterway tourism and services to users, with special thanks to Aurélie Millot, Nicolas Delaporte and Adrien Quivoron. VNF is to be credited for its efforts to develop 'green' navigation by providing battery charging stations on the waterways of the northeast: the Canal de la Sarre and Canal de la Marne au Rhin. With significant post-pandemic recovery funding by the French Government, agreed in 2021 with the Grand Est region, it is to be hoped that the rest of the system – both the VNF network and the waterways managed by the regions and départements – will be similarly equipped as soon as possible, gradually making navigation greener and quieter.

The author is also grateful to the many contributors of photographs as well as information updates and corrections since the last edition was produced.

I would like to thank here my family and friends who have accompanied me in my own travels on the waterways in the last 10 years, Padraic Neville, who cycled with me on the towpaths from Givet to Paris in 2017, and Thierry and Catherine Eschbach, owners of the 1600-tonne *Bucentaure*, for the memorable voyage on the Seine from Tancarville to the Port of Gennevilliers in February 2019.

Finally, my thanks to all boaters, *plaisanciers* and *Sportsschiffer* – and the surviving *mariniers* in their 220-tonne barges – for their confidence and continued reference to this work.

David Edwards-May, July 2021

For Irène
For Raymonde and in memory of Edouard Desouche

A single-barge sand push-tow heads upstream out of Poses lock. The Seine is tidal below this lock.
© PIERRE CHEUVA/DOC VNF

Introduction

FRANCE IS THE WORLD'S number one holiday destination, and the country's waterways have become increasingly popular with tourists from across the world. River cruise ships ply all the high-capacity (*grand gabarit*) waterways, making up one fifth of the network of around 8500 km; hotel barges offer all-inclusive cultural and gastronomic cruises on the smaller canals; comfortable self-drive boats may be hired at nearly a hundred locations. Considering the value of all these products and the €2 billion of economic activity generated annually, there is understandably a keen awareness among decision-makers – in the French Government and in the various regions concerned – of the importance of maintaining the waterway infrastructure for all these operators, as well as for the commercial traffic, their prime vocation, and providing moorings and services to meet the constantly increasing demand. While hopefully of value also to these other waterway interests, this book – since its first edition in 1956 – has been addressing the particular needs of a user that has often received less attention than the commercial waterway tourism operators: the private boat owner. This is the user category that commands respect for having started waterway tourism in France all those years ago. The boats have changed, becoming larger and more comfortable for living aboard, and the cruising practices even more so, becoming slower and more sustainable, but it is striking how the enthusiasm of boat owners for France as a destination to enjoy through her waterways seems to endure all the possible causes for discouragement. And there have been a few such causes over the years.

When the previous edition of this work was produced, the national managing body *Voies Navigables de France*, set up in 1991, had recently been instructed by the Government to concentrate its efforts on the commercially viable routes, making up less than half of the national network. The canals of Burgundy had been handed over experimentally to Burgundy Region, a move that seemingly announced the dismemberment of the national network. In fairness to the policy-makers, the principle of transfer of management or even ownership simply takes one stage further the process of devolved administration that began with the concessions to the *départements*, starting with the Brittany canals and Anjou rivers in the 1960s, continuing with the Nivernais in 1971 and the Somme west of Péronne in 1992. However, there is a fundamental difference between these concessions and the situation in the period 2010-2013. In the above examples, local authorities voluntarily accepted to manage the waterways on behalf of the State for a fixed concession period, to keep them open. The Government allocated budgets to renovate structures as required, and made available State employees through the public works administration for each *département*. In short, there was plenty of sugar to help the medicine go down. In recent years, the State has been presenting to regional or local authorities what amounts to an ultimatum: 'take over this sensitive and vulnerable infrastructure, or we close it down'! The experimental management by Burgundy Region was stopped after two years, after it was found by the regional council to be unfeasible. This is the administrative echelon with the least resources, the most recently created (1983) and with neither the organisation nor the experience required to take on such responsibilities. This created a hiatus, and concern among all parties involved in boating and development of waterway tourism. In the absence of any agreement on transfer, all progress in resolving the difficulties inevitably arising on the network was blocked.

In 2013 another significant change was made, when VNF was made an administrative arm of the State, still empowered to collect revenue but no longer a purely commercial body (*établissement public d'intérêt industriel et commercial*, EPIC). The change was brought about largely by a typically French struggle with all the accompanying industrial action and drumbeating. The thousands of public servants on the Ministry's payroll, 'made available' to the commercial body since 1991, refused to give up their *fonctionnaire* status to be employed directly by VNF. The change of status to an *établissement public administratif* enabled a return to a more unified management.

The waterways (in any country, it should be added) are under permanent threats that are more real than the consequences of any administrative and policy decisions: deterioration of the structures, under the combined effects of age and aggression by extreme climate events. This has been the case for a number of canals in recent years. The deal proposed by the Government, through VNF, to the regions and *départements* crossed by little-used rural canals was already unattractive for many while the canals were operating. Imagine how much more difficult the negotiations became after structures failed or the canals silted up, making them impassable!

The French political culture takes brinkmanship to extremes. The worst possible outcome feels certain to occur. Then, at the eleventh hour, pragmatism kicks in and all is resolved! The processes are fascinating to observe, and I have had the privilege of being involved for more than 35 years, but for the foreign boaters whose plans may be thwarted by closure of part of their intended route, the short-term picture may seem bleak.

Fortunately, in 2021, several dramatic situations have been turned round and waterways restored, and with some local nuances the show goes on. I predict that there will be a heightened appreciation of French waterways and all they have to offer as the world comes out of the COVID-19 pandemic that has changed so much in our lives. More

French boaters will hopefully join the ranks of the boaters from many other countries, especially the UK, Germany, the Netherlands, Belgium and the Scandinavia, and grow the numbers of boats cruising through most of the year. After the overview of recent developments on the smaller waterways, I will come back to the main VNF network of high-capacity waterways.

Regional and local waterways

After a series of closures of French waterways in recent years, it is heartening that two routes were reopened in 2021.

The **Canal de la Sambre à l'Oise** welcomed boats for the first time in 15 years on July 1, 2021, following a €23.5 million programme of works including the reconstruction of its two aqueducts, dating from 1836 and 1837, renovation of 25 locks on the Oise side of the summit level, and dredging to a depth of 1.60m for the passage of recreational boats. The locks were equipped for automatic operation, and a large volume of marsh pennywort (*hydrocotyle vulgaris*) had to be removed: 30 000 m² was cleared of the weed in 2020.

This success was obtained by vigorous local campaigning and lobbying, and underlined how the future of the waterways can only be guaranteed by bringing together the widest possible partnership. VNF, under pressure from the Ministry of Finance in Bercy, would have let the canal fall into ruin without substantial co-funding of the restoration project by the Hauts-de-France region and the *département* Aisne. The lobbying by local authorities was supported by the international boating community, including DBA The Barge Association and Inland Waterways International, whose members signed an on-line petition. This took the local stakeholders by surprise, and helped them to obtain the exceptional contribution from the Government, enabling VNF to commit to three quarters of the cost.

Local bodies including *Réussir notre Sambre* designed a tourism development strategy to maximise the benefits of the restored waterway. This includes rehabilitating lock cottages to give them new use, improving tourism infastructure and developing the canalside cycleway (*véloroute voie verte*). The partners agreed to share the annual operating costs, estimated at €2.3 million, for a period of 20 years, during which it is hoped that the itinerary will become a magnet and generate economic benefits for the seven districts and the region as a whole.

The **Canal des Ardennes** was closed for a shorter period – just three years – after a lock wall the collapsed at Neuville-Day during an extreme flood on a small stream, and was reopened to navigation on May 1st 2021. Here too, the canal would have been sacrificed by the number-crunchers in Bercy without a concerted effort by the region and Ardennes *département*. VNF signed a 'contract for the territory' with the Grand Est region in October 2020, injecting €43 million into waterway investments in the vast region over the following two years. To be eligible for part of this fund, the *département* Ardennes and the local districts (groups of communes) were required to submit a coherent tourism development plan, with services and activities that will attract tourists to the canal, both by boat and along an extension of the highly successful Trans-Ardennes cycle route, which runs 121 km from above Sedan to Givet. Again, the successful conclusion of this project demonstrates how real the risk of dismemberment of the network has been in recent years. Even before the flood damage occurred at Neuville-Day, this canal was on the list of little-used routes to be 'remaindered', to use the English word in use during the late 1960s, when the equivalent axe was poised above many English canals. Up to 20% of VNF's waterways were under threat of being no longer operated, hence the new French word *dénavigation*, which for several years was on the lips of every civil servant involved in setting VNF's budget.

The **lower River Lot** was extended in April 2021 by the opening of the restored lock at Saint-Vite. This is the eighth lock from the Garonne at Nicole, and was rebuilt in a combined investment with construction of a new adjacent hydropower plant. A grouping of local and international associations has been formed to promote restoration of the remaining missing links upstream.

The first boat through Saint-Vite lock in April 2021

Studies are in progress for a travel-lift solution at Fumel dam, estimated at €500 000 for the lift itself, plus €3.5 million for road access, the actual ramps down into the river above and below the dam, and cutting an approach channel to the ramp from downstream. The project would be funded 50% by the *département* Lot-et-Garonne. A lock here would cost €16 million, which it is believed would have no chance of being approved in the short term. The *tour de table* securing investment in the waterway is more complex than in the two cases examined above. Despite the spectacular progress overall (three quarters of the total length restored and navigable), there are marked contrasts between the 'grand scheme' promoted at the interregional level and the agendas of each *département* involved. For several years the Lot *département* adopted

Introduction

One of the most emblematic sites on the French waterways is the Briare aqueduct on the Canal latéral à la Loire, opened in 1896. © SYLVAIN CAMBON

a short-sighted policy, being content to reap the benefits of its 64 km long section with 14 locks opened in 1991. Downstream, Lot-et-Garonne theoretically had the advantage of being connected to the main network. This left Aveyron, upstream, in isolation. When local politicians succeeded in getting the *département* to apply for funding to start restoration at the upstream end of the 266 km waterway, this was opposed by the Lot council, its downstream neighbour! The latter was under pressure from its own local authorities to extend the navigable length, in particular on a new section around Puy-l'Évêque, and tried to divert the funds allocated to Aveyron on the grounds that navigation was not feasible upstream. Their arguments were rejected, and the first 11 km section of the river in Aveyron was opened in 2010. This inside story is only an anecdote, but it serves to underline the risks inherent in the current situation, with planning responsibilities inadequately defined and distributed. The *départements* are also continuing to refuse outright ownership of the waterway, which is maintained and operated by each of the three authorities under the legal regime of *authorisation*. The implications of the change in the river basin authority, from an *entente* to a *syndicat mixte*, are too complex and subtle to develop here; suffice it to say that the political force of the five *départements* of the Lot valley has diminished, while both the French Government and the European Commission have pulled the plug on further investments to complete the project started in 1987. *La lutte continue!*

The history of the **Roubaix Canal** restoration project is also revealing of the difficulty in securing the long-term future of canals for inland navigation. In September 2003, when the EU's INTERREG secretariat suggested that the restoration project could be submitted for funding, the local partners were willing to go ahead, but the owner VNF was reluctant to commit itself in contradiction with national policy. Instructions from the ministry were to focus exclusively on the priority network. The mayor of Roubaix succeeded in persuading VNF to be lead partner of the Blue Links project, but VNF insisted that a new owner and operator had to be identified and in place within two years. The *Région* Nord-Pas de Calais refused, which left Lille Métropole as the only 'candidate'. Here the incentive of the EU funding and the cross-border nature of the project meant that the dynamic was maintained despite this difficulty. Eventually *Lille Métropole* agreed in October 2009 to take over canal operation and maintenance for an experimental period of two years starting in May 2010. Boaters and readers of this guide played no small part in this successful outcome, by turning up in significant numbers at the highly successful 'Blue Days' rally at the Union site in Roubaix on September 19-20, 2009. The onerous tasks of operating this essentially urban canal, with its 12 locks and 8 moving bridges, and water supply by back-pumping, has forced the Lille metropolitan council to the brink of a decision to close the canal to navigation, on several occasions in recent years.

The 'northern branch' of the **Canal du Rhône au Rhin** was to be reopened by 2010, establishing a direct connection for boats between Strasbourg and Colmar, but unlike the Roubaix Canal, this project was not completed. This itinerary, avoiding the Rhine, would be open to the hire boats operating in the region. The canal had already been closed, which made it impossible for VNF to operate the completed waterway, even temporarily; it could only be project engineer for the restoration works. These started in 2006, but a year later Alsace regional council interrupted the works. The decision was motivated partly by escalation of costs; the final bill was going to be double the €7 million originally budgeted. But the main reason was that operation and maintenance were going to be entirely at the local authorities' expense, without any contribution or staff available from the French Government, through VNF. The region's intention was then to explore how the half-restored canal could be made to work as an asset without being navigable. The regional council agreed to fund the works after Colmar led a vigorous campaign, securing the support of all riparian municipalities for a sensible compromise solution: Alsace would foot the bill for the works, but the local councils together would operate and maintain the canal. This sequence of events underlined several aspects of the situation throughout the network: first, the *région* was ill-equipped to take on the management of inland waterways; secondly, the economic benefits of waterway tourism are perceived more keenly at the local than at the regional level; consequently, local authority groupings are likely to be increasingly involved in future governance models. This project is now unlikely to be completed in the near future, also because one completely new lock is required to connect the old canal with the lowered pound above lock 75, where the connecting canal from the Rhine enters.

The sorry spectacle of lock 67 on the Canal du Rhône au Rhin in 2017, just north of Marckolsheim; The lock is fully restored while the canal itself remains impassable. Bank consolidation is required before the canal could be filled to its normal depth, but the Region Grand Est no longer wants to complete this project

The **Brittany canals** are complex, because there is an additional level of authority between the *région*, which owns the system, and the *départements*. Public institutions were set up in the 1960s and 1970s to operate and maintain some waterways, while others continued to be managed directly. These bodies were rendered redundant after the *Région Bretagne* took over. Prospects are now good for the system, since the regional council has recognised their importance for tourism inland, and is continuing to make substantial investments in restoration and dredging. There remains a threat to integrity of the network because of an ongoing campaign to demolish the weirs on the canalised rivers. The main advocates of weir demolition on the Aulne and the Blavet are the angling community and their representative organisations, who want to encourage migrating fish species to return to these rivers. After careful study of the impacts of weir removal, the idea was abandoned as unfeasible. Regional ownership of the waterways has been instrumental in avoiding this scenario of demolition, but the 'return to nature' movement is constantly in ambush, which means that vigilance and education are also a constant challenge. On the other hand, the region is not pursuing the project to build a bypass at the 1923 Guerlédan dam on the **Canal de Nantes à Brest**. The possible solution shown in this book is to be considered as a 'local project'. Local politicians are indeed still pushing hard, and have suggested that the bypass could be completed by about 2025, where the region's reluctance could perhaps be compensated by EDF, owner of the structure. It was EDF's duty under their original concession to ensure the continuity of navigation. In the absence of an act of parliament relieving them of that obligation, it remains in force.

The partnership needed to keep a canal properly maintained and operating, as in the above examples, can never be a foregone conclusion. One VNF waterway that has regrettably been downgraded to canoeable status is the **Scarpe inférieure** between Douai and Saint-Amand-les-Eaux. This was another closure forced by a structural failure, the lift-bridge at Lallaing, in the early 2000s. This made the newly opened *port de plaisance* at Saint-Amand-les-Eaux a *cul-de-sac*. Making the port accessible at least from the downstream junction with the Escaut was indispensable, and a practical solution was found relatively quickly in this case. Operating staff were provided by the community of communes for the Porte du Hainaut district, and are assigned during the season to the lowest two locks on the river. Saint-Amand nevertheless sees little traffic, but the authorities refuse to spend the €15 million required to dredge the waterway and restore its locks and lift bridges. In the absence of local commitment equivalent to that for the Canal des Ardennes, for example, the Scarpe inférieure remains closed. VNF continues to monitor the waterway for hydraulic continuity, and carry out minimal maintenance to ensure efficient conveyance of flood flows, and may count the occasional canoe. This is a sad destiny for the once essential industrial waterway featuring in the novels of Émile Zola.

In other parts of the network, the *départements* have been pursuing their projects without regional support. This is the case of the *Région* Centre, which does not appear to have a strategy for its historic waterways. This may be because they form a disparate and disconnected network, but it is no less regrettable. The **canalised River Cher** suffered a serious setback when the upstream *département* Loir-et-Cher stopped all works on the construction of two new gated weirs, designed to replace dangerous needle weirs. As on the Canal du Rhône au Rhin south of Strasbourg, described above, the authority was alarmed by the escalating cost of the works. A further difficulty stemmed from the local interpretation of the EU's Water Framework Directive. Civil servants, prompted by anglers and environmentalists, saw the possibility of downgrading the river from a canalised or 'heavily modified' state to a natural water body, in other words free-flowing. The downstream *département* of Indre-et-Loire has been resisting this move, supported by the Association *Les Amis du Cher Canalisé*, but negotiations are complex. The State bodies which issue authorisations for works on rivers are insisting that all weirs, old or new, should not be raised until the end of the fish-spawning season on 1st July each year, which naturally calls into question the feasibility of the weir rebuilding programme. The current situation is an unsatisfactory stalemate.

The neighbouring *département* of Loiret has made remarkable progress in restoration of the **Canal d'Orléans**, although the difficulties of water supply to the central summit level section have to date prevented completion of this valuable project. This narrow canal is expected to be opened to electrically-powered craft only, but even that now appears to be a remote prospect.

Another case where spectacular progress was made in the period 2000-2010 is the **Upper Rhône**, which remains a State-owned waterway, theoretically in the priority network for development of navigation, despite having been abandoned more than 70 years ago! Two-lock bypasses were built at the hydropower plants built by CNR at Chautagne and Belley. The Upper Rhône, like the river Loire, serves to cool a nuclear power station, and that is the argument for maintaining the 'officially navigable' status, while navigation is an optional extra to be negotiated on a case-by-case basis. The Upper Rhône scheme faced opposition from environmentalists, whose main concern was to kill for ever any prospect of a Rhine-Rhône waterway by this route and through the Swiss lakes and the canalised river Aar to the Rhine. When the Upper Rhône project was studied in 1999-2000, the *Verts* wanted the locks to be built to smaller than Freycinet dimensions, precisely to prevent any commercial use of the waterway. Recreational boating, in their short-sighted view, could be tolerated as being intrinsically more compatible with protection of the environment. Fortunately this attempt to downgrade the project was resisted, and the new locks were built to Freycinet dimensions, like the earlier lock at La Feyssine in Lyon, built in the 1980s. Despite the lack of navigable connection with the main system at Lyon, the new locks opened up a remarkable cruising area in the heart of the Alps, extending 75 km with five locks, and this is my local waterway, with the delightful canalside village of Chanaz on the natural Canal de Savières. Works are to start soon on construction of a new lock to bypass the hydropower plant at Brégnier-Cordon, which will add 30 km to this navigation.

The **Upper Canal de la Somme** is another missing link in the network, which could receive funding as a spinoff from the Seine-Nord Europe Canal project, to restore the 16 km long canal with four locks through the small town of Ham. The canal became silted up and closed in 2006.

These are just a few examples of recent developments on the system. Many other stories could be told, of projects successfully completed or frustrated by political or funding difficulties, as may be experienced in any country. Overall, the situation in France is no more alarming than, say, in Germany or the UK. The risk of cuts in public spending, whether for investments or to subsidise bodies giving a public service, is universal. The main challenges are environmental: to ensure that water resources are not diverted from canal supply to other functions, and to prevent 'downgrading' of river navigations to free-flow conditions by the removal of weirs, as promoted by those who assume, often without foundation, that demolition of structures built 200 years ago will automatically make the rivers more appealing for shad, salmon and other migrators.

To conclude this overview of the smaller waterways, the fact that tourism is France's biggest export industry has justified enormous investments in waterway restoration schemes, adding hundreds of kilometres to the length of the waterway network. It is not unreasonable to predict that the institutional difficulties outlined here will eventually be resolved, as long as we users keep making our voices heard. The inevitable questioning of budget commitments at the State level, and the brinkmanship mentioned above, will doubtless lead to more scares in the future, adding to those caused by extreme climate events.

There will inevitably be some frustrations, as boaters encounter stoppages or cutbacks in service and have to change their plans accordingly. The most frequent incidents are likely to be restrictions on the use of locks across the summit level canals, even closure during extreme drought, but there can be no doubt that the waterways provide the key to enjoyment of many French regions, with all their diversity, their history and culture, their gastronomy and wines. Towns and villages alike have awoken to the vast potential, and are gradually developing boat moorings of varying configurations and size, from the landscaped quay or pontoons, generally referred to by the term *halte nautique*, to the fully-equipped boat harbour or *port de plaisance*. We use the French terms in this guide because they are are so conveniently descriptive. These facilities and the associated information, activities and services will help the boater to get the maximum enjoyment from the cruising experience.

Integrated network for water transport

It feels strange to be heralding impending change in this edition in almost the identical terms to those used in 2010, when I referred to the 'imminent start of works on the new Seine-Nord Europe Canal' but such is the reality of the French Government's seemingly chronic hesitations regarding the waterways and the future role of inland water transport. At least now, works on the first of four sections of the 107 km long canal between Compiègne and Aubencheul-au-Bac, are genuinely taking place. Interconnecting the high-capacity (*grand gabarit*) waterways in the interests of Europe as a whole remains VNF's objective and *raison d'être*. A *société de projet* was created by Government decree in December 2016, and a parallel European Economic Interest Group for financial management including toll collection. Management of the project was transferred from the State to the region Hauts-de-France and its four *départements* in 2019. This is a strategic EU infrastructure project. The European Commission is convinced of the intrinsic value of this investment, along with others in the 'Connecting Europe Facility', justifying a 50% contribution to the total cost.

A carefully conducted process of studies and consultations had resulted in a consensus among all parties, massively in favour of the project. That was before the economic crisis, followed by the change of government in 2012. The projected cost, based on a public-private partnership, had by then increased from €4.2 to nearly €7 billion. A commission was set up to study possible savings. Its report was presented in late 2013, and suggested a route following the existing Canal du Nord for 8 km and eliminating one lock, lowering the summit level by 18.5 m. This modified route was formally adopted in 2018. The canal is divided into four distinct sections for the works and contracts, starting from the southern end. The first section along the river Oise should open in 2027, and the rest of the canal in 2028.

The link is projected to increase waterborne traffic on the Paris-Lille axis from 4 million to 13-15 million tonnes per year by 2030. Nearly all this traffic would be transferred from the A1 motorway, the busiest in France.

Implementation of the project should confirm a deep trend, which shows waterway projects as giving a greater overall return on investment than when analysis was based on freight transport alone. A major factor in gaining favour among all politicians was full consideration of the external costs of transport (including accidents, congestion and pollution), which economists and waterway lobbyists had been campaigning for since the 1960s. It was gratifying to see that the arguments were at last taken into consideration. The European Commission and Parliament have played a major role in this process, by pushing for proper accounting of these external costs, estimated at 8% of Europe's GDP.

Environmental concerns, particularly in the Somme valley, are met by routing the canal on the flank of the valley instead of along the bottom. The canal will have 5 locks, their depth ranging between 13 and 26 m, with a sixth lock (6 m rise) on the river Oise above Compiègne.

At least two other significant projects are going ahead. The first, now practically complete, is upgrading to Class Va of the **Canal du Rhône à Sète**, to improve the competitive position of the port of Sète; the second is upgrading to Class Vb of the **Upper River Seine** from Bray to Nogent.

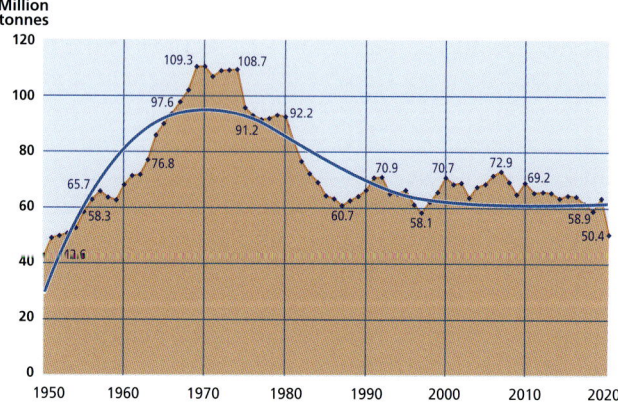

The graph for freight traffic on French waterways, including transit on the Rhine, shows a relative stagnation since the mid-1980s: approximately 65 million tonnes transported annually, for around 8.2 billion tonne-kilometres. The boost expected from the Canal Seine-Nord Europe is now on the horizon, but 2020 showed a significant decline on account of the pandemic.

When the entire Seine basin (a quarter of the French population and economy), already served by high-capacity waterways, is interconnected with the main European network, the mindset of politicians and industry will be radically transformed, and the climate could change for the other major project first conceived by the Roman General Vetus: the North Sea-Mediterranean link between the Moselle and the Saône. Discussions to revive this project started at the regional level a few years after the original project for the Rhine-Rhone waterway was abandoned by Environment Minister Dominique Voynet in 1997. It is premature to talk of a replacement project, because Alsace is not prepared to abandon its interest. Accordingly, the preliminary investigations of the potential for a new Saône-Moselle waterway include the possibility of a branch across the Vosges to link up with the high-capacity waterway in the Mulhouse area. This would roughly correspond to the historic Canal de Montbéliard à la Haute-Saône, which was never completed. The first timid move was made by the *Régions* Lorraine and Rhône-Alpes in 2004, when the question asked of consultants, with support from central Government and the other regions concerned (Bourgogne and Franche-Comté) was simply: is it worth studying the feasibility of a high-capacity waterway to link the Rhine and Rhône basins? The answer was yes, and the Ministry of Sustainable Development approved the subject for a national public debate which was supposed to be organised by VNF in 2012. Although the debate was cancelled, the broad vision of a French waterway system fully integrated in the European waterway network, used for bulk freight and combined transport, remains alive.

In the meantime, the bulk of VNF's investment programme concerns improvements to ageing infrastructure on the existing high-capacity network. New gated weirs have been built on the Oise and bridges are being rebuilt on the Liaison Dunkerque-Escaut to offer the new standard headroom of 7.00m, although some bottlenecks with bridges at 5.25m are likely to remain for at least 10 years.

The limited improvements made to the existing network have proved successful, contributing to a significant increase in overall traffic on the French waterways in recent years. As the graph shows, a 25% increase in tonnage transported was achieved by inland water transport between the low in 1997 and the pre-recession peak in 2007, and the industry has fared better than railway freight since then.

The owner-skippers of *péniches* carrying about 220 tonnes also continue to provide a useful service, but would like to see more maintenance of the canals they operate on. They are concerned that the current policy could gradually make commercial operation unfeasible on the smaller waterways.

On the bigger picture, the long-term trend suggests that the post-war peak of the early 1970s could be reached again by around 2030 or 2035, and the new Seine-Nord Europe Canal would clearly make a significant contribution to this growth.

Part I – Planning a cruise

9000 kilometres of cruising waterways

France has the most extensive waterway network in Europe, offering an extraordinary variety of scenery, tourist interest and cruising conditions. Water-borne transport remains the prime function over about a third of the network and remains a minority user over another quarter. That leaves almost half the above total maintained essentially for tourism and other functions not related to commercial navigation. The current situation and recent developments are described in the *Introduction*.

Recreation is accepted as one of the main justifications for maintaining the waterways, and considerable development has taken place accordingly. Harbours and attractive moorings for boats have sprung up at an astonishing rate, here as well as on all the busiest waterways: Rhine, Seine, Moselle, Saône and Rhône. In short, commercial traffic is no obstacle to safe and pleasant cruising, provided certain precautions are taken. This having been said, it is obvious that readers without previous cruising experience (or having only cruised on the English canals, for example) should study the CEVNI rules to be fully acquainted with all navigation signs and rules of the road. It is preferable to keep initially to the smaller waterways, if possible, where commercial traffic has ceased or is very slight. Inevitably mistakes will be made, but these are better made on the quiet canals of Burgundy, amongst fellow boaters, than in the centre of Paris amongst the *bateaux-mouche* and commercial barges.

Regulations – an overview
Notes by Tam and Di Murrell

(a) Registration documents

Formalities for boats entering France have been greatly simplified. Boat owners wishing to cruise in France, regardless of where and how they arrive, will need the boat's registration documents. Along with the other requirements set out on the following paragraphs, this will permit a stay without fiscal or other complications. The restriction on movements of UK citizens entering France, whose stay is now limited to 180 days, does not apply to their boats permanently moored in France.

Registration is a legal requirement. A boat takes its flag normally from either the nationality of the owner or the country of residence of the owner. Most countries have a simple register and a more complex one, which involves further checks, and tonnage and measurement surveys. In the UK, the Small Ships Register is the simple form of registration, and the Part 1 is the more involved register. Both have the same legal validity throughout the world, and they are both issued by the Registry of Shipping and Seamen in Cardiff (02920 747 333).

(b) VAT documentation

VAT paid in one EU country is recognised throughout the EU and import can be made for an indefinite period without complication. The only conclusive proof that a boat is 'VAT paid' is the original VAT certificate, which is issued to the original owner of a new boat and subsequently passed on to future owners. However, a variety of VAT exemptions apply to boats, and it is important for the traveller to become familiar with these rules prior to going abroad. For readers in the UK, the best place to get hold of this information is from the Revenue and Customs website, where various notices are available on line and can be downloaded. The address for Revenue and Customs is **http://customs.hmrc.gov.uk**. Particularly relevant is Notice 8 *Sailing your pleasure craft to and from the United Kingdom*. This summarises the main VAT rules, including the possibility of applying for exemption from VAT in the UK if the boat is to be permanently located in the EU under the 'Sailway' scheme. Then of course VAT will have to be paid in the destination country, as well as import duty. The site also explains the rules relating to temporary importation. Owners may bring their boat into the EU and use it for up to 18 months in a 2-year period without being liable for VAT.

HMC Notice 200 gives further details on temporary import, while notice 728 now applies only to boats moved from Northern Ireland to the EU, pending the drafting of the equivalent rules for the rest of the UK as a third state.

The general rule that remains applicable is that VAT is payable either in the country of purchase at that country's rate, or at the rate applicable in country of destination.

(c) Marine insurance

Insurance is compulsory on the inland waterways of Europe. In some cases it may be a requirement for the insurance documents to be translated. For further details refer to the relevant countries listed in the RYA's Foreign Cruising Guides, published jointly with The Cruising Association. These publications detail the regulations for European countries and list the documentary requirements of both the boat and the crew, including a section on inland waterways.

(d) Ship's radio licence

A radio telephone ship licence is required for every British ship with radio telephonic equipment installed, intended for public correspondence use. For British registered ships, this licence is available from the Radio Licensing Centre. The user should also have an operator's licence for the appliance.

(e) Helmsman's licence

Skippers of craft navigating inland need to hold a valid certificate of competence, and inland waterway regulations come into effect once a vessel is upstream of the seaward limit of each estuary. The category of licence required is determined by the size of craft and the power of the engine. There is an exemption for boats less than 5m with no cabin and with a power factor T less than 1, calculated by the formula T = hp of the engine multiplied by 1.9, this sum then divided by the square of the boat's length. By this formula a 4.9 m long boat with a 12.5 hp engine just qualifies for exemption. The helmsman must be 16 or over.

(f) International Certificate of Competence

UN Resolution 40 introduced a Europe-wide helmsman's licence, known as an International Certificate of Competence (ICC). It is issued after a test of practical ability and knowledge of the 'rules of the road', and is available for cruising with a sail boat and/or a motor-driven one, with the test being taken on an appropriate craft. To gain an ICC with coastal endorsement requires a test of knowledge of the International Regulations for Preventing Collisions at Sea (COLREGS), and for an inland endorsement a test of the CEVNI rules, which govern inland boating. In the UK the ICC is issued by the Royal Yachting Association.

In 2011 the European Boating Association and DBA The Barge Association, along with the RYA, succeeded in getting an amendment to Resolution 40. Non-EU residents can be issued an ICC by countries which have accepted the Resolution. Residents/nationals of an EU country can only get theirs from the country where they live. A valuable study book for the ICC inland endorsement is the *RYA Book of European Waterways Regulations*. This book should be carried on board, but a copy of the CEVNI rules in the language of the country one is cruising is also worth having on board, as a courtesy towards the navigation authority.

Inland boating certificates issued by non-EU countries are not generally accepted, as the CEVNI rules are specific to the interconnected European inland waterways, and differ in significant ways from the COLREGS in use at sea. The study book for the ICC Inland endorsement is the RYA Book of *European Waterways Regulations*, which will also satisfy the requirement that a copy of the CEVNI rules is carried on board.

(g) French Certificates of Competence

French helmsman licences were reorganised in 2008. There are two categories of inland licence for recreational craft: a *Permis Plaisance* for craft between 5m and 20m, and an *Extension Grande Plaisance* for craft 20m and over. They can be held by persons of any nationality. The *Permis Plaisance* requires brief practical instruction on a small craft, and then a computerised multichoice test of knowledge of the CEVNI rules, in French. A person requiring the Extension Licence, whether for a larger craft or as a first step to a commercial licence for taking passengers on board, *must* first gain the small craft licence. There is then a minimum of nine further hours demonstrating ability to carry out common boating manoeuvres on an appropriate-sized vessel, plus instruction on various safety matters. The minimum age for holders of an Extension licence is 18.

A special temporary certificate called *Carte de Plaisance* is issued by the boat hire firms to all clients not in possession of one of the above, for cruising on waterways that are considered relatively safe. The hire firm is obliged to spend sufficient time with each client to explain the boat's operation and handling.

(h) Community Inland Navigation Certificate (ES-TRIN, formerly TRIWV))

This originates with the 2006 and ongoing UN Resolution No. 61. Various countries previously had their own rules for construction and equipping craft, and the ES-TRIN are intended to harmonise standards throughout the jurisdiction of the ECE, now including the Rhine. All craft over 20m on European inland waters must have a Certificate of Conformity, which will be issued by authorised bodies of any of the countries concerned (this does not have to be the country of registry).

VNF LICENCE RATES (VIGNETTE) 2021

Categories	I <8m	II 8<11m	III 11<14m	IV ≥14m
Liberté [1]	8.90 x L + 89.00	8.90 x L + 205.90	8.90 x L + 392.10	8.90 x L + 511.80
Loisirs [2]	7.80 x L + 28.60	7.80 x L + 41.60	7.80 x L + 54.40	7.80 x L + 69.50
7 days [3]	4.20 x L + 15.90	4.20 x L + 24.00	4.20 x L + 31.90	4.20 x L + 39.70
Per day [4]	3.20 x L + 11.70	3.20 x L + 17.60	3.20 x L + 23.10	3.20 x L + 28.70

[1] Issued for the calendar year (1st January to 31st December)
[2] Issued for 30 consecutive days
[3] Issued for 7 consecutive days
[4] Issued for any specified day

The amount is calculated according to the duration of navigation and the vessel's length. It is rounded up to the nearest decimal point. The calculation of the price of the vignette includes a variable part depending on the length of the boat (as indicated on the certificate of registration) and a fixed lump-sum part.
A discount of 17% is applied to the «Liberté» vignette only, if acquired before March 31.

Introduction

(i) Boat licences – péage plaisance

Licences were introduced when Voies Navigables de France (VNF) was set up in 1991. The *péage* is payable by all boats for use of the waterways managed by VNF, per day of navigation, with or without passage through locks. Boats are divided into four categories, defined by length. (Regrettably, this penalises English narrow boats.) The table below gives the rates in € applicable in 2021 for each licence period: liberté or freedom, corresponding to the former annual licence, loisirs or monthly (30 days), 7 days and 1 day. The facsimile reproduced here shows the current vignette, which where the category, year and date of validity are clearly displayed.

The vignette is now easily purchased online – **vnf.fr/vnf/services/acheter-sa-vignette** – and printed at home, entering the boat owner's name and address, the boat's name and draught, length overall, the boat's registration number, or failing that, its serial number, the category of *vignette* required and the corresponding start date (for the *Loisirs*, 7-day and 1-day *vignettes*), a scan of the navigation permit, sea permit or French registration certificate, as well as proof of engine capacity. Payment is by debit or credit card. It is also possible to acquire the vignette at one of VNF's 31 designated customer service offices, which often correspond to the local offices listed in this guide.

The formalities indicated above are a small price to pay for the freedom enjoyed while cruising through the French waterways. Occasionally, generally at a lock, a boat owner will be asked for his ship's registration papers in order to furnish basic information; the boat's name, number and port of registry, and ownership details. He may also be asked to show his vignette.

The distinction between time spent navigating and time spent at a long-term mooring is important. The licence gives the right to moor free of charge for up to 48 hours anywhere on the network, or until asked to move on (a very rare occurrence, although charges are made at harbours leased to a public or private operator).

Long-term moorings are subject either to the charges applied by the harbour concessionary, or to a mooring lease or *autorisation d'occupation temporaire* (AOT) to be obtained from VNF.

Mast unstepping

A common experience seems to be that boatyards that offer this may be friendly and know how to operate a crane, but are not in business to provide a 'de-rigging' service. You may (as we were) be expected to undo and generally prepare everything, then they will attach a strop to the mast, lift it up and lay it onto the supports you have provided on the boat. In that respect they do not 'look after one' as one might hope. A shame, since for most of us unmasting does not happen often and is a worrying event – problems at the time maybe and maybe problems stored up for the future. We taped the positions of all our shroud and stay bottle-screws and took photographs of all the critical bits of our rig, hopefully to reassemble it correctly in the future.

Trailer sailing

Owners of trailed craft will find it much easier than in the past to launch on the French waterways. Facilities for boats have mushroomed, and the *ports de plaisance* are usually equipped with a slipway or crane suitable for most trailed boats. Hire firms also welcome private boats to make use of their facilities, except out of season or at weekends when they are busy turning round their own boats. Generally speaking, boat harbours with slipways are encountered more frequently on river navigations than on canals. Most facilities are indicated in the route descriptions, but reference may also be made to the individual waterway guides listed under *Guides and publications*.

If you are planning on trailer-sailing, the maximum authorised dimensions of vehicle and trailer without special permission and documentation are as follows: height, no restriction (but 4m is the practical maximum); overall width, 2.50m; overall vehicle length 12m, and overall trailer length, 12m. The vehicle/trailer combination should not exceed 18.5m. The RYA legal department publishes a booklet on trailer sailing.

Boat transport

An increasingly popular method of having a vessel delivered to the continent is by truck and trailer using a haulage firm with experience in transporting heavy, oversize loads, especially boats to continental Europe. The haulier arranges competitive ferry prices, selects the appropriate route and obtains the necessary transport permits and *Convoi Exceptionnel* documents and escorts where required. Documents to be supplied to arrange the transport of privately owned vessels are (a) documentation showing the vessel's VAT paid, or exempt, status and (b) a copy of the registration documents. This method of relocating your boat has a number of advantages. There is not the wear and tear of a Channel crossing, there are no forced delays waiting for favourable weather, and the cruise starts where you want, avoiding the occasionally awkward first week's navigation from a busy commercial port through high-capacity waterways shared with heavy inland shipping. For example, the normal delivery time from the UK to Laroche-Migennes is 48 hours.

Part I

Hire boats

A convenient way of discovering France through her waterways is to hire a comfortable cruiser (*houseboat* in French), ideally suited to inland navigation. There are about 100 hire bases operating on the French waterways, belonging to 50 separate companies, with a total of about 1800 boats. It is thus now possible to plan a week's cruise virtually anywhere on the network. Only the waterways between the Seine basin and north-eastern France remain poorly represented.

Listing all hire firms is a risky exercise, for changes occur from one season to the next, but it worth setting out all the details, for hire bases are such an important part of the French waterway scene. Bases are listed in alphabetical order by region. These include a number of relay bases which are operated mainly to allow clients to cruise one-way only. The possibility of one-way cruises is indicated.

Compared with the situation 10 years ago, there has been significant contraction and reorganisation of the hire fleet. The two largest firms, Crown Blue Line (itself the result of a merger) and Connoisseur, merged under the name Le Boat. The table also shows the bases at Nieuwpoort and Kuurne in Flanders, Belgium, because they give access to the waterway network of northern France, where there is still sadly no hire base.

There is no point in contacting the individual bases of the bigger firms for reservations, which are all centralised. These companies, which have bases throughout France, are listed under the first heading 'Central reservation offices'. Their web sites are not repeated under the individual entries.

Many of the smaller firms can offer high-quality boats at reasonable prices. Generally speaking, where lower prices can be obtained for a boat with the same number of berths, clients will get less for their money (older, smaller, less well-equipped and less comfortable boats).

Given the considerable choice of cruising areas, decide first which waterway and which region appeal to you most, and then consult the web sites or ask to be sent the brochures of the various firms operating in the area. Study carefully the characteristics of the boats and their equipment, and compare the dimensions of boats rather than taking for granted the spaciousness apparent in the wide-angle photographs.

Central reservation offices

Name	Tel	Website	Details
FPP Travel	03 85 53 76 70	fpp.travel	agency for a network of several small French operators
Le Boat	04 68 94 42 80	leboat.com	combines former Crown Blue Line and Connoisseur
Locaboat Holidays	03 86 91 72 72	locaboat.com	14 bases throughout France
Nicols Locations	02 41 56 46 56	nicols.com	8 bases throughout France, and agent for others

Northern and eastern France

Name	Location	Website	Details
BBoat	Kuurne (BE)	bboat.be	on the Lys (Leie) close to the Kortirjk and the border
Le Boat	Nieuwpoort (B)		In Belgium, allowing circular cruise in northern France
Picardie Boat	Long	locpicardieboat.wordpress.com	the only base on the Somme

Burgundy and central France

Name	Location	Website	Details
Aqua Fluvial	Baye	aquafluvial.fr	former Saint Line base at Nivernais summit
France Fluviale	Tonnerre	francefluviale.com	on the Canal de Bourgogne
France Fluviale	Vermenton	francefluviale.com	at Vermenton, one-way cruises to Marigny-sur-Yonne
Canalous Plaisance	Châtillon-en-Bazois		Nivernais, one-way to Coulanges-sur-Yonne
Canalous Plaisance	Mailly-le-Château	canalous-bourgogne.com	Nivernais, one-way to Châtillon-en-Bazois
Canalous Plaisance	Digoin		Centre, Loire lat., Roanne one-way to Châtillon-en-Bazois
Canalous Plaisance	Châtillon-en-Bazois		Nivernais, one-way to Coulanges-sur-Yonne
Charmes Nautiques	Briare	charmes-nautiques.com	Loire latéral and Briare
Le Boat	Saint-Jean-de-Losne		Saône, one-way to Fontenay-le-Château
Le Boat	Decize		Loire lateral Canal, Loire, Nivernais, one-way to Tannay
Le Boat	Châtillon-sur-Loire		Loire lateral Canal, Briare
Le Boat	Tannay		Nivernais, Yonne, one-way to Decize or Migennes
Le Boat	Migennes		Yonne, Canal de Bourgogne, one-way to Tannay
Locaboat Holidays	Corbigny		Nivernais and one-way to Joigny and Dompierre
Locaboat Holidays	Joigny		Yonne, + one-way to Nivernais, Bourgogne, Loire lat.
Locaboat Holidays	Montbard		C. de Bourgogne
Locaboat Holidays	Dompierre-s-Besbre		Loire lateral Canal and one-way to Briare or Corbigny

Locaboat Holidays	Briare		Briare, Loire lateral Canal, one-way to Dompierre
Locaboat Holidays	Saint-Léger-s-Dheune		Canal du Centre
Nicols	Brienon-s-Armançon		western end of C. de Bourgogne, one-way to Venarey
Nicols	Venarey-les-Laumes		near summit of C. de Bourgogne, one-way to Brienon
Snaily (L'Escarg'eau)	Chagny	snaily.com	Canal du Centre
Tourisme Fluvial du Centre	Rogny-les-7-Écluses	bateaux2bourgogne.com	Briare and Loing, one-way to Plagny or Brienon

Navigable dimensions

The waterways of France may roughly be divided into three categories.

High-capacity (grand gabarit) waterways (Class IV or larger)

These are the Seine and Oise, the Liaison Dunkerque-Escaut and lower Escaut, the Moselle, the Rhine, the Rhône and the Grande-Saône, as well as the maritime navigations in the Loire and Gironde estuaries.

Navigable dimensions obviously present no constraint for boats and barges on these waterways, which offer lock dimensions of at least 144m by 12m, a minimum navigable draught of 2.50m and a minimum air draught of 4.50m (generally much more).

'Freycinet' waterways, including Canal du Nord and the lower river Yonne (Classes I and II)

Most of the waterways come into this category, offering standard dimensions established in 1879 by the Minister of Public Works Charles Louis de Saulces de Freycinet. Here too, the dimensions are ample for most boats, with minimum lock dimensions of 38.50m by 5.10m, minimum navigable draught of 1.80m and a minimum air draught of 3.40m (generally 3.50m). It must be noted, however, that the available depth on many canals is far short of the theoretical 2.20m, and that barges are increasingly forced to waste valuable energy ploughing their furrow through the thick layer of sediment that has deposited on the bed over the years. The remaining commercial carriers are even forced off the routes restored for recreational navigation, where the funding was agreed for dredging for a loading depth of 1.60m instead of the historic 1.80m. This reduced draught also of course excludes many recreational craft, especially yachts.

Smaller waterways (Class 0)

Here dimensions are more critical, especially for barges or deep-keeled yachts. There are only two routes in this volume that are affected by restricted dimensions:

Route	Length	Beam	Draught	Air Draught
Canal du Nivernais	30.15	5.10	1.20	3.00
Canal de l'Ourcq (Paris canals)	58.80	3.10[1]	0.80[2]	2.40

1 One lock (Varreddes) remains to be rebuilt to allow passage of broader-beam boats (3.70m)
2 Up to 1.00 or 1.10m at the risk and peril of the navigator

The owners of large motor yachts and barges will regularly be nudging through low bridges like this one on the Canal d'Ille-et-Rance in Brittany. © PHILIP COOK

Rules of the road

The rules of the road are relatively easy to comply with, and the ability to handle one's boat precisely and confidently is just as important as theoretical knowledge of the waterway code. The rules to be observed by boaters are documented thoroughly in the RYA *Book of European Waterway Regulations* by Tam Murrell, but some of the main points are summarised in the following paragraphs.

Priority to commercial traffic and other barges

Smaller boats must at all times leave room for barges to proceed on their course and to manoeuvre. Barges must never be forced by small boats to steer clear. Skippers of boats must constantly bear in mind this priority to working boats, including trip boats. They must also steer well clear of all craft under way, dredgers and other maintenance vessels, and any work sites on the waterways.

Meeting other craft (croisement)

Boats may pass each other only when the channel is wide enough, taking into account local circumstances and other traffic movements. Boats whose respective courses are such that there is no risk of collision must not alter their course or their speed in a manner likely to cause a risk of collision. Boats meeting must normally keep to the right (passing port to port). There is an exception to this rule (more important for barges than for small boats) on wider river navigations, where it is normal practice for boats heading upstream to keep to the inside of the channel in bends to take advantage of the slacker water, while boats heading downstream keep to the middle of the channel.

This practice is covered by the international 'blue flag' rule, under which the upstream-bound barge wishing to keep to the left makes its intention clear by displaying a blue flag or panel on the right-hand side of the wheelhouse (or by night, a flashing white light). The barge heading downstream acknowledges by displaying its blue flag or flashing white light, and adopts the corresponding course. If the skipper of the first barge fears his intention has not been understood, he sounds two short blasts (to pass on the left), and this signal must be acknowledged. (Similarly, one short blast confirms the intention to pass normally on the right, and must be acknowledged.) Small craft are not bound to observe this rule, but being aware of it makes it that much easier to comply with the number one rule of priority to commercial craft.

On French river navigations, there are certain sections where all craft are forced by these conventional signs to cross over or keep to the 'wrong' side of the channel and pass oncoming boats starboard-to-starboard. Here too, the blue flag is normally displayed. At points where the course thus changes sides it is the boat heading downstream which has priority, the upstream-bound boat slowing down or stopping as necessary. Where there is insufficient width for two barges to pass abreast, this prohibition sign is often displayed. On encountering this sign, a boat must not proceed until the skipper has satisfied himself that the channel in the restricted section is not occupied. Barge skippers communicate by radio at such locations, using the ship-to-ship channel 10; boaters should proceed cautiously, sounding a long blast on their horn as appropriate. Generally speaking, it is the boat heading downstream which has priority over that heading upstream.

Overtaking (dépassement or trématage)

Overtaking normally takes place on the left. Only on wide river navigations may overtaking on the right be envisaged. The skipper of the overtaking boat must strictly indicate his intention by displaying a blue flag at the bow. If the overtaken vessel has to modify its course or speed to facilitate this manoeuvre, the overtaking one shall sound two long blasts followed by one short one to signal he is overtaking to starboard, or two long blasts followed by two short ones for overtaking to port. Boaters must not accelerate momentarily for the exclusive purpose of passing another boat or barge, and should bear in mind that it is forbidden to overtake (a) whenever it is not certain that the manoeuvre can be effected safely, (b) within 500m from a lock and (c) wherever these prohibition signs are displayed. Generally speaking, never try to overtake a barge on the 'Freycinet' canals unless invited to do so by the barge skipper, since this can be a dangerous manoeuvre. If no such invitation is forthcoming, and the boat skipper is certain that there is time to get far enough ahead of the barge before the next lock is reached not to cause any delay (in practice, this means that the next lock must be at least 2 or 3 kilometres away), he may signal his intention to overtake by sounding two long blasts and two short (to overtake normally to port).

It is then permitted to overtake unless the barge skipper sounds one short blast, meaning that he would prefer to be overtaken to starboard, or five short blasts, meaning that he considers it unsafe or inappropriate to be overtaken at this point. However, only experienced navigators with loud horns should indulge in such dialogue; it is simpler, especially on a heavily-locked canal, to moor when the opportunity arises and let the barge get well ahead.

Turning (virement)

When a boat wishes to turn to head in the opposite direction, notice of the intention is to be given by one prolonged blast on the horn, followed by one short blast if swinging to the right and two short blasts if swinging to the left.

Navigation signs

The most common navigation signs are shown opposite.

Speed limits

The special regulations for each waterway (*règlement particulier de police de la navigation intérieure*) lay down speed limits, and the owner of any boat exceeding the authorised limit renders himself liable to prosecution. Throughout the smaller canal network the limit is 6km/h (3.7 miles/hour) for barges and pleasure boats displacing more than 20 tonnes, reduced to 4km/h for the passage of movable bridges and navigation at night (where allowed). The limit is eased to 8km/h and in some cases 10km/h for boats of less than 20 tonnes. One of the uses of the tables, with distances precise to within 100m, is to allow speed to be checked. In practice, however, speed in the smaller canals should constantly be adapted to local conditions, the basic rule being to ease off whenever the boat causes wash to break on the banks, as well as when passing moored boats and anglers, thus avoiding damage in the first case and unpleasantness in the second.

On canalised rivers, higher speeds are authorised in river sections than in lock-cuts or canal sections. For example, the limits are respectively 15km/h and 6km/h on the Marne, on the Saône above Auxonne and on the Yonne, while the maximum on the smaller river navigations is 10km/h.

On the large-scale waterways, much higher limits are applied, generally 15km/h in canals or lock-cuts and up to 35km/h in open river sections. Speeds higher still, up to 60km/h, are allowed on specified short reaches for the practice of water-skiing and small power boating only. It must be underlined that local restrictions may be applied on any waterway, and indicated by the conventional speed limit sign shown in the section on navigation signs.

Locks

Different recommendations must be given for negotiating locks according to the four main types of lock encountered on the network.

Introduction

LIGHTS AT LOCKS

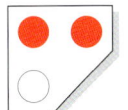    

Wait | Wait (lock in operation) | Wait, lock is being prepared | Enter the lock now | Lock not operational

OTHER LIGHTS

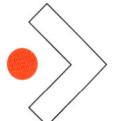

No entry to basin or channel indicated by white arrow

MANDATORY & WARNING SIGNS

No entry | No over-taking | No meeting or overtaking (i.e. single lane) | No mooring or anchoring | No anchoring | No mooring | No turning (winding) | Do not create wash | Motor boats forbidden

Proceed in direction indicated | Stop | Speed limit | Make a sound signal | Unspecified hazard | Major waterway ahead | Headroom limited | Width of passage or channel limited | Keep this distance from bank

Make radio contact with waterway staff* | Cross channel to pass boats starboard to starboard | Cross channel to pass boats port to port (normal) | Keep to port | Keep to starboard | Channel moves to port | Channel moves to starboard | No passage outside marked limits

* Note that channel 10 is the ship-to-ship channel on inland waterways throughout the continent.

OTHER SIGNS (RECOMMENDATORY OR INFORMATIVE)

Weir | Ferry | Chain ferry | Side turning | Tributary waterway | Priority waterway | Berthing permitted | Anchoring permitted | Making fast permitted | Turning

Recommended direction | Electricity cable | End of prohibition or restriction

SIGNS ON BRIDGES

Keep within limits (green) | Recommended channel (in both directions) | Passage only in direction indicated (other direction prohibited)

SOUNDS

—	Attention	••••••	(6 very short) Imminent danger of collision
•	I am moving (or holding) to starboard	— — — —	(repeated) Distress signal
• •	I am moving (or holding) to port	— •	I am turning to starboard
• • •	I am going astern	— • •	I am turning to port
• • • •	I am incapable of manœuvring		

Part I

High-capacity (grand gabarit) waterways

The big locks on these waterways (as defined under navigable dimensions) are all controlled by lock-keepers, normally from a control tower located midway in the lock basin on one side or the other. The automatic lock filling or emptying sequences (and corresponding light displays for navigators) are subordinated to the lock-keepers' decisions, based on the observed or announced traffic situation. A boat navigating singly may thus be kept waiting for 20 minutes or longer if the lock is ready for a barge announced in the other direction. This is allowed for by the regulations, so do not be surprised if the double red light display persists for that time. In case of doubt, moor at one of the dolphins providing access to the bank and approach the lock-keeper to announce your arrival. Alternatively, a VHF radio call number is listed in the route descriptions for locks on these large-scale waterways, and lock-keepers may be called on VHF for an inquiry or to announce your arrival time. A single red or red and green lights side by side mean that the lock is being prepared. Wait until the double green light is displayed before entering the lock. If there are barges or other craft queueing at the lock, take your place in the queue, but in any event when the double green light shows, allow all barges to enter the lock first. When traffic is heavy, the lock-keeper will generally wave or use a loud-hailer to call boats into the spaces remaining in the lock chamber. Avoid coming close to a barge's stern until she has stopped in the chamber, in case there is an unexpected last-minute use of reverse at high revs causing pronounced turbulence for some distance behind the prop.

Don't forget to put on your lifejackets when passing locks on the high-capacity waterways! This is **Pacific** *skipper Samuel in Dracé lock on the Saône.*

The deepest locks have floating bollards or a series of bollards set in the wall vertically at intervals of one or two metres. These are referred to as 'step bollards' and require a certain amount of juggling with the bow and stern lines as the water level rises or falls. The recommended procedure here is to have two lines available or one lengthy line with an eye at each end at both bow and stern. This allows use of the 'one on - one off' method as you rise or fall. It is forbidden to make fast to the rungs of a ladder between two sets of bollards. It is sometimes more convenient to come alongside a barge (with the skipper's permission) and make fast to its bollards.

Automated locks on smaller waterways

To reduce operating costs on the smaller canals and canalised rivers (for example, the Canal de Garonne, the Canal du Centre, the Canal de la Marne au Rhin, the upper Saône), a large number of locks have been equipped for fully automated or semi-automatic operation. These locks, often grouped together and referred to as a *chaîne* or flight, are equipped with lights, with the same meanings as above: red = wait, red plus green = lock in preparation, and green = proceed into lock. A system of advanced detection registers the boat's arrival some distance before the lock. This system may be automatic (radar) or will involve using a remote control supplied by the lock-keeper at either end of the flight. Some canals still have the simple device of a pole suspended above the water, which needs to be given a quarter turn.

A flashing orange light near the detector, or the red plus green light display at the lock, means that the boat has been detected. When the green light is displayed, proceed slowly into the lock. Some locks have a chamber entry/exit detector, either a photoelectric sensor or on older locks a horizontal pole to be pushed forwards by your boat for at least 5 seconds. Once the boat is safely moored in the chamber, raise the blue rod situated on the edge of the lock, to start the automatic lock filling or emptying sequence. It will take a few seconds for the command to be registered. The red rod is be pulled in a case of emergency only. This not only stops the sequence, but shuts down the entire system, and requires intervention by waterway staff to set it up again. If it is an actual case of emergency requiring a rapid response you should also call on the interphone to advise someone of this, or your problem will simply be treated as a lock out of action, and an itinerant lock keeper will come to repair it in due course. At the end of the cycle, the gates open automatically. It is important to clear the chamber promptly. It should be noted that a group of boats locking together should pass the radar detector in close file. If the lock fails to start or fails in mid-sequence, use the telephone (interphone) outside the lock cabin.

Once in a flight it is important to maintain a constant speed between locks, and if it is decided to stop, if only for lunch, before the flight is completed, the lock-keepers must be notified of this intention. They are normally stationed at each end of the flight. In an emergency or in case of breakdown, they can be also be contacted by two-way telephone outside the small control cabinet beside each lock. If conditions are extremely difficult (strong wind or heavy rain, for example), the section lock-keeper will often be seen on the towpath on his scooter ascertaining that all is well.

Locks operated by lock-keepers

Staff cutbacks everywhere – on the VNF network and on the other waterways – combined with the cheap technology available for mechanal operation, whether automated or not, mean that there are now precious few locks on the 'Freycinet' network that are still operated by lock-keepers.

It is not usually necessary to warn the lock-keeper of your arrival, but a short, polite beep on the horn may be required if there is no sign of any activity. Be sure not to do this during the lunch break, however! No action is necessary if other traffic is moored up waiting to lock through. In any event, it is advisable to make a complete stop 50m from the lock, to wait until the lock-keeper signals permission to enter, or until the gates are completely open. While waiting, if it is preferred not to moor up to the bank, care should be taken not to obstruct the passage of any boat which may emerge from the lock when the gates are opened. On entering the lock (at low speed), arrange for one of the crew to alight on the side opposite the lock-keeper, normally the towpath side, or whichever side he is not working. Having attended to the boat's lines it is customary to assist in working the lock (closing one of the gates when the boat has entered the lock, possibly working the gate paddles and opening the gate on the same side when the lock is ready). Some of the older locks on the Seine and Yonne have sloping sides, requiring particular caution, especially when descending. It is often possible and preferable to pass your mooring lines to the lock-keeper as you enter these particular locks. Be ready to bear off with boat-hooks, preferably one forward and one aft. Many of these sloping-sided locks have been upgraded in recent years, with a floating pontoon inside the chamber. This facility is suitable only for smaller vessels, unfortunately!

A recent development which is changing the practical arrangements for passing locks on considerable lengths of canal is the complete reorganisation of waterway personnel, the numbers of permanently-posted lock-keepers being drastically reduced (by non-replaced departures or transfers to maintenance staff). Locks on designated sections are thus attended by mobile teams, which follow boats through successive locks, in some cases only two but perhaps as many as 20. This makes the boater a little less free to move as he pleases, for the team's movements obviously have to be programmed, and a spontaneous decision to stop between two locks will create confusion and perhaps even delay commercial traffic. Boaters are thus requested to cooperate by giving reasonable notice of their movements and stops.

Finally, it is worth noting that tipping the lock-keepers is not normal practice. Lock-keepers are State or local authority employees and are paid a fair salary for their job. On the other hand, they often do more than is strictly required of them, and in such cases the navigator should use his discretion and imagination in judging the best way of showing appreciation. In some cases a euro will suffice, or perhaps a cool drink on a hot day? Cash will obviously be appreciated if water is supplied from the lock-keeper's private tap, say €1.50 or €2, but water is generally provided by VNF at locks as part of the service paid for by the licence fee.

Unmanned locks on the smaller waterways

'Do-it-yourself' lock operation has become the system on a number of waterways that are used only by tourist traffic. This is the case on the western section of Canal de Nantes à Brest, the Charente, the Seille and the Lot, for example.

In all cases the lock operating gear is already installed, and a leaflet of instructions on lock operation is issued to navigators.

Observations by a seasoned canaller

The reflections by the late Robert Somerville that were included in previous editions of this work remain relevant today. The increasing popularity of the canals and rivers of France means an increased responsibility for all users, not just the long-term, perhaps retired, year-round navigator who will tend to know the ropes, the waterway etiquette, not to mention half of the entire family of seasoned canallers, but also the first-time family vacationer hiring a self-drive vessel for the first time, or perhaps the navigators passing through the system from or to the Mediterranean with their motor yacht or sailing boat for the one and only time.

Why have you been moored to that quay for three weeks? One should not expect to stay moored indefinitely to a public quay, usually where the services are superior and possibly free. A stay of two or three days is normally tolerated but by then it is time to move on and allow others to enjoy those same facilities, the sights and sounds that have kept you staying for as long as you have. Especially if others are being turned away daily! Have you considered breasting up? Perhaps the extended stay should be made in a privately-managed port. There are suitable facilities at or near most popular locations, and by paying the going rates you acquire the right to stay as long as you wish.

Why have you got your screwdriver out, to pry open the security door on the service panel? A charge of €2 for water is not excessive, nor is €3 for a nightly power hook-up. Once the services have been vandalised to save some small change, in all likelihood they will be unusable for the next user and probably will not be serviceable at all the following year.

Why are you moored in the middle of the quay? Snuggle up to the boat ahead of you or to one of the ends of the pontoon and leave some room for others who are certain to come along later. If the most recent arrival is having difficulty getting a line ashore and securing their vessel – take a minute or two to assist in securing the vessel – being careful not to trip over your own lines which may have been carelessly coiled on the pontoon!

Why are you cruising so fast? More importantly you're on holiday. Take a moment and have a look at your bow wave and behind at your wake! All canals and rivers have speed limits. They are designed to preserve the banks, respect the speed limit and the waterways' navigable depths will not be rapidly reduced as a result of collapsing banks.

Why is that other vessel owner yelling at you? Have you raced ahead to get to the next lock first? Have you overtaken in a dangerous location? Have you had too much to drink? There are 'rules of the road'; know what they are and follow them, but more importantly, respect your fellow boater!

On a completely different issue which I have found to be critical, canal guides make frequent reference to the concept of a *bassin* or canal basin. They come in various shapes and sizes and are normally found downstream of a lock, close to a small village or town, a loading quay or silo, or for no apparent reason in the middle of nowhere. In the past they were an important part of the commercial life on the canal and river system. They allowed *péniches* to turn around and proceed in the opposite direction to load or unload cargo or to return to a favoured port without having to travel great distances in the opposite direction to do so. Where situated in the middle of nowhere, their function was often to allow barges to moor while waiting for a new load. The biggest were given the more important title of *gare d'eau*.

Unfortunately, with the decline of commercial traffic these basins fell into varying degrees of disrepair. Many became silted up, overgrown with weed or worst of all served as a dumping ground for abandoned vessels or even cars. Consequently, a number have been staked off or have signs to indicate that entry is neither possible nor recommended. However, the majority have no indication of their suitability for turning or mooring.

This means that if it is contemplated to use a basin it is advisable to approach with extreme caution and expect the worst! Proceed slowly, bow first, ideally with a person up at the bow paying special attention to what is ahead. That stone quay just inside might look very inviting but in all likelihood there are no services and the risk of damage to your vessel is just not worth it. Look for a more suitable turning location or mooring a little further on.

Hours of navigation

It is as well when planning a cruise to realise that for all practical purposes there is no navigation after dark or, during the lighter months of the year, after 19:30. Locks are generally open between 06:30 and 19:30 in summer, and the working hours progressively shorten as the nights close in. However, now that many waterways are being handed over to regional councils or other local bodies, it is to be expected that operating hours will vary much more widely than in the past. Councils are known to be seeking to reduce the financial burden of operating costs, so boaters should expect some disappointments in the coming years. While it is possible to run between locks during the dark hours (the proper navigation lights being shown and the regulation reduction in speed being observed), there is little advantage for boats in doing so, except in an emergency.

Time of year

The season suitable for pleasure cruising extends from March to November, depending on how comfortable and well heated your boat is. The weather in France, being of the continental type, tends to be more settled than that of the British Isles, and long periods of high temperature are not infrequent in the summer. Before about the end of April, cold weather and night frosts may occur. Moreover, it is always colder on the water than on the land and, owing to the higher humidity, it feels colder. The weather is often fine in September and October, when the autumn colours make the scenery particularly beautiful. However, morning mists on the canals and rivers will often delay a planned early morning departure.

In the late autumn and winter, the intrepid navigator must be prepared for floods (from November to March, but often also in the spring months through to May) and also for icing (December to February). Bear in mind that some of the canals rise to a considerable height above sea level, and with the increase in altitude the fall in temperature is accentuated. Such severe conditions do not usually extend beyond the month of March.

Seasonal restrictions in the coming years will not be a question of climate, but of canal operating conditions, as indicated in the previous paragraph on hours of navigation. Some authorities will want to close their canals completely during the winter months, and some vigorous campaigning is likely to be required, before new waterway authorities will accept to pay for more staff time. The cause will be difficult to defend, since the resulting additional traffic will seem not to have been worth the effort.

Out-of-season cruising has become a genuine trend on the Canal du Midi, where it is seen by private boat-owners as the ideal way to enjoy the canal's charms without having to struggle with the large numbers of hire boats on the busiest sections of the canal.

Mast lowering

One important aspect of planning to enter the inland waterways, for sailing yachts, is mast lowering or stepping. This will benefit from some preparatory work. The marinas at Dunkerque, for example, whilst helpful and able to provide craneage, may not be as familiar with the techniques as the yard at Rouen. They cannot be relied on to know and do everything required. It might be advisable to talk to an experienced yard in your home country about the practicalities and the sequence: disconnecting electrics, the order in which shrouds and stays and their bottle screws should be loosened and released, how and where the lifting strop on the mast should be attached (to avoid the wrongly balanced mast tipping end over end), and how the mast should actually be lifted and laid down.

Introduction

Planning a cruise

Feedback received from readers suggests that the most vital information is the location of quayside fuelling points and wastewater pump-outs. Hence the two maps on the following pages. The following through routes are commonly used. (Note that there is some overlap with Volume 2.)

Calais to Paris via Canal de Saint-Quentin
470km, 60 locks
This route carries quite heavy commercial traffic, especially on the high-capacity sections (Liaison Dunkerque-Escaut and Oise), but presents much of interest, notably the towns of Cambrai and Saint-Quentin, and the tunnels on the summit level of the Canal de Saint-Quentin. Between the industrial towns the countryside is often pleasant, especially in the Escaut valley above Cambrai and along the river Oise.

Calais to Paris via Canal du Nord
425km, 37 locks
This alternative is for navigators in a hurry, for the Canal du Nord was built to provide a shorter route from northern France to the Paris region and to relieve saturation on the Canal de Saint-Quentin. On the other hand, the scenery is less attractive and there are less sites to visit than on the parallel route, with the exception of Péronne. This route will be subject to major upheaval during construction of the Seine-Nord Europe Canal, in 2022-2028 (see under that waterway).

Calais to Lyon via Saint-Quentin and Reims
897km, 218 locks
This is the most direct route from Calais to Lyon, via the canal which has been renamed 'entre Champagne et Bourgogne'. It joins the Marne route from Paris at Condé-sur-Marne. For those who take the short Channel crossing and who do not wish to visit Paris, this is a useful alternative. Commercial traffic over the summit level is very sporadic, and the canal is little used even by boats. The countryside is very pleasant, and the towns of Langres and Chaumont have plenty of interest for tourists.

Paris to Lyon via Canal de Bourgogne
629km, 219 locks
This is the shortest of the three main routes, but also the slowest on account of the large number of locks. The Canal de Bourgogne passes through some stunningly beautiful countryside, as well as offering the greatest variety of cultural and heritage sites of the three Paris-Lyon routes.

Paris to Lyon via Bourbonnais (Loire)
643km, 157 locks
This is only slightly longer than the Burgundy route, but has far fewer locks. It passes through pleasant agricultural countryside, with some industrialised sections, notably in the former mining region of Montceau-les-Mines. This route is used by some barges on hauls between the Seine and Saône, but encounters with *péniches* will be rare.

Paris to Lyon via Nivernais
706km, 225 locks
This alternative route combines parts of the Bourgogne and Bourbonnais routes, linked by the Canal du Nivernais. This is the slowest route, but it is strongly recommended for navigators with time to spare (and draught not exceeding 1.20m) for the Nivernais is one of the most remote and attractive waterways in France.

Paris to Lyon via Marne
713km, 155 locks
This is the longest route, but that with the least number of locks. In practice, it will take only slightly longer to cover than the Bourbonnais route, while the scenery is much more attractive, both on the river Marne and on the Canal entre Champagne et Bourgogne.

Paris to Strasbourg
564km, 190 locks
This is the direct route from Paris to the Rhine, which is reached at Strasbourg. The Marne is attractive, as is the Canal de la Marne au Rhin where it crosses the Vosges. Elsewhere the scenery is gently rolling countryside and there remains little evidence of the canal's former industrial character.

Note In calculating route lengths, it should be borne in mind that Paris, denoted here by the junction with the Canal Saint-Martin (which has a large marina just beyond the entrance lock from the Seine), is 72km upstream of the Oise confluence at Conflans-Sainte-Honorine and 5km downstream of the Marne confluence at Charenton.

Guides and publications

Much of the basic data for the route descriptions, particularly the kilometre distances or *points kilométriques*, was originally taken from the *Guide de la Navigation Intérieure*, a comprehensive two-volume guide published by Berger-Levrault in Paris in 1965. This continues to be my favourite reference work, at least where there has been no change in basic configuration of the waterways since that date. Imray's general map of the waterways of France, Belgium and the Netherlands, scale 1:1.500.000, produced by the author, is useful for cruise planning and for the overview it gives of the network in the three countries.
Jane Cumberlidge has prepared a map broken down into regions in another Imray publication – *Waterway Routes Through France*. Éditions du Breil also offers a good French waterways map.

Part I

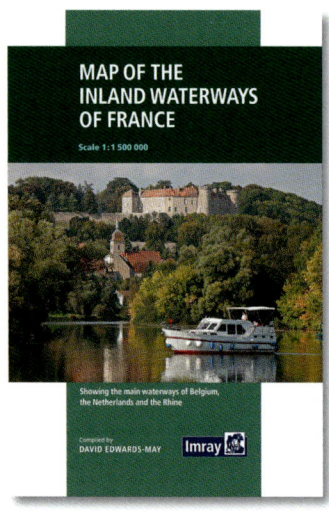

For a wealth of detailed information on navigable conditions, sites to visit, restaurants and practically everything else you might need to know while cruising, there is a choice of specialist guides. The most thoroughly researched and best-documented are those published by Éditions du Breil, the company founded by John Riddel in 1997.

Éditions du Breil
The maps in these guides are at 1:50 000 for canals and 1:25 000 for rivers, with the exception of the Saône (1:40 000) and the Charente (1:12 500). We list here those that cover the waterways in this volume.

Another useful and popular map is the *European Waterways Map and Concise Directory* (sixth edition, 2021), compiled by the author and now also published by Imray. The map now becomes one of the 'family' of waterway publications. It covers the whole of Europe at scales of 1:3 800 000 (for the overview from Portugal and Ireland to the Caspian Sea) and 1:1 500 000 (for the main network from Dublin to Bratislava), and is accompanied by a 64-page directory with brief descriptions for each country.

No. 2   Loire/Nivernais
No. 11 Bourgogne/Nivernais
No. 19 La Marne
No. 20 Picardie
No. 21 Seine

New titles are planned for Nord-Pas-de-Calais and the river Sambre.
503 chemin Notre-Dame, 11400 Castelnaudary, France
+33 (0)4 68 23 51 35   editionsdubreil.com

Fluviacarte
Fluvial, the French monthly waterways magazine, publishes a useful *Guide du Plaisancier* every two years. It is like a condensed version of the present guide, and gives up-to-date information on nearly 700 mooring locations and more than 100 boatyards. Their *Fluviacarte* series includes the following guides covering waterways in the present volume:

No. 1   La Seine Aval, du Havre à Paris
No. 2   La Seine Amont, de Paris à Marcilly
No. 3   La Marne, de Paris à Vitry-le-François
No. 8   Champagne-Ardenne
No. 17 Canaux de Marne au Rhin
No. 20 Bourgogne Ouest, d'Avon à Digoin
No. 24 Picardie

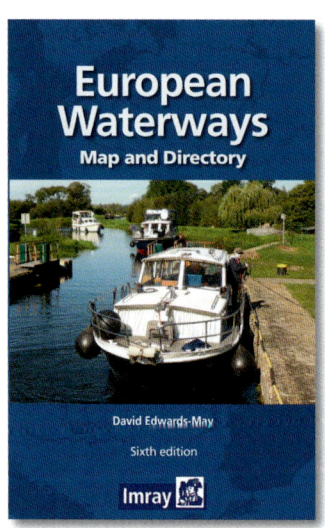

A prime source of information is the online version of the present publication, included, by agreement with Imray, within the website **french-waterways.com**. The 'hands on' (or practical navigation) section of the website contains valuable guidance and recommendations, complementing those set out in this introduction, while the descriptions of each waterway or each chapter may be downloaded as pdfs, as well as compilations of through routes. We hope that boat owners will appreciate having the actual book at home or on board, despite the availability of much of its content in digital format! The site also sells the Imray, Éditions du Breil and Fluviacarte publications.

Introduction

Some other guides are currently out of print. It is not known when they may again be available.
Marina Del Rey - Bât. A, 2 rue des Consuls - CS 30031, 34973 Lattes Cedex   fluvialnet.com

All the above guides have English and German texts alongside the French. They are available from specialised bookshops, from **imray.com** and from **french-waterways.com**. Inland Waterways International also has a useful online shop selling the main titles, but not the individual waterway guides: **inlandwaterwaysinternational.org**.

Other sources

The DBA website **barges.org** has a wide range of information for cruising on the continent, including a mooring guide and updates on current legislation, much of it available to non-members.

The Cruising Association **cruising.org.uk** also publishes *Cruising the Inland Waterways of France and Belgium*, compiled by Gordon Knight. This is an invaluable publication, formerly edited by Dr Roger Edgar. Now in its 25th edition, the 216-page guide is regularly updated via reports from members actively cruising the waterways. It supplements rather than replaces the above publications. Described as their 'Bible' by regular users and yacht skippers planning routes to and from the Mediterranean, the guide contains a wealth of information on cruising routes, cruising preparations, supplies, equipment, licences and documents, useful addresses, books and websites as well as listing around 250 mooring places throughout France and Belgium, with comments upon facilities (including where fuel may be obtained either alongside or within easy jerry can distance), depths, prices, closest shops and restaurants and nearby attractions.

The Cruising Association, CA House, 1 Northey Street, Limehouse Basin, London E14 8BT, +44 (0)20 7537 2828

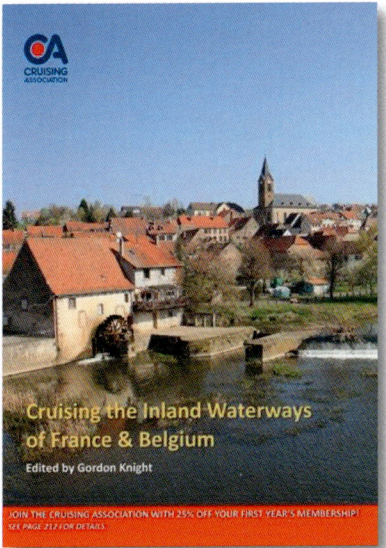

For approaching the French waterway system from the coast the following publications are available (published by Imray, with partners as indicated):

Shell Channel Pilot Tom Cunliffe (Imray)
River Seine Cruising Guide Derek Bowskill
Channel Islands, Cherbourg Peninsula and North Brittany Royal Cruising Club Pilotage Foundation
Atlantic France   Royal Cruising Club Pilotage Foundation (Imray)
Mediterranean France and Corsica Pilot
   Rod and Lucinda Heikell (Imray)
Cruising Almanac The Cruising Association (Imray)
Mediterranean Almanac Rod and Lucinda Heikell (Imray)
Votre Livre de Bord   an almanac in French (with some English) available in two volumes: *Méditerranée* and *Mer du Nord Manche Atlantique*   Bloc Marin

Part II – Route descriptions and maps

The route descriptions and accompanying maps and plans are designed to be of use both for planning and during the actual cruise. Distances are given precisely to within 100m, and possible mooring places are highlighted in bold type. The distance from the mooring to the centre of the locality is also indicated. This is not to be interpreted as a guarantee that mooring will be practicable at this point, but may be useful in emergency situations, as well as for all users of the towpath or riverside cycle itinerary. Junctions are readily identifiable by the use of a distinctive style with white text on a blue background. The route descriptions include sections that are not navigable, either because restoration is in progress or at least envisaged, or for continuity of the cycling itinerary where feasible.

The abbreviations u/s and d/s are used for upstream and downstream, and r/b and l/b for right bank and left bank. These abbreviations are also used on canals, the downstream direction being implicit in relation to the summit level or parallel river. On summit levels or tidal waters, geographical directions are used instead, to avoid confusion.

Boat harbour entries (*ports de plaisance*) will be valuable for users of this guide, and have been researched in detail. Changes take place rapidly, however, so readers are invited to take the information as indicative only. 'Fuel' means that both diesel and petrol are available. The price indicated for visitor moorings is the average charge per night in season, for a boat of 10m length. Where a range of prices is given, the lower figure corresponds to boats up to about 7m, and the higher figure for the maximum length of boat accommodated, which may vary from 15 to 24 or even 38m. Prices will of course change over time. In most cases the local *taxe de séjour* will be charged, usually between 20 and 50 cents per person on board.

The index map shows the position of the waterway in the network, and the strip map, which is precise despite the relatively small scale, enables immediate identification of the boat's position in relation to the overall route, and to the towns and villages where it may be proposed to stop. Partial distances on these maps are shown between pin markers, with the number of locks in italics.

Most junctions and locations where alternative routes are possible are covered by detailed plans at a scale of approximately 1:15 000. These distinguish navigable and unnavigable water areas and give route indications, positions of moorings, main sites of interest and other useful information.

Details of the engineers responsible for each waterway – the local *unité territoriale* or *subdivision* – are given, and in case of specific enquiries or difficulties en route, they may be contacted. Otherwise the regional headquarters listed here will forward any queries to the appropriate office. For the waterways that are not managed by VNF, we distinguish the managing authority and the agency in charge of operation and maintenance.

VNF Regions

VNF Nord-Pas-de-Calais
37 rue du Plat, BP 725, 59034 LILLE
03 20 15 49 70   **dt.nordpasdecalais@vnf.fr**

VNF Bassin de la Seine
18 Quai d'Austerlitz, 75013 PARIS
01 83 94 44 00   **dt.bassindelaseine@vnf.fr**

VNF Rhône Saône
2 rue de la Quarantaine, 69321 LYON 05
04 72 56 59 00   **dt.rhonesaone@vnf.fr**

VNF Centre-Bourgogne
13 avenue Albert Premier, 21000 DIJON
03 45 34 13 00   **dt.centrebourgogne@vnf.fr**

Head office
Voies Navigables de France
175 rue Ludovic Boutleux
B.P. 820, 62408 BÉTHUNE CEDEX
03 21 63 24 24

Paris office
156, rue du Faubourg Saint-Denis, 75010 PARIS
01 44 89 65 00

CHAPTER I – NORTHERN FRANCE

Routes south from the English Channel ports and Belgian border crossings

THIS SECTION COVERS THE ROUTES INTO FRANCE for hundreds, if not thousands, of boatowners each year, plus a few clients of hire boat companies based across the border in Belgium. The most obvious choice of port of entry is Dunkirk (Dunkerque), where boat owners are encouraged to plan on taking time to discover the fascinating Dunkirk canals* before continuing on the high-capacity Liaison Dunkerque-Escaut towards Lille and Douai, then heading south… or not! After a lifetime of promotion and consultancy for restoration of the Canal de Roubaix, and many other projects throughout the Nord-Pas-de-Calais and Picardie regions (now Hauts-de-France), the author can state unequivocally that this region, historically marked by its heavy industry and coal mines, is one of the friendliest and most welcoming in France. The landscapes, the treatment of urban waterfronts and the mooring facilities offer a great variety of experiences; not all satisfying, it is true, but considerable efforts have been made in recent years and investments are continuing today, for example in Dunkirk and Lille.

As a high-capacity waterway (*grand gabarit* in French), the Liaison Dunkerque-Escaut is used by a sizeable fleet of barges of 1500 tonnes and more, and passing them may be challenging because when the canal was widened in the 1960s, it was to much less than the standard width for modern European waterways. That is why the whole canal is being enlarged again, and additional, longer locks being built. This is part of the package of priority investments for French and European waterways related to the new Seine-Nord Europe Canal. The canal is to be built, roughly on the line of the Canal du Nord, in the seven years from 2022 to 2028.

The majority of boats from the Netherlands and Belgium cross at one of the five points shown here: the Canal de Furnes parallel to the coast; the Lys (Leie in Flanders), the Canal de l'Espierres, Canal de Roubaix, the Escaut and the Sambre, the latter route reopening in 2021 after 12 years of closure because of the risk of collapse of its two aqueducts.

The most spectacular route into France within the vast new region of 'Hauts-de-France' is the Somme estuary. Although there is a limited tidal window for access to William the Conqueror's port of Saint-Valery-sur-Somme, the Canal de la Somme is a wonderful waterway to continue inland. Amiens itself is well worth the detour for those coming south on the Canal du Nord.

* This term is suggested by the author to group together the three canals to Furnes, Bergues and Bourbourg.

Cruising on the Canal de Roubaix at Grimonpont

I – Northern France

1. Dunkirk port and canals

DUNKIRK IS THE PREFERRED PORT of entry to French waterways for most boaters crossing the Channel from England or coming from other countries via the North Sea. See under 'Dunkirk as entry port' the description of the approach through the port and and its short **Canal de Jonction** to the three 'Dunkirk canals'. These lead out from the port in three directions: (1) the **Canal de Furnes** runs along the coast east to the Belgian border, a distance of 14.5km, and the beautiful town of Furnes (Veurne) is only 7.5km beyond the border; (2) the **Canal de Bergues** extends for just over 8km south to the small town of Bergues, where it used to connect with the Canal de la Colme, but this waterway fell into disuse in the 1960s; (3) the **Canal de Bourbourg** provides a 21km link from the Canal de Junction through to the river Aa. Formerly a key link between the port and its hinterland, extending to the Paris region, it was superseded in the 1960s by the high-capacity Liaison Dunkerque-Escaut. A 1.6km section in the middle of the Canal de Bourbourg was upgraded and incorporated into the larger waterway between the Colme diversion canal (dérivation de la Colme), PK 9.3, and the Mardyck diversion canal (dérivation de Mardyck), PK 10.9. For further details see under the Liaison Dunkerque-Escaut. For convenience the distances on all three canals are given, starting from Dunkirk.

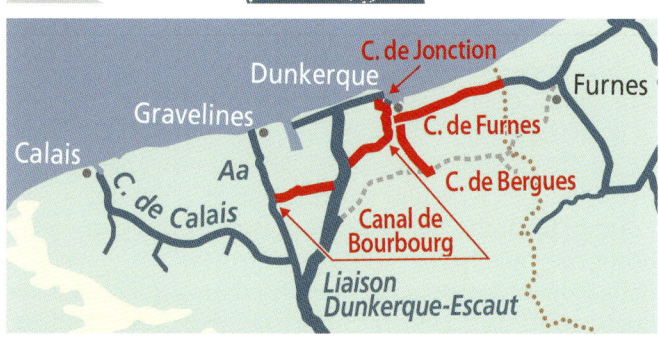

The **Canal de Furnes** is part of the complex network of wateringues (drainage channels) established since the Middle Ages. It was navigated prior to 1634. The canalisation was initiated by the Spanish, then rulers of Flanders, in 1669. The single lock was lengthened to 44m around 1818. Yet, the square lock at Jeu du Mail in Dunkerque, which gives access to the canal, was only 36m long. The canal's present depth was negotiated with Belgium in 1890.

The **Canal de Bergues** is one of the oldest canals in Flanders, shown on a map dating from the 9th century. The town itself, heavily fortified by Vauban in the late 17th century, is the main attraction for boats, which moor in a dramatic location just outside the fortified walls. The site acquired worldwide fame in 2008 as the location for the cult film Bienvenue chez les ch'tis. The local dialect and out-of-tune belfry chimes contributed to making Bergues a destination for tourists from near and far. Restoration of the Canal de la Colme would increase the number of visiting boats, but there is opposition from the authority that manages all the local drainage canals.

Key dimensions (m)	
Length	38.50
Beam	5.25
Draught	1.80
Air draught	3.50

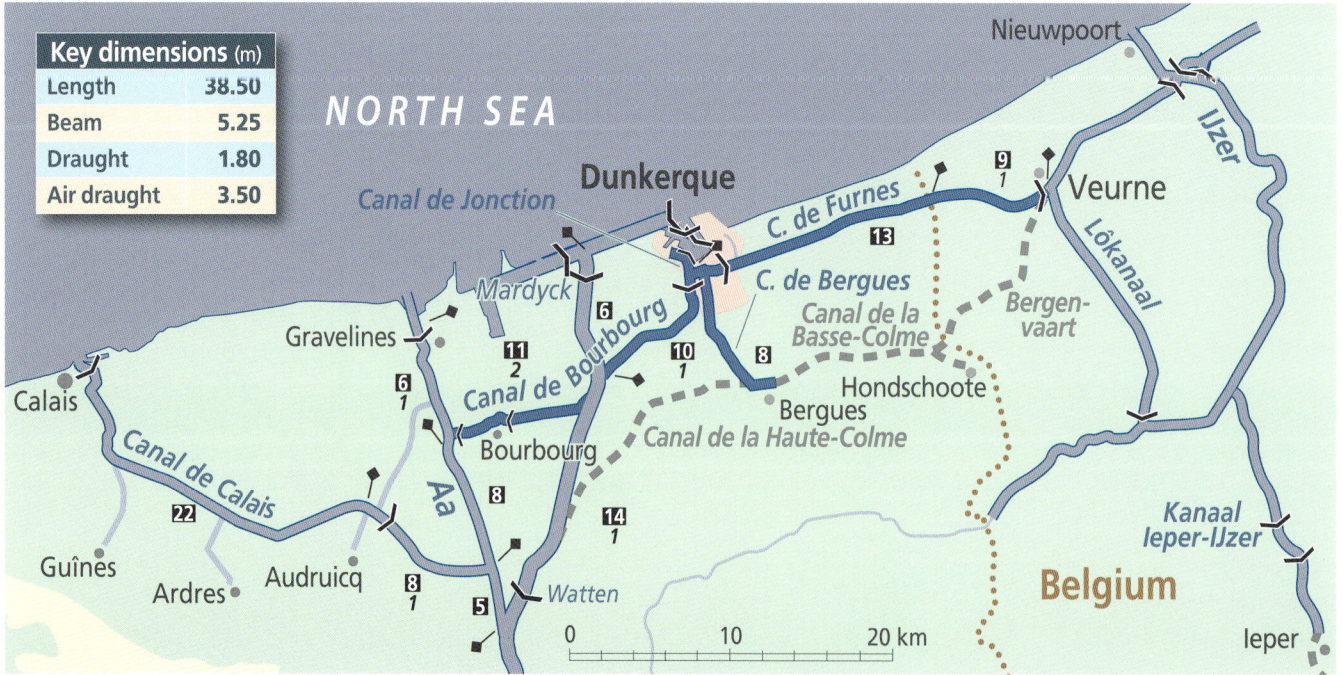

Dunkirk port and canals

*Work on the **Canal de Bourbourg** started in 1679, from Dunkerque to the Aa river. The present locks were built between 1846 and 1855, then enlarged to the Freycinet gauge. The 'Jeu du Mail' lock in Dunkerque is a curiosity. It was rebuilt to European Class IV standards around 1960, but there is no high-capacity link to the port basins downstream, only a Freycinet tide-lock. The high-capacity link is now through the Mardyck diversion canal, part of the Dunkerque-Escaut waterway.*

Dunkirk as entry port

The plan shows the slightly tortuous route into the canals from the outer harbour of Dunkirk. Call up on VHF 73 to make arrangements with the harbourmaster. If the port will allow, leave the main tide lock (Trystram) to the right, to proceed through the more interesting old basins of the port, passing or using the services of four separate *ports de plaisance*. A passage north from the corner of the Bassin de la Marine leads back into the commercial basins of the port, here Darse n° 1. Turn left here to approach the barge lock that leads into the Canal de l'Île Jeanty. From this point, an extensive basin where *péniches* used to congregate, continue south to the Canal de Jonction. This is where the 'inland' adventure begins, VNF's Canal de Bourbourg being straight ahead. Turning left, the Canal de Jonction (part of the port of Dunkirk) leads to the Canal de Bergues and Canal de Furnes.

Navigation

Once on the VNF network, navigation is straightforward. Encounters with commercial traffic will be limited to the port of Dunkirk and the Canal de Bourbourg, especially the section incorporated in the Liaison Dunkerque-Escaut. Note that the very infrequent movements on the other canals can lead to problems with weed and invasive species such as the water hyacinth.

Locks

There are no locks on the Canal de Bergues, and only one lock on the Canal de Furnes, situated at the entrance from the Canal de Jonction. Authorised dimensions are 38.50m by 5.05m. There are three locks on the Canal de Bourbourg. The one at Jeu de Mail in Dunkerque (see plan) is 110m by 12m. The other two, situated on the section between the upgraded length and the river Aa, have dimensions of 38.50m by 5.20m.

Draught

The maximum authorised draught is 2.20m in Dunkirk and along the Canal de Bourbourg to PK 10.9, and 3.00m on the upgraded length incorporated in the Liaison Dunkerque-Escaut, otherwise 1.80m.

Headroom

All the fixed bridges leave a clear headroom of 3.20m above the highest navigable water level (3.50m above normal level). There are no bridges on the upgraded section of the Canal de Bourbourg.

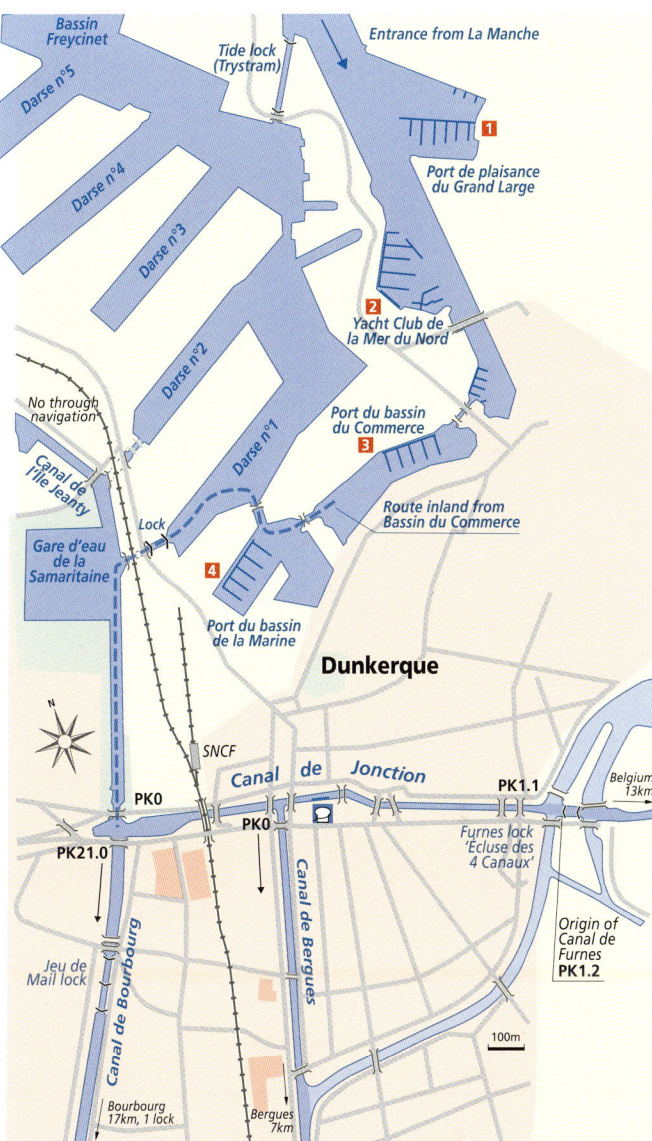

The Port du Grand Large **1** has a full range of facilities including a boatyard. The Yacht Club de la Mer du Nord **2** is recommended, as it has good facilities (03 28 66 79 90). Through the lock are the Bassin du Commerce **3**, spectacularly located in the town centre, and finally the Bassin de la Marine **4**, with more limited facilities.

Lock connecting Darse n° 1 to the Canal de l'île Jeanty. Once through this lock, it is 700m south to enter the inland waterways.

© FRÉDÉRIC ADANT

I – Northern France

Towpath
A metalled public road replaces the former towpath on the south bank from Dunkirk through to Bourbourg (with a 2km long bypass at the junction to cross the Liaison Dunkerque-Escaut), then on the north bank through to the Aa. The towpaths on the Canal de Furnes and Canal de Bergues have also been transformed into local roads.

Authority
Grand port maritime de Dunkerque
- Terre-plein Guillain, BP 6534, 59386 Dunkerque cedex 1
  03 28 28 78 78 (Canal de Jonction and Canal de l'Île Jeanty)
VNF Nord-Pas de Calais
- Terre-plein de l'Écluse du Jeu de Mail, 59375 Dunkerque
  03 28 58 71 10 (all three canals)

Route description

Canal de Jonction
Canal de l'Île Jeanty to Canal de Furnes

PK 0.0	Junction with the Canal de l'Île Jeanty (north) and Canal de Bourbourg (south), the former gives access from and to the semi-tidal basins of the port through a lock 700m to the north, the latter leads off to the south
PK 0.2	Railway bridge and bridge
PK 0.4	Bridge, Junction with the Canal de Bergues, south side, bridge
PK 0.6	Dunkerque footbridge (Passerelle Saint-Martin), *halte* (pontoon on south bank), town centre 500m
PK 0.8	Bridges
PK 1.0	Bridge
PK 1.1	Bridge, crossing of flood relief channel (no access)

Canal de Furnes
from Dunkirk to Belgian border

PK 1.2	Lock (Furnes), automatic
PK 1.7	Footbridge (Corderies)
PK 2.0	Footbridge and bridge (Dunkerque express road)
PK 2.6	Bridge (Pont Neuf)
PK 2.7	Pipeline crossing
PK 2.9	Road bridge (Maraîchers)
PK 2.9	Railway bridge (Rosendaël)
PK 3.5	Bridge (Chapeau Rouge)
PK 5.9	Bridge (Leffrinckoucke)
PK 7.1	Private basin, 500m branch to the north, serving steelworks (Usine des Dunes)
PK 7.4	Pipeline crossing
PK 9.7	Zuydcoote lift bridge, village north bank

Note that 48 hours' notice of passage is to be given to VNF, for this lift-bridge and the one at Ghyvelde, PK 11.6. The mobile phone number to call is 06 60 59 04 28. This is particularly relevant for boats entering from Belgium, of which VNF operating staff will be unaware.

PK 10.9	Road bridge (D947)
PK 11.6	Ghyvelde lift bridge (automatic), pipeline crossing, village 1200m south, Bray-Dunes 1km north
PK 13.3	Canal widens north side
PK 14.5	Belgian border, connection with Kanaal Nieuwpoort-Dunkerque in West Flanders, Belgium (*port de plaisance* in Furnes/Veurne, 8.3 km)

Canal de Bergues
from Dunkirk to Bergues

PK 0.0	Junction with Canal de Jonction, km 0.4 on the Canal de Furnes. Dunkerque boat moorings (base fluviale) 200m to the east
PK 0.0	Bridge (Pont Rouge)
PK 0.4	Footbridge (Batardeau)
PK 0.6	Bridge (Coq)
PK 0.7	Flood relief canal, r/b (not navigable)
PK 1.1	Railway bridge (Coudekerque)
PK 1.3	Bridge (Saint-Georges, downstream or 2nd bridge)
PK 1.4	Bridge (Saint-Georges, upstream or 1st bridge)
PK 1.6	Bridge
PK 1.8	Motorway bridge (A16)
PK 2.4	Mooring east bank
PK 3.1	Bridge (Sept-Planètes), quay u/s l/b, Capelle-la-Grande
PK 4.9	Fort Vallières (historic fort) r/b
PK 7.7	Junction with the Canal de la Haute-Colme (disused, except for boat moorings for Bierne 50m up the canal)
PK 7.9	Bergues basin, boat mooring along quay or 36m pontoon below town wall, 03 28 68 71 06, night €8, water and electricity included, maximum 5 days, restaurant, town centre with all services 300m
PK 8.1	Junction with Canal de la Basse-Colme (disused)

The author studied the feasibility of restoring this canal in 2006, but no decision is to be expected in the near future. It would open up an ideal circular cruising itinerary in the charming fenland region south of Dunkirk, and would bring many more boats to Bergues.

Dunkirk port and canals

Canal de Bourbourg
From Dunkerque to the river Aa

PK **21.0** Junction with Canal de l'Ile Jeanty and Canal de Jonction
Waterways managed by the Port of Dunkerque

Heading back to Dunkirk, turn right along Canal de Jonction for the boat moorings.

PK **20.7** Footbridge
PK **20.6** Lock (Jeu de Mail), bridge, VHF 22, quay d/s r/b

Heading inland, the canal skirts the southern industrial areas of Dunkerque, not exactly picturesque.

PK **20.0** Private basin and public quay (Petite-Synthe), l/b
PK **19.2** Motorway bridge (A16)
PK **19.1** Railway bridge, public quay d/s l/b
PK **18.8** Turning basin l/b, private basin through bridge r/b
PK **16.0** Petite-Synthe bridge, public quay u/s l/b
PK **15.6** Bridge (N225)
PK **15.2** Old line rejoins canal, l/b (access to Usine des Deux-Synthes)
PK **14.7** Water pipeline crossing
PK **13.1** **Spycker** bridge, quay u/s l/b, village 2.5 km r/b, **Grande-Synthe** (Dunkerque suburb) 3000 m l/b
PK **11.2** Gas pipeline crossing
PK **10.9** Junction with Mardyck diversion canal (liaison Dunkerque-Escaut), l/b

Caution required, beware of traffic coming up the Liaison Dunkerque-Escaut from Mardyck lock.

PK **9.3** Junction with Liaison Dunkerque-Escaut r/b
PK **8.3** **Coppenaxfort** bridge, quay u/s l/b, private quays d/s
PK **5.7** Road bridge (D600)
PK **4.0** Lock (Bourbourg)
PK **3.9** **Bourbourg** quay and mooring for 2 boats on bypassed section of old canal, water, electricity, slipway, small town r/b
PK **3.7** Lift bridge (Louis Manier)
PK **3.1** Lift bridge (Maisonneuve), private quays
PK **2.8** Site of former railway bridge (industrial siding), quays
PK **0.1** Lock (Le Guindal), bridge
PK **0.0** Junction with river Aa

The ideally located pontoon moorings just outside the Vauban fortress of Bergues

Landing stage (left) and small pontoon (right, in what remains of an old loop of the canal) in the village of Bourbourg

Le Guindal lock, at the western end of the canal de Bourbourg, is one of many in urban areas throughout France that have received protective railings; it is not certain that these are a bonus for personal safety. © JEAN-MARC GFP

I – Northern France

2. Liaison Dunkerque-Escaut

THE DUNKERQUE-ESCAUT WATERWAY WAS COMPLETED in the late 1960s to provide a route for high-capacity barges between the busy North Sea port and the industrial towns of Denain and Valenciennes on the Escaut. The waterway (referred to by barge skippers simply as *la liaison*) extends over a distance of 143 km from Mardyck lock, linking with the basins of the port of Dunkirk, to its junction with the Escaut (conventionally considered to be at Pont-Malin lock, 500m from the actual junction). The large-scale waterway and its branch to Lille and the river Lys (Canal de la Deûle) incorporate a number of earlier canals, which were widened, realigned and linked by new cuts as necessary. The **Mardyck diversion canal** (PK 143-137), **Colme diversion canal** (PK 136-127) and **Canal de dérivation de Saint-Omer** (PK 113-107) were new cuts built for the high-capacity waterway. The detailed map distinguishes the canals making up the through route, and also shows the numerous connections and branches.

The **Canal de Beuvry** is another attractive branch canal, remarkably rural in character since coal mining ceased in the area. Originally 2.5km long, it is navigable from the junction with the main canal at PK 66.9 through to the culverted bridge at Beuvry, 200m short of the terminal basin. The lift bridge at PK 1.9 has been restored.

The **old canal through La Bassée** offers another opportunity to escape into calmer waters, branching off from the through route at PK 61 and rejoining it at PK 58.6. The 2.6km of the old line includes a *halte* conveniently located in the centre of this small town.

The most important branch is the **Canal de Lens**, extending 8.6 km from its junction with the through route (PK 44) to its terminal basin east of Lens. Most of the industrial quays in this former coal-mining area are no longer in use, and the canal is much more attractive than in the past; it is also less polluted, following a programme of dredging works.

At the end of the waterway, the **old line of the Canal de la Sensée** is of interest. It extends over a distance of 3.7km starting from the main canal at PK 3.0 and connecting with the river Escaut. It includes the remarkable *Bassin Rond*, a tranquil canal basin which is wide enough to allow dinghy sailing and other water sports. The quay along the south side of the basin makes an ideal mooring.

Navigation

Barge traffic is intense, and since some sections remain relatively narrow, particular care should be taken when meeting or overtaking the bigger barges which operate on the waterway. Advantage should be taken of the opportunities to moor in wash-free water off the through route.

Locks

There are seven locks, falling towards Dunkirk from an elevation of about 34m at Pont-Malin, plus the sea lock at Mardyck in the port of Dunkirk. Their dimensions are 144.60m by 12.00m. In some cases the original 38.50m lock

The liaison *is made up of all or part of six original canals. The common thread of their history was linking up the navigable rivers which flow north off the Artois plateau. The* **Canal de la Sensée** *(PK 0-23.6), linking the Escaut to the Scarpe, was completed in 1820 by a private company under a concession from the State. The Deûle and Lys were linked by the* **Canal d'Aire à La Bassée** *(PK 54-93), built under a concession in 1822-1825, with both economic and military functions. The* **Canal de Neuffossé** *(PK 93-112.6) was first built as a military ditch in 1046-54 under Count Baudouin of Lille. Vauban proposed in 1688 to enlarge it for navigation as well as improved defences, but works did not begin until 1753. The canal was completed in 1774. For notes on the other waterways included in the liaison – the* **Aa** *(PK 112.6-121), the* **Canal de la Colme** *(PK 121-127.1) and the* **Canal de Bourbourg** *(PK 136-137), see the separate entries for those waterways. In 2016, nearly 50 years after completion of the high-capacity waterway, an ambitious programme of enlargement works is now under way, as part of the overall Seine-Scheldt Waterway project, a priority transport infrastructure project for the EU. This means rebuilding 35 bridges eventually to provide a headroom of 7.10m, so that containers can be carried on three tiers. New, longer and slightly wider chambers will also eventually be built at each lock, but probably not for a number of years.*

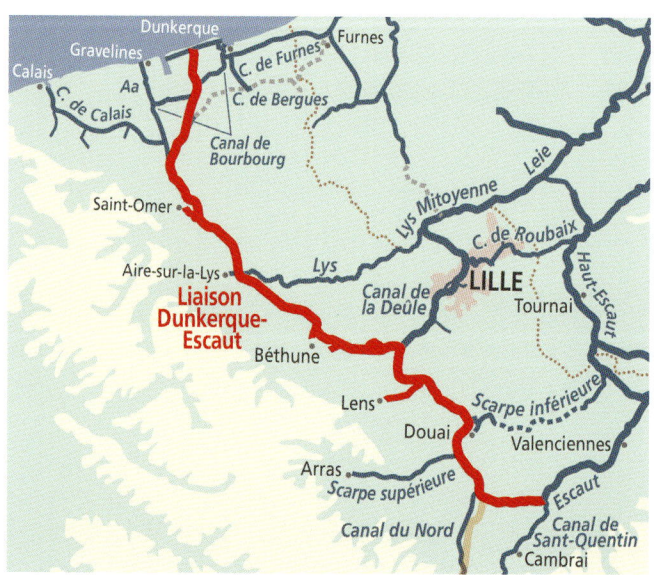

remains in operation alongside the bigger chamber. The lock-keeper's instructions should be followed. There are no locks on any of the branches.

Draught
The maximum authorised draught is 3.00m. On the branches the maximum authorised draught is 1.80m, except on the Canal de Lens (2.20m).

Headroom
After some recent rebuilding, all fixed bridges now leave a minimum headroom of 5.25m above the highest navigable water level. New bridges are built to provide a headroom of 7.00m, to allow barges to load three levels of containers. The least headroom on the Canal de Lens is 4.20m, on other branches 3.20m.

Towpath
There is a good service road throughout.

Authority
VNF Nord - Pas de Calais
- 16, route de Tournai, BP 26, 59119 Waziers 03 27 95 82 50 (PK 0-54)
- Rue de l'Écluse Saint-Bertin, BP 353, 62505 Saint-Omer 03 21 12 95 30 (PK 54-121)
- Terre-plein de l'Écluse du Jeu de Mail, BP 1008, 59375 Dunkerque 03 28 58 71 10 (PK 121-143)

Route description

Mardyck diversion canal

This section, 6km long, is given for reference only, as it is forbidden to recreational craft. Boats join the Liaison Dunkerque-Escaut from the port of Dunkerque via the Canal de Bourbourg.

PK 143.1	Mardyck maritime lock, VHF 18, navigation enters the inland waterway from the basins of port of Dunkerque
PK 142.5	Pipeline crossing and bridge (Fortelet)
PK 141.7	Pipeline crossing
PK 140.7	Main road bridge (D601)
PK 140.1	Dunkerque canal basin (Port Fluvial), l/b

The author in a rented pénichette *regretted closure of the lift bridge at Beuvry, back in 1988. It has now been restored.*

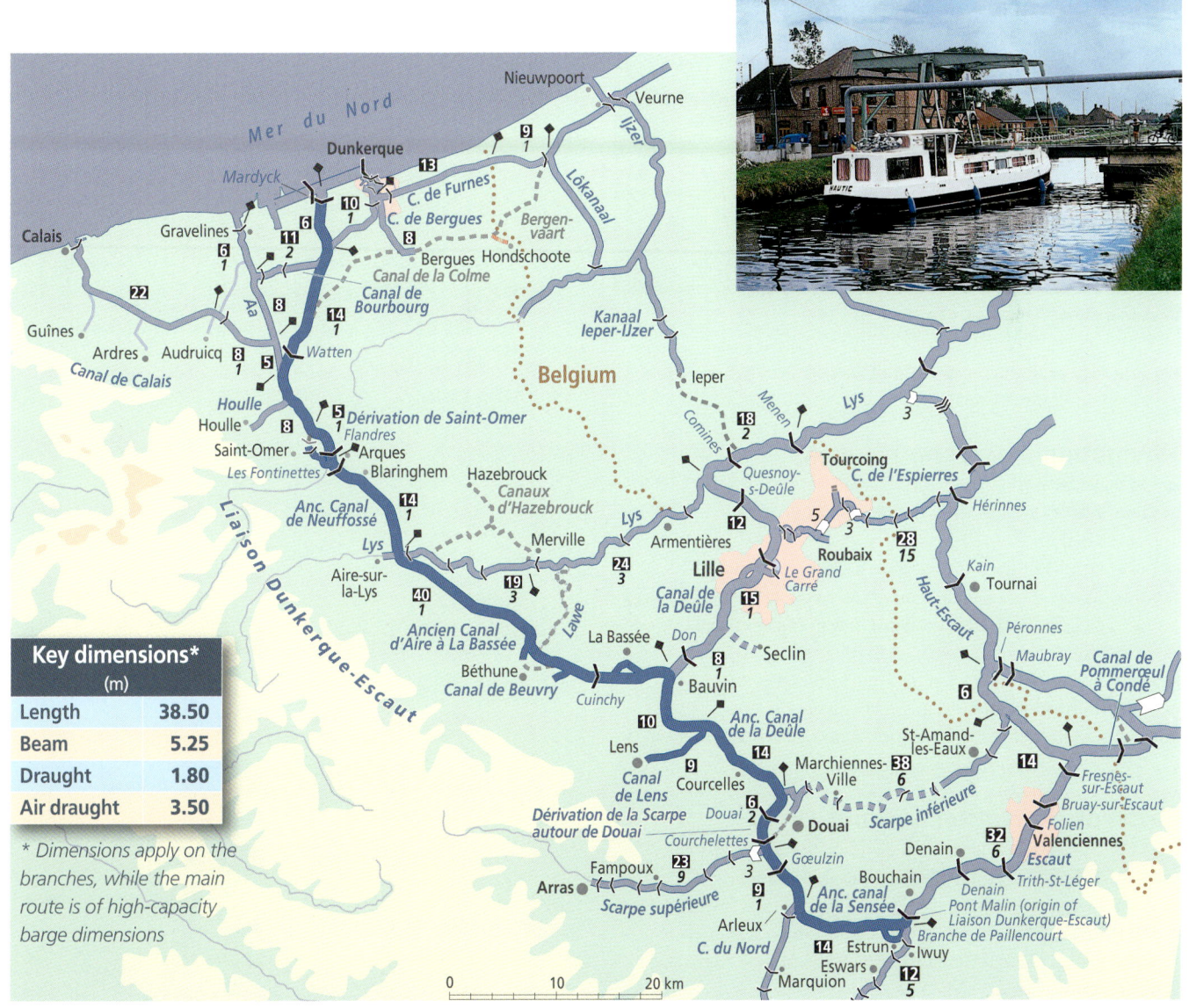

Key dimensions* (m)	
Length	38.50
Beam	5.25
Draught	1.80
Air draught	3.50

* Dimensions apply on the branches, while the main route is of high-capacity barge dimensions

I – Northern France

PK 139.5 Railway bridge (Mardyck)
PK 139.4 Motorway bridge (A16)
PK 137.3 Bridge (Basses-Brouckes)
PK 137.0 End of Mardyck diversion canal, Junction with Canal de Bourbourg r/b

Former Canal de Bourbourg
PK 135.6 Navigation continues in a section of Canal de Bourbourg
PK 134.9 Bridge (Coppenaxfort), raised to 7.00m
PK 133.1 Bridge (Dieppe-Straete)
PK 130.7 Bridge (Looberghe)
PK 128.2 Bridge (Lynck)

Former Canal de la Haute-Colme
PK 127.1 Junction with Canal de la Haute-Colme, navigation continues in Colme diversion canal, l/b
PK 126.5 Bridge (Pont l'Abbesse)
PK 126.2 Cappelle-Brouck quay l/b, village 2700m l/b
PK 124.7 Millam quay r/b, village 2 km r/b
PK 123.0 Basin
PK 121.6 Railway bridge (TGV/Eurostar Paris-London)
PK 121.2 Lock (Watten), VHF 22

Barge heading out of Flandres Lock towards Dunkirk

Watten lock, PK 121. © Jean-Marc GFP

PK 121.0 End of diversion canal, Aa branches off l/b, navigation continues in Canal de la Colme

Navigation in widened river Aa
PK 121.0 Bridge (D3)
PK 120.0 **Watten** bridge, quay d/s r/b, entrance to Watten diversion canal l/b
PK 119.4 Port l'Ermitage former boat harbour, slipway, r/b
PK 118.1 Cutoff (bypassing a bend in the river) r/b, junction with river Houlle, l/b (navigable 4.0km to the village of Houlle, see under Aa)
PK 117.8 End of cutoff
PK 114.5 **Saint-Momelin** bridge, small village r/b
PK 114.3 Confluence of Moerlack, r/b (entrance to Wateringues canal system used by small craft)

Canal de dérivation de Saint-Omer
PK 112.6 Navigation enters Canal de dérivation de Saint-Omer, junction with river Aa, disused, silted up
PK 111.9 Bridge (Doulague)
PK 110.2 Bridge (D209), quay d/s l/b, Saint-Omer 2.5 km l/b
PK 108.9 Bridge (Marais Platiau), turning basin d/s
PK 108.6 Railway bridge (Malhove)

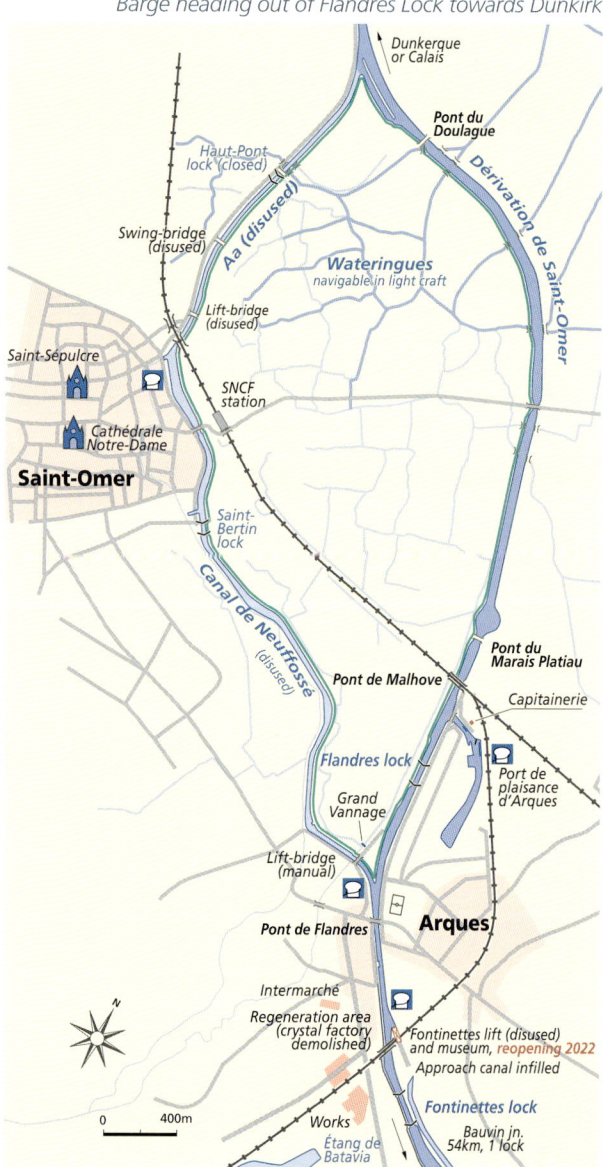

Liaison Dunkerque-Escaut

PK 108.4	Boat harbour in basin r/b, through bridge, 03 21 98 35 97, 06 80 05 77 35, 50 berths, night €12, water, electricity, showers, slipway €3-5, repairs, restaurant
PK 107.9	Lock (Flandres), VHF 18, water
PK 107.3	Junction with Canal de Neuffossé l/b, navigable to Saint-Bertin lock
PK 107.2	Arques bridge (Flandres), town l/b
PK 106.6	Widening at junction with former cut to Fontinettes boat lift, r/b
PK 106.5	Railway bridge
PK 106.0	Lock (Fontinettes), VHF 22, 03 21 38 08 84, water
PK 105.0	Private quays l/b
PK 104.5	Private quays r/b
PK 104.2	Bridge (Arques bypass, D942)
PK 103.4	Bridge (Campagne)
PK 101.2	Bridge (Asquin), quay u/s l/b
PK 98.2	Blaringhem bridge, quay d/s l/b, village 800m r/b
PK 97.2	Private quays r/b
PK 95.3	Bridge (Garlinghem), quay u/s l/b
PK 93.7	Pipeline bridge
PK 93.6	Boat moorings at canal widening, l/b (formerly junction with old line of Canal de Neuffossé)
PK 93.2	Bridge

Former Canal d'Aire à La Bassée

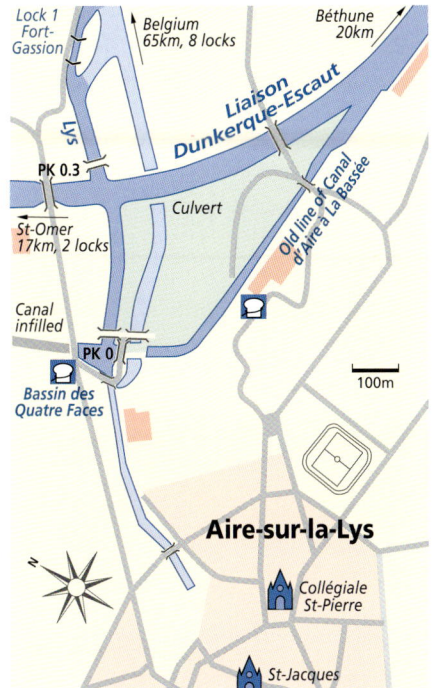

PK 93.1	Junction with canalised river Lys, access to Aire-sur-la-Lys, projected new port de plaisance l/b, see under Lys
PK 92.7	Bridge (D194)
PK 92.5	Junction with old line of canal, access to halte on south bank
PK 91.0	Pipeline bridge
PK 90.7	La Lacque bridge, small village l/b
PK 89.2	Isbergues bridge, quay u/s l/b, village 1 km l/b
PK 88.9	Railway bridge, basin u/s
PK 88.5	Footbridge (Bray)
PK 88.2	Steel works, private basin l/b (through bridge)
PK 86.3	Guarbecque bridge, quay u/s r/b, village 500m l/b
PK 85.9	Public basin l/b, d/s entrance
PK 85.3	Public basin l/b, u/s entrance
PK 85.2	Railway bridge
PK 83.7	Bridge (Épinette)
PK 82.1	Bridge (Biette)
PK 80.6	Robecq bridge (Eclemme), quay u/s l/b, village 500m r/b
PK 79.3	Bridge (Saint-Venant)
PK 78.1	Bridge (Suppli)
PK 75.7	Hinges bridge, village 1.5 km l/b
PK 74.5	Bridge (Hingettes)
PK 73.5	Bridge (Avelette)
PK 72.6	Junction with old line through Béthune, l/b, access to Béthune boat harbour at end of basin, free moorings (pontoon, 18m), 03 21 68 26 06, water, electricity, slipway

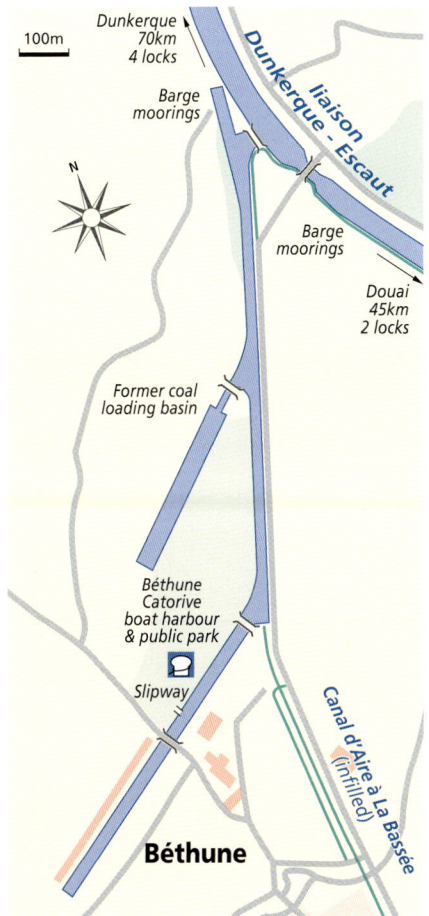

PK 72.4	Bridge (Long Cornet)
PK 72.0	Quays, l/b
PK 71.3	Bridge
PK 70.5	Public quay l/b
PK 69.3	Basin l/b
PK 68.7	Bridge (Gorre)
PK 68.4	Footbridge (Gorre)
PK 67.9	Gorre quay r/b, small village 400m r/b
PK 66.9	Junction with Canal de Beuvry, l/b, access to halte, see branch below
PK 65.0	Pipeline crossing
PK 64.2	Cuinchy bridge, quay d/s l/b, village l/b
PK 63.6	Lock (Cuinchy), VHF 18, two chambers
PK 62.5	Bridge (Crêtes)
PK 61.0	Canal divides, new cut l/b, junction with old line through La Bassée, La Bassée r/b

33

I – Northern France

PK 60.9	Skew railway bridge
PK 60.2	Bridge (D941)
PK 59.3	Bridge
PK 58.6	New cut rejoins old line, basin d/s l/b
PK 57.9	Footbridge (Blanc-Ballot)
PK 57.8	Road bridge (N47), quay (Douvrin) d/s l/b
PK 54.8	Billy-Berclau bridge, village 400m l/b
PK 54.4	Triangular junction with Canal de la Deûle

Keep right to continue on the *Liaison*

Former Canal de la Deûle

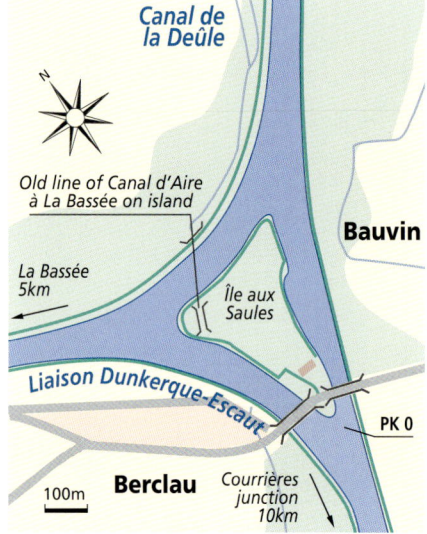

PK 54.0	Bauvin bridge (D163), village 1km r/b
PK 53.9	Triangular junction with Canal de la Deûle north towards the Lille and the Lys
PK 51.2	Meurchin bridge, quay d/s r/b, village 500m r/b
PK 50.6	Basin l/b
PK 50.5	Bridge (D165)
PK 49.8	Basin (Pont-à-Vendin) and boatyard r/b, quay l/b
PK 48.7	Railway bridge
PK 48.6	Pont-à-Vendin bridge, village r/b
PK 47.8	Annay basin and quays l/b, small town 100m l/b
PK 46.5	Bridge (Pont Maudit, D917), private quay u/s r/b
PK 44.2	Courrières bridge, quay d/s l/b, small town 1.5 km l/b
PK 44.0	Disused railway bridge
PK 43.9	Junction with Canal de Lens, l/b

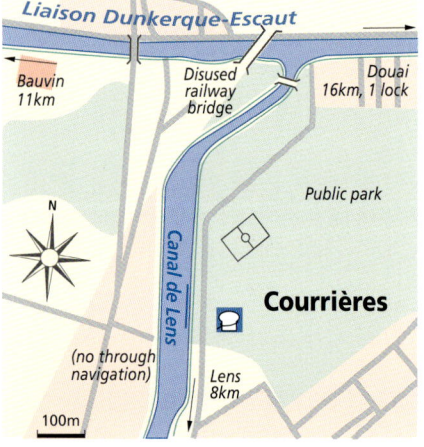

PK 42.2	Oignies bridge (Batterie), quay d/s r/b, town centre 1700m r/b (site of the last working mine in northern France, shut down in 1990)
PK 41.4	Railway bridge (TGV Paris-Brussels/London)
PK 41.2	Motorway bridge (A1, Autoroute du Nord)
PK 40.6	Bridge
PK 40.1	Dourges multimodal port platform Delta 3, quays
PK 38.8	Bridge (Pont-à-Sault), Dourges 1 km l/b
PK 38.4	Railway bridge (SNCF), basin d/s
PK 37.1	Basin (Houillères) l/b
PK 36.3	Courcelles bridge, Evin-Malmaison 1.5 km r/b
PK 35.5	Entrance to basin l/b, Courcelles *port de plaisance* in former dry dock on south side of basin, 03 61 19 74 00, 10 berths, night €20, 2 visitor moorings without water or electricity, shower, slipway (free)

Mooring here many years ago, boats were packed inside the tiny basin, and these berths are all taken up by long-term residents. Visiting boats moor to two small pontoons in the main basin.

PK 33.9	Footbridge (pipeline crossing), quay l/b
PK 33.8	Basin r/b
PK 32.6	Auby footbridge (with pipeline crossing), quay d/s r/b, small town 700m l/b
PK 32.0	Footbridge

Douai bypass (*dérivation de la Scarpe autour de Douai*)

PK 31.5	Junction with old line of Canal de la Deûle, r/b (enclosed 1 km long basin with former industrial quays), navigation continues in Scarpe diversion canal (bypassing Douai)
PK 30.9	Road bridge (N455 Douai North bypass)
PK 30.8	Bridge (Flers)
PK 30.3	Boatyard (Polygone), water
PK 29.9	Bridge (Polygone)
PK 29.8	Junction with Canal de Jonction (link with the Scarpe Moyenne d/s of Douai)

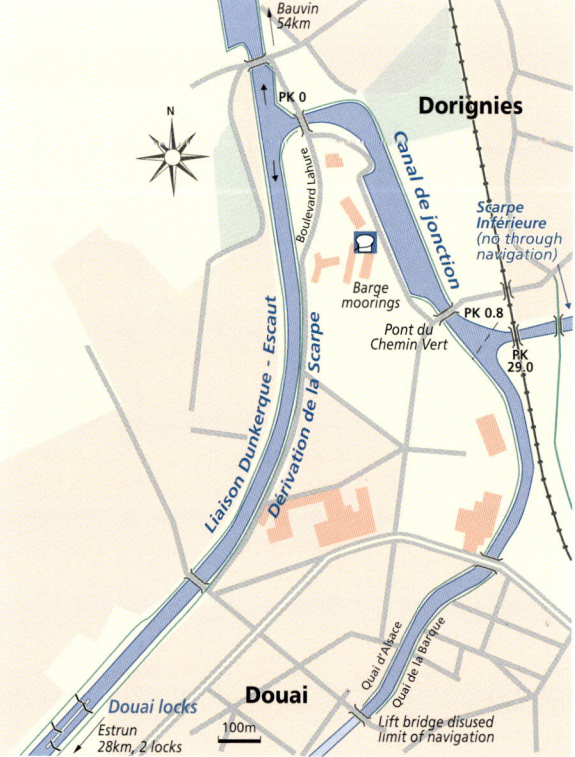

Liaison Dunkerque-Escaut

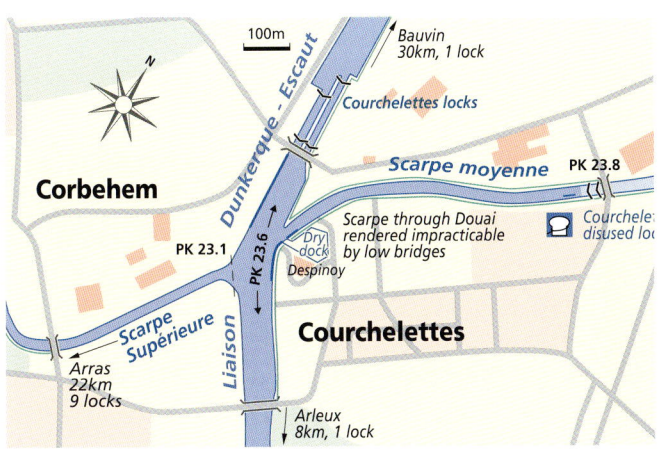

PK 10.1	**Junction with future Canal Seine-Nord Europe**, l/b, at Aubencheul-au-Bac, works to start 2024
PK 7.9	**Fressies** bridge, village l/b
PK 6.2	Hem-Lenglet bridge, quay u/s r/b, village 500m l/b
PK 5.8	**Hem-Lenglet** village and church l/b, footbridge
PK 3.5	Wasnes-au-Bac bridge (Pont Rade), village 1200m r/b
PK 3.0	**Junction with former line of Canal de la Sensée**, l/b
PK 2.0	Bridge (Marlettes)
PK 1.7	Culvert (Pré Piton) for river Sensée
PK 0.5	**Junction with river Escaut** (see plan)
PK 0.0	End of liaison at upstream entrance to Pont Malin lock, navigation continues on river Escaut

PK 29.7	Quays
PK 28.5	Bridge (Ocre)
PK 28.4	Footbridge (Ocre)
PK 28.0	Lock (Douai), VHF 22, 03 27 88 95 12, two chambers, water
PK 27.7	Esquerchin bridge, **Douai** centre 500m r/b
PK 26.9	Quay r/b
PK 25.6	Main road bridge (Arras road, D950)
PK 25.2	Road bridge (D621 Douai bypass, Rocade Minière)
PK 24.7	Turning Basin
PK 24.2	Railway bridges
PK 23.8	Lock (Courchelettes), VHF 18, 03 27 88 14 38, two chambers, bridge, water

Former Canal de la Sensée

PK 23.6	**Junction with river Scarpe**, navigable d/s to old lock

Just upstream of the junction on the *liaison* is the extensive Despinoy boatyard, 03 27 91 87 80, where many barges are repaired, maintained or reconditioned.

PK 23.3	Corbehem bridge
PK 22.5	Férin basin
PK 21.2	Férin bridge, quay d/s r/b, village 500m r/b
PK 20.2	Lock (Gœulzin), VHF 22, 03 27 89 60 49, two chambers, water

PK 18.6	Bridge (Moulinet), quay u/s r/b, Gœulzin village 1200m r/b
PK 17.8	Industrial quay r/b (cement works)
PK 16.3	Public quay r/b
PK 15.5	Arleux bridge, boat moorings u/s l/b, village 1200m l/b
PK 15.1	**Junction with Canal du Nord**, l/b
PK 12.3	Bridge (Abbaye du Verger), Oisy-le-Verger 2km l/b
PK 11.1	Railway bridge (Aubigny, SNCF -Douai)
PK 11.0	Main road bridge (Aubigny, D643), Aubencheul-au-Bac village 200m l/b
PK 10.8	Aubigny-au-Bac basin, quay r/b, village 500m r/b

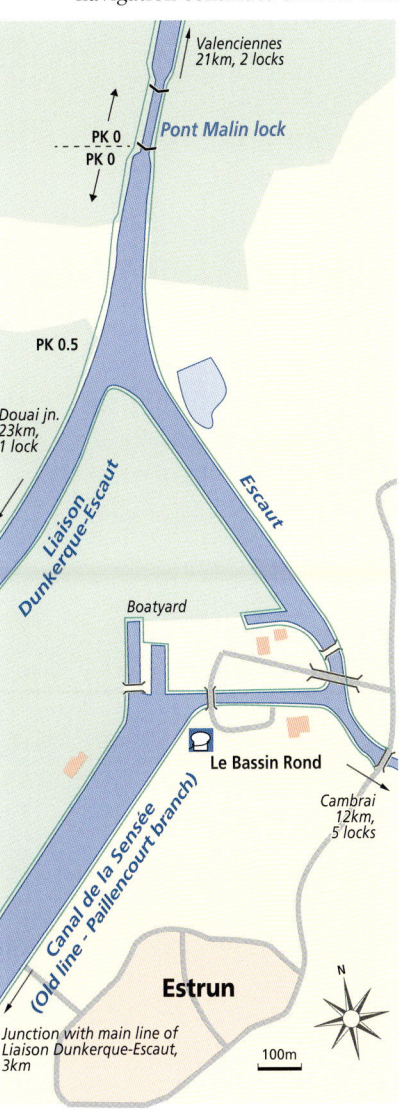

I – Northern France

The privately-run halte on the Canal de Beuvry © GONTRAND BAYART

Branches of Liaison Dunkerque-Escaut

Canal de Beuvry

PK 2.5	Junction with liaison Dunkerque-Escaut (PK 66.9)	
PK 2.4	Footbridge and railway bridge	
PK 2.0	**Beuvry** *halte* run by association, both banks, 40 moorings, 3 visitor moorings, free (maximum 48 hours), water, electricity	

If there is 'room at the inn', this privately-run facility is an ideal spot to moor away from the main canal with its heavy commercial traffic

PK 1.9	Lift bridge (rue des Plantes), café
PK 1.5	Large canal basin (150 x 120m) r/b
PK 1.1	Disused lift bridge (rue Thomas), limit of navigation
PK 0.4	Former coal loading quays l/b, camp site r/b
PK 0.2	Bridge (Planche Wattel), culverted, last 200m of canal inaccessible, Beuvry town centre 400m

Canal d'Aire à La Bassée, old line

PK 0.0	Junction with liaison Dunkerque-Escaut at PK 58.6
PK 1.0	Basin r/b
PK 1.1	Railway bridge
PK 1.2	Basin r/b
PK 1.5	Bridge (Avenue de la Gare)
PK 1.6	**La Bassée** *halte* on pontoon r/b, supermarket 200m

La Bassée is another excellent place to moor in calm waters out of the main canal, and the town offers all shops and services.

PK 1.6	Bridge (D941)
PK 2.6	Junction with liaison Dunkerque-Escaut at PK 60.1

Canal de Lens

PK 8.6	Junction with liaison Dunkerque-Escaut
PK 8.0	Boat moorings alongside public park r/b
PK 7.4	**Courrières** bridge, small town r/b
PK 7.1	Disused railway bridge (Vert Gazon)
PK 5.1	Bridge, former coal loading quays d/s r/b
PK 4.6	Footbridge (Harnes)
PK 4.5	**Harnes** quay l/b, town centre 300m l/b
PK 3.9	Bridge (Fouquières)
PK 3.2	Footbridge (former railway bridge)
PK 1.6	**Noyelles-sous-Lens** bridge, quay u/s r/b, town 500m r/b
PK 0.8	Turning basin
PK 0.6	Railway bridge, basin d/s r/b
PK 0.0	Head of navigation at road junction 1.5 km east of **Lens**, industrial quays (2.7km from original head of navigation)

Old line of Canal de la Sensée (Paillencourt branch)

PK 0.0	Junction with the canalised river Escaut at PK 12.2
PK 0.3	Bridge (Bassin Rond)
PK 0.4	Beginning of Bassin Rond basin (100m wide), quay l/b
PK 0.5	Former junction canal on r/b, boatyard
PK 1.3	End of Bassin Rond widening
PK 2.0	**Paillencourt** bridge, village 200m l/b
PK 3.7	Junction with liaison Dunkerque-Escaut at PK 3.0

3. Calais Port and Canal de Calais

The canal de Calais is 29.5km long from the canal lock in the port of Calais to its junction with the River Aa at Le West. It has three branches, extending to the small towns of Guînes (6.2km), Ardres (4.8km) and Audruicq (2.4km), lying on the edge of the Flanders plain. The canal is still regularly used by commercial traffic, and has been upgraded throughout to accommodate 600-tonne barges. The works, completed in the 1990s, included the reconstruction of Hennuin lock, demolition of the iron swing-bridge at the junction, and the automation of lift-bridges. Despite these changes, the canal remains an attractive cruising waterway, but the situation on the branches leaves a lot to be desired. The lift bridges on the Guînes branch are disused, so that only the first 900 metres is accessible, while silting limits the available draught on all three branches to about 1.00m.

Calais as entry port

Calais is the closest port to the UK (Dover or Ramsgate are the usual nearest departure ports) and an interesting town that tends to be bypassed by the vast numbers who transit through the functional terminals (car ferry and Eurotunnel) each year. For navigators it is a convenient point of entry into the French inland waterways network. The marina in the Bassin Ouest is entered through a sea-lock, which has waiting buoys outside. Call Port of Calais VHF 17 harbour control (or 03 21 34 55 23, to arrange for passage either into the marina or through the sea-lock and its lift bridges into the Bassin Carnot: email **calais-marina@calais.cci.fr**. From here it is right into the Bassin Arrière and through the canal lock into the Bassin de la Batellerie. This is possible approximately 1.5hrs either side of HW, which might guide the planned passage time if you do not need to enter the marina, for example for mast unstepping (see *Introduction*).

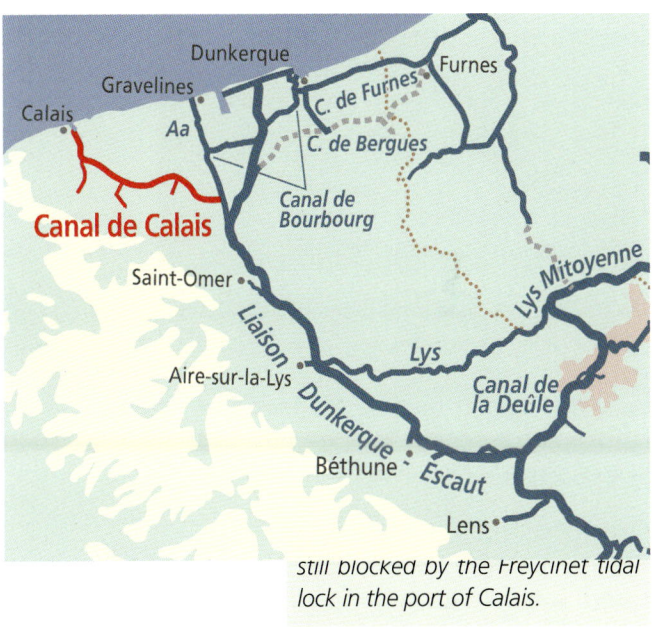

still blocked by the Freycinet tidal lock in the port of Calais.

Navigation

There are mooring pontoons near the VNF office at 45 quai de la Meuse (03 21 34 03 49). This may be useful to purchase a *vignette*, although this is now much easier on-line. VNF will also arrange for a travelling bridge-keeper to open the six lifting bridges on the canal out of Calais.

Key dimensions (m)	
Length	38.50
Beam	8.00
Draught*	2.20
Air draught	3.45

* Through route only, branches silted up

Locks

The canal lock in Calais is part of the Port of Calais. On the inland waterway there is only one lock, situated at Hennuin, with a rise of about 1m in the direction of

I – Northern France

The lift-bridge at Hennuin (top), and canal landscape near Ruminghem. © JEAN-MARC GFP

the river Aa. The former 38m lock here was replaced by a modern lock for high-capacity barges, 92.00m long and 8.00m wide.

Draught
The maximum authorised draught is 2.20m. The three branch canals have silted up and offer a depth of no more than 0.80m.

Headroom
All the fixed bridges on the through route leave a minimum headroom of 3.17m above the highest navigable water level (3.47m above normal level). The corresponding dimensions for the branches are of academic interest only, since none of them is maintained for navigation. They are respectively: Guînes 3.40m, Ardres 3.10m and Audruicq 3.70m. Vessels exceeding 28m in length could not enter the branch to Ardres on account of the difficulty in turning under the Sans-Pareil bridge at the junction.

Towpath
There is a metalled towpath throughout.

Authority
VNF Nord Pas-de-Calais, UTI Flandres-Lys
– Rue de l'Écluse Saint-Bertin, BP 20353
  62505 Saint-Omer cedex, 03 21 12 95 30

Route description

PK **29.8** Lock, VHF 10, and bridge, entrance from the Bassin Carnot of Port of Calais (2.3 km from the Bassin Ouest marina and 2.5 km from the English Channel), 03 21 34 55 23, night €27.10, fuel, water and electricity included, shower, repairs, restaurant *plaisance-opale.com*

The main port is in one of the tidal basins some distance from the entrance to the inland waterway.

PK **29.5** Bridge (Pont Mollien) and railway bridge, limit of inland waterway, moorings d/s
PK **29.3** **Calais** public quay r/b, water
PK **29.0** Footbridge (Vic)
PK **28.9** Automatic lift bridge (Vic), two separate decks
PK **28.4** Bridge (Saint-Pierre)
PK **27.7** Automatic lift bridge (Curie), footbridge
PK **27.4** Railway bridge
PK **27.2** Motorway bridge (A16, Calais bypass)
PK **26.8** Industrial quays
PK **26.2** **Coulogne** automatic lift bridge, footbridge
PK **25.6** Junction with Guînes branch, l/b
PK **24.5** Bridge (Pont de Briques)
PK **22.4** Turning basin
PK **21.1** **Les Attaques** automatic lift bridge, quay u/s r/b
PK **18.1** **Le Pont d'Ardres** bridge (Sans-Pareil), junction with Ardres branch, l/b, quay d/s r/b

Calais Port and Canal de Calais

The 'Sans Pareil' was a charming four-way stone bridge built in 1745 and set at 45° from the canal alignment (main line and Ardres branch). It has been replaced by a modern structure that is far from unique.

- PK 17.2 Sugar mill, pipeline crossings and quay, l/b
- PK 15.9 Motorway bridge (A26)
- PK 10.8 **Fort-Bâtard** bridge, quay u/s r/b
- PK 8.1   *Junction with Audruicq branch*, l/b

After 15km of open fenland countryside, approaching Hennuin, announce your arrival on VHF 18: the lock-keeper will first open the bridge, then continue to operate the lock.

- PK 6.6   **Hennuin** lift bridge, automatic, quay d/s l/b, small village

Village quayside mooring (the lock-keeper should be told if it is intended to stop here).

- PK 6.0   New lock (Hennuin), VHF 18/22, water
- PK 2.1   **Ruminghem** bridge. quay u/s l/b, village 1200 l/b
- PK 0.0   *Junction with river Aa* at Le West (PK 13.7)

The junction is near the village of Watten. Turn left (north) on the Aa to reach either Gravelines or the pleasant village of Bourbourg via the Canal de Bourbourg, then and on to Dunkerque. Turn right (south-east) to head along the Liaison Dunkerque-Escaut towards Douai, Paris and the Mediterranean.

Branches off the Canal de Calais

The three branches are listed hereafter for reference, and for possible exploration on foot or by bicycle. They are all heavily silted, and VNF does not allow navigation.

Guînes branch

The branch to the village of Guînes has to be explored by the towpath. It runs close to where the Field of the Cloth of Gold meeting between King Henry VIII and François I happened in 1520.

- PK 0.0   *Junction with Canal de Calais* (PK 25.6), railway bridge
- PK 1.1   Lift bridge (Planche-Tournoire)

Current limit of navigation in shallow-draught boats, as none of the lift-bridges are operated.

- PK 2.1   Lift bridge (Écluse Carrée)

There is no longer any superstructure for this bridge, which means that a crane has to be brought in to lift it for the occasional passage of a weed-cutting vessel.

- PK 3.8   Lift bridge (Banc-Valois), disused
- PK 5.0   Turning basin
- PK 5.8   **Guînes** public quay, town centre 500m
- PK 6.2   Terminal basin (filled in)

Ardres branch

- PK 0.0   *Junction with Canal de Calais* (PK 18.1) at Sans-Pareil bridge
- PK 0.1   Railway and road bridges
- PK 3.6   Brick works and quay l/b
- PK 3.8   Swinging footbridge (Brêmes), disused
- PK 4.8   **Ardres** quay, canal ends in cul-de-sac, town 500m

Audruicq branch

- PK 0.0   *Junction with Canal de Calais* (PK 8.1)
- PK 1.2   Bridge (Pont Rouge)
- PK 2.4   **Audruicq** canal basin

I – Northern France

4. Port of Gravelines and River Aa

THE CANALISED RIVER AA was like a 'back door' into French waterways from the port of Gravelines, until the tide sluices and movable bridges in the port were closed in 2017. The river is now navigable from just south of Gravelines to Saint-Omer, a distance of 27km. The 0.7km long 'maritime waterway' formerly managed by the Port of Gravelines is now closed since the authority was formally wound up in 2017. At the other end, the Aa formerly connected in Saint-Omer with the Canal de Neuffossé (or Canal d'Arques à Saint-Omer), but the waterways in the area were completely transformed when the high-capacity Dunkerque-Escaut waterway was built in the 1960s. Saint-Omer was bypassed, and part of the former through route was closed to navigation, with the result that access to the centre of Saint-Omer is from upstream (see Dunkerque-Escaut waterway).

Gravelines

Although no longer an entry port, Gravelines is a historic village port that contrasts with its bigger neighbours Calais and Dunkirk. The half-tidal marina basin dries partly, but does so to very soft mud of a depth not to compromise even fin keel yachts. The tidal lock at Saint-Folquin, at the end of the marina (see plan, opposite), is no longer operated.

The passage up the entrance channel to Gravelines is quite feasible and straightforward approximately 2 hours either side of HW, although this will depend on draught. It is not to be attempted in adverse conditions, including on-shore breezes more than force 4. There is 1km of concrete breakwater protected channel through the beaches, then another 3km to the marina entrance itself.

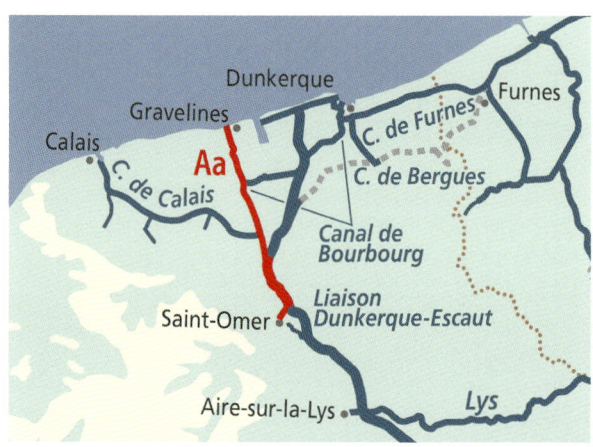

Works to make this fenland river navigable were started in 1114 under the Count Baudouin VII of Flanders. They were completed in 1320 under Jean III. Navigation developed in this part of France before the invention of the pound lock, and made use of primitive inclined planes or over-drach. The Aa and the port of Gravelines were vital to commerce in Flanders from the mid-17th century, when Vauban drew up the first plans for the Canal de Neuffossé to link with Lille. Today the river remains in the strategic national network despite its mixed identity: part of it belongs to the high-capacity waterway, while the lower section below the junction with the Canal de Calais is a tranquil recreational waterway which deserves to see more use. The River Houlle is also a delightful branch and well worth the detour. Restoration of the disused section to link with the old Canal de Neuffossé in Saint-Omer was envisaged by the local authority, but the project is currently on hold.

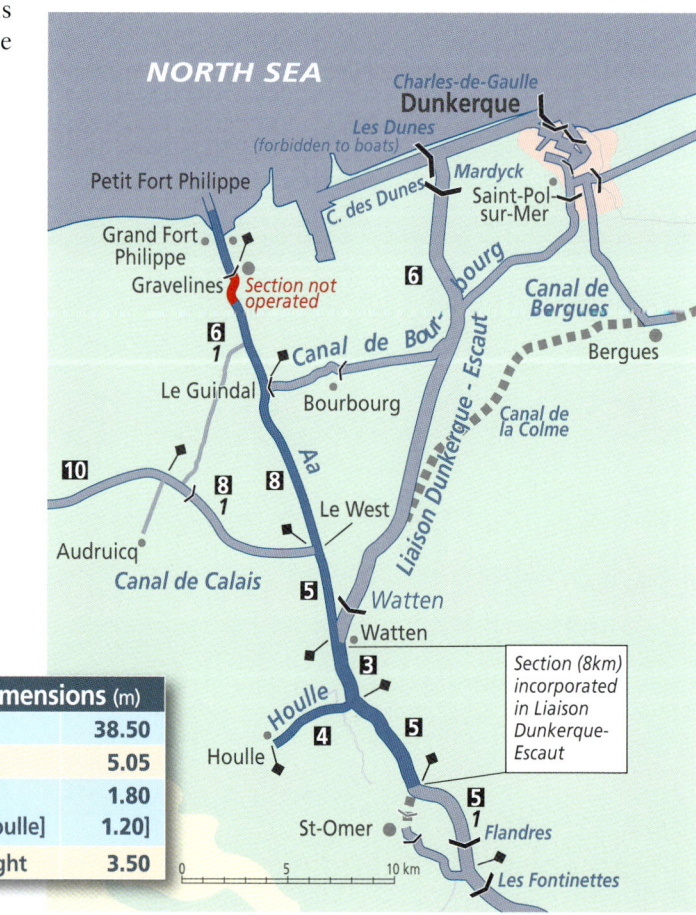

Key dimensions (m)	
Length	38.50
Beam	5.05
Draught	1.80
[River Houlle]	1.20
Air draught	3.50

River Aa and Gravelines Port

Navigation
South from Gravelines, the Aa is a tranquil fenland river, connecting with the Canal de Bourbourg and the Canal de Calais. Then from PK 11, over a distance of 8km, the river is incorporated in the Liaison Dunkerque-Escaut, and it is the PK of this waterway that are shown on the posts on the right bank. The route description is continued here throughout from Gravelines to Saint-Omer, ignoring these 'official' distances of the *Liaison*. Within this section, an attractive lock-free branch, the river Houlle, extends 4km from the Aa to the village of Houlle.

The last 2.1km section of the Aa to Saint-Omer from the junction off the through route of the Dunkerque-Escaut waterway is closed to navigation. The lock at Haut-Pont has been out of use for many years, and the whole section has silted up badly. It is to be hoped that the local authorities will recognise the value of the old waterway through Saint-Omer for tourism and find the means to restore this disused section.

Locks
The complex system of tide sluice gates in Gravelines, which ensures automatic discharge of the river flow to the sea and protection against high water, is no longer in operation for boats. Navigation is lock-free from Gravelines to the former lock (Haut-Pont) at Saint-Omer (now closed).

Draught
The maximum authorised draught is 3.00m in the upgraded section (PK 2 to PK 11), then 2.00m to the junction with the Canal de Calais, finally 1.80m from here down to Gravelines. The maximum draught on the Houlle is 1.20m.

Headroom
Fixed bridges leave a minimum headroom of 4.20m above the highest navigable water level, increased to 5.25m in the improved section, and 5.40m between PK 15.1 and Gravelines (respectively 4.45m, 5.55m and 5.65m above normal levels).

Towpath
There is a good towpath from Gravelines along the left bank, changing to the right bank at Le Guindal, but interrupted where the Liaison Dunkerque-Escaut joins the Aa from the left, forcing a long detour by local roads to Watten.

Authority
VNF Nord - Pas de Calais
UTI Flandres-Lys
- Rue de l'Écluse Saint-Bertin, BP 20353
  62505 Saint-Omer cedex 03 21 12 95 30 (PK 0-10)
- Terre-plein de l'Écluse du Jeu de Mail, rue du 11 Novembre,
  BP 1008, 59375 Dunkerque cedex 1,
  03 28 58 71 10 (PK 10-28.4)

Route description

Looking inland from the outer sluice structure (Vannes Vauban), the river entrance is off to the left. © JEAN-MARC GFP

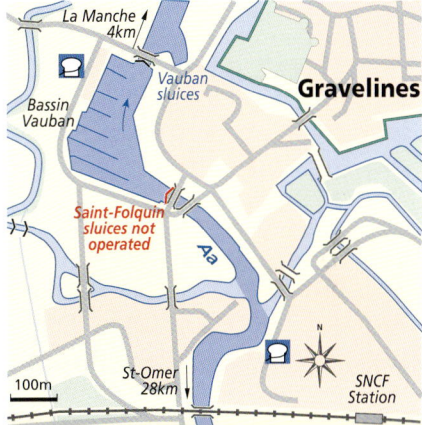

The town itself is historic as it lay on the border between France and the Spanish Netherlands. It has a fortified star plan, surrounded by a moat that can nowadays be rowed around. The Spanish Armada anchored off Gravelines in 1588, preparatory to taking on experienced fighting troops and launching an invasion of England, foiled by the (far smaller) Royal Navy's action using fire-ships that effectively destroyed the Armada and sent it on a calamitous voyage around the British Isles.

PK 29.1	Gravelines tide sluice gates, swing bridge, access to harbour and North Sea
PK 28.9	Bassin Vauban, yacht harbour, 03 28 23 13 42, 30 visitors' berths, night €19.40, water and electricity included, crane 7t, slipway, pump-out, wifi, repairs, restaurant

Port de Plaisance: VHF 9 harbour control for the lock gates, 03 28 65 45 24 The marina offers all services, good restaurant on the quayside and more shops, restaurants and bars in the town. email ***port.de.plaisance.gravelines@wanadoo.fr***. N.B. There is at present no connection between the main port and the river Aa. The following entries are given for reference, and for small craft that can pass under the lift bridges.

PK 28.7	Saint-Folquin tide sluice gates and fixed bridge
PK 28.6	Bridge
PK 28.5	**Gravelines** quay and boat moorings r/b, village 500m
PK 28.1	Railway lift bridge, industrial quays u/s
PK 27.5	Automatic lift bridge (D940)

Craft heading for Gravelines will not be able to proceed beyond this point.

I – Northern France

PK 24.7	Motorway bridge (A16)
PK 24.5	Junction with Canal de Mardyck l/b (small craft)
PK 23.6	**Saint-Folquin**, lift bridge, village 2 km l/b
PK 22.9	Junction with Canal de Bourbourg , r/b (Le Guindal)

The lift bridges between Gravelines and Le Guindal are opened by a travelling lock-keeper, from Le Guindal onwards they are manned. The Canal de Bourbourg that enters the Aa here has its starting point at Dunkerque; a short detour along it from here to the pretty village of Bourbourg is worthwhile (see section 1. Dunkirk canals).

PK 20.5	Lift bridge (Saint Nicolas)
PK 17.4	Lift bridge (Bistade), private quay d/s l/b
PK 15.1	Junction with Canal de Calais , l/b (Pont du West)
PK 11.6	Bridge (Ruth)
PK 11.3	LGV railway viaduct (line to Channel Tunnel)
PK 11.2	Pipeline crossing
PK 11.0	Road bridge (D600 Saint Omer-Dunkerque)
PK 10.7	Junction into Liaison Dunkerque-Escaut (PK 120.9)

The Liaison Dunkerque-Escaut joins the Aa from the left, interrupting the towpath. Cyclists have to make a long detour to join the towpath again at Watten.

PK 9.6	Boat moorings (*relais fluvial*) on La Bombe, l/b
PK 9.5	**Watten** bridge, quay d/s r/b, navigation continues in Watten diversion canal l/b
PK 8.9	Port L'Ermitage former boat harbour r/b, slipway
PK 7.6	Cutoff (bypassing bend in river) and junction with river Houlle l/b, navigable 4.0km to the village of Houlle (see below)
PK 7.2	End of cutoff, r/b
PK 4.0	**Saint-Momelin** bridge, small village r/b
PK 3.8	Confluence of Moerlack, r/b (entrance to Wateringues canals navigable in small craft)

PK 2.1	Junction off Liaison Dunkerque-Escaut (PK 112.6) r/b, end of section of the Aa incorporated in the *Liaison*, possible mooring for Saint-Omer in basin r/b
PK 1.2	Lock (Haut Pont), disused, restoration envisaged in 2010, then project abandoned
PK 0.0	**Saint-Omer** basin, former junction with Canal de Neuffossé, accessible only from u/s (branch of Liaison Dunkerque-Escaut)

River Houlle

PK 0.0	Lowestel bridge, junction with liaison Dunkerque-Escaut at PK 118.1, (Aa PK 7.6)
PK 0.1	Railway bridge
PK 0.2	Junction with river Muissens (small boats only), r/b
PK 0.4	Junction with La Serque, r/b (small boats only) r/b
PK 0.5	Junction with river Reninghe (small boats only) l/b
PK 1.3	Café l/b, moorings
PK 1.9	Road bridge (D600)
PK 2.1	Disused basin (former brick factory) l/b
PK 3.3	Camp-site l/b
PK 3.5	**Houlle** moorings l/b, village with shops, café, restaurant 300m
PK 3.6	Former grain loading basin, r/b
PK 3.7	Camp site, r/b, mooring possible
PK 4.0	Moulin de Lafoscade, limit of navigation but inaccessible on account of silting

Junction between the river Houlle (in the foreground) and the river Serques, part of the vast wateringues drainage system. EPAULARD59

5. River Lys

THE NAVIGABLE RIVER LYS extends from the junction with the Dunkerque-Escaut waterway (PK 93) near Aire-sur-la-Lys to the confluence with the Scheldt/Escaut at Ghent in Belgium. The length of waterway given in the route description below is 65km, ending at the point where the river enters Belgium at Halluin/Menin. The river itself forms the border over a distance of almost 24km downstream from Armentières, the right bank being in France and the left bank in Belgium (hence the official name of this section: Lys *mitoyenne*). The two countries have upgraded this shared section to provide a direct high-capacity link with the Canal de la Deûle, a branch of the Dunkerque-Escaut waterway. The Deûle joins the Lys at Deûlémont (PK 48). The Lys also used to connect with the Hazebrouck canals on the left bank at PK 5 and at PK 19, but these have long been closed to navigation.

Between Aire-sur-la-Lys and Armentières the river flows quietly through rural Flanders and makes a very attractive cruising waterway, while the towpath has also been carefully landscaped and planted for the enjoyment of cyclists and walkers. *Ports de plaisance* have been developed on the bypassed loop of the river at Prés Duhem, near Armentières, and at the border town of Halluin, and attractive moorings at many other locations.

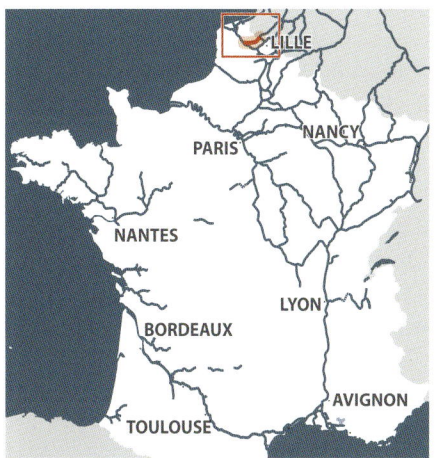

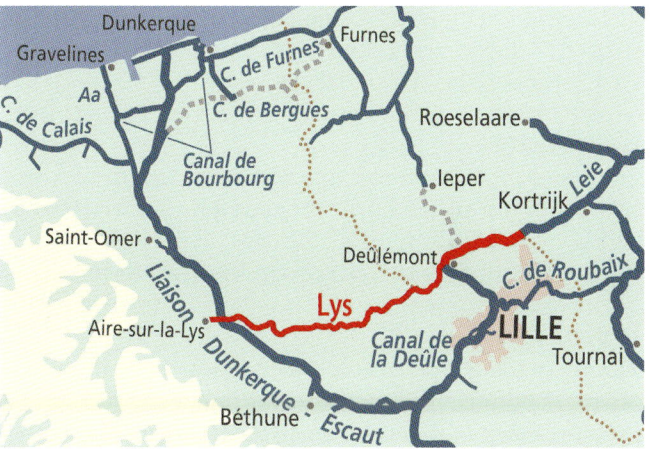

The Lys was a commercial navigation from the Middle Ages, but it was the river's devastating floods rather than navigation improvements which justified major works and meander cutoffs started around 1670. The 9m difference in elevation between Aire-sur-la-Lys and the border was gradually overcome by six locks and weirs, completed in 1780. The river carried a heavy traffic in grain and linen through to Ghent and Antwerp. The navigation was leased out to a company around 1825, and the locks upgraded to 5.20m wide, for a draught of 1.60m. The river was given its present depth by the Freycinet programme.

The section below Armentières was enlarged to Class III from 1930, and the border section was improved to Class Va starting from 1960. This section is part of the EU's priority Project 30 for the Seine-Scheldt waterway. The upstream (western) section, by contrast, is used almost exclusively by recreational craft, and is at present heavily silted. The Lawe, a tributary of the Lys shown on the map below, had four small locks, built starting in the 18th century, but fell into disuse, and has long been abandoned.

Key dimensions (m)	
Length	38.50
Beam	5.15
Draught	1.80
Air draught	3.60

I – Northern France

Navigation
Commercial traffic will be encountered downstream of Armentières, and especially on the high-capacity waterway downstream of Deûlémont. Above Armentières the *plaisancier* will be practically alone to enjoy the river and its charming villages.

Locks
There are eight locks between Aire-sur-la-Lys and Halluin/Menin, overcoming a difference in level of 11.00m. The first five are of standard 300-tonne barge dimensions, 38.50m by 5.18m. Armentières lock is of Campenois barge dimensions, 85 by 8m. The last two locks at Comines (PK 54) and Menin (PK 63), come under Belgian administration and have been rebuilt to European Class Va dimensions.

Draught
The maximum authorised draught is 1.60m from Aire-sur-la-Lys to Armentières, 2.20m from here down to Deûlémont, then 3.50m on the Lys mitoyenne.

Headroom
The fixed bridges offer a minimum headroom of 3.90m above normal water level, reduced to 3.60m above the highest navigable water level. Bridges on the Lys mitoyenne leave a clear headoom of 5.25m (to be raised to 7.10m).

Towpath
The towpath is practicable throughout for walking and off-road biking, following substantial works under the Lys sans Frontières development programme. This natural approach to treatment of the banks was preferred to the cycle path solution that is prevalent on many French canals, but in recent years a conventional paved cycle itinerary has been completed throughout the river.

The attractive moorings laid out as part of the Lys Sans Frontières development programme at Sailly-sur-la-Lys, PK 30. © LYS SANS FRONTIÈRES

Lys Sans Frontières
Lys Sans Frontières is a transnational body promoting the river under the slogan *Cap sur la rivière d'or!* ('where the river runs gold!'). The organisation has worked hard to make the river an attractive destination for all users, and runs a trilingual marketplace for ecolodges, boat rental and other water activities. It also organises an annual stand-up paddle race.

Authority
VNF Nord - Pas de Calais
– 113 avenue Max Dormoy, BP 56, 59004 Lille   03 20 17 06 10
Lys sans Frontières, Espace Françoise Dolto, 3385 Rue de la Lys, 62840 Sailly-sur-la-Lys   03 21 25 86 55
www.capsurlarivieredor.com/en

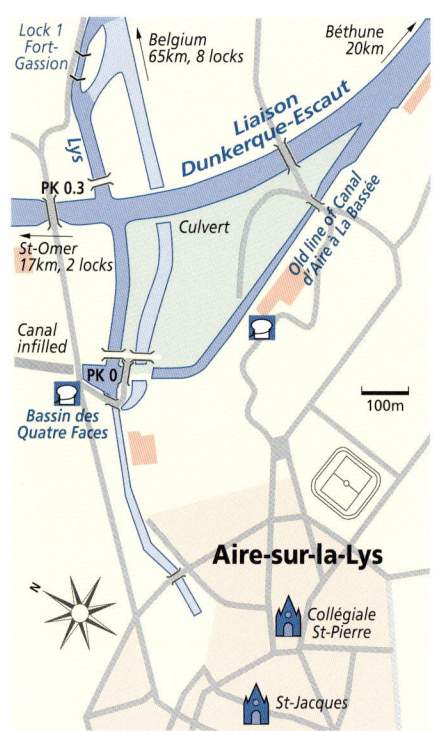

Route description

PK 0.0	**Aire-sur-la-Lys** basin (Bassin des Quatre Faces) and pontoon mooring, projected *port de plaisance*, footbridge (currently inaccessible), 500m from town centre
PK 0.3	*Junction with Liaison Dunkerque-Escaut*
PK 0.6	Lock 1 (Fort-Gassion)
PK 3.7	**Thiennes** lift bridge, quays upstream, village 1km l/b
PK 4.1	Footbridge (Oxyduc)
PK 4.5	Railway bridge
PK 4.6	Junction with Canal de la Nieppe (disused), l/b
PK 5.4	Houleron quay r/b, small village
PK 6.7	Lock 2 (Cense à Witz) and weir
PK 10.6	Footbridge (passerelle rouge Haverskerque-Saint-Venant)

River Lys

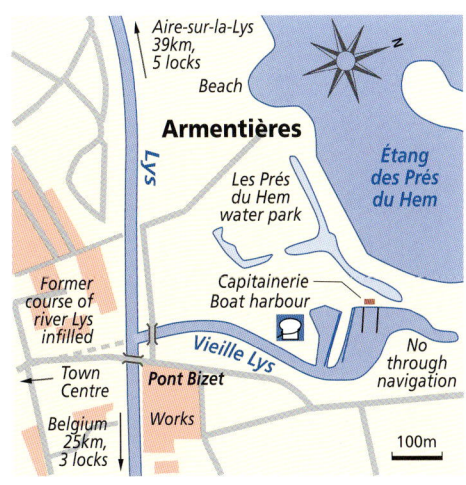

PK 12.4 **Haverskerque** *Port de plaisance* Flandre-Lys l/b, 03 28 41 33 12, 06 78 61 46 47, 6 visitors' berths, night €11, water €6.20/m³, electricity €11/60 kWh, showers €2, slipway €5, wifi, **Saint-Venant** village 300m r/b

A charming, compact *port de plaisance* in a small basin on the left bank, with shops, restaurants and services on site and across the bridge in Saint-Venant. Boats longer than 15m moor on the right bank (grass bank with bollards).

PK	
PK 12.6	Lock 3 (Saint-Venant)
PK 12.7	Road bridge (D916, Saint-Venant bypass)
PK 14.5	**Saint-Floris** village 500m r/b
PK 17.4	Le Sart quay, village 500m l/b
PK 19.0	Footbridge (Basse-Boulogne)
PK 19.2	Confluence with Bourre and entrance to lock-cut r/b
PK 19.4	Lock 4 (Merville), lift bridges u/s and d/s, small town
PK 19.9	Confluence of **Merville** arm of Lys, navigable u/s 800m
PK 20.1	Site of a former railway swing bridge, pipeline bridge
PK 22.3	Private commercial quay r/b and private footbridges
PK 24.4	Confluence of Lawe (formerly navigable) r/b
PK 24.6	**La Gorgue** bridge (Pont de la Lys), village 500m r/b
PK 25.7	**Estaires** bridge (Pont de la Meuse), quay u/s l/b, small town 300m l/b
PK 26.6	Private footbridge
PK 26.7	Bridge (Pont d'Estaires)
PK 30.2	**Sailly-sur-la-Lys** bridge, *halte* on pontoon d/s r/b, capacity 4 boats, village 400m r/b
PK 32.5	Lock 5 (Bac-Saint-Maur) and weir
PK 32.9	**Bac-Saint-Maur** bridge, small village r/b
PK 33.9	Entrance to Erquinghem-Lys cutoff, r/b
PK 34.9	Railway bridge (high-speed line to Channel Tunnel)
PK 35.7	End of Erquinghem-Lys cutoff
PK 36.1	Bridge (D945)
PK 36.2	Entrance to cutoff, l/b
PK 37.1	Motorway bridge (A25), end of cutoff
PK 37.9	Railway bridge
PK 38.5	Entrance to cutoff, r/b
PK 39.1	Armentières bridge (D933), centre 800m r/b
PK 40.2	End of cutoff, **Armentières** marina (Prés du Hem) and water sports centre on old course of river, l/b (see plan), 03 20 63 11 27, 06 07 08 62 22, 68 berths, night €15, water and electricity included, showers, pump-out, slipway

The pontoon for visiting boats at the popular Prés du Hem port de plaisance run by a former marinier   © LYS SANS FRONTIÈRES

PK	
PK 40.2	Bridge (Bizet)
PK 40.4	Armentières industrial quays
PK 40.6	Bridge (Pont Aristide Briand)
PK 41.1	Footbridge (Bayard)
PK 41.4	Lock 6 (Armentières) and weir, VHF 18, beginning of Lys mitoyenne (border with Belgium)
PK 41.8	Railway bridge (Houplines), disused, entrance to Ploegsteert cutoff, l/b
PK 42.3	Bridge (Ploegsteert)
PK 43.6	End of cutoff
PK 43.8	Bridge (belgian N58)
PK 44.9	**Frelinghien** bridge, village 200m r/b
PK 47.1	Footbridge (Pont Rouge), cycle itinerary changes bank
PK 47.7	**Junction with Canal de la Deûle)** r/b
PK 50.5	**Warneton** bridge, village l/b (in Belgium)
PK 54.0	Lock 7 (Comines) and weir, quay u/s r/b
PK 54.6	Former junction with disused Canal de Comines à Ypres, l/b
PK 55.1	**Comines** bridge, town centre 200m l/b
PK 55.6	Industrial quay d/s r/b
PK 56.8	Bridge
PK 57.5	Footbridge, pontoon l/b
PK 58.6	**Wervicq** bridge, quay d/s r/b, town 400m r/b
PK 61.6	**Bousbecque** r/b
PK 63.1	Lock 8 (Menen)
PK 64.7	Bridge
PK 65.3	**Halluin** boat harbour, 06 08 36 15 13, 35 berths, night €18, water €4 for 1000 litres, electricity, shower €2, slipway, restaurant, end of Lys mitoyenne, Belgian border, Menin bridge 200m d/s

The historic town of Courtrai (Kortrijk) is just 11km from the border, with no intermediate locks. It is part of the European metropolis of Lille-Kortrijk-Tournai, and an ideal short-stay round cruise via the Canal de Roubaix.

45

I – Northern France

6. Canal de la Deûle

THE CANAL DE LA DEÛLE is a branch of the high-capacity Liaison Dunkerque-Escaut. It is 35km long from the triangular junction with the main through route at Bauvin (PK 54) to the river Lys. It passes through the regional capital city Lille, potentially by two different routes: the old 19th century line and the modern bypass. Restoration of the old line is a project the author advised on for many years, but progress is slow because of the substantial investments required. The extensive basin at Lomme, at the start of the old line, is soon to become Lille's badly-needed *port de plaisance*, which will provide a unique mix of facilities for residential barges and visiting boats. Downstream of Lille, at Marquette (PK 23), is the junction with the Canal de Roubaix, reopened to navigation in 2011 after nearly 15 years of restoration works. The Canal de la Deûle is thus in the middle of several attractive cruising loops. Although officially a branch of the Liaison Dunkerque-Escaut, prosaically named 'from Bauvin to the Lys', VNF itself now prefers to use the only name that is recognised by the population of Lille and the region (for whom it is simply 'La Deûle'). The Canal de la Deûle is the highly engineered course of what used to be a small winding river.

The Canal de la Deûle, designed by Vauban to link the Scarpe to the Deûle, was opened in 1693. The canal was rebuilt in the 19th century and extended down through Lille, where barges previously had to transship from the 'Haute' Deûle to the 'Basse' Deûle. It was incorporated in the Liaison Dunkerque-Escaut, so the canal described here is only part of the original course. There are plans to restore navigability of the old arms of the canal through Lille.

Key dimensions* (m)	
Length	38.50
Beam	5.25
Draught	1.80
Air draught	3.50

* Dimensions apply on the branches

The 49m long barge Ushuaïa *leaves Don lock on the Canal de la Deûle heading for Lille.* © LILLE MÉTROPOLE/MAX LEROUGE

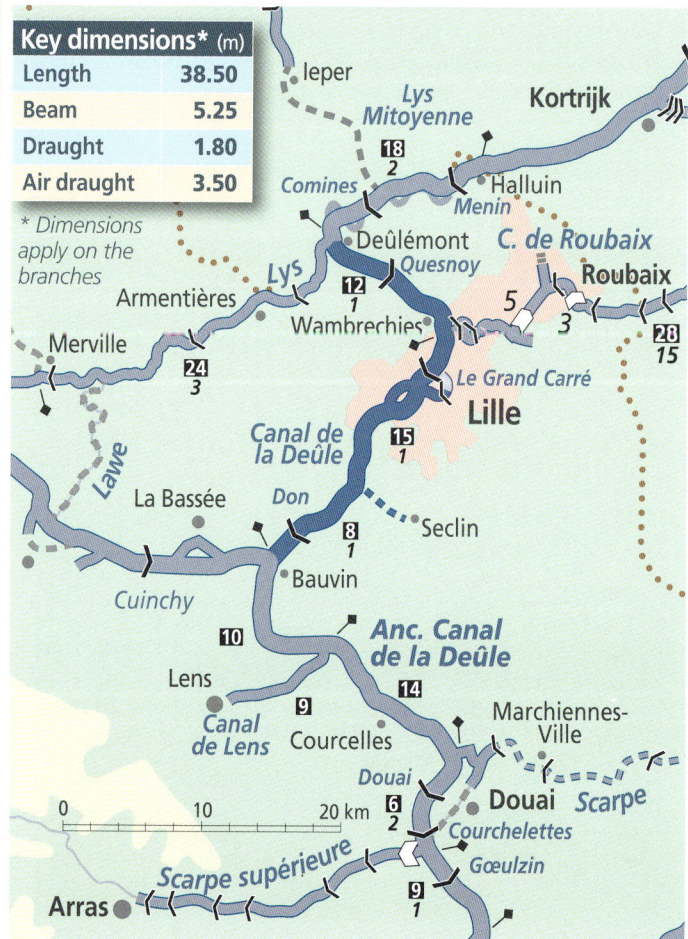

Canal de la Deûle

Navigation
The canal is seeing increasing commercial traffic, particularly to and from the port of Lille with its imposing container terminal just south of the city. Due care should be taken also because of the intense water sports activities, based just inside the Canteleu arm of the old canal. Substantial works will be encountered downstream from Lille in future years, as the waterway is widened and deepened to the European Class Vb dimensions (185 by 12m).

Locks
There are three locks on the canal, with the same navigable dimensions as on the Liaison Dunkerque-Escaut, 144.60m by 12.00m, built in the period 1965-1980: Don, Lille (*écluse du Grand Carré*) and Quesnoy, allowing elimination of Wambrechies lock, while Comines lock and weir on the high-capacity river Lys made the old lock at Deûlémont redundant. The former locks here and at Wambrechies have been redeveloped as boat harbours. The lock (38.50m by 5.25m) on the old canal through Lille (*écluse* de la Barre) is operational but rarely used because the canal downstream is a dead end. The old lock at Don is on a by-passed length of the former canal, but could be restored to navigation, as part of the works to upgrade the canal to handle much heavier commercial traffic.

Draught
The maximum authorised draught is 3.00m down to the port of Lille (PK 18). From here to the Lys the maximum draught is 2.50m, to be increased to 3.00m on completion of upgrading works. On the old canal through Lille the maximum authorised draught is 1.80m. The Seclin branch is regrettably no longer accessible (draught 0.80m).

Headroom
Bridges leave a minimum headroom of 5.25m above the highest navigable water level. The old line of the canal through Lille regrettably has a low fixed bridge in place of a lift bridge, limiting the headroom to less than 1.50m.

Towpath
There is a good service road throughout most of the length of the canal, interrupted by a fenced port area where local roads will need to be taken, downstream of Wambrechies.

Authority
VNF Nord - Pas de Calais
– 113 avenue Max Dormoy, BP 56, 59004 Lille, 03 20 17 06 10

Route description

PK 0.0	Junction with through route of Liaison Dunkerque-Escaut (PK 54), triangular junction, see plan
PK 0.1	**Bauvin** bridge, quay d/s r/b, village 1km r/b
PK 0.6	Junction with through route towards Dunkerque, l/b
PK 1.0	Basin (former *gare d'eau*, see plan), r/b, u/s entrance
PK 1.7	Basin r/b, d/s entrance
PK 2.6	Pipeline bridge
PK 2.7	Railway bridge
PK 3.0	Former canal through Don branches off, l/b

The old line including a 38.50m lock is expected to be restored in the near future, opening up new potential for the village of Don as an overnight mooring.

PK 3.5	Lock (Don), VHF 22
PK 3.8	Bridge (Don)
PK 4.7	Former canal rejoins through route l/b, **Don** moorings, slipway, water, 800m up the old line r/b, but reported to be in poor condition

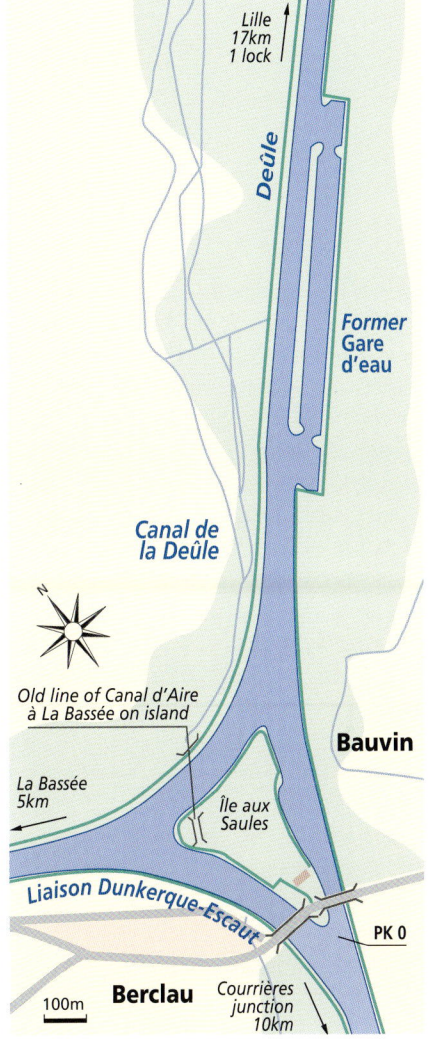

PK 5.5	Pipeline crossing
PK 6.2	Ansereuilles bridge
PK 8.0	**Wavrin** bridge, village 2km l/b
PK 8.4	Junction with Seclin branch, r/b

This branch is very narrow, has not been dredged, and is barely navigable. Regrettably, keeping this branch open for navigation is practically a lost cause.

PK 9.5	Bridge (Houplin)
PK 11.6	Road bridge (Santes)
PK 11.7	Old line of canal branches off r/b (dead end)
PK 11.9	Footbridge (Santes)
PK 12.2	Railway bridge, basin u/s
PK 12.4	Old line of canal branches off r/b (site of)
PK 12.6	Bridge (avenue du Comte d'Hespel)

I – Northern France

PK 12.8	Footbridge
PK 13.0	**Haubourdin** bridge, town centre r/b
PK 13.4	Old line of canal branches off, r/b (dead end)
PK 13.7	Motorway bridge (A25)
PK 13.7	Railway bridge
PK 14.3	Bridge

Lille has until recently been not quite the welcoming place for boaters that it should have been, but major changes are under way in 2021. The City and Metropolitan Councils (Métropole Européenne de Lille, MEL) have drawn up ambitious plans for restoration of the two old arms of the original Canal de la Deûle, as well as the former basin in the city centre (Bassin de Wault) and the arm of the Vieille Deûle leading to the Roubaix pumping station. It was planned to rewater the latter arm through to the centre of Vieux Lille at the Avenue du Peuple Belge **1**, but the idea, the brainchild of Mayoress Martine Aubry, has been shelved. The focus now is on developing a substantial *port de plaisance* in the Bois Blancs basin **2**. The original plans for a conventional facility were amended to be more inclusive of the activities historically developed in the basin by local associations and residential *péniches*.

The author has recommended restoration of the old line throughout Lille since 1988, to attract more waterborne tourists to the city. These involve building a movable bridge in the middle of the Canteleu arm **3**, and adding a three-way circular lock at the end of the Moyenne Deûle, thereby completing the bypass of the modern cut and the Grand Carré lock **4**; a second 185m long chamber will eventually have to be built here. Boats may take advantage of informal moorings along the Quai Léon Jouhaux upstream of the La Barre lock.

PK 14.8	Sequedin power station, quay l/b
PK 15.3	Footbridge, numerous industrial quays d/s
PK 16.0	Bridge (D48, Avenue Kuhlmann), navigation enters **Port of Lille**
PK 16.2	Port basin r/b (Darse No 1)
PK 16.4	Link with Canteleu branch), l/b

Access is currently blocked by a chain, pending development of the basin as a long-awaited, fully-equipped *port de plaisance* for Lille.

PK 16.7	Former basin r/b (Darse No 2, infilled)
PK 17.0	Basin r/b (Darse No 3), container terminal
PK 17.6	Bridge (Pont de Dunkerque)
PK 18.3	Bridge (Avenue Léon-Jouhaux)
PK 18.5	**Lille**, junction with Canteleu branch and Moyenne Deûle (see plan), access to city centre via Moyenne Deûle, 800m to mooring u/s of the lock (Écluse de la Barre, not in use)
PK 18.6	Footbridge (Colisée)
PK 19.3	Footbridge (République)
PK 19.7	Lock (Grand Carré), VHF 18
PK 20.0	Road bridge (Pont Royal)
PK 20.4	Railway viaduct (TGV Nord/Eurostar)
PK 20.8	Bridge (Sainte-Hélène)
PK 21.6	Pipeline crossing and rail bridge (La Madeleine)
PK 22.2	Bridge (L'Abbaye), industrial quays d/s
PK 22.3	Pipeline crossing
PK 22.4	Pipeline crossing
PK 23.1	Junction with Canal de Roubaix, r/b

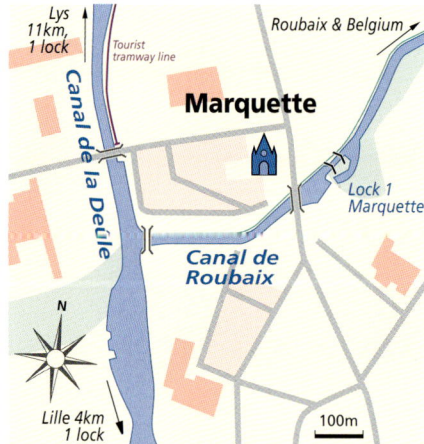

PK 23.3	**Marquette-lez-Lille** bridge, quay d/s r/b, town r/b (Lille suburb)
PK 24.0	Bridge (D652 Lille northern bypass)
PK 24.9	**Wambrechies** bridge, quay for 8 visiting boats u/s l/b, 03 20 15 85 37, 06 12 31 03 14, night €15, water and electricity (not included), shower, wifi, slipway €5, restaurants, town l/b

Wambrechies is a delightful location, a busy village with a waterside *brasserie* and shops, a short bus ride from Lille city centre, and the principal *port de plaisance* for Lille until completion of the development in the Bois

Canal de la Deûle

Blancs basin. Good services and some shelter from the wash of passing traffic for those lucky enough to moor inside the former lock chamber. The Claeyssens gin distillery adjacent to the port is well worth visiting.

Deûlémont port de plaisance just before the junction with the Lys
© Lille Métropole/Max Lerouge

Branches off Canal de la Deûle

Canteleu branch

PK 0.0	**Junction off the 'grand gabarit' canal** (Port of Lille) at PK 16.4
PK 0.1	Pipeline crossing (possibly blocked by chain)
PK 0.3	Basin (Bassin des Bois Blancs)

Formerly occupied by residential barges (retired *mariniers*), to be developed as a *port de plaisance*

PK 0.5	Automatic lift bridge
PK 1.0	Footbridge (Bois-Blancs)
PK 1.3	Fixed low bridges (Canteleu), shops Avenue de Dunkerque l/b, no through navigation
PK 1.8	Bridge (Léo-Lagrange), canoe and rowing club moorings d/s r/b
PK 1.9	Footbridge
PK 2.0	**Junction back into the main line**

Wambrechies port de plaisance

PK 25.0	Private quay (distillery) l/b
PK 27.7	Turning basin
PK 28.4	New lock (Quesnoy), VHF 22
PK 29.9	**Quesnoy-sur-Deûle** bridge, quay d/s l/b, capacity 14 boats, 03 20 63 11 89, night €10.60, water, electricity, slipway, restaurant small town r/b

The facilities are mainly used for water sports (dinghy sailing, canoeing and day boats).

PK 30.4	Railway bridge
PK 33.8	Former lock (Deûlémont) l/b, bypassed by new channel
PK 33.9	**Deûlémont** footbridge, quay l/b, boat harbour, 42 berths, 3 visitor berths, 03 20 42 78 69, night €12, water and electricity (metered), shower, slipway, village 1.5 km r/b
PK 34.6	Bridge (D945)
PK 34.8	**Junction with canalised river Lys**

Turn left here for Armentières and the delightful river Lys up to Aire-sur-la-Lys and the Liaison Dunkerque-Escaut. The high-capacity waterway to the right is officially the Lys mitoyenne, which means that it is shared by Belgium and France under a specific treaty.

Barges on the Canteleu arm of the Canal de la Deûle in Lille, with the Bois Blancs basin in the background. As part of the new port de plaisance, the central jetty visible on the left will be rebuilt.
© Ville de Lomme

7. Canal de Roubaix

THE CANAL DE ROUBAIX CONNECTS two high-capacity (*grand gabarit*) waterways: the Canal de la Deûle branch of the Liaison Dunkerque-Escaut) and the river Escaut (8.4 km and three locks beyond the border, via the Canal de l'Espierre in Belgium). The length of the canal from the junction with the Deûle at Marquette-lez-Lille to the border at Leers is 20km. The first 3.6km on the Deûle side is used daily by barges unloading at the Lesaffre yeast factory in Marcq-en-Barœul, and remains in the VNF-managed national network. The rest of the canal has been transferred to the Lille metropolitan council (MEL).

Thanks first to a determined campaign (in which the international waterways movement played a part, alongside local associations), then to strong political support both locally and in the EU, a project for complete restoration of the cross-border canal link was submitted for EU funding in 2003 and approved the following year. The 'Blue Links' programme of works, for a budget which finally reached €50 million (including the cost of an initial phase of works carried out in 1999-2002), was completed and the canal reopened to navigation for the 'Blue Days' event in September 2009.

There are two branches, both now with abandoned sections. Navigation extends from the through route to the *port de plaisance* at Wasquehal (0.6km) and to the fixed-deck former lift bridge in Tourcoing (0.9km) respectively. The first section of the Tourcoing branch is a charming, deep tree-lined cutting.

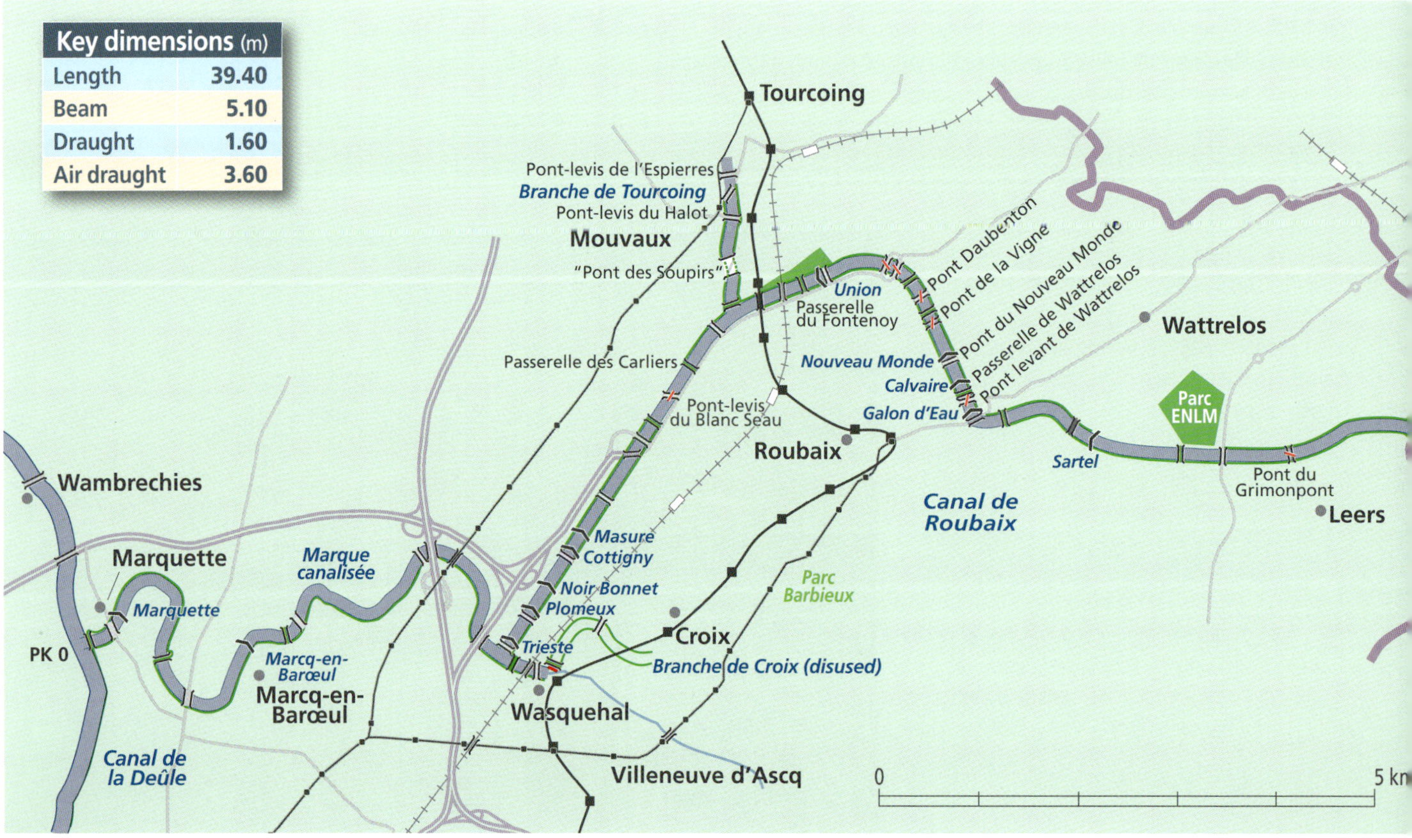

Key dimensions (m)	
Length	39.40
Beam	5.10
Draught	1.60
Air draught	3.60

Canal de Roubaix

In 1821 local manufacturers and merchants promoted a canal to link France to Belgium. The wool and textile industries were developing rapidly in the Roubaix-Tourcoing area, and needed secure supplies of water and coal, both essential to their activity. The first section, canalising the river Marque from the Deûle to Croix, was completed In 1831, to Freycinet dimensions. In 1843, the section linking Roubaix to the Belgian border was opened, at the same time as the Espierre Canal in Belgium. The project was then delayed by the difficulty of tunnelling under the watershed in Roubaix. New plans were made for the watershed section, routed further north, thus serving Tourcoing, and the connection was made in January 1877, when the first barge loaded with coal, 'La Décidée', reached Roubaix from the Deûle. The Tourcoing branch was completed In 1893. The canal was closed after structures failed in 1985, but it was not long before the campaign to save the heritage was started. Restoration was completed in 2009 and the canal was reopened in 2011 under new management by the Lille metropolitan authority.

A mussel-boat moored in front of what used to be the Descente des Mariniers *café at Roubaix during the 'Blue Days' event in September 2009. The same boat had moored here in the 1930s, transporting its improbable cargo of mussels from the Scheldt estuary.* © PAUL VERMAUT/TOLERANT

Navigation

The canal has been found by all *plaisanciers* who use it to be a delightful navigation, with its locks and lift-bridges operated by friendly and attentive staff. A secure overnight mooring has been provided on the summit level just above the lock at L'Union, with four water and electricity connections. Because of operating constraints, it is important to allow two days to make the transit.

Locks

There are 2 locks on the canalised river Marque (or *Marque Urbaine*). Five more climb from the Marque to the summit level, while the remaining five fall towards the Escaut. The lock dimensions are 39.40m by 5.10m.

The lock on the Croix branch just before the Wasquehal basin is permanently open, following construction of a new weir beyond the harbour and lowering of the intermediate section. All locks (and bridges, see below) have been mechanised and are operated by staff of Métropole Européenne de Lille.

Draught

The maximum draught is 1.80m from the Deûle junction up to the industrial quay at PK 3.3. Over the remaining length, the dredging was completed to a depth of 1.90 m, for a draught of 1.60m. However, the back-pumping system at each lock means that there is a slight drawdown during busy days, so the full depth may not be available later in the day.

Headroom

The minimum headroom is 3.60m above normal water level. There are eight lift bridges and one swing bridge, all operated by waterway staff. The original EU-funded Blue Links project provided for remote control and monitoring equipment at an operations control centre beside Union lock, but this project has been shelved for the time being.

Towpath

There is a good towpath throughout, which has been attractively developed for use by pedestrians and cyclists.

Authority

VNF Nord-Pas de Calais
- 113 avenue Max Dormoy, BP 56, 59004 Lille, 03 20 17 06 10 (PK 0-4).

Métropole Européenne de Lille – Direction Nature Agriculture Environnement, 2 boulevard des Cités Unies, CS 50749, 59034 Lille cedex

Canal management: 202 rue de Roubaix, 59200 Tourcoing 03 20 63 11 39 (PK 4-20)

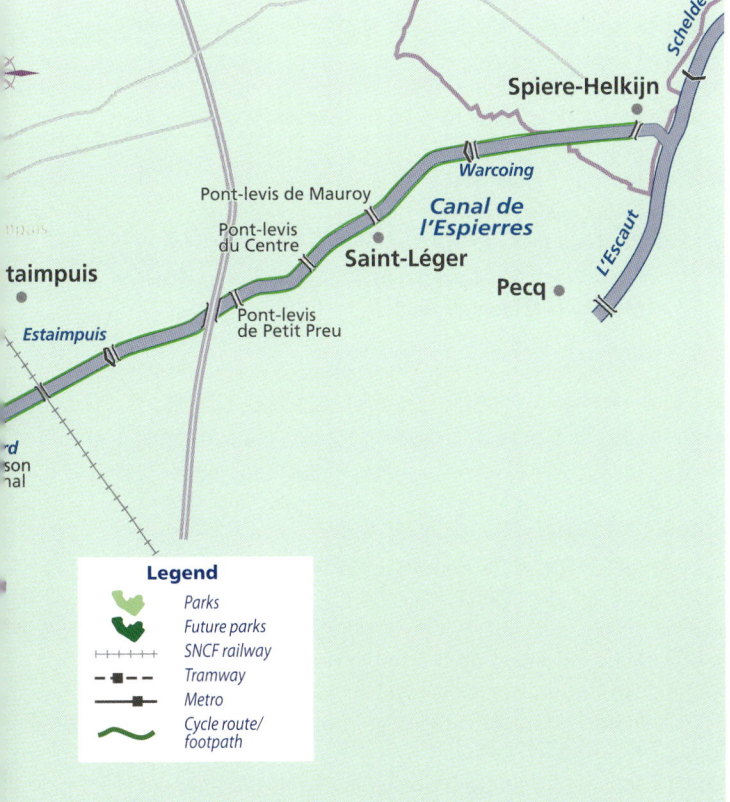

I – Northern France

Route description

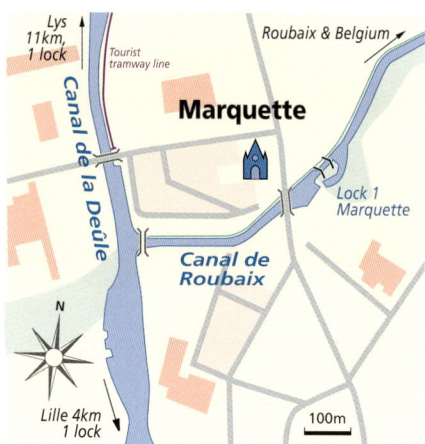

PK **0.0** *Junction with Canal de la Deûle*, footbridge

This footbridge also carries the Amitram tram line which follows the Deûle down to Wambrechies.

PK **0.3**	Bridge (Épinette), D108	
PK **0.4**	Lock 1, **Marquette**	
PK **2.1**	Bridge	
PK **2.6**	Bridge (Marcq-en-Barœul), D617	
PK **3.3**	Lesaffre fertiliser works and loading quay r/b	
PK **3.7**	Lock 2, Marcq-en-Barœul, footbridge, mooring to landing stage 200m u/s r/b	
PK **4.1**	Footbridge (Risban)	
PK **4.3**	Bridge (Risban)	
PK **4.6**	**Marcq-en-Barœul** public library (Médiathèque) gardens and moorings r/b (for 4 boats)	

Informal moorings, a hose to fill with water may be supplied on request.

PK **6.0**	Bridge (Collège)
PK **6.2**	Motorway bridge (A22)
PK **6.3**	Overhead power lines
PK **6.5**	Bridge (Château-Rouge), tramway line T
PK **7.4**	Motorway bridge (D656)

The delightfully rural aspect of the flight of locks in Wasquehal

PK **7.6** *Junction with Branche de Croix*, access to former *Port du Dragon* harbour in **Wasquehal**

No access pending dredging and redevelopment of basin, planned in 2016. The ugly weir will eventually be removed and the former branch 'downgraded' to a narrow free-flowing arm of the river Marque. A whole new *écoquartier* is to be built here, and boats will be able to navigate a short distance up the river.

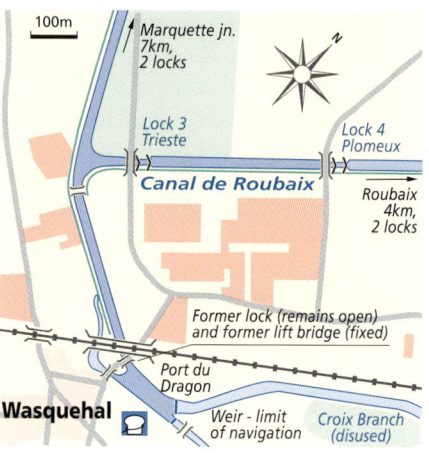

PK **7.8**	Lock 3 (Trieste), bridge (Marie-Curie)
PK **8.2**	Lock 4 (Plomeux), bridge (Molinel)
PK **8.5**	Lock 5 (Noir Bonnet)
PK **8.9**	Lock 6 (Cottigny), *guinguette*, bridge
PK **9.2**	Lock 7 (Mazure), beginning of summit level
PK **9.5**	Bridge (Mazure)
PK **9.8**	Skew road bridge (D656 express road)
PK **10.1**	Bridge (access to expressway)
PK **10.2**	Footbridge
PK **10.7**	Pipeline crossing and lift bridge (Blanc-Sceau)
PK **11.1**	Footbridge
PK **11.5**	Bridge (Fresnoy)
PK **11.7**	*Junction with Branche de Tourcoing*
PK **12.1**	Bridge (Pont de la République), **Roubaix** centre 1.5 km south
PK **12.4**	Railway bridge (SNCF Roubaix-Tourcoing)
PK **12.5**	Swing bridge (Fontenoy)
PK **12.8**	**Roubaix** halte on quay u/s of Union lock, 03 20 63 11 39, 5 moorings, free (maximum 4 nights), water, electricity, *relaiscanal@lillemetropole.fr*

The *halte* is in middle of the 'Union' urban regeneration area, where the 'Blue Days' rally was organised in September 2009 to celebrate the canal's restoration. At that time, pending development, the site was regularly occupied by travellers and appeared unwelcoming. Now the whole site has been radically transformed, with a public park and arboretum opened in 2020. Beside the *halte* is the former lock-keeper's house, which is being converted into a canalside bistrot (*guinguette*). The adjacent land is being landscaped as a wetland oasis of biodiversity.

PK **12.9**	Lock 8 (Union), bridge, end of summit level
PK **13.6**	Two lift bridges (Couteaux) on roundabout, headroom limited to 1.50m with bridges closed
PK **13.8**	Footbridge (Hutin)
PK **14.2**	Modern lift bridge (Daubenton), limited headroom in closed position

Canal de Roubaix

The Union rally site during the 'inauguration in September 2009
© LMCU

A sediment-laden barge pushed by a small Ghent Dredging push-tug passes through Grimonpont lift bridge during the dredging works in the autumn of 2008. © LMCU

PK 14.3	Lift bridge (Vigne)
PK 14.7	Lock 9 (Nouveau Monde), bridge
PK 15.0	Lock 10 (Calvaire)
PK 15.1	Lift bridge (Wattrelos)
PK 15.2	Lock 11 (Galon d'Eau), bridge
PK 15.3	Bridge (Nyckès)
PK 15.6	Footbridge (Soies)
PK 16.1	Disused railway bridge
PK 16.4	Bridge (Sartel)
PK 16.5	Lock 12 (Sartel)
PK 17.2	Disused railway bridge
PK 17.6	Footbridge (Sainte-Marguerite)
PK 18.0	Bridge (D700)
PK 18.7	Lift bridge (Grimonpont), public quay, restaurant 'La Guinguette' r/b
PK 20.0	Border, *junction with Canal de l'Espierres* in Belgium (8km and 3 locks to junction with canalised river Escaut)

Branches off the Canal de Roubaix

Branche de Croix

PK 0.0	*Junction off the Canal de Roubaix* (PK 7.6)
PK 0.1	Footbridge and pipeline crossings
PK 0.4	Railway bridge (SNCF Lille-Roubaix)
PK 0.4	**Wasquehal** bridge, former lock, basin u/s included in urban regeneration scheme but not expected to be dredged, small craft only, town centre l/b
PK 0.6	Fixed weir (to be demolished, free-flowing landscaped stream to replace former canal)

Branche de Tourcoing

PK 0.0	*Junction off the Canal de Roubaix* (PK 11.7)
PK 0.1	Towpath bridge
PK 0.4	Entrance to short tunnel (former railway viaduct)
PK 0.5	End of tunnel (Carliers)
PK 0.9	Lift bridge (Halot)
PK 1.2	Former lift bridge (Tourcoing tramway), fixed, no through navigation, **Tourcoing** basin, former terminus of navigation and town centre, 400m

Spring scene upstream of lock 9, Nouveau Monde, PK 15 © ÉPAULARD 59

The hydraulic lift bridge below lock 11, Galon d'eau, PK 15. © M. CLARKE

I – Northern France

8. River Scarpe

THE NAVIGABLE RIVER SCARPE BEGINS at the canal basin in Arras (linked to the river by a short length of canal) and ends at the confluence with the Escaut at Mortagne. It is divided into three sections: the upstream Scarpe (*supérieure*) from Arras to Corbehem (23km), the middle Scarpe (*moyenne*) from Corbehem to the lock at Fort-de-Scarpe (7km), and the downstream Scarpe (*inférieure*) from Fort-de-Scarpe to Mortagne (36km). Most of the second section through the town of Douai was closed following construction of a bypass canal (the *dérivation de la Scarpe autour de Douai*) as part of the Liaison Dunkerque-Escaut, which branches off from the left bank of the Scarpe opposite the junction with the Canal de la Sensée, skirts the west of the town and joins the former Canal de la Deûle on the northern outskirts. Continuity of navigation on the Scarpe is ensured by a short (800m) link canal (*Canal de Jonction*), leaving the bypass at PK 6.2 and joining the Scarpe moyenne downstream of the Pont Vauban in Douai. The distances in the route description below are those of the original line of navigation, making a total of 66km from Arras to Mortagne. The newer route bypassing Douai is 1km longer.

In 2021 the Scarpe inférieure regrettably remains closed in the absence of an agreement between the Government and local authorities on funding the necessary restoration works.

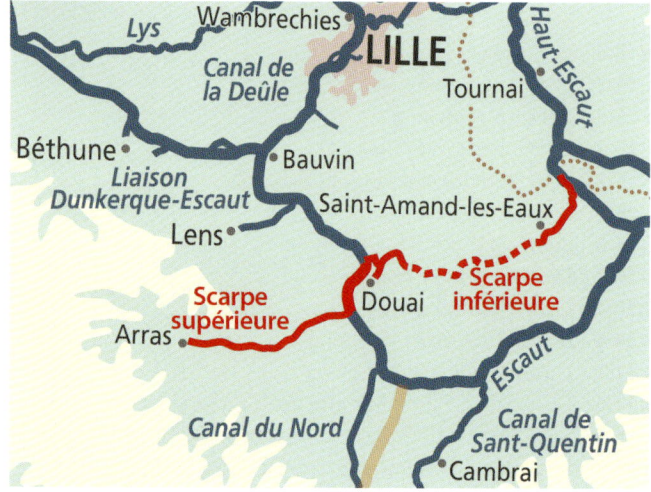

This river was navigated from the Escaut up to Douai as early as 638, but improvements with flash locks were required to give access to the important town of Arras, reached in 1613. This remained a shallow navigation, with locks of varying width and length, until it was improved to the Becquey gauge in the 1840s. The enlargement to Freycinet dimensions was completed by about 1890.

Navigation

The Scarpe supérieure is a 'navigation on demand' waterway on account of the very limited traffic, but it is well worth planning to make the detour up the river to Arras, where dredging works have recently been completed

Key dimensions (m)	
Length	38.50
Beam	5.20
Draught	1.60
[to reach Arras	1.10]
Air draught	3.65
[to reach Arras	3.50]

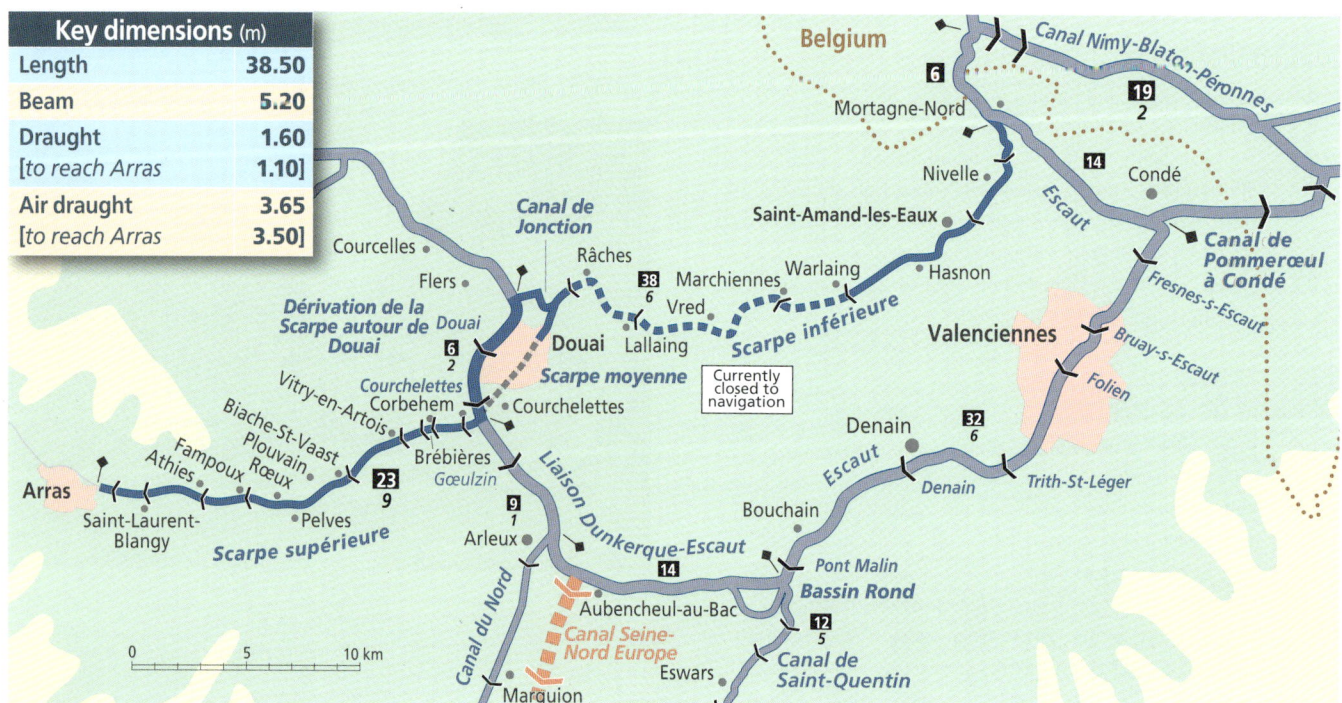

54

Scarpe

to remove the accumulated silt at Saint-Laurent-Blangy. The Scarpe inférieure has been closed since 2005 following a serious failure at Lallaing lift bridge, and has become heavily silted. A major dredging programme would need to be implemented before the waterway could be reopened throughout. Local authorities are currently reluctant to commit to such a project, estimated to cost €15 million. Part of the lower Scarpe may however be navigated from the confluence with the Escaut, for access to the *port de plaisance* at Saint-Amand-les-Eaux.

Locks
There are 9 locks on the Scarpe supérieure, of standard barge dimensions (38.50m by 5.20m), all of which have been equipped for automatic operation. The locks on the Scarpe moyenne have been taken out of use, while those on the bypass canal, at Courchelettes and Douai, each have two chambers 144.60m by 12.00m and 91.60m by 12.00m. There is no lock on the link canal. The six locks on the Scarpe inférieure are also of standard barge dimensions (38.70m by 5.20m). Only the lowest two locks are currently operated by local authority staff, giving access from the Escaut to Saint-Amand-les-Eaux.

Draught
The maximum authorised draught is 3.00m on the bypass canal. On the Freycinet-gauge sections the official draught is 1.80m, but this is unlikely to be maintained in the future on the sections no longer used by commercial traffic. Dredging works required in the terminal section towards Arras and throughout the lower Scarpe are expected to provide a draught limited to 1.60m. Access to Arras is currently limited to boats drawing no more than 1.10m.

Headroom
Below the Pont des Grès in Arras, with a headroom of 3.50m, all fixed bridges offer a clear headroom of 3.95m above normal water level, reduced to 3.75m during flood flows on the Scarpe supérieure and 3.65m on the Scarpe inférieure. The least headroom on the bypass canal is 5.25m.

Towpath
There is a crushed gravel service road throughout, including on the Scarpe inférieure, which remains open for cycling.

Authority
VNF Nord - Pas de Calais
- 16, route de Tournai, BP 26, 59119 Waziers 03 27 95 82 50 (PK 0-51) 06 32
- 22 chemin du halage, BP 2025, 59321 Valenciennes Cedex 03 27 32 22 80 (PK 51-66)

Boats, canoes and a riverside housing development compose an attractive landscape at Saint-Laurent-Blangy, in the suburbs of Arras. © VNF/YVELINE DRUELLE

Route description

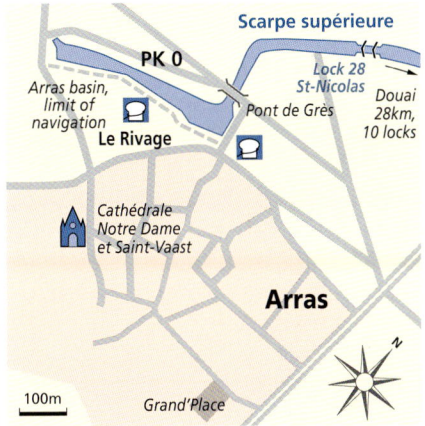

Scarpe supérieure

PK 0.0	**Arras** basin, public quays, town centre 300m
PK 0.2	Bridge (Pont des Grès), boat moorings u/s r/b
PK 0.6	Lock 1 (Saint-Nicolas), automatic, navigation enters Scarpe
PK 0.9	Main road bridge (D917), public quay u/s l/b
PK 1.3	Basin r/b, new port of Arras
PK 2.3	Lock 2 (Saint-Laurent-Blangy) in short cut l/b, bridge
PK 2.5	**Saint-Laurent-Blangy** pontoon for 6 boats r/b, 3 visitor moorings, night €7.50, water, electricity, shower (8:00 to 20:00), pump-out *basenautique@saint-laurent-blangy.fr*

The whitewater canoeing course using the fall of the lock and weir at Saint-Laurent-Blangy is both spectacular and highly popular.

PK	
PK 3.9	Railway viaduct
PK 4.0	Chemicals factory r/b, quay
PK 5.0	Lock 3 (Athies), automatic, in short cut l/b, bridge, **Athies** 300m l/b
PK 7.3	Lock 4 (Fampoux), automatic, in short cut r/b, bridge
PK 7.9	**Fampoux** quay l/b, village 800m l/b
PK 8.1	Railway viaduct
PK 8.6	Railway viaduct (TGV Nord)
PK 8.7	Motorway viaduct (A1)

I – Northern France

The arts barge Hydroplane *moored at Saint-Laurent-Blangy, to take part in a water festival*

PK 10.1	**Rœux** bridge, quay d/s l/b, village 300m l/b
PK 11.1	Pelves quay r/b, village 400m
PK 11.6	Plouvain basin, boat moorings l/b, village 1700m
PK 12.3	Motorway viaduct (A26)
PK 14.1	**Biache-Saint-Vaast** pontoon l/b for 2 boats, water, electricity, 03 21 50 07 27, night €8, small town 400m l/b
PK 14.2	Lock 5 (Biache-Saint-Vaast), automatic, in cut r/b, bridge
PK 14.3	Basin l/b (former cement works)
PK 17.3	**Vitry-en-Artois** bridge, quay u/s l/b, town l/b
PK 17.7	Bridge (Vitry-en-Artois)
PK 18.0	Lock 6 (Vitry), automatic, r/b, weir
PK 20.1	Lock 7 (Brébières-Haute-Tenue), automatic, in short cut l/b
PK 20.6	Lock 8 (Brébières-Basse-Tenue), automatic, bridge
PK 21.0	**Brébières** quay l/b, village 400m
PK 21.3	Bridge
PK 22.0	Overhead pipeline and conveyor belt crossings (five crossings)
PK 22.4	Lock 9 (Corbehem), automatic
PK 22.6	**Corbehem** bridge, village l/b
PK 23.1	**Junction with Liaison Dunkerque-Escaut** (at PK 23.6)

Navigation continues on the Canal de dérivation de la Scarpe section of the high-capacity waterway, left. Turn right here for the Escaut (via the former Canal de la Sensée). Straight ahead is the short length of the Scarpe moyenne leading to the *halte* at Courchelettes (700m), but beware of silting (see plan below).

Scarpe diversion canal (Douai bypass)

The PK distances here are those of the Liaison Dunkerque-Escaut

PK 23.8	Lock (Courchelettes), VHF 18, 03 27 88 14 38, two chambers, bridge, water
PK 24.2	Railway bridges
PK 24.7	Turning Basin
PK 25.2	Road bridge (D621, Douai bypass, Rocade minière)
PK 25.6	Bridges (Arras road, D950)
PK 26.9	Quay r/b
PK 27.7	Esquerchin bridge, Douai centre 500m r/b
PK 28.0	Lock (Douai), VHF 18, 03 27 88 95 12, two chambers, water
PK 28.4	Footbridge (Ocre)

PK 28.5	Bridge (Ocre)
PK 29.7	Quay l/b
PK 29.8	**Scarpe navigation continues in Canal de Jonction** (link with the Scarpe moyenne and Scarpe inférieure d/s of Douai)

Scarpe

Canal de Jonction

PK 0.0	*Junction off the Scarpe diversion canal*
PK 0.1	Bridge (Boulevard Lahure)
PK 0.4	Basin
PK 0.7	Bridge (Chemin Vert)
PK 0.8	*Junction with Scarpe moyenne*

Scarpe moyenne

Navigation continues for 1km in the Scarpe moyenne before joining the Scarpe inférieure at Lock 1 Fort-de-Scarpe.

PK 29.0	*Canal de Jonction connects with Scarpe moyenne*

The Scarpe moyenne is navigable 1100m upstream from this point to moorings beside a former lift bridge in Douai, along the picturesque Quai d'Alsace and Quai de la Barque (see plan left). Quayside moorings free, but without services.

PK 29.1	Railway bridge
PK 29.2	Pedestrian/cycle path bridge (formerly a railway bridge)
PK 29.3	Basin r/b
PK 29.5	Basin r/b
PK 29.9	Basin l/b

The delightful river Scarpe in the cetre of Douai, passing the old parliament building © GIORGIO PANECK

Scarpe inférieure

Included for reference and as a route for canoeists and cyclists, since all the lift-bridges and locks are currently closed down to Saint-Amand-les-Eaux.

PK 30.0	Lock 1 (Fort-de-Scarpe)
PK 30.4	Bridge (Pont Rouge)
PK 31.1	Motorway bridge (A21, Douai north bypass)
PK 33.3	**Raches** lift bridge, village l/b
PK 36.4	**Lallaing** lift bridge, small town 400m l/b
PK 36.8	Lock 2 (Lallaing)
PK 37.6	Quay l/b
PK 37.9	Lift bridge (Germignies)
PK 40.3	Pumping station r/b
PK 41.1	Pipeline crossing
PK 41.5	**Vred** swing bridge, out of operation, former boat moorings d/s l/b (for 5 boats) slipway, village l/b
PK 45.3	Lock 3 (Marchiennes)
PK 45.5	**Marchiennes** bridge, public quay d/s r/b, former boat mooring d/s l/b, small town with all facilities l/b
PK 46.9	Disused railway bridge
PK 47.2	Overhead gas pipeline crossing
PK 47.8	Pipeline crossing
PK 49.7	Lock 4 (Warlaing), lift bridge, village 500m l/b
PK 54.2	**Hasnon** bridge, village r/b
PK 54.5	Motorway bridge (A23)
PK 57.6	Railway bridge (Saint-Amand)
PK 58.2	Saint-Amand-les-Eaux lift bridge (rue de Valenciennes), footbridge u/s, quay u/s l/b, not accessible
PK 58.6	**Saint-Amand-les-Eaux** port de plaisance in basin l/b, 03 27 30 44 35, 07 85 25 79 52, night €13, water €2, electricity €3, shower, slipway, wifi, pump-out, town centre 500m l/b *tourisme-porteduhainaut.fr*

The Lower Scarpe gives access to this port and busy small town from downstream only.

PK 58.6	Alternative boat moorings for Saint-Amand, l/b
PK 59.1	Lift bridge (route de Condé), footbridge d/s
PK 59.3	Lock 5 (Saint-Amand)
PK 59.9	Road bridge (D169, Saint-Amand bypass)
PK 62.3	**Nivelle** bridge, village 800m l/b
PK 63.7	Lock 6 (Thun)
PK 65.8	Mortagne lift bridge
PK 66.1	*Confluence with Escaut*

Continue downstream to enter Belgium or moor at the pontoon at Mortagne-du-Nord, otherwise turn right to head up the Escaut towards Valenciennes.

The modern port de plaisance at Saint-Amand-les-Eaux, near the town's popular casino. © CRT NORD-PAS DE CALAIS

9. Canal du Nord

This 95 km-long canal has been a curiosity since it was first planned, the only canal to be built in France to intermediate dimensions between the 250-tonne Freycinet and the modern high-capacity standards. It is now to be abandoned within a few years, after an operating lifetime of less than 60 years, taken over by the future Seine-Nord Europe Canal.

The distance of 95 km from Arleux, near Douai on the Canal de la Sensée (now the Liaison Dunkerque-Escaut), south to the junction with the Canal latéral à l'Oise at Pont-l'Evêque, is divided into three sections:

Section 1 extends from Arleux on the Canal de la Sensée to Péronne on the Canal de la Somme (PK 45).
Section 2 is a redeveloped length of the Canal de la Somme from Péronne to a junction near Rouy-le-Petit (PK 65). **Section 3** connects the Canal de la Somme to Pont-l'Evêque on the Canal latéral à l'Oise (PK 95).

The first and third sections cross low watersheds, and their summit levels have impressive tunnels. The Grand Souterrain de Ruyaulcourt, on the summit level of the first section (PK 25-29) has a total length of 4354m. It is divided into three sections. The first 1600m from each portal is of single barge width (6.30m), while the 1150m middle portion is of double width (12.30m). Thus north and southbound barges enter simultaneously at each end, pass each other in the middle portion and exit simultaneously from each end. There is a remote monitoring and traffic control system with lights, ensuring minimum delays to barges on this busy route. The Souterrain de la Panneterie, on the summit level of the third section, is 1040m in length. Its dimensions provide for one-way working only, with entrance controlled by lights as at Ruyaulcourt.

Excavation for the canal started in 1908, when the parallel Canal de Saint-Quentin had reached saturation, despite its paired locks throughout. By 1914 three quarters of the earthworks, as well as a number of the locks and bridges, had been completed. Following wartime destruction several attempts were made to restart the project, but little was achieved in the inter-war period. The rapid economic growth experienced by France in the 1950s saw a marked increase in bulk transport requirements between the Seine basin and the north, and it again became urgent to complete the project. The works were carried out in the early 1960s and the canal opened to navigation in 1966.

Navigation

The canal is a busy commercial waterway, and boaters may prefer the parallel Canal de Saint-Quentin. Imposing civil engineering works will be in progress throughout almost the entire length from 2024 until the new canal is opened in 2028 (as currently projected). A new lock will give access to a short length of the current canal with two locks down to the Canal de la Somme at Péronne. This future connection is shown in the route description. Access to Marquion from the northern end may also be maintained.

Locks

There are 12 locks in the first section (7 up from the Sensée to the summit and 5 down to the Somme), 2 in the second section and 5 in the third section (one up from the Somme to the second summit level and 4 falling towards the Oise).

The mini-push-tow comprising two Freycinet barges has always been a distinctive feature of the Canal du Nord, with its long, narrow locks. ©VNF

Canal du Nord

All measure 91.60m by 6.00m and accommodate push-tows made up of two 38.50m barges, as well as some 700-tonne barges designed specifically to operate between the Seine basin and northern France. There may be delays at certain locks, for example at lock 12 for vessels proceeding upstream, as the lock-keepers attempt to rationalise the transit of commercial vessels in groups.

Draught
The authorised draught is 2.40m.

Headroom
All the bridges leave a minimum headroom of 3.98m above the highest navigable water level (4.28m above normal level).

Authority
VNF Nord - Pas de Calais
- UTI Deûle - Scarpe, 16 route de Tournai, 59119 Waziers, 03 27 95 82 50
  UTI-Deule-Scarpe.DT-Nord-Pas-de-Calais@vnf.fr (PK 0 - 1)
- UTI Escaut - Saint-Quentin, 22 chemin de halage - 59300 Valenciennes, 03 27 32 22 80
  uti-escaut-saint-quentin.DT-Nord-Pas-de-Calais@vnf.fr (PK 1-25)

VNF Bassin de la Seine
- UTI Seine-Nord Compiègne, 2 boulevard Gambetta, BP 20053, 60321 Compiègne cedex, 03 44 92 27 00,
  uti.seinenord@vnf.fr (PK 25-95)

Route description

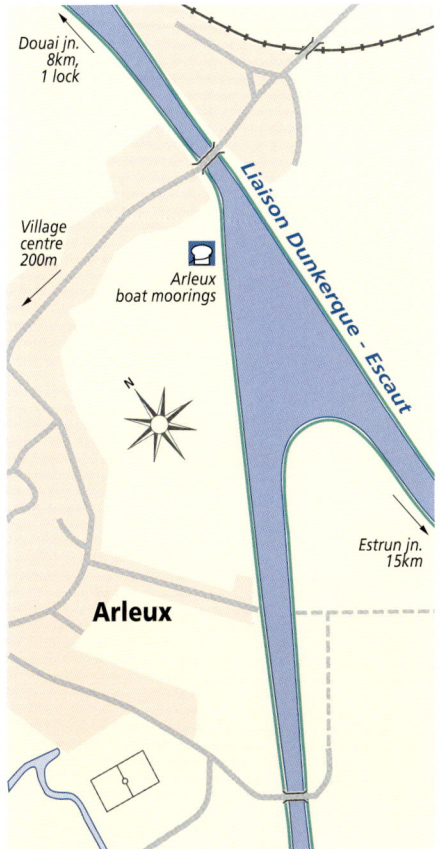

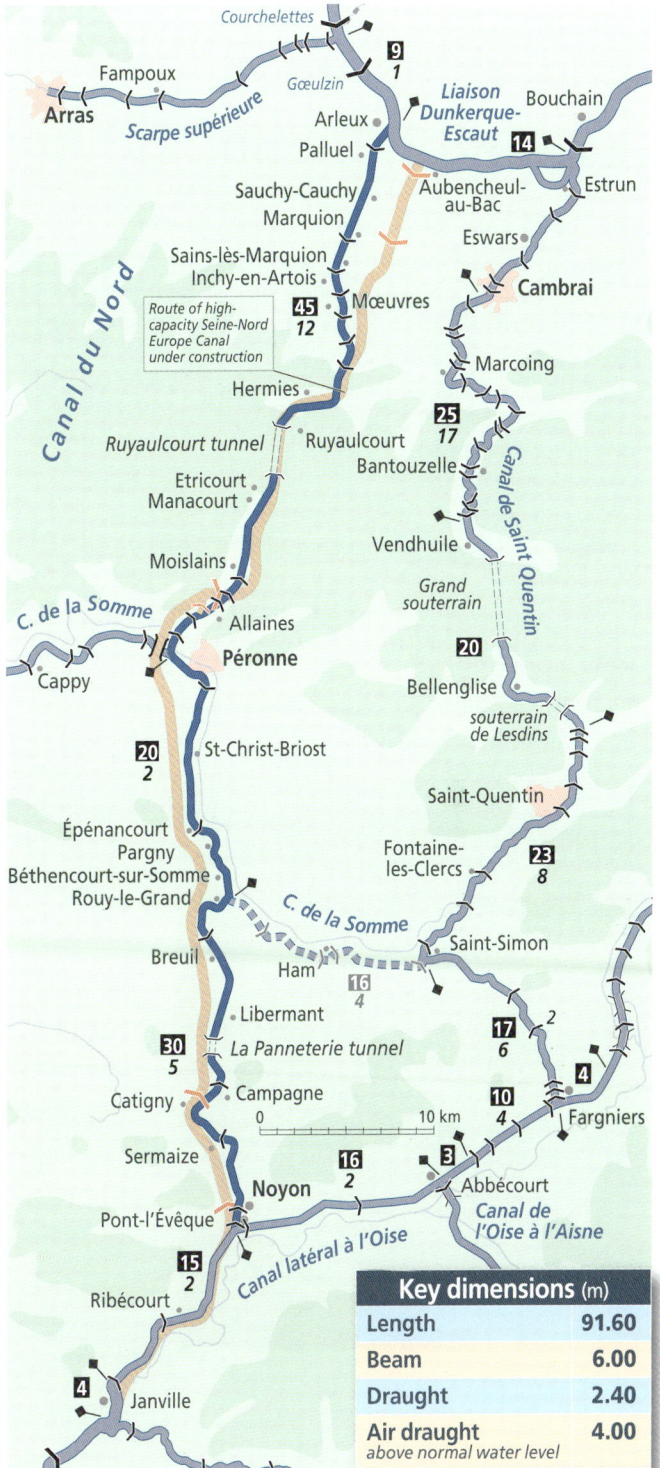

Key dimensions (m)	
Length	91.60
Beam	6.00
Draught	2.40
Air draught *above normal water level*	4.00

PK	
PK 0.0	**Junction off the Liaison Dunkerque-Escaut** PK 15, beginning of first section, boat moorings
PK 0.6	**Arleux** bridge, village 1km l/b
PK 0.9	Private basin (Malderez) l/b (length 560m)
PK 1.4	Lock 1 (Palluel), VHF 18
PK 1.8	**Palluel** bridge (D21), village 400m l/b
PK 3.5	Bridge (Oisy-le-Verger)
PK 5.1	Sauchy-Cauchy bridge, village r/b
PK 6.6	Motorway bridge (A26)
PK 7.0	Turning basin

I – Northern France

PK **7.7** **Marquion** bridge (D939), *halte* d/s l/b, 3 visitor berths (free), water, village 500m r/b

This is a popular quayside mooring. Access to Marquion may be expected to survive the opening of the new Seine-Nord Europe Canal.

PK **8.0**	Lock 2 (Marquion), VHF 22, water
PK **10.0**	**Sains-lès-Marquion** bridge, village 300m r/b
PK **10.7**	Lock 3 (Sains-lès-Marquion), VHF 18
PK **11.2**	**Inchy-en-Artois** bridge, quay u/s l/b, village 800m l/b
PK **12.0**	Bridge
PK **12.3**	Lock 4 (Sains-lès-Marquion), VHF 22
PK **13.4**	**Mœuvres** bridge, village 500m l/b
PK **14.0**	Lock 5 (Mœuvres), VHF 18
PK **14.3**	Bridge
PK **15.3**	Bridge (D930)
PK **15.8**	Lock 6 (Graincourt-lès-Havrincourt), VHF 22
PK **16.5**	Bridge
PK **17.5**	Lock 7 (Graincourt-lès-Havrincourt), VHF 18, beginning of summit level
PK **17.9**	Bridge
PK **19.8**	**Havrincourt** bridges (two high cantilever bridges 30m apart, D5), village 1200m r/b

Deep cutting at Havrincourt, PK 20 © MARCO MENEI

PK **21.3**	Turning basin
PK **21.6**	Bridge
PK **22.7**	**Hermies** bridge, private quay u/s l/b, village 1200m l/b
PK **23.6**	Bridge
PK **24.5**	Bridge
PK **25.1**	Ruyaulcourt tunnel control post, l/b
PK **25.2**	Ruyaulcourt tunnel, northern entrance

Well-lit, controlled by lights, there is a 1km long passing-place in the middle.

PK **27.4**	Ventilation shaft
PK **29.6**	Ruyaulcourt tunnel, southern entrance
PK **30.4**	Bridge (D58)

View from the bridge at PK 30.4 towards Ruyaulcourt tunnel. © PIR6MON

PK **31.0**	**Étricourt-Manacourt** bridge, village 200m r/b
PK **31.8**	Bridge
PK **32.7**	Bridge (D72)
PK **34.2**	Turning basin
PK **35.5**	Bridge
PK **36.8**	Bridge
PK **37.2**	**Moislains** bridge (D184), quayside mooring d/s l/b, water and electricity, village 400m r/b
PK **37.6**	Lock 8 (Moislains), VHF 10, end of summit level
PK **38.1**	Turning basin
PK **38.4**	Bridge (D43)
PK **38.7**	Lock 9 (Moislains), VHF 10
PK **39.7**	Lock 10 (Allaines), VHF 10
PK **40.0**	**Allaines** bridge, small village 300m l/b
PK **40.7**	Bridge
PK **41.5**	*Future junction with Canal Seine-Nord Europe* (for reference, expected to be opened 2028)

The plan on page 69 shows how the new canal will be connected to the existing canal, to give access to the Somme at Péronne. The lock will have a lift of 11.27m. Péronne will become a mecca for waterway enthusiasts in the coming years, as the new canal and the Somme Aqueduct are built.

PK **41.7**	Bridge (D1017)
PK **42.0**	Lock 11 (Feuillaucourt), VHF 10, water
PK **43.3**	Bridge (D938), quay d/s r/b, no services
PK **43.8**	Lock 12 (Cléry-sur-Somme), VHF 10, water
PK **45.4**	*Junction with Canal de la Somme*, beginning of second section (common to Canal de la Somme) quay with water u/s l/b
PK **47.8**	**Péronne** port de plaisance, 03 22 84 19 31, night €14, diesel on commercial quay, water included, electricity €2.50/day, showers at campsite, washing machine €4.80, dryer €3, slipway, wifi, restaurant

Convenient sheltered moorings in a spur off the main canal. PK **48.2** Bridge (D1017), quays d/s, private quay u/s r/b with all services but limited space, Péronne 1300m r/b

PK **48.6**	Railway bridge
PK **49.5**	Lock 13 (Péronne), VHF 10, water
PK **53.2**	Bridge (Pont-lès-Brie), D1029

Canal du Nord

- PK 55.9 **Saint-Christ-Briost** bridge, quay u/s l/b, no services, village 300m
- PK 57.8 Motorway bridge (A29)
- PK 58.9 Épenancourt l/b
- PK 59.7 Lock 14 (Épenancourt), bridge, VHF 10, water, private quay u/s l/b
- PK 60.9 **Pargny** bridge, village l/b
- PK 63.7 **Béthencourt-sur-Somme** bridge, quay d/s r/b
- PK 65.3 Junction with Canal de la Somme, end of section common to Canal de la Somme, beginning of third section

The regrettably closed section of the quiet and peaceful Canal de la Somme branches off eastwards.

- PK 67.8 **Rouy-le-Petit** bridge, small village 400m r/b
- PK 68.8 Railway bridge, private quay u/s and d/s l/b, no services
- PK 68.9 **Nesle** bridge (D930), quays u/s, village 2km l/b
- PK 69.6 Lock 15 (Languevoisin), VHF 10, beginning of summit level
- PK 69.9 Bridge (D89), quay u/s l/b, no services
- PK 71.5 **Breuil** bridge, small village l/b
- PK 72.7 **Buverchy** bridge, small village r/b
- PK 74.6 Bridge (D186), quay u/s r/b, no services, turning basin d/s r/b, **Ercheu** 2.5km l/b
- PK 77.1 **Libermont** bridge, small village 800m r/b
- PK 78.5 Tunnel (La Panneterie), northern entrance

Like Ruyaulcourt, the tunnel is lit. Entrance controlled by lights.

- PK 79.6 Tunnel (La Panneterie), southern entrance
- PK 81.2 Bridge (Frétoy-le-Château)
- PK 81.9 Lock 16 (Campagne), VHF 10, water, end of summit level
- PK 82.9 **Campagne** bridge, small village l/b
- PK 84.3 **Catigny** bridge, small village r/b
- PK 86.2 Bridge (Béhancourt)
- PK 87.1 **Sermaize** bridge, village 400m r/b
- PK 87.7 Lock 17 (Sermaize-Haudival), VHF 10, water
- PK 89.2 **Beaurains-lès-Noyon** bridge, village 500m r/b
- PK 91.2 Bridge (D934)
- PK 91.8 **Noyon** quay l/b, water and electricity, town centre 1300m
- PK 93.1 Bridge (D938)
- PK 93.4 Lock 18 (Noyon), VHF 10, water
- PK 93.8 Bridge (avenue Jean Jaurès)
- PK 94.2 Bridge (D1032, Noyons bypass)
- PK 94.4 Lock 19 (Pont-l'Évêque), VHF 10, water
- PK 94.7 **Pont-l'Évêque** bridge, village 800m l/b
- PK 94.8 Railway bridge
- PK 95.0 End of third section, junction with Canal latéral à l'Oise (PK 18.6)

A péniche leaves lock 19, Pont-l'Évêque, the last on the canal.
© FALCONER DAVE LONG

I – Northern France

10. Seine-Nord Europe Canal

THE SEINE-NORD EUROPE CANAL, planned since the mid-1970s, will replace the existing Canal du Nord and part of the Canal latéral à l'Oise. The *plaisancier* should be aware of this project, because the main works – starting in 2022 and expected to last 6 years – will inevitably have an impact on conditions of navigation through the Canal du Nord and the Canal latéral à l'Oise. Preliminary environmental works including tree planting began in 2020. The new canal will provide a missing link of European importance, by connecting the Seine basin to the Rhine basin and the main inland waterway network of Europe via the Hauts-de-France region. The European Commission is convinced of the intrinsic value of this investment, along with others in the 'Connecting Europe Facility', justifying its 40% contribution to the total cost. This percentage may be increased to 50%. The canal will extend 107 km from Aubencheul-au-Bac on the Liaison Dunkerque-Escaut to Compiègne on the river Oise. Its line was dramatically prefigured by preventive archeological excavations which started in October 2008, although the summit level section has since been redesigned.

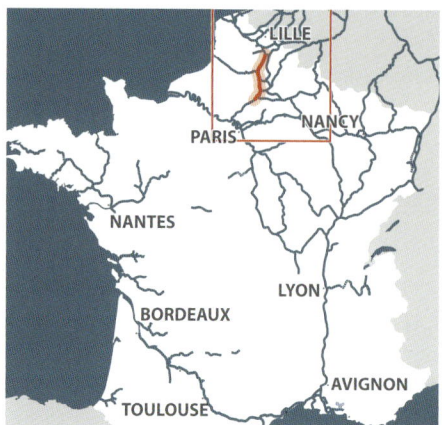

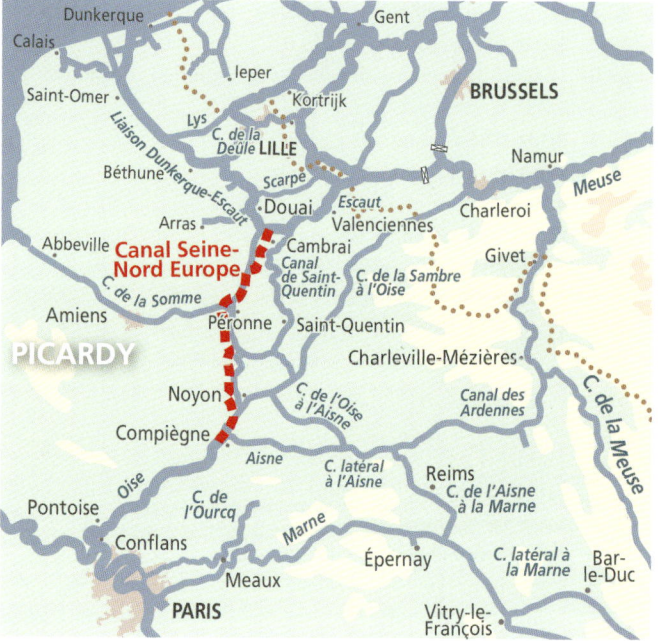

Why a new canal?

The existing waterways on this route are of limited capacity (barges of 250 to 650 tonnes). The new canal will remove this capacity bottleneck, to form a major high-capacity transport corridor for barges and push-tows up to 4400 tonnes (European Class Vb), from Le Havre to Dunkirk, Benelux and the Rhine. The presence of the bottleneck on one of the Europe's principal transport arteries is reflected in the current statistics: where the market share of inland water transport measured in tonne-kilometres reaches 18% in the Seine-Oise basin and 14% in Nord-Pas de Calais, and even more than 50% on the major waterways of Germany and Benelux, the constraints of carrying capacity on the North-South waterway route limit the waterway market share to between 3 and 4% (peaking at about 5 million tonnes). Traffic is projected to reach between 15 and 18 million tonnes per year a few years after the waterway has opened. Designs provide for a second lock chamber to be built at each of the six locks. Land is reserved in the local land use plans for this future extension of capacity.

Montmacq lock (PK 107.1) will be the first to be built on the new waterway. With a lift of 6.41m, the lock is provided with a pumping station to supply the canal with water abstracted from the river Oise. SCSNE - TEAM O+ - PIXXIM

Multimodal port platforms

A key to success of the new waterway is the simultaneous construction of four inland ports on the route, two of them given new railway connections to the existing rail freight network (with a third railway connection planned at Péronne). Covering 360 ha, they are to become high-performance logistics hubs serving economic development of entire regions. The canal will be a source of industrial water supply, and is expected to be a powerful lever for the development of tourism and recreational activities throughout the corridor.

Link with the Canal de la Somme

The new canal will have a link with the existing waterway system at Allaines. Here a new lock will be built, dropping

Canal Seine-Nord Europe

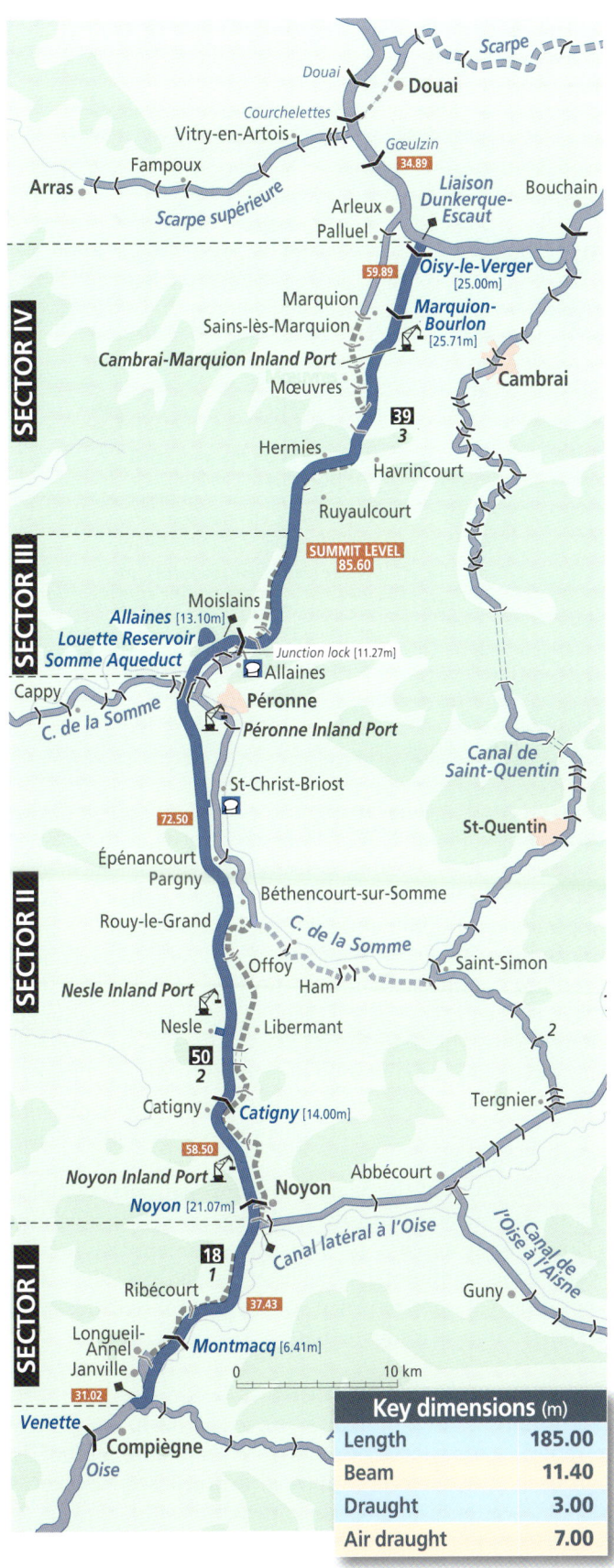

Canal de la Somme as a whole. The Conseil Départemental is negotiating transfer of ownership from VNF (see under Canal de la Somme).

Gigantic works, closure of most of the existing canal

The total volume of earthworks is 57 million m³, or 36 million m³ of cut and 21 million m³ of fill. Land acquisition totals 2450 ha, including surplus earth fill disposal areas and the inland ports.

Transit time will be less than 21 hours for 90% of all commercial traffic, depending on traffic density. Boats will be allowed to use the waterway, giving priority to commercial traffic. Boat harbours and passenger vessel moorings are currently planned at Allaines, off the main canal, and at Saint-Christ-Briost, and are positioned in the route description.

Preliminary works have been under way for several years, but the actual excavation of the new canal is expected to start in 2022, for completion by 2028.

Locks

There will be six locks on the waterway, 195m long and 12.50m wide. All except Montmacq lock in the Oise valley will be provided with water-saving basins. The highest locks will be Oisy-le-Verger and Marquion-Bourlon at the northern end: respectively 25m and 25.71m deep.

Draught

The canal will be 54m wide at the surface and 4.50m deep. The loading depth will be up to 3.50m, but 3m is expected to be the maximum.

Headroom

Bridges will offer a minimum headroom of 7m above the normal navigable water level.

Aqueducts

There will be three aqueducts on the canal. The Somme aqueduct will be 1330 m long and 25 m high above the water level of the navigable river Somme. The other two aqueducts will cross over the A29 and A26 motorways respectively.

Planning

A carefully conducted process of studies and consultations produced a consensus among all parties, massively in favour of the project. That was before the economic crisis, followed by the change of government in 2012. The projected cost based on a public-private partnership had by then increased from €4.2 to nearly €7 billion. A commission was set up to study possible savings. Its report was presented in 2013, suggesting a route following the existing Canal du Nord for 8 km and eliminating one lock, lowering the summit level by 16.90m. This modified route was formally adopted in 2017. The canal is divided into four distinct sections for the works and contracts, starting from the southern end. The first section along the river Oise received final authorisation in regard to its environmental impacts and treatment in April 2021, and should open in 2027, and the rest of the canal in 2028. As shown

from the 72.50m level to that of lock No. 11 (Feuillaucourt) on the existing Canal du Nord, at 61.23m. The lock will have the same dimensions as the existing Canal du Nord locks.

The Canal de la Somme east of the new canal is expected to be restored by the *département* by 2024, since it is forecast to play an important role in attracting boats to the

I – Northern France

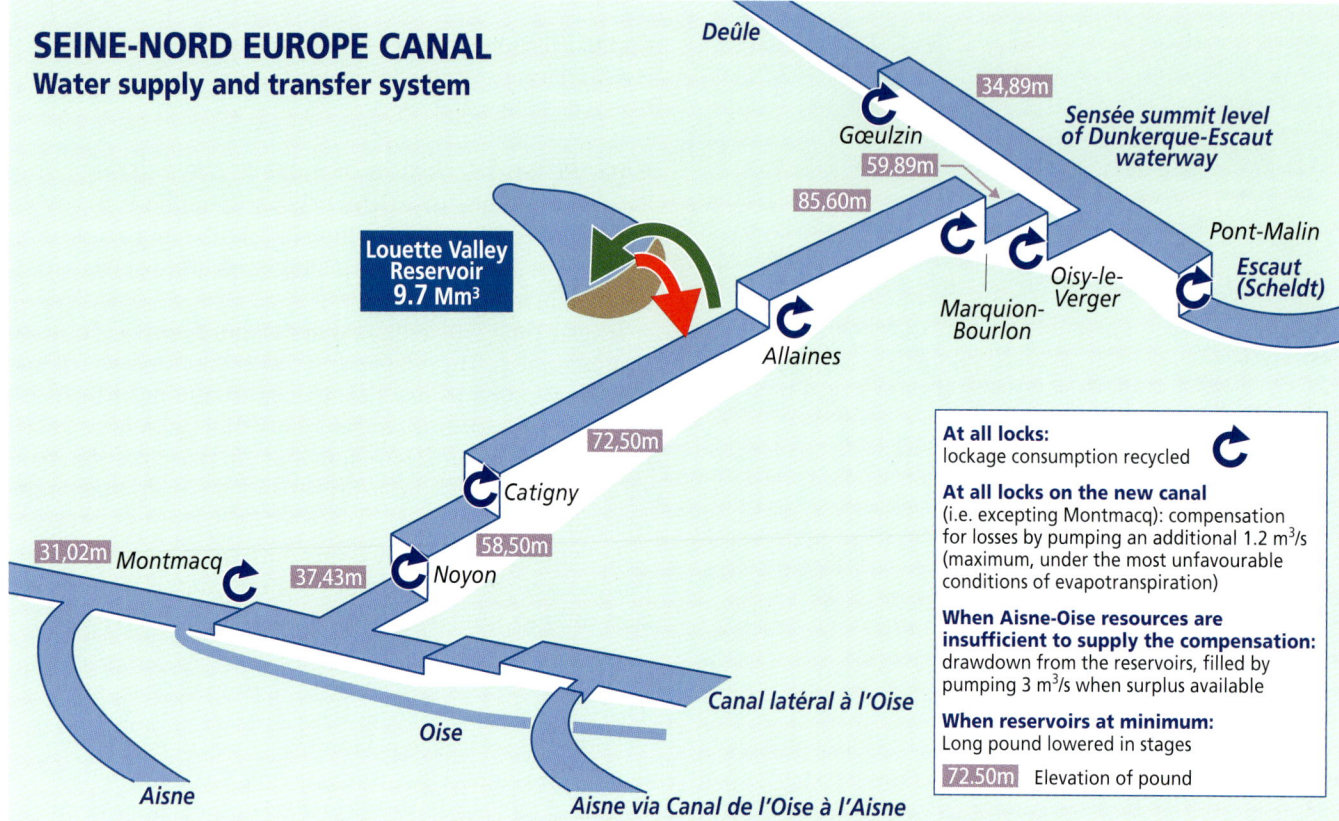

on the map, there will be a junction with the existing Canal du Nord and the Canal de la Somme through a new 92 by 6m lock at Allaines.

Water supply

Details of water supply would not normally find their place in an inland waterway guide, but water is such a critical issue in the modern world that it was thought useful to summarise here the detailed studies of water supply by the Société du Canal Seine-Nord Europe (with several consultants). Even on small canals, boaters will occasionally be affected by measures to reduce water consumption during periods of drought, and an understanding of how this new canal will work serves to illustrate the issue of water supply to all summit level canals.

The volumes consumed in lockage on the Seine-Nord Europe Canal will be limited by the water-saving basins, and the rest will be entirely recycled by back-pumping (see diagram above). Watertightness of the bed will be guaranteed by a clay lining 40cm thick. Permanent losses through evaporation will be made up by a large reservoir in the Louette valley filled by pumping whenever there is surplus water available. The volume thus consumed, corresponding to a maximum discharge of 1.2 m³/s under the most unfavourable conditions, is met by the resources of the catchment area of the rivers Oise and Aisne.

The discharge of 1.2 m³/s will only be abstracted if the flow in the river Oise is above a threshold defined as the sum of the current mean monthly low-flow discharge of five-year return period plus the increase in water requirements over the next 30 years (drinking water supply, industrial water and irrigation) throughout the catchment areas of the rivers Oise and Aisne. Under these conditions, the required discharge would be guaranteed 95% of the time on average. When abstraction from the Oise is impossible, the following measures will be implemented in succession: abstraction from the Louette valley reservoir (14 million m³), built alongside the first pound down from the summit. When the capacity of this reservoir has been used up, the final measure is lowering of the long pound itself, in stages. Vessels will then be required to programme their transits loading to less than full capacity, but this should not call into question the value nor the use of water transport. This system offers a high level of reliability, and the risk of interruption of navigation is limited to a return period of 60 years.

Construction of the Seine-Nord Europe Canal will also bring modifications to the existing canals of northern France, with impacts on their management. Savings in water consumption may thus be envisaged, and the corresponding volumes returned to the natural hydrographic system to improve aquatic life.

Environmental treatment

The canal has been formally approved by the national body responsible for assessing the environmental impact of major infrastructure projects. Approval in April 2021 concerns the first section, 18.6km long in the Oise valley.

Since this is in many respects the most sensitive section, the decision augurs well for approval of the other three sections. Environmental works include side basins, lagoons, new woodland, grazing meadows, created by spreading the surplus of excavated material over broad areas, and a dedicated bridge for wild animals across the deep cutting in the summit level.

Canal Seine-Nord Europe

Project authority
Société du Canal Seine-Nord Europe
– 23 place d'Armes, 60200 Compiègne, 03 44 40 74 96
canal-seine-nord-europe.fr

Route description

PK **98.7** *Origin of first section in the river Oise*
PK **99.8** Viaduct (N31)
PK **102.0** *Junction with Oise branch* to Janville

The Canal latéral à l'Oise will remain open to navigation up to Janville locks for at least one year after opening of the new canal.

PK **105.3** Bridge (D15)
PK **101.3** Bridge (D81)
PK **105.4** **Thourotte** quay, 200m long
PK **106.3** Bridge (Thourotte-Montmacq)
PK **107.1** Lock (Montmacq), lift 6.41m
PK **108.6** Bridge (D66)
PK **108.9** Turning basin

PK **109.6** **Ribécourt** quay, length 150m, r/b
PK **109.9** Skew bridge (D40)
PK **110.7** Bridge (D40 bis)
PK **110.8** **Pimprez** quay, 200m long
PK **114.5** Bridge (D48)
PK **115.6** Sloping banks both sides allowing wild animals to cross the canal
PK **117.6** *Junction with canal latéral à l'Oise*, turning basin

Boats will have convenient access to the halte at Pont-l'Évêque, 800m from the junction.

Halte *at Pont L'Évêque, close to the new canal*   © FRANK BAUER

PK **118.1** Bridge (D64)
PK **118.7** Bridge (D1032)
PK **119.0** Bridge (D932)
PK **119.7** Bridge (D938)
PK **119.8** Lock (Noyon), lift 21.07m
PK **120.2** Water level compensating basin r/b
PK **121.6** Bridge (D934)

Extensive lagoon treatment of the banks in this section.

PK **123.4** Bridge (D611/91)
PK **124.6** Mooring quay l/b
PK **125.6** Bridge (Béhancourt)

This rendering of the bridge and turning basin at Ribécourt (PK 108.6) shows a backwater on the right bank, leading to lock 3, Belleville, on the Canal latéral à l'Oise.   SCSNE - TEAM O+ - PIXXIM

Special treatment of the canal banks at Chiry-Ourscamps allowing wild animals to swim across. Note the continuity – for the wild animals – with the bridge over the parallel main road.
SCSNE - TEAM O+ - PIXXIM

I – Northern France

PK 125.8	Turning basin
PK 126.0	**Noyon** inland port l/b
PK 128.1	Bridge (D39)
PK 128.2	Lock (Catigny), lift 14.00m
PK 130.1	Bridge (D76)
PK 130.8	Mooring quay l/b
PK 135.3	Bridge (D186), Cressy-Moyencourt
PK 139.6	Bridge, Languevoisin-Breuil
PK 140.3	Languevoisin quay (300 m)
PK 140.6	Bridge (D89)
PK 141.0	Turning basin
PK 142.1	Bridge
PK 143.2	**Nesle** multimodal port platform r/b
PK 143.5	Bridge (D930C)
PK 144.0	Mooring quay
PK 145.4	Road underpass in culvert (D930)
PK 147.2	Bridge (D103), **Morchain**
PK 148.6	Bridge Morchain-Épenancourt

This bridge may not be built, depending on the results of discussions in progress with the local councils.

PK 150.3	Bridge (D62), **Licourt**
PK 150.7	Aqueduct (over A29 motorway)
PK 151.6	Road underpass in culvert, Licourt-Cizancourt
PK 152.5	Road underpass in culvert (D45)
PK 152.6	**Saint-Christ-Briost** moorings, l/b

Moorings for two hotel barges and 10 boats of up to 15m length. Small village on the other side of the Canal de la Somme and river Somme.

PK 155.3	Bridge (D1029), **Villers-Carbonnel**
PK 156.7	Bridge (D1017), **Éterpigny**
PK 157.7	Bridge (D4164)
PK 158.2	**Péronne** inland port l/b, turning basin
PK 158.9	Bridge (D79)
PK 159.4	Moorings
PK 160.3	Bridge Flaucourt-Biaches
PK 161.4	Bridge (D1), **Biaches**
PK 162.3	Southern entrance to Somme aqueduct
PK 163.6	Northern end of Somme aqueduct
PK 165.8	Bridge (D1017)
PK 166.5	**Junction with branch to Somme** via a section of the former Canal du Nord considered here as the Somme branch of the new canal (see plan below)

Just downstream of the junction there will be two berths for river cruise ships up to 135m long. On the Canal du Nord there will be four moorings for hotel barges and 20 moorings for boats of up to 15m length. It remains to contract with a concessionary for management of the port of Allaines.

PK 167.3	Bridge (Allaines-Bouchavesnes)
PK 167.4	Lock (Allaines), lift 13.10m

The embankment retaining the 14 million m³ Louette valley reservoir will be an imposing feature of the landscape on the west side of the lock.

PK 169.0	Road underpass in culvert (D43)
PK 170.1	Turning basin
PK 170.2	**Moislains** quay, 200m long
PK 170.4	Bridge (D184)
PK 174.8	Bridge (D72), **Manancourt**
PK 177.3	Bridge (D58)
PK 179.6	Bridge (D7E, **Ytres**)
PK 184.0	Motorway viaduct (A2)
PK 185.0	Bridge (Hermies-Ruyaulcourt)
PK 185.2	Bridge (D7, **Havrincourt-Hermies**)
PK 185.5	Bridge for wild animals crossing the deep cutting
PK 187.8	Bridge (D5, **Ruyaulcourt**)
PK 191.5	Bridge (D15), Graincourt-lès-Havrincourt)
PK 192.3	Graincourt quay (300 m)
PK 192.7	Bridge (D930)
PK 193.1	Turning basin
PK 194.5	Road underpass in culvert (Rue d'en Haut, **Mœuvres**)
PK 195.4	Bridge (D16)
PK 196.5	Bridge (D939)
PK 196.7	Aqueduct (over A26 motorway)
PK 198.3	Lock (Marquion-Bourlon), lift 25.71m
PK 199.3	**Marquion** multimodal port platform r/b
PK 201.1	Bridge (D21 E1)
PK 203.7	Bridge (D21)
PK 204.9	Lock (Oisy-le-Verger), lift 25m
PK 206.0	**Junction with Dunkerque-Escaut waterway**

66

Canal Seine-Nord Europe

Branch off the SNE Canal

PK **0.0** Junction off Canal SNE on the long pound, PK 169.2
PK **0.2** New lock 10 (Allaines), lift 11.27m
PK **0.5** Navigation joins old line of Canal du Nord at PK 41.5

The old canal will remain accessible upstream from this junction for 800m, up to the bridge in Allaines. and developed as a *port de plaisance*, one of several facilities along the 107km canal.

PK **0.7** Bridge (D1017)
PK **1.1** Lock 11 (Feuillaucourt), VHF 10, water
PK **1.8** Bridge (D938)
PK **2.1** Lock 12 (Cléry-sur-Somme), VHF 10, water
PK **3.0** Somme crossing (culverts)
PK **3.4** Junction with Canal de la Somme

Turn right here for the Somme towards Amiens and Saint-Valery, left for the port de plaisance in Péronne. The Canal du Nord beyond Péronne will be a dead end until the Canal de la Haute-Somme is restored, connecting with the Canal de Saint-Quentin.

Barge enters lock 12, Cléry-sur-Somme, approaching the Somme valley, marked by the trees in the background. This lock will continue to be operated as part of the branch from the new canal to the Somme. © FALCONER DAVE LONG

11. Canal de Saint-Quentin

THE CANAL DE SAINT-QUENTIN WAS for 150 years France's only navigable link from the industrial north to the Paris region. It connects the canalised river Escaut at Cambrai to the Canal latéral à l'Oise at Chauny, a distance of 92.5km. It also has junctions with the Canal de la Somme near Saint-Simon (PK 68), and with the Canal de la Sambre à l'Oise via the branch to La Fère, which leaves the through route at PK 85. The canal crosses the watershed between the Escaut and Somme basins by a 20.4km long summit level at an altitude of 83m, between locks 17 (Bosquet) and 18 (Lesdins). There are two tunnels on the summit level (see below). The branch to La Fère leaves the through route at a junction just below lock 31 (Fargniers) and connects with the Canal de la Sambre à l'Oise between Beautor and La Fère. Its length is 3.8km.

In 1724 the Sieur de Marcy obtained authorisation to build the Canal de Picardie (later Canal Crozat) from Saint-Quentin to the Somme and then the Oise at Chauny. When he ran out of funds, the concession passed in 1732 to the rich Antoine Crozat, who succeeded in finding subscribers to 10 000 shares; the canal was opened in 1738, but fell into disrepair after Crozat died the same year. In 1766 it was bought by the king from Crozat's heirs, as part of the projected through route to the Escaut. The need to handle coal traffic from Belgium led to proposals by Devicq and Laurent for the extension through the ridge of high ground to the Escaut near Cambrai. Laurent's line was agreed in 1769 on the duc de Choiseul's initiative. It included an enormous 13 682m tunnel which, if it had been built, would have been the world's longest. The section from the Oise to Saint-Quentin was opened in 1776, but works on the link across the watershed had been interrupted in 1773. Napoleon revived the project, choosing De Vicq's line, and personally opened the canal in 1810. It was upgraded to its current dimensions in the 1830s. Heavy traffic meant that all the locks had to be doubled. The canal found itself in the centre of the fighting of the World War I. There are many poignant reminders.

Navigation

This canal is attractive for cruising, especially the northern section in the Escaut valley, the spectacular summit level with its tunnels and the *port de plaisance* in the basin at Saint-Quentin. Commercial traffic declined dramatically after opening of the Canal du Nord, and it is now consistently quiet and peaceful, although a few Freycinet barges still use this scenically attractive route.

Tunnels

There are two tunnels. The first, at Riqueval, also called the Grand Souterrain, is 5670m long, the longest still in use on the French waterways. The second, Lesdins or Tronquoy, is 1098m in length. The tunnels have a navigable width of 6.75m and a headroom of 3.58m. The Riqueval tunnel has been equipped with improved ventilation and the electric tugs were withdrawn in 2021, so that vessels now proceed through both tunnels under their own power. This was the last tunnel in France where towage was compulsory. Times of passage remain as previously. The departure times are:
- **northbound** (from Riqueval), **07:30** and **15:00**,
- **southbound** (from Vendhuile), **09:30** and **17:00**.

All craft are to maintain a maximum speed of 4 km/h through the section comprising the two tunnels. Navigation is one-way only, controlled by lights.

Characteristic double lock on the canal: lock 15, Honnecourt.
© LDM PROVINSBLOGSPOT

Canal de Saint-Quentin

Key dimensions (m)	
Length	39.30
Beam	6.00
Draught	2.20
Air draught	3.70

Locks

There are 35 locks, of which 17 fall towards Cambrai and 18 towards Chauny. All the locks are paired, with two chambers separated by a central quay. Lock dimensions are 39.30m by 6.00m and maximum vessel dimensions are 38.50m by 5.60m. Locks 7 to 12, 18 to 21 and 26 to 30 have been equipped for automatic operation, with sensors and lock entry lights. There are no locks on the La Fère branch.

Draught
The maximum authorised draught is 2.20m.

Headroom
All the fixed bridges offer a minimum headroom of 3.70m, although it should be noted that Saint-Quentin bridge (PK 52) is on a gradient and offers 3.58m on one side and 3.83m on the other. Headroom is reduced by up to 0.30m when the canal drains storm waters.

Towpath
There are towpaths on both banks.

Authority
VNF Nord - Pas de Calais
- Place Marcelin-Berthelot, BP 371, 59407 Cambrai cedex 03 27 82 25 25   (PK 0-26)

VNF Bassin de la Seine, UTI Seine-Nord
- 44 rue du Gouvernement, BP 616, 02321 Saint-Quentin 03 23 05 78 00   (PK 26-92)

Route description

The *port de plaisance* in Cambrai, with water and electricity, and fuel (diesel only), just downstream of the bridge is strictly on the river Escaut. See details and plan under Escaut (p.73)

PK	
0.0	**Connection with canalised river Escaut**
2.2	Lock 1 (Proville)
3.8	Lock 2 (Cantigneul), bridge d/s, Proville 2km
4.4	Lock 3 (Noyelles), aqueduct
5.3	Bridge (Râperie), quay, Noyelles 700m
7.3	Lock 4 (Talma), quay d/s r/b
7.7	**Marcoing** bridge, quay d/s l/b, village 700m
7.8	Lock 5 (Marcoing)
8.1	Railway bridge
9.4	Lock 6 (Bracheux)
10.7	**Masnières** bridge, quays above and below r/b, village 300m
11.5	Lock 7 (Masnières), automatic
12.7	Lock 8 (Saint-Waast), automatic, aqueduct u/s
13.8	**Crèvecœur-sur-l'Escaut**, quay r/b, village 500m
14.1	Lock 9 (Crèvecœur), automatic, bridge
15.0	Lock 10 (Vinchy), automatic, bridge, **Les Rues-des-Vignes** l/b
15.4	Lock 11 (Tordoir), automatic
17.9	Lock 12 (Vaucelles), automatic, bridge d/s, Vaucelles abbey 700m
19.3	Bridge (Grenouillère), D644, main road Cambrai-Saint-Quentin
19.8	Private basin l/b
20.0	Lock 13 (Bantouzelle)
20.5	Lock 14 (Banteux), bridge, Banteux l/b, Bantouzelle r/b
23.2	Lock 15 (Honnecourt), bridge, village l/b

I – Northern France

Now consigned to history, the electric tug with three péniches in tow approaches the Grand Souterrain from the Macquincourt entrance.
© LUCIEN DEFAWE

PK 24.2 Lock 16 (Moulin-Lafosse)
PK 24.8 Lock 17 (Bosquet), beginning of summit level
PK 26.6 Grain loading quay in former canal arm
PK 26.9 **Vendhuile** bridge and village
PK 27.6 Macquincourt basin (for southbound tow)
PK 29.0 Riqueval tunnel (Grand Souterrain), Macquincourt (northern) entrance

The *Grand Souterrain* tunnel has finally made the inevitable concessions to modernity. Its venerable electric chain-tugs have been withdrawn. Improvements to safety measures and ventilation allowed VNF to abandon the compulsory towage, so that vessels now proceed under their own power. Transit at 4 km/h now takes less than 80 minutes, instead of 2 hours behind the tug. The canal runs in a deep cutting from here to Lesdins tunnel.

PK 34.7 Riqueval tunnel (Grand Souterrain), Riqueval (southern) entrance
PK 35.9 Basin for northbound tow
PK 36.0 Riqueval bridge
PK 37.3 Basin (former tow passing point)
PK 38.0 Grain loading quay
PK 38.2 **Bellenglise** bridge and village, basin south side
PK 39.5 Bridge (D1044), main road
PK 41.0 **Le Haucourt** bridge, quays either side, village 400m
PK 41.9 Lesdins tunnel, Le Haucourt (northern) entrance
PK 43.0 Lesdins tunnel, Le Tronquoy (southern) entrance
PK 43.7 Basin (formerly for tow formation)
PK 44.5 Public quay, water points
PK 45.2 Lock 18 (Lesdins), end of summit level
PK 45.5 Lock 19 (Pascal), bridge
PK 45.6 **Lesdins** bridge, village 1 km
PK 45.9 Private basin r/b
PK 46.7 Lock 20 (Omissy), bridge, village r/b
PK 48.7 Lock 21 (Moulin-Brûlé), bridge
PK 49.5 Bridge
PK 50.9 Lock 22 (Saint-Quentin)
PK 51.7 **Saint-Quentin** bridge, quay and *port de plaisance* r/b, 60 berths, 8 visitor moorings, free (maximum one week), water, electricity, restaurant 300m, town centre 800m

PK 52.7 New road bridge (Viaduc de Picardie), D1029 (road uses infilled bed of former canal basin)
PK 52.8 Entrance to basin (Vieux Port)

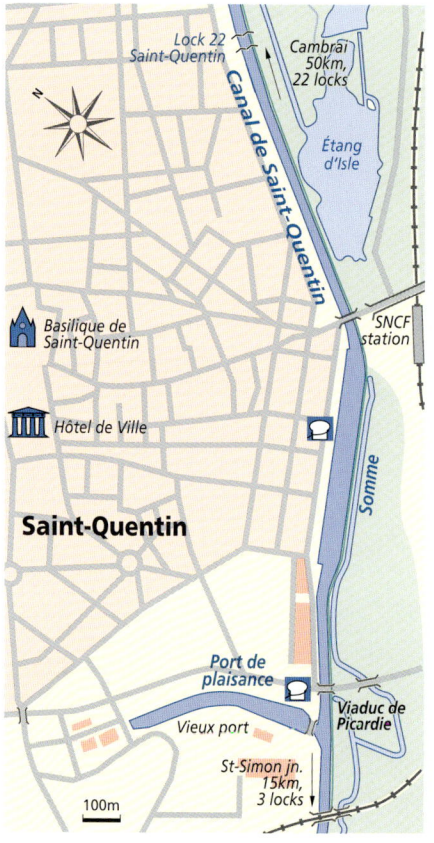

Unfortunately the *port de plaisance* has recently been closed and the harbour fenced off from the town, although still available to moor within. There are also attractive places to moor along the banks beyond the port.

PK 53.0 Railway bridge, quays r/b
PK 54.9 Bridge (Œstres)
PK 55.6 Motorway bridge (A26)
PK 56.9 Dallon bridge, village r/b
PK 58.3 Lock 23 (Fontaines-les-Clercs), bridge, village r/b
PK 60.7 Bridge
PK 61.1 **Seraucourt-le-Grand** *halte* on pontoon in former canal arm l/b, moorings for 5 boats, 06 85 97 72 82, night €12, water and electricity included, showers (€3.50 for 2 persons), slipway, village 600m

Recommended *halte* along a quiet spur branch.

PK 61.7 Bridge
PK 62.8 Lock 24 (Seraucourt-le-Grand), aqueduct u/s
PK 64.4 Artemps bridge, village l/b
PK 66.1 Entrance to former canal arm r/b
PK 66.3 Pont-de-Tugny bridge
PK 66.5 Lock 25 (Pont-de-Tugny), d/s entrance to Pont-de-Tugny arm, quays 300m
PK 68.0 Triangular junction with Canal de la Somme, Point Y, r/b

The Canal de la Somme branches off to the west. This section is currently closed, but restoration is being envisaged by the Somme *département*.

Canal de Saint-Quentin

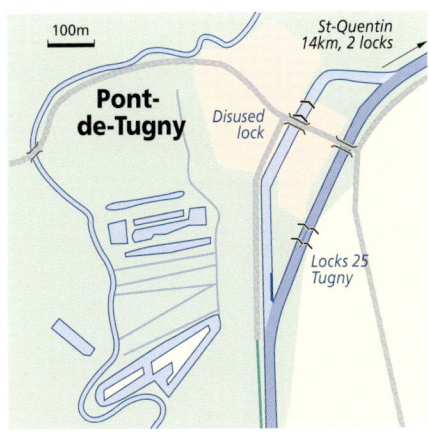

The port de plaisance at Saint-Quentin in its heyday; its revival is eagerly awaited by regional boatowners. © VILLE DE SAINT-QUENTIN

PK 69.0	**Saint-Simon** bridge, village l/b
PK 74.2	Jussy basin r/b and quay l/b
PK 74.5	Jussy bridge, village r/b
PK 76.4	Railway bridge (Paris-Valenciennes line), footbridge
PK 77.1	Lock 26 (Jussy)
PK 78.6	Main road bridge (D1)
PK 79.6	Lock 27 (Mennessis), bridge
PK 80.2	Lock 28 (Voyaux)
PK 83.0	Quessy bridge, quay d/s l/b, village 300m
PK 83.8	Lock 29 (Fargniers I)
PK 84.1	Lock 30 (Fargniers II)
PK 84.2	Fargniers bridge
PK 84.8	Lock 31 (Fargniers III), railway bridge d/s
PK 84.9	Junction with Branche de La Fère, l/b

Tergnier and Fargniers are both small industrial towns at the canal T-junction. La Fère branch leads east to join the Canal de la Sambre à l'Oise. Turn right to continue to the Canal latéral à l'Oise.

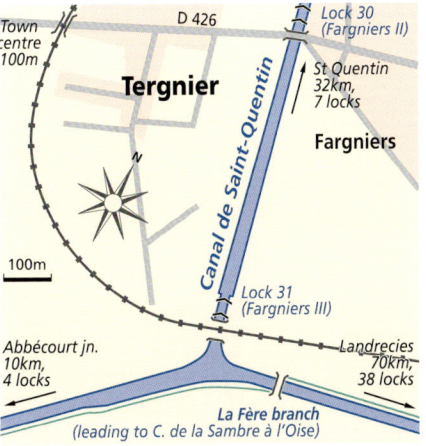

PK 85.8	Lock 32 (Tergniers), bridge
PK 87.1	Bridge (D53), public quay u/s l/b, Condren 800m
PK 88.3	Bridge (D1032)
PK 88.4	Lock 33 (Viry)
PK 89.7	**Viry-Noureuil** bridge, railway station 500m, village 1km
PK 90.7	Bridge (Senicourt)
PK 90.8	Lock 34 (Senicourt)
PK 91.8	Railway bridge
PK 92.0	Junction with Branche de Chauny, with one lock down to the Oise, navigable for 500m (branch now disused)

Halte fluviale at the junction, water and electricity, 12 visitor moorings.

PK 92.3	Lock 35 (Chauny)
PK 92.5	**Chauny** bridge, town r/b, connection with Canal latéral à l'Oise

Branch off the Canal de Saint-Quentin

Branche de La Fère

PK 0.0	**Fargniers** junction off the through route
PK 0.2	Pipeline crossing
PK 0.9	Bridge (Frette)
PK 1.5	Disused railway bridge, power station and numerous overhead power lines, industrial quays
PK 3.2	**Beautor** bridge
PK 3.3	Railway bridge, quay
PK 3.5	Disused railway bridge
PK 3.8	Junction with Canal de la Sambre à l'Oise d/s of **La Fère** bridge

12. River Escaut

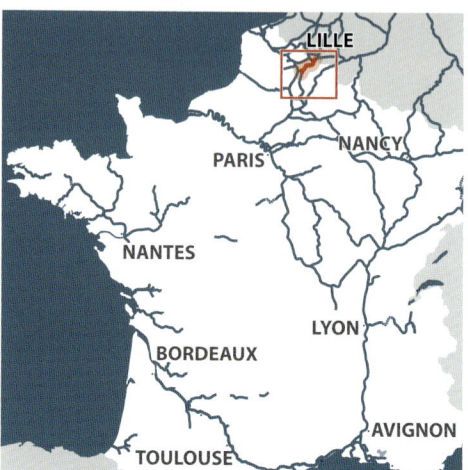

The RIVER ESCAUT BECOMES NAVIGABLE at Cambrai, where it connects with the northern end of the Canal de Saint-Quentin. It runs through the towns of Denain and Valenciennes before crossing the Belgian border at Mortagne, a distance of 59km. The Escaut subsequently flows past Tournai (Wallonia) as the Haut-Escaut and Ghent (Flanders) as the Bovenschelde then Antwerp before debouching in the North Sea. The river has always carried heavy barge traffic, since it forms part of the route from the Paris region to Northern France, Belgium, the Netherlands and the Rhine, and its importance as a commercial waterway increased after it was widened to European waterway standards (1350-tonne barges) from its junction with the Dunkerque-Escaut waterway to the Belgian border. The Escaut connects with the soon to be restored Canal de Pommerœul à Condé on the right bank at PK 32 and with the navigable river Scarpe on the left bank at PK 44 (currently closed to through navigation). The straightening of the river left numerous minor arms, most of which were subsequently filled in. Despite its importance for commercial navigation, the Escaut is an attractive waterway. Many of the factories which used to line its banks have been demolished, and the river is pleasantly rural throughout much of its length.

The Escaut was developed first in Belgium from Antwerp to Tournai, then extended to Valenciennes. Canalisation upstream from Valenciennes to Cambrai was completed in 1788 with locks 44m by 5.20m and a draught of 1.20m. Napoleon saw the benefits of linking Paris to Belgium and promoted the Canal de Saint-Quentin to the south. The locks were deepened and doubled, as coal became the essential commodity of the industrial revolution. Upgrading downstream from Bouchain was started in the 1960s, but the waterway is still not fully compliant with international standards. For many centuries, Belgian traffic from Mons to Tournai used the Haine and Escaut rivers through France, paying a high toll, hence the idea of the Nimy-Blaton-Péronnes canal, a short cut in Belgian territory, built in the late 19th century. All the locks on the high-capacity section are to be doubled by European Class Vb size locks, 185m by 12m, as part of the overall European Seine-Scheldt waterway project.

Navigation
The Escaut is divided into two sections. From Cambrai to Étrun (13km) it has the standard Freycinet *péniche* dimensions, then the high-capacity (*grand gabarit*) waterway from Pont-Malin lock to the Belgian border (46km).

Locks
There are 5 locks on the first section, each with twin chambers measuring 40.50m by 6.00m. In the second section there are 6 locks, all of 3000-tonne push-tow dimensions (144.60m by 12.00m).

Draught
The maximum authorised draught is 2.20m in the first section and 3.00m on the high-capacity waterway down to the Belgian border.

Headroom
In the first section the headroom under fixed bridges is 3.80m at normal water level. Throughout the second section this is being increased to offer a minimum of 5.25m above the highest navigable water level (5.55m above normal level). The lowest bridge at present is 4.80m (5.10m). The target headroom for the Seine-Escaut waterway is 7.00m, but 5.25m is likely to remain the maximum available for at least 15 years. The Pont Jacob in Valenciennes is the principal difficulty, since it carries the Valenciennes tramway.

Towpath
There is a good towpath throughout the first section and a metalled service road along the high-capacity waterway.

Authority
VNF Nord-Pas-de-Calais
- Place Marcellin Berthelot, BP 371, 59407 Cambrai Cedex 03 27 82 25 25 (first section)
- 22 chemin du halage, BP 2025, 59321 Valenciennes Cedex

Escaut

PK 1.0	Lock 2 (Selles), two chambers, bridge
PK 1.4	Bridge (Pont Rouge)
PK 1.5	Railway bridge (Cambrai)
PK 3.6	Lock 3 (Erre), two chambers, bridge, water, boatyard u/s r/b
PK 6.6	**Eswars** bridge, quay u/s l/b, village 600m l/b
PK 7.9	Lock 4 (Thun-l'Evèque), two chambers, bridge, village 300m l/b
PK 8.3	Quay r/b
PK 10.0	Lock 5 (Iwuy), two chambers, water, quays u/s r/b, village 1km r/b
PK 10.8	Motorway bridge (A2)

Key dimensions (m)

Length	40.50
Beam	6.00
Draught	2.20
Air draught	3.80

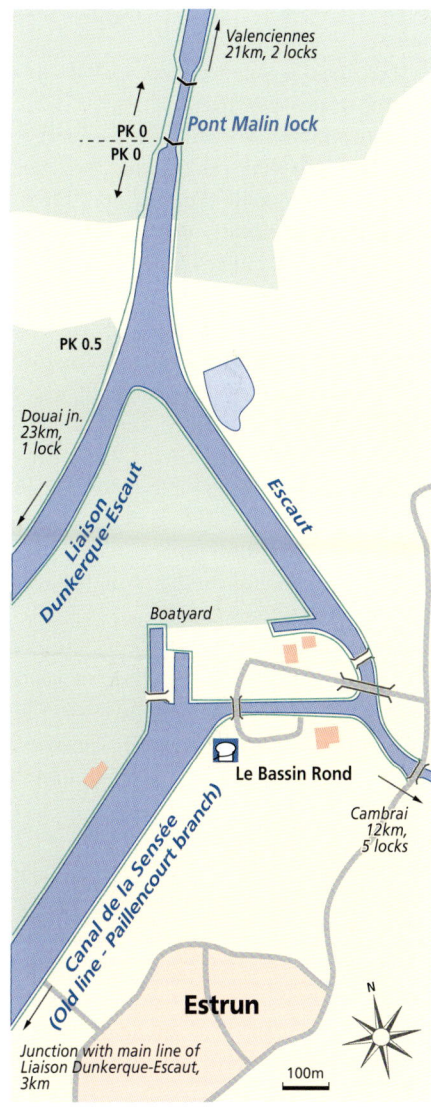

Route description

Cambrai to junction with Liaison Dunkerque-Escaut

PK 0.0	Cambrai bridge (Pont de Marquion) and footbridge, *connection with Canal de Saint-Quentin*
PK 0.1	**Cambrai** Cantimpré basin, boat harbour l/b, 20 berths, 8 visitor moorings, 03 27 81 41 87, night €8.40, diesel, water and electricity included, showers, wifi, slipway

A popular *port de plaisance*, but with limited capacity; it is recommended to book in advance. The town is delightful, and famous for its sweets called *bêtises*. The town centre is only a short walk from the basin.

PK 0.2	Lock 1 (Cantimpré), two chambers, bridge, water, town centre 500m r/b
PK 0.6	Cambrai-Selles basin l/b

Cambrai is one of the longest-established and most attractive boat harbours in the Nord-Pas de Calais. © CRT

PK 12.0	**Estrun** bridge, village 800m l/b
PK 12.2	*Junction with original line of Canal de la Sensée*, l/b

Enter this original section of the Canal de la Sensée (Branche de Paillencourt) to discover the superb basin (Bassin Rond) with idyllic tranquil moorings and a boatyard, otherwise limited facilities.

PK 12.2	Bridge
PK 13.0	*Junction with Liaison Dunkerque-Escaut*, l/b
PK 13.5	Lock (Pont-Malin) (these last 500m in the Liaison Dunkerque-Escaut)

73

I – Northern France

Escaut (Pont Malin to Belgian border)

- PK 0.0 Lock (Pont Malin), VHF 18 (considered to be the end of the Liaison Dunkerque-Escaut)
- PK 2.3 **Bouchain** bridge, quay d/s r/b, village l/b
- PK 4.7 Railway bridge
- PK 5.4 **Neuville-sur-Escaut** bridge, village r/b
- PK 6.2 Turning Basin
- PK 6.9 **Lourches** bridge, town 1200m l/b
- PK 7.2 Bridge (N455 motorway access)
- PK 8.1 Junction with Rivière des Moulins l/b, boat moorings 760m down this branch on r/b
- PK 8.7 Lock (Denain), two chambers, VHF 22, water
- PK 9.2 **Denain** bridge (Pont de l'Enclos), town centre 1 km l/b
- PK 9.6 Footbridge
- PK 10.2 Bridge (Abattoir), quay d/s l/b
- PK 11.5 Railway bridge
- PK 11.7 Motorway viaduct (Rouvignies), A2
- PK 12.0 Bridge (Pont de l'Escaut), D630
- PK 13.5 Private footbridge and quay l/b
- PK 13.6 Railway bridge (Prouvy)
- PK 13.7 **Thiant** bridge, village 1 km r/b
- PK 15.4 Lock (Trith), VHF 18
- PK 15.6 Gas pipeline crossing
- PK 15.9 **Trith-Saint-Léger** footbridge, town 700m l/b
- PK 17.1 Bridge (Pont de la Fontenelle), D59, turning basin u/s
- PK 18.8 Motorway viaduct (Trith), A2
- PK 18.9 Railway bridge (Vert Gazon), turning basin d/s
- PK 19.5 Boat moorings l/b level with dinghy sailing centre on adjacent lake (Étang du Vignoble)
- PK 20.6 Bridge (Notre Dame)
- PK 21.3 Valenciennes bridge (Pont Saint-Waast), quay u/s r/b
- PK 22.0 Bridge (Pont Jacob)
- PK 22.1 **Valenciennes** port de plaisance 'Valescaut' in left-bank arm, 64 berths, 40 visitor moorings on pontoons, 06 33 32 24 72, night €11, water (50 litres) and electricity (10 kWh) included, showers, pump-out, slipway, valescaut@valenciennes-metropole.fr. Town centre 500m (tram stop at Pont Jacob).

The new port de plaisance at Valenciennes

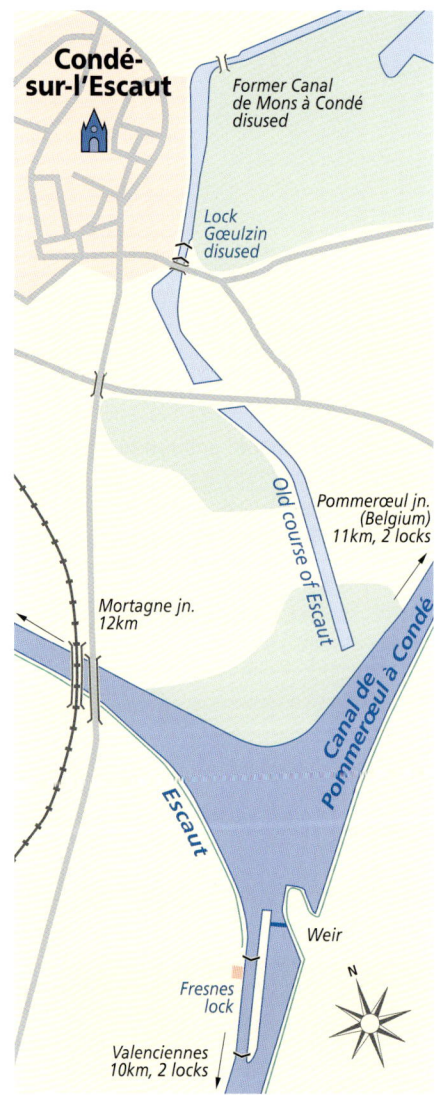

Splendid port de plaisance opened in 2015 in the weir arm of the Escaut in Valenciennes. This is fancy 'pretending-to-be-a-barge' architecture, with a guide wall to protect the capitainerie against ramming by barges. The photo is looking south towards the through route and the approach to Folien lock (on the other side of this island). The pontoon on the far side is open, but on this side (to the north) it has been fenced it off for boaters' security. Larger craft (more than 18m long) are invited to moor on the opposite bank where dolphins are available, and the mooring charges are reduced.

- PK 22.1 Lock (Folien), VHF 22, water
- PK 23.1 Railway bridge (Bleuse-Borne)
- PK 24.0 Overhead power lines
- PK 24.7 Railway bridge (Saint-Guillaume)
- PK 24.9 Lock (Bruay) in new cut, l/b, VHF 18
- PK 25.4 Bridge (Pont des Vaches), Bruay-sur-l'Escaut 500m l/b
- PK 28.7 Bridge (Marais), D50
- PK 32.0 Bridge (Masys)
- PK 32.1 Disused railway bridge (Moulin)
- PK 34.2 Bridge (Sarteau), **Vieux-Condé** 700m r/b
- PK 32.0 Bridge (Masys)
- PK 32.1 Disused railway bridge (Moulin)
- PK 34.2 Bridge (Sarteau), **Vieux-Condé** 700m r/b
- PK 36.7 Boat moorings r/b
- PK 37.8 **Hergnies** bridge, village r/b
- PK 44.1 **Mortagne-du-Nord** bridge, village r/b
- PK 44.3 Boat moorings and public park, l/b
- PK 44.4 Confluence with navigable river Scarpe, l/b
- PK 45.7 Belgian border

13. Canal de Pommerœul à Condé

THE CANAL DE POMMERŒUL À CONDÉ was opened in 1980 to link the busy commercial waterway networks of Northern France and Belgium, but had to be closed 10 years later after the river Haine dumped huge quantities of silt into the entire length of the canal in France. The large-scale dredging works and other improvements on the canal are under way as part of the overall Seine-Scheldt project, with with 42% EU funding, and are expected to be completed in 2022. The canal is 11.6km long from Pommerœul, on the Nimy-Blaton-Péronnes canal in the Wallonian Region of Belgium, to Condé, on the canalised river Escaut. The French part is 5.5km long, but for convenience the whole length is given in the route description. The modern canal completely bypasses the former route through the historic walled town of Condé-sur-l'Escaut. This attractive site is therefore no longer accessible by boat, but it is shown on the large-scale plan of the junction (opposite, under the Escaut) for reference.

The cross-border Canal de Mons à Condé was started by order of Napoleon in 1807, when Belgium was part of France, and inaugurated in 1818. It was re-routed in 1968 to make way for a motorway in Belgium. Originally built with locks of Freycinet size (the péniche flamande is the craft from which the Freycinet gauge was derived), the new cut from Pommerœul to Condé was built to Class IV dimensions in 1980, but soon fell into disuse due to silting from the river Haine. The canal is to be dredged and reopened in 2022 as part of the Seine-Scheldt waterway incorporating the new Seine-Nord Europe Canal.

Navigation
The canal is designed for use by large commercial craft, but boats may be locked through, subject to having the *vignette* paperwork for the destination network, VNF or the waterways of Wallonia (Service Public Wallon) or Flanders (De Vlaamse Waterweg).

Locks
The canal has two large locks, 145 by 12m with intermediate gates, both on the Belgian section.

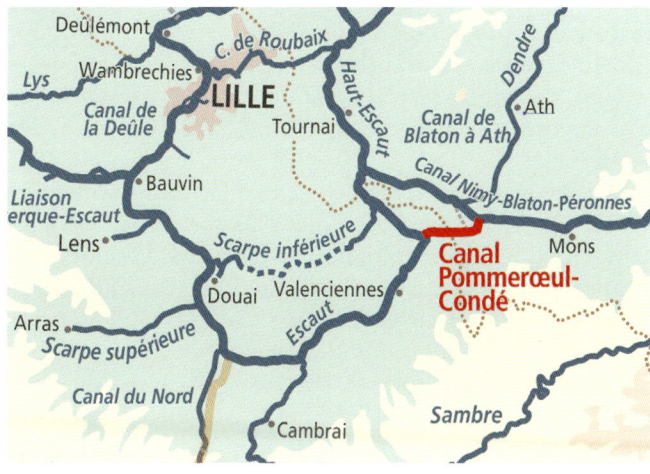

Key dimensions (m)	
Length	185.00
Beam	12.00
Draught	3.00
Air draught	5.25

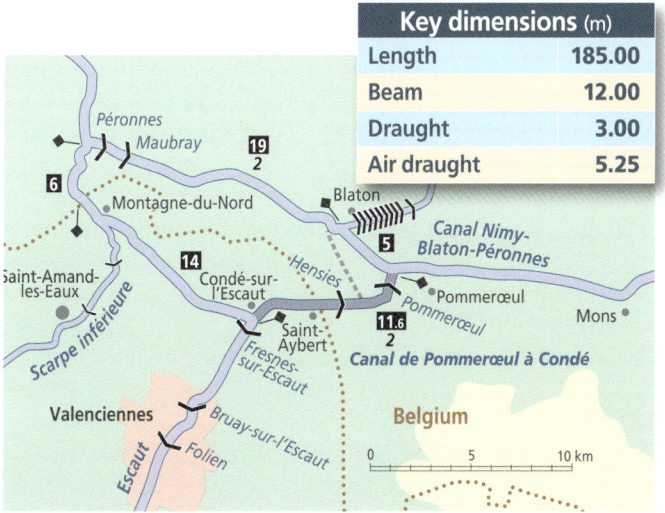

Draught
3.00m on completion of the dredging works.

Headroom
The bridges offer a minimum headroom of 5.25m at highest water level.

Authority
VNF Nord - Pas de Calais (for the French section) – 22 chemin du halage, BP 2025, 59321 Valenciennes cedex 03 27 32 22 80

Route description

PK 0.0	**Junction with canalised river Escaut** d/s of Fresnes lock
PK 0.8	Bridge (Pont du Bastringue, D935)
PK 2.3	Basin
PK 4.9	**Saint-Aybert** bridge, small village 200m l/b
PK 5.5	Belgium-France border
PK 6.2	Lock (Hensies)
PK 7.0	Bridge (Sartis)
PK 9.7	**Pommerœul** bridge, village 1km l/b
PK 10.9	Railway bridge, basin d/s
PK 11.1	Lock (Pommerœul), bridge
PK 11.6	**Junction with Nimy-Blaton-Péronnes Canal** in Belgium

Turn left here for the charming Canal de Blaton à Ath and the river Dendre.

14. River Sambre and Canal de la Sambre à l'Oise

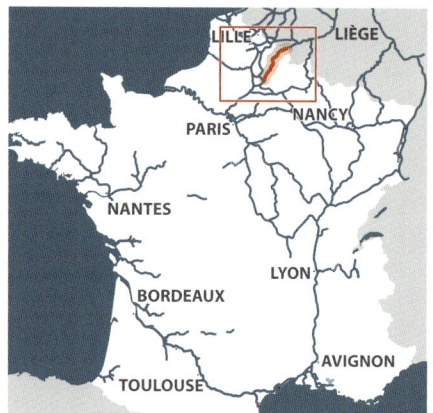

THE NAVIGABLE RIVER SAMBRE and Canal de la Sambre à l'Oise together form the most popular route for *plaisanciers* entering France from Belgium and the Netherlands. Publication of this edition coincides with the reopening of this route in July 2021, following reconstruction of the aqueducts at Vadencourt and Macquigny. The French Government paid for half the cost of restoring the canal, the rest of the €23.5 million investment being covered by the local authorities. For 15 years, boat owners were deprived of this 'back door' into France. Starting from Charleroi, the Sambre is a very attractive winding river navigation, despite its historic association with the heavy industry that lined its banks in towns in both Belgium and France. Hautmont, for example, had steelworks that have now vanished and given way to a splendid *port de plaisance* which itself justifies making this a cruising destination during the year or for wintering.

The navigable river Sambre extends from the Belgian border downstream of Jeumont to the small town of Landrecies, a distance of 54km with 9 locks. Various rectification works cut almost 2km from the course of the river, so that the actual distance is just over 52km. The route description below retains the original distances, corresponding to the kilometre posts on the river. Meander cutoffs shorten the route slightly downstream of Berlaimont (PK 19) and downstream of Sassegnies (PK 12-15).

From Landrecies, navigation continues on the Canal de la Sambre à l'Oise, which passes through a profoundly rural area of northern France. The canal is 67km long from Landrecies to La Fère, where it joins the La Fère branch of the Canal de Saint-Quentin. The canal includes a summit level at an altitude of 137.40m, near Landrecies. Throughout most of the descent towards La Fère, the canal follows the upper valley of the river Oise.

Navigation

The canal was reopened to through navigation in July 2021, and dredging has restored a navigable depth of 1.60m. The local authorities have made great efforts to meet the needs of tourists (re)discovering this itinerary.

Boats gather at Catillon-sur-Sambre for a rally to celebrate reopening of the canal on July 1st, 2021 © RÉUSSIR NOTRE SAMBRE

A company was set up in 1826 to canalise the river Sambre under the Becquey programme. Some flash locks had been built in the 17th century. A canal to link the Meuse with the Seine was envisaged from the late 17th century, but it was only after the Becquey programme was approved that the canal was let to private concessionary Urbain et Piard in 1833. Works were carried out in 1834-39, while the river canalisation works were also completed within this period (1835-1837). Closed for 15 years after two aqueducts threatened to collapse, the through route was reopened to navigation in 2021.

During the season, from mid-May to mid-September, the locks are operated from 9:00 to 19:00, with the usual hour-long break for lunch. The rest of the year, operating hours are 8:30 to 17:30, and advance notice must be given to VNF 48 hours before passage: by 15:00 for passage Wednesday to Saturday, and by 15:00 on Friday for passage Sunday to Tuesday. The numbers to be called are 03 27 58 81 70 for the sector from Jeumont to Rejet-de-Beaulieu (the summit level); 06 03 23 40 67 for the sector from Étreux to Noyales (locks 1-21); and 06 12 26 09 99 for the sector from Macquigny to Travecy (locks 22-35).

Locks

There is a standard 38.50m by 5.20m lock beside each of the nine movable weirs on the river Sambre, overcoming a total difference in level of 11.35m. The 38 locks on the

Sambre and Canal de la Sambre à l'Oise

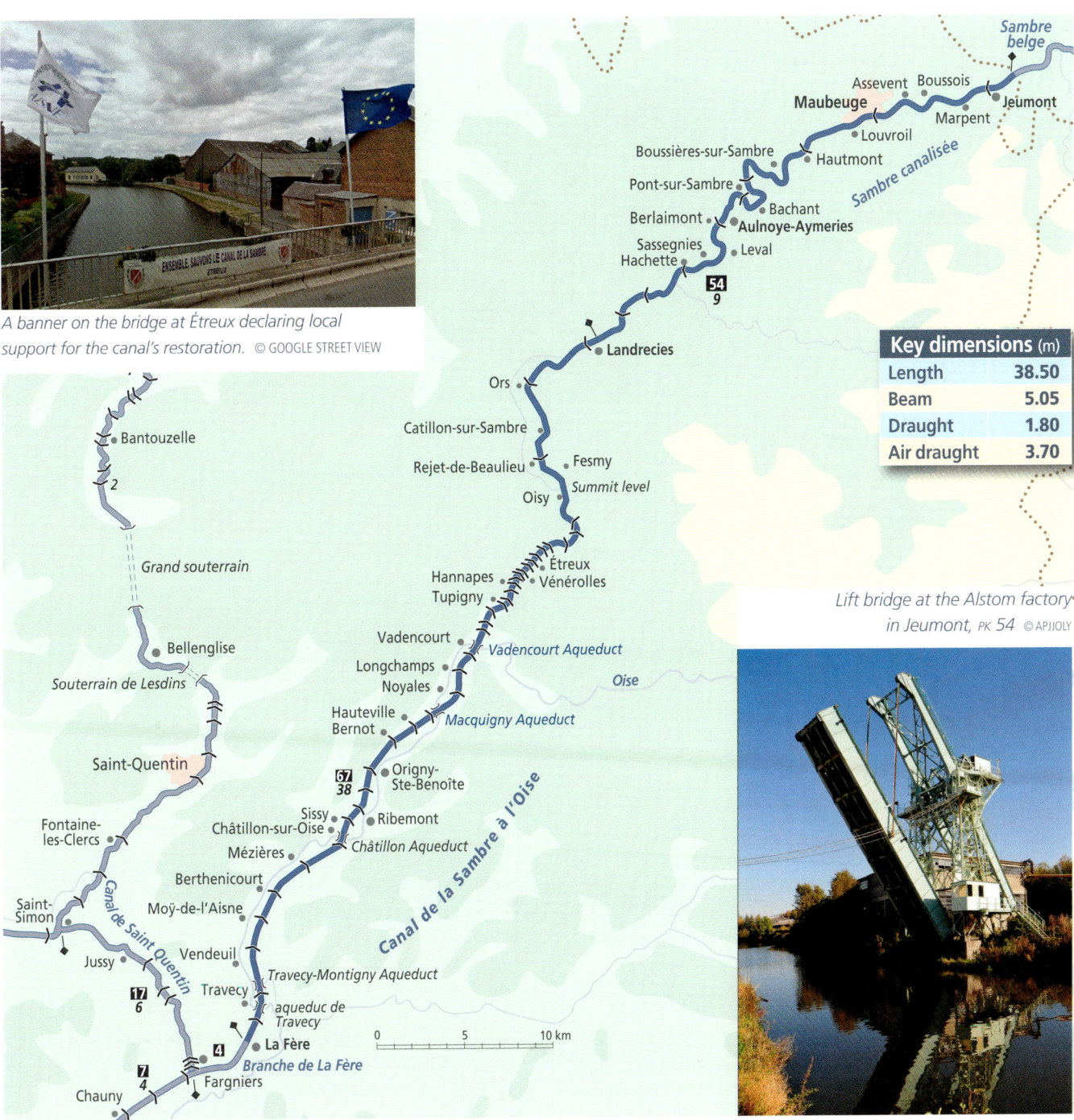

A banner on the bridge at Étreux declaring local support for the canal's restoration. © GOOGLE STREET VIEW

Lift bridge at the Alstom factory in Jeumont, PK 54 © APJJOLY

Key dimensions (m)	
Length	38.50
Beam	5.05
Draught	1.80
Air draught	3.70

canal have the same dimensions. Three locks rise the 5.70m from Landrecies to the summit level. The other 35 fall towards La Fère (difference in level 86.65m). Coming from Belgium, the welcome at Marpent lock (9) is a challenge, because it means walking along the sheet piling guide wall to the lock, where there is an intercom to announce your arrival. You will be registered by the VNF staff, who will deliver your remote control for use on the river and the canal up to the summit level. You may obtain your *vignette* either from VNF at Berlaimont or at the *port de plaisance* at Hautmont. Locks 1 to 7 at Étreux are operated in an automatic sequence. Locks 8 to 21 are operated by mobile lock-keepers. The remote control is again used for locks 22 to 35, but operation of the two lift-bridges is by waterway staff.

Draught

The maximum authorised draught is 2.00m from the Belgian border to Landrecies, and from lock 25 Originy-Sainte-Benoîte to the junction with the Canal de Saint-Quentin. This is reduced to 1.60m throughout the recently-restored central section.

Headroom

The fixed bridges on the canalised river Sambre leave a minimum headroom of 3.95m, reduced to as little as 3.00m when the river is in flood. The canal offers a slightly reduced headroom of 3.60m, reduced to 3.40m when the rivers supplying the canal are in flood.

I – Northern France

Towpath
There is a good towpath throughout, developed as a cycle itinerary.

Authority
VNF Nord Pas-de-Calais
Unité territoriale Escaut-Saint-Quentin
- 2 chemin du Halage, 59620 Aulnoye-Aymeries, 03 27 58 81 70 (Sambre PK 54-0 and canal PK 0-19)

VNF Bassin de la Seine, UTI Seine-Nord
- 44 rue du Gouvernement, BP 616, 02321 Saint-Quentin 03 23 05 78 00 (PK 19-67)

The attractive port de plaisance *at Hautmont* © MAIRIE DE HAUTMONT

Route description

Sambre

PK 54.2	Belgian border, 39km and 10 locks from the junction with the Canal de Charleroi à Bruxelles at Charleroi
PK 54.1	Private pipeline bridge (Alstom factory)
PK 53.9	Private lift bridge (Alstom factory)
PK 53.2	**Jeumont** bridge, quay and pontoon moorings on quay u/s l/b, 03 27 62 11 93, slipway, small border town r/b
PK 53.0	Railway bridge, private quays u/s
PK 51.8	Lock 9 (Marpent) r/b and weir

The staff from the VNF office at Berlaimont provide here the remote control for the locks on the river and the canal (but not locks 8 to 21 on the canal south of the summit level, which are operated by waterway staff).

PK 50.9	**Marpent** bridge, small town 400m r/b
PK 50.1	Conveyor bridge
PK 47.7	**Boussois** bridge, *halte* on quay 40m, village 200m l/b, water, electricity, **Recquignies** r/b
PK 47.0	Railway bridge (private)
PK 45.3	**Assevent** bridge, village l/b
PK 43.5	Bridge
PK 42.2	Road bridge (boulevard Charles De Gaulle)
PK 41.5	**Maubeuge** bridge (Pont Franco-Belge), *halte* d/s, 03 27 62 11 93, quay and 48m long pontoon, free, water, electricity, town l/b
PK 41.4	Lock 8 (Maubeuge) r/b and weir
PK 41.1	Bridge (Europe)
PK 39.9	Railway bridge
PK 39.5	Bridge
PK 39.4	**Louvroil** bridge (Pont Michaux), town r/b
PK 39.0	Bridge (avenue du 19 mars 1962)
PK 38.7	Bridge (Usinor railway siding, disused)
PK 37.5	Bridge
PK 37.3	Bridge
PK 36.9	Expressway bridge (N2, Maubeuge bypass)
PK 35.7	Disused railway bridge and new road bridge (D95d), industrial quays
PK 35.4	Lock 7 (Hautmont) l/b and weir, bridge
PK 35.2	**Hautmont** marina l/b, 06 08 69 44 31, night €10, all services, electricity and water on pontoons (metered), gated access and videosurveillance, fuel, pump-out, slipway, wintering, town centre r/b

This fine marina opened in 2014. It is an attractively landscaped former industrial site, with residential development around the harbour. There are 65 berths for boats up to 15m long, 3 dolphin moorings for 38m *péniches* and a 150m long quay for visiting boats.

PK 34.5	Railway bridge and footbridge
PK 33.9	Bridge (D800)
PK 32.0	**Boussières-sur-Sambre** bridge, village l/b
PK 26.2	Lock 6 (Quartes) r/b and weir
PK 26.0	Bridge (Quartes)
PK 23.2	Bachant bridges, village r/b
PK 22.0	Pont-sur-Sambre bridge, village l/b
PK 21.7	Lock 5 (Pont-sur-Sambre) and weir
PK 19.9	Aymeries bridge, small village r/b
PK 18.1	**Berlaimont** bridge, quay u/s l/b, 03 27 67 31 63, water, electricity, small town 400m l/b

Mooring to long quay partly in weir stream above the lock, beware of possible current pulling towards the weir.

PK 17.8	Lock 4 (Berlaimont) and weir
PK 17.6	Bridge (Montbard), private quay u/s r/b
PK 15.7	Railway bridge
PK 14.8	**Leval** mooring r/b to 25m landing stage, village 700m

Mooring beside a nature conservation area in a bypassed loop of the river.

PK 13.0	Bridge
PK 12.5	Pipeline crossing
PK 11.1	Lock 3 (Sassegnies) and weir
PK 7.7	Lock 2 (Hachette) and weir

Mooring d/s l/b on quay backed by grass bank with picnic tables.

PK 5.9	Bridge (Hachette)
PK 3.0	Lock 1 (Étoquies) and weir, lift bridge
PK 0.0	**Connection with Canal de la Sambre à l'Oise** (300m d/s of Landrecies), turning basin

Canal de la Sambre à l'Oise

PK 0.0	Connection with the canalised river Sambre, turning basin
PK 0.2	**Landrecies** bridge, small town
PK 0.3	Lock 3 (Landrecies), weir, municipal *halte* u/s r/b (pontoon, 48m), 03 27 77 52 52, night €5 (maximum 72 hours), water, electricity, slipway

The flottilla celebrating the reopened canal is seen here at Landrecies on July 18th, 2021. © ELIAS CONGIU, L'AVESNOIS VU D'EN HAUT

Good moorings to quay backed by grass, with pontoons for smaller craft closer to the lock. The remote control supplied at Marpent works for the locks on the canal.

PK 5.8	Lock 2 (Ors), bridge, village l/b
PK 8.6	**Catillon-sur-Sambre** lift bridge, municipal *halte* on quay u/s r/b for 4 boats, 03 27 77 61 16, night €5 (maximum 72 hours), water, electricity, pump-out, village 500m l/b

Good mooring with picnic area.

PK 12.0	Lock 1 (Bois l'Abbaye), beginning of summit level

Just beside the lock is the reputed fish restaurant Le Paradoxe.

PK 13.9	**Fesmy** bridge, village 1300m
PK 16.0	**Oisy** bridge, village 200m
PK 18.6	Railway bridge
PK 18.9	Lock 1 (**Gard**), overflow weir, end of summit level, Boué bridge, pontoon moorings, village 2km
PK 19.3	Lock 2 (Étreux), overflow weir, quay u/s l/b
PK 20.1	Lock 3 (Étreux), overflow weir
PK 20.8	Lock 4 (Étreux), overflow weir
PK 21.1	Lock 5 (Étreux), overflow weir
PK 21.5	Lock 6 (Étreux), overflow weir, bridge
PK 21.8	**Étreux** swing bridge, *halte* on quay u/s r/b, 03 23 60 60 19, free, slipway, water, electricity, pump-out, village l/b
PK 22.1	Lock 7 (Étreux), bridge
PK 22.5	Lock 8 (Étreux)
PK 23.0	Lock 9 (Vénérolles)
PK 23.2	**Vénérolles** bridge, small village l/b
PK 23.8	Lock 10 (Vénérolles), private footbridge
PK 24.5	Lock 11 (Vénérolles)
PK 25.0	**Hannapes** swing bridge, village r/b
PK 25.1	Lock 12 (Hannapes), quay d/s r/b
PK 26.5	Lock 13 (Hannapes)
PK 27.0	Lock 14 (Tupigny)
PK 27.2	Lock 15 (Tupigny)
PK 27.3	Swing bridge, river Noirieux enters canal, r/b, quay r/b
PK 27.7	**Tupigny** swing bridge, village r/b
PK 28.0	Weir (Tupigny) r/b, Noirieux leaves canal
PK 28.4	Lock 16 (Tupigny)
PK 29.2	Lock 17 (Grand-Verly)
PK 30.0	Lock 18 (Grand-Verly), bridge, village 500m r/b
PK 30.9	**Vadencourt** swing bridge, turning basin, village 800m r/b
PK 31.5	Vadencourt aqueduct over Oise (rebuilt)
PK 31.6	Lock 19 (Vadencourt), quay d/s r/b
PK 31.9	Bridge (Bohéries)
PK 33.2	Lock 20 (Longchamps), bridge, water
PK 35.2	Lock 21 (Noyales), bridge, village 400m r/b
PK 37.3	Macquigny aqueduct over Oise (rebuilt)
PK 37.5	Lock 22 (Macquigny), bridge
PK 38.6	Lock 23 (Hauteville), bridge
PK 40.9	Lock 24 (Bernot), bridge, village 700m r/b
PK 42.4	Turning basin l/b
PK 43.2	Neuvillette swing bridge, quay u/s l/b
PK 43.6	Lock 25 (Origny-Sainte-Benoîte), water
PK 44.1	**Origny-Sainte-Benoîte** bridge (D1029), quay u/s l/b, village 900m l/b, basin r/b
PK 44.4	Pipeline crossings (factory on both banks)
PK 45.9	Lock 26 (Thenelles), bridge
PK 48.1	Lock 27 (**Ribemont**), bridge, quay and turning basin d/s l/b, small town 1200m l/b
PK 49.7	Lock 28 (Sissy), bridge, village 600m r/b
PK 51.3	Châtillon aqueduct over Oise
PK 51.6	Lock 29 (Châtillon), bridge, small village 600m r/b
PK 52.9	Lock 30 (**Mézières-sur-Oise**), bridge, quay d/s l/b, village 500m r/b
PK 53.6	Railway bridge (preserved railway)
PK 54.5	Lock 31 (Berthenicourt), bridge
PK 55.3	Alaincourt bridge, quay d/s r/b
PK 56.4	Motorway bridge (A26)
PK 56.8	Lock 32 (Hamégicourt), bridge, water, quay d/s r/b, **Moÿ-de-l'Aisne** 700m r/b
PK 57.8	Bridge (Brissy)
PK 58.4	Lock 33 (Brissy)
PK 60.7	**Vendeuil** bridge, quays, village 1200m r/b
PK 62.2	Travecy-Montigny aqueduct over river Serre, overhead power line
PK 62.6	Lock 34 (Travecy-Montigny)
PK 63.5	Turning basin and quay l/b
PK 63.8	**Travecy** swing bridge, quay d/s l/b, village 500m r/b
PK 64.3	Travecy aqueduct over Oise
PK 65.1	Lock 35 (Travecy), bridge, water
PK 66.1	Bridge (D1044)
PK 67.2	**La Fère** bridge, centre 1200m l/b, connection with Branche de La Fère of Canal de Saint-Quentin

It is a further 3.7km, without locks, to the junction with the main line of the Canal de Saint-Quentin, where the route leading to the Oise and the Seine is straight ahead.

15. Saint-Valery and Canal de la Somme

The canal de la Somme, built in 1770-1843 to provide an outlet to the sea from Saint-Quentin, is in effect the canalised river Somme throughout the greater part of its course. It is one of the most attractive waterways of northern France, passing through a marshy valley dotted with lakes, peat marshes and gravel pits, and is ideal for pleasure cruising. Commercial traffic has all but ceased. The waterway extends 156km from Saint-Valery to a junction with the Canal de Saint-Quentin at Saint-Simon. The last 16km between the Canal du Nord and Saint-Simon have been closed to navigation since 2006, but the Somme département plans to take over this section from VNF and restore navigation by 2024. The waterway is divided into four sections. From the sea lock (PK 156) to Abbeville (PK 142) is the Canal maritime d'Abbeville à Saint-Valery-sur-Somme, designed to be used by coastal ships. From Abbeville to the junction with the Canal du Nord near Péronne (PK 37) navigation is mainly in the river, with occasional lock-cuts. In this length the river is abandoned in favour of a lateral canal over the last 17km. The third section from Péronne to Béthencourt-sur-Somme doubles up as a section of the Canal du Nord. The fourth section is the above-mentioned projected restoration.

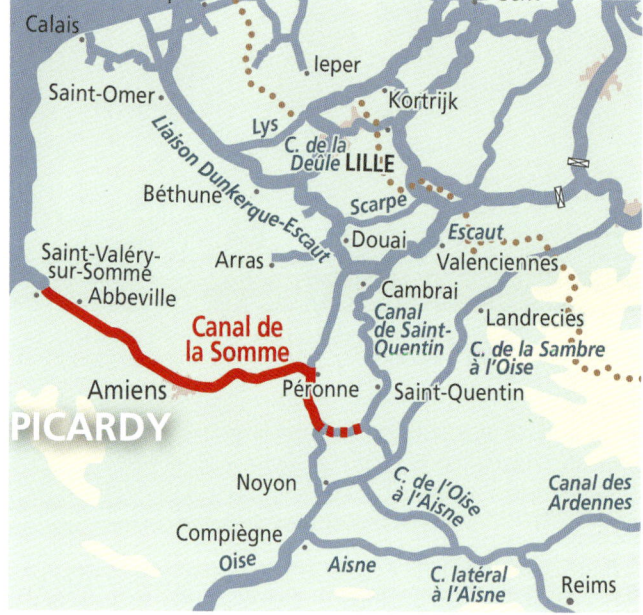

Saint-Valery as entry port

Although the approach from the English Channel is a little difficult and demands care and preparation, the rewards from visiting Saint-Valery and using the Somme route into France's river and canal system are substantial. For mast lowering and stepping, see the notes in the *Practical Navigation introduction*.

The approach from the Channel must be made in the correct tidal, wind and weather conditions because of the extensive shoals and drying areas of the Baie de la Somme. The access channel twists and turns and is well marked with buoys, but the channel's route changes so charts may not be completely accurate. Inward bound, be at the ATSO safe-water mark around HW-2, preferably not at neaps if the draught is more than 1.50m and not in an on-shore breeze greater than F4. The harbourmaster advises to keep close to the red port-hand marks. A keen look-out and a depth-sounder are vital. There is a subsidiary small-craft channel north to Le Crotoy. Time from sea to Saint-Valery is approximately 2 hours. If proceeding directly into the canal, entrance through the sea lock is possible only for 30 minutes or one hour before high tide.

Navigation

From 1st April to 1st November, operating hours are 0900-1800. Lock-keepers (locks 25 to 7 inclusive) accompany boats after passage has been notified by calling the central control office (PCE) on 06 74 83 60 69. This number may be used in season from 08:30 to 18:00. From 2 November to 31 March, 36 hours' notice of passage is to be given, and operating hours are reduced to 09:00 - 17:00, with no service on weekends or public holidays. In all cases operating staff have a break from 1230 to 1330. The 'Somme en poche' app can be downloaded to your smartphone and will prove invaluable for booking passages, as well as for countless other tips and suggestions.

The Pont du Cange is the gateway to the historic Saint-Leu quarter of Amiens, where boats with limited air draught may moor on the quai Bélu. © S. BOULNOIS

Canal de la Somme and Saint-Valery

The river Somme was for centuries considered a strategic route for navigation inland to Picardy and Paris, potentially faster and more reliable than the Seine, particularly for trade with England. The first comprehensive plan for canalisation was produced in 1729. The meandering river was not easily tamed, however, and the Intendant of Picardy reporting in 1763 found the navigation to be in a 'pitiful state'. Complete canalisation was authorised under Louis XVI in 1785, but works were interrupted by the Revolution. The project revived by Napoleon in 1810 included a canal maritime between Saint-Valery-sur-Somme and Abbeville. The waterway was opened to navigation above Abbeville in 1827, while the ship canal was completed in 1835. Locks were 34m by 6.25m wide, later enlarged to Freycinet dimensions. The two locks on the section incorporated in the Canal du Nord were rebuilt in 1964 to the dimensions adopted for that project, 90m by 6m. The canal was among the first to be conceded to a local authority, in this case the Somme département, in 1992, but the concession was limited to the section west of Péronne. The Somme will be crossed by a 1300m long aqueduct, the landmark structure of the Seine-Nord Europe Canal.

Locks
There are 25 locks, including the sea lock at Saint-Valery. They rise to the Saint-Simon pound of the Canal de Saint-Quentin, 65m above sea level. Lock dimensions vary, but the smallest are 38.50m by 6.35m.

Draught
The maximum authorised draught is 1.80m in the *canal maritime* (which used to allow small coasters to trade up to Abbeville), then 1.50m from Abbeville to Frise supérieure, 1.40m to Sormont, then 2.40m on the section common to the Canal du Nord.

Headroom
There are four swing bridges and one lift bridge on the *canal maritime*. These are equipped with gauges displaying the headroom available with the bridges in the closed position. The normal headroom under the numerous fixed bridges on the rest of the route is 3.70m, but the bridge upstream of lock 17 in Amiens may present a reduced headroom of 3.43m.

Towpath
There is a towpath throughout. developed as a cycle path (the Véloroute Vallée de Somme).

Authority
VNF Bassin de la Seine, UTI Seine-Nord
– 19, route de Paris, BP 1053, 80201 Péronne cedex 03 22 84 74 40 (PK 0-39, but transfer of PK 0-16 planned)
Conseil Départemental de la Somme
– Direction du Fleuve et des Ports, 1 rue Baillon, 80000 Amiens   06 74 83 60 69 (PK 39-156)

Route description

Somme estuary to Canal de Saint-Quentin
PK 156.4 Downstream tidal gates, railway swing bridge d/s, end of canal maritime, **Saint-Valery- sur-Somme** harbour in estuary below lock, 03 22 60 24 84, *portsaintvalery.com*, 25 berths (non-drying) up to 2.30m draught, night €26, water and electricity included, showers, wifi, crane 10t, slipway, repairs, email *contact@portsaintvalery.com*

Saint-Valery grew as a seaport during the 10th and 11th centuries and William the Conqueror assembled his fleet here before sailing to England in 1066. During many wars the village passed between French, English and Burgundian ownership. The English destroyed the abbey and cloister to strengthen the nearby Saint-Valery castle. In 1431, Joan of Arc was held prisoner by the English in the local prison where she was then conveyed to Rouen and burnt at the stake. The cell in which she stayed is near part of the old village walls. Saint-Valery has a station of the narrow gauge 'Chemin de Fer de la Baie de Somme', which runs around the entire length of the bay, connecting with Le Crotoy, Noyelles-sur-Mer and Brighton Plage.

Key dimensions (m)	
Length	38.50
Beam	5.45
Draught	1.80
Air draught	3.40

A delightful bucolic mooring on the Somme at Bray © JULIE DEAN

I – Northern France

PK **156.1** Lock 25 (Saint-Valery), 06 15 33 34 43, upstream sluice gates, boat repair yard, yacht and boat moorings u/s r/b

Canal pontoon moorings inside the sea-lock.

PK **155.6** Lift bridge (Pinchefalise), headroom 4.20m, D940
PK **153.0** Swing bridge (**Boismont**), village 1 km l/b, headroom 2.70m, municipal bridge manually operated
PK **148.2** Swing bridge (Petit-Port) headroom 2.43m
PK **145.2** Swing bridge (Laviers), headroom 2.50m
PK **144.0** Motorway bridge (A28)
PK **143.1** Swing bridge (Sur-Somme), headroom 2.93m
PK **142.9** Private quay l/b
PK **142.3** Railway bridge (Boulogne-Paris), end of canal maritime, headroom 6.50m
PK **142.1** Bridge (D928 Abbeville bypass)
PK **142.0** Towpath bridge, end of lock-cut
PK **142.0** Junction with bypassed river Somme navigable a few hundred metres upstream towards the town centre (trip boat mooring)
PK **141.9** Bridge (Hocquet)
PK **141.7** Lock 24 (Abbeville), water
PK **141.0** **Abbeville**, bridge (Gare), *relais nautique* d/s r/b for 10 boats, 03 22 24 27 92, free for 3 days, water, electricity €2 for 4h, pump-out, railway station l/b, town centre r/b
PK **140.7** Bridge (Portelette), entrance to lock-cut, l/b
PK **140.6** Bridge (Boulevard des Prés)
PK **139.5** Disused railway bridge (Béthune)
PK **136.0** Bridge (Épagnette)
PK **134.2** Bridge (Épagne)
PK **133.0** Bridge (Eaucourt-sur-Somme)
PK **131.3** Lock 23 (Pont-Remy)
PK **131.0** Bridge (D901)
PK **130.6** **Pont-Remy** *halte* r/b for 2-3 boats, 06 88 61 33 05, free, water €2, electricity €2/4 hours, slipway
PK **130.3** Towpath bridge
PK **127.5** Bridge (Cocquerel)
PK **124.8** Lock 22 (Long)
PK **124.7** **Long** bridge, municipal *halte* d/s l/b, 4-5 boats, free, water, electricity (€2 per unit), slipway, small town r/b
PK **120.6** Bridge (Étoile)
PK **118.0** Railway bridge (Flixecourt), disused
PK **117.9** Railway bridge (disused) and overhead power lines
PK **117.5** Lock 21 (La Breilloire)
PK **115.0** **Bourdon** bridge, industrial quay u/s l/b, **Hangest** l/b

The lock at Longy (PK 124) © BINNENVAARTINBEELD

PK **108.0** Lock 20 (**Picquigny**), *halte* u/s on quay, 50m, free, water, electricity, bridge, village l/b
PK **106.0** **La Chaussée-Tirancourt** *halte* for visiting Samara archeological site, water, electricity €2 for 4h
PK **102.5** Lock 19 (**Ailly-sur-Somme**), bridge, *halte* for 3 boats, free for 48 hours, water, electricity, shower in lock building,
PK **100.0** Bridge (**Dreuil**), village l/b
PK **98.7** Motorway bridge (A16)
PK **97.7** Lock 18 (Montières), bridge
PK **97.1** Railway bridge
PK **95.8** Bridge (Blanc)
PK **95.0** Bridge (Cagnard), private quay u/s l/b
PK **94.3** Footbridge (Saint-Maurice), quay d/s l/b
PK **94.0** Lock 17 (Amiens), water, bridge
PK **93.8** Bridge (Maulcreux), lowest on the Somme
PK **93.6** Bridges (Saint-Pierre)
PK **93.4** Bridge (Célestins)
PK **93.0** Footbridge
PK **92.7** Footbridge (Samarobriva), Saint-Pierre park r/b
PK **92.6** Junction with Somme through Amiens, attractive quay accessible through very low arch bridge (Pont du Cange)
PK **92.4** **Amiens** bridge (Beauvillé), quay d/s l/b (Port d'Amont), 03 22 71 69 50, 4 berths, free for 48 hours, water, electricity, pump-out, slipway, town l/b

The Port d'Amont quayside *halte* is close to Amiens Cathedral, a world heritage site: the tallest and 'purest' of the large Gothic churches of the 13th century. Boats with a limited air draught can pass through the Pont du Cange to moor along the Quai Belu in the historic Saint-Leu quarter.

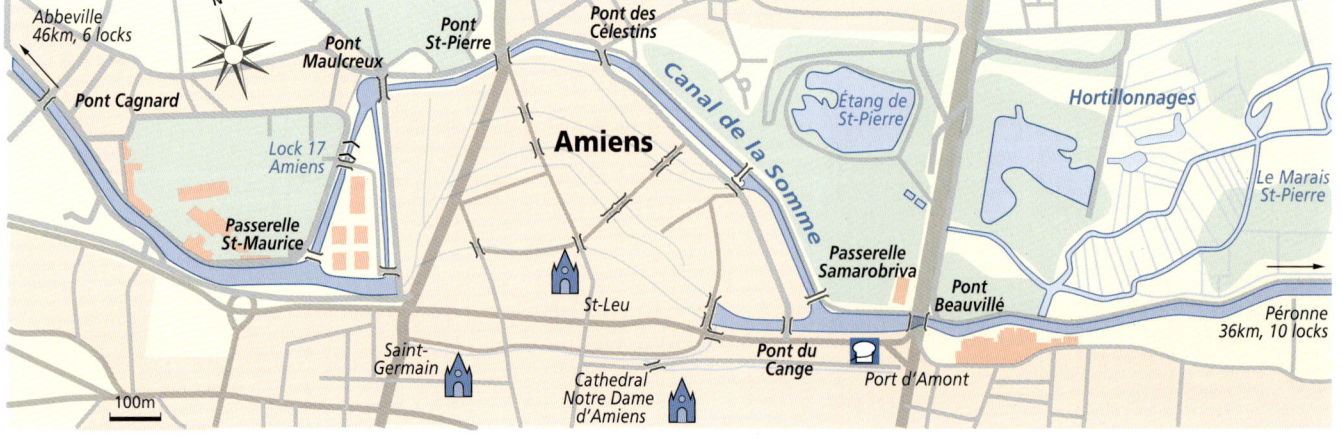

Canal de la Somme and Saint-Valery

PK 90.1	Bridge (Camon)
PK 88.7	**Camon** bridge (Longueau), boatyard u/s r/b, 03 22 46 30 83, repairs, chandlery, private slipway, village r/b
PK 87.1	Main road viaduct (Jules Verne), N25 Amiens bypass
PK 85.6	Railway bridge (Amiens-Lille)
PK 84.3	Lock 16 (**Lamotte-Brebière**) in short lock-cut r/b, halte for 3 boats, free for 72 hours, water, electricity
PK 83.9	Pipeline crossing
PK 80.7	Private footbridge
PK 80.5	Private quay r/b
PK 80.1	Railway bridge (Amiens-Lille)
PK 79.7	Lock 15 (Daours)
PK 79.3	Bridge (Daours/Vecquemont)
PK 77.2	Railway bridge (Amiens-Lille)
PK 74.5	**Corbie** lock 14, water, bridge, *halte* u/s l/b, mooring for 3 boats, 03 22 48 23 35, water €2/4 hours, electricity €2/4 hours, wifi and showers at camp site, town r/b

Corbie is a busy small town steeped in history, well worth visiting.

PK 70.7	Bridge (Vaire-sous-Corbie)
PK 66.8	**Sailly-le-Sec** r/b (track to village, 600m)
PK 65.3	Lock 13 (**Sailly-Laurette**), bridge, village 600m r/b
PK 63.7	Bridge (Cerisy l/b)
PK 62.4	**Cerisy/Chipilly** bridge, quay u/s r/b
PK 58.6	Lock 12 (**Méricourt-sur-Somme**), bridge, village 1300m
PK 57.1	Étinehem arm r/b (no longer used)
PK 54.1	Navigation enters Somme (Bray arm r/b)
PK 52.9	Lock 11 (Froissy), quay d/s r/b
PK 52.8	**Froissy** bridge, quays d/s
PK 52.5	Quays, l/b, tourist railway (Froissy-Dompierre) and museum

Good informal moorings near the lock and bridge and also immediately adjacent to the light railway.

PK 51.0	Lock 10 (Cappy)
PK 50.4	**Cappy** lift bridge, quay u/s r/b, 03 22 76 12 12, 14 berths, night €12, water and electricity included, showers €2.50, crane, slipway, pump-out €4/m3, repairs, restaurant

Formerly a Locaboat hire base, the whole quay is now available to visiting boats. Upstream from here to the Canal du Nord the canal sections are narrow due to overhanging trees, and may be shallow.

Port of Cappy, with the lift bridge in the background SOMME TOURISME

PK 46.9	**Éclusier-Vaux** lift bridge
PK 46.0	Quay l/b
PK 44.7	Lock 9 (Frise inférieure), footbridge
PK 43.6	Lock 8 (**Frise**, supérieure), bridge, quay u/s r/b
PK 41.3	**Feuillères** lift bridge (automatic, with radar detection), quay u/s l/b
PK 40.0	Railway bridge (TGV Nord), basin d/s
PK 39.9	Motorway bridge (A1)
PK 39.1	Lock 7 (Sormont), bridge, quay r/b
PK 37.1	Aqueduct carrying Seine-Nord-Europe Canal across the Somme valley (works to start in 2023)
PK 36.9	Bridge (Bazincourt)
PK 36.7	Junction with Canal du Nord r/b, beginning of common section
PK 33.9	**Péronne** port de plaisance, 03 22 84 19 31, 20 berths, night €9.45, diesel on commercial quay, water, electricity, showers at campsite, slipway, restaurant

The *port de plaisance* is in a spur off the main canal, which still carries a fair amount of commercial traffic. Passing *péniches* (especially the empty ones, which travel faster) can cause wash and movement in the basin.

PK 33.5	Bridge (D1017), quays d/s, quay u/s r/b with all services but limited space, Péronne 1300m r/b
PK 33.1	Railway bridge (disused)
PK 32.9	Lock 6 (Péronne), VHF 10, water
PK 28.4	Bridge (Pont-lès-Brie), D1029
PK 25.7	**Saint-Christ-Briost** bridge, quay and turning basin d/s r/b
PK 23.8	Motorway bridge (A29)
PK 22.7	**Épénancourt** l/b
PK 22.2	Lock 5 (Épénancourt), bridge, VHF 10, water, quay u/s l/b
PK 20.7	**Pargny** bridge, quay u/s l/b
PK 17.9	**Béthencourt-sur-Somme** bridge, quay d/s r/b
PK 16.4	Junction with Canal du Nord l/b, end of common section

The Canal de la Somme east from this junction has been closed since 2003, but the *département* is planning to take over the waterway from VNF and restore it to full navigability.

PK 14.8	**Voyennes** bridge, village 300m
PK 12.5	Lock 4 (Offoy), bridge, quay d/s l/b, **Offoy** 300m
PK 11.2	**Canizy** l/b (windmill)
PK 10.0	Footbridge
PK 8.3	Footbridge
PK 7.9	Quays l/b
PK 7.2	Lock 3 (Ham inférieure), bridge
PK 6.6	Lock 2 (Ham supérieure), bridge
PK 6.1	**Ham** basin l/b, small town

Ham, proud of its history and medieval château, is rightly pressing the Somme *département* to fund the complete restoration of this abandoned section of the waterway.

PK 3.1	**Sommette-Eaucourt**, l/b
PK 1.6	Bridge (D56)
PK 0.1	Lock 1 (Saint-Simon), bridge
PK 0.0	**Saint-Simon**, 'Point Y', triangular junction with the Canal de Saint-Quentin, (*see junction plan p.71*)

CHAPTER II – RIVER SEINE
AND CONNECTING WATERWAYS, NORTH AND EAST

This chapter covers the country's major waterway artery, the river Seine throughout its lower course to Paris, along with the waterways that connect eastwards from the capital to the Champagne region. There is a 'north-south' logic that applies to the other regions in this guide, following the imaginary migration of the North European boatowner from the Channel ports or the land border crossings heading down south. In contrast, geography, culture and the often-derided Jacobine centralism of Paris here dictate a west-to-east logic. The *plaisancier* will not argue with the Parisian: entering the French system from the Seine estuary, the itinerary takes the boat eastwards to Paris, one of Europe's finest waterway destinations; many would argue *the* finest.

First, there is a choice to be made, especially by yachts needing to lower (or 'unstep') their mast. Three options are familiar to the author. The first is Le Havre, continuing on the Canal du Havre à Tancarville. Boats are no longer allowed through this canal, but Le Havre as port of entry is described in the pages on the associated canal, for commercial vessels. The second is Honfleur, described as the possible port of entry to the Lower Seine (Seine *aval*). However, there is little doubt that the third option, Rouen, is the most convenient to prepare for the inland voyage.

At Conflans-Saint-Honorine, barge capital of France, the Seine is joined by the river Oise, the first part of the route that is to link the Seine with the Scheldt and the Rhine basin for high-capacity barges, by means of the Canal Seine-Nord Europe now under construction. Preliminary works are under way, while the heavy digging and building will be from 2024 to 2028.

The river Oise also leads to the river Aisne and four canals that provide important connections for both north-south and east-west itineraries. They will take the navigator beyond the limits of the Île-de-France capital region and into the 'Grand Est' region, which includes Champagne. As connections, in vast rolling landscapes, these have never received the attention they merit. One of these, the Canal latéral à l'Oise, will be replaced over almost half its length by the future high-capacity canal.

This chapter naturally includes the three canals that are managed by the city of Paris. The popular Port de d'Arsenal is just behind the entrance lock to the Canal Saint-Martin. Most boats never venture beyond this excellent facility, which is a pity, for all three of these canals are fascinating and well worth discovering, all the way through to the impossibly remote location of Port-aux-Perches.

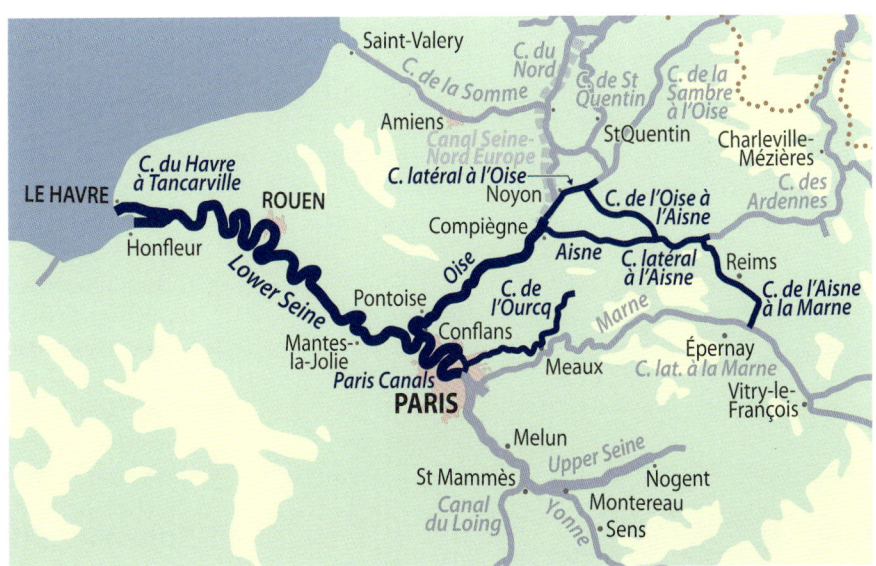

Chalk cliffs overlooking the Seine at Val-Saint-Martin, PK 275, in February 2019.

II – River Seine and routes north and east

16. Lower River Seine (Honfleur to Paris)

THE SEINE RISES IN THE hills of the Côte d'Or and discharges into the English Channel near Le Havre after a course of nearly 800km. It is a major transport artery, navigated by a substantial fleet of high-capacity barges and push-tows, and now a dozen or so river cruise ships. In the tidal estuary up to the seaport of Rouen, inland craft share the 11m-deep channel with ships of up to 120 000 dwt. This entry covers the Lower Seine (Seine *aval*) from Honfleur to Paris, a distance of 356km. For Paris to Marcilly, see under Petite-Seine (or Seine *amont*), part of the Central France network (Chapter III). The Lower Seine navigation officially begins at a point between Honfleur and the confluence of the Risle, 10km upstream, but for convenience the route description starts in Honfleur.

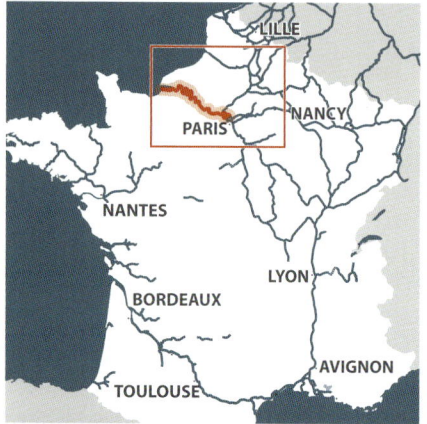

> The Seine was notoriously difficult to navigate under free flow conditions because of the limited depths during low flows. There were several proposals to dredge a reliable channel in the late 18th century, but no significant progress was made until Poirée's successful experiment building a movable weir suggested use of this technique to canalise the river. The five locks and weirs on the Lower Seine were thus built from the 1840s, guaranteeing a draught of 1.60m. A first improvement was started in 1860, raising the weirs to allow a draught of 2m, also adding three new locks and weirs. The third phase, raising the draught to 3.20m, was started in 1880. The fourth major phase of works was in 1957-64, new lock chambers being given a sill depth of 5m up to Paris.

Honfleur as entry port

The entrance lock from the Seine **1** is marked by a distinctive control tower. The lock is closed during low water, which is important to note for both entry and exit. The deepest channel lies towards (but not hard by) the tower itself. Entering from the river at LW, the lock can appear intimidatingly high and the water ingress quite fast. Boats should be prepared to manoeuvre and tie up promptly. To take advantage of the Seine's flood tide up the river to Rouen, it is necessary to pass out of the lock back into the river as early as possible after LW, taking care not to

The Vieux Bassin in Honfleur. © GEOTHEQUE.ORG

ground on the shallows. The *Vieux Bassin* **2** is accessed through the inner lock, open at set times, and has 30 visitor moorings. There is a boatyard **3** in the *Bassin Carnot*. To get there one has to pass from the *avant-port* through the opening bridges into the *Bassin de l'Est* and then into the *Bassin Carnot*. These bridges also open according to timetable (consult the harbour office in the tower house by the Vieux Bassin).

Rouen as entry port

Rouen is the most convenient entry port for all logistical purposes, especially mast stepping/unstepping. Navigation is tidal for 105km up to the inland waterway limit at Rouen (PK 242). Maritime navigation in the Seine estuary follows the corresponding rules of navigation, as well as lights and

Lower Seine

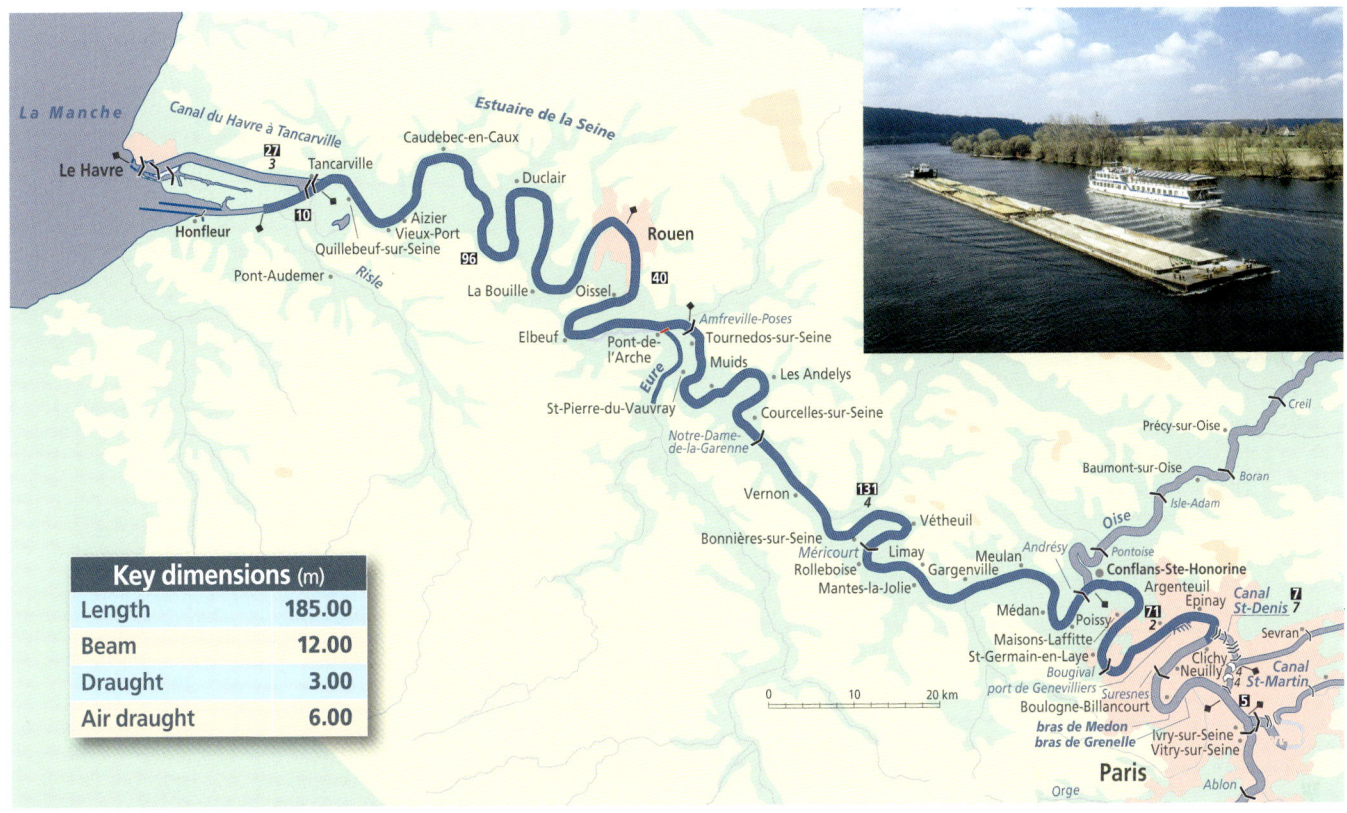

Key dimensions (m)	
Length	185.00
Beam	12.00
Draught	3.00
Air draught	6.00

channel markings. The river is still tidal up to the first lock at Amfreville-Poses (PK 202), and allowance must be made for the rise and fall of the tide when mooring to avoid the risk of grounding. If caught by the turning tide, there are a number of possibilities for mooring before reaching Rouen: anchor in the drying, shallow river Risle at PK 346; or moor alongside at Caudebec PK 310, Duclair PK 278 or la Bouille PK 260. All these moorings may be subject to severe wash from passing shipping. The Vigicrue website http://vigicrues.gouv.fr provides excellent data for the tides at Tancarville and Rouen. The pattern of times and heights can be seen for these two critical places (plus others on the river), essential for passage planning in conjunction with a tide table for Le Havre. Use of the Éditions du Breil guide to the Lower Seine is also recommended.

Navigation

The river carries heavy traffic, and navigation is complicated by the numerous bridges and several islands, which generally have to be passed on one side by boats heading downstream and on the other by those heading upstream. The route description clearly indicates the route to be followed in each case, as well as those arms that are forbidden to navigation.

The lower Seine connects with the Canal du Havre à Tancarville, which offers sheltered access for commercial shipping to the port of Le Havre from the northern shore of the estuary at PK 338. Closer to Paris, it connects with the river Oise at the waterway capital of Conflans-Sainte-Honorine (PK 71), and with the Canal Saint-Denis (one of the Paris canals) on the right bank at PK 29.

Among the many recommendations and regulations, it is worth noting that night-time navigation on the tidal river is forbidden to pleasure craft. The contrast on reaching the non-tidal River Seine above the first lock at Poses is striking. One immediately enters a 'middle earth' of leafy side channels and islands. There are multiple options of channels to choose and explore (but be alert to depths). There are a number of places that can be busy with dinghies, rowing, sculling and canoeing. Large barges and small ships continue to use the main channels.

Locks

There are six groups of locks on the lower Seine. At Amfreville-Poses there are two chambers (220m by 17m and 185m by 12m), similarly at Notre-Dame-de-la-Garenne (185m by 24m and 185m by 12m). At Méricourt there are three chambers (185m by 12m, 160m by 17m and 141m by 12m). Two chambers also at Andrésy (185m by 24m and 160m by 12m) and at Suresnes (187m by 18m and 176m by 17m, but 12m at the gates). At Bougival the two chambers measure 220m by 17m (12m at the gates) and 112m by 12m. Navigation may bypass Bougival locks by using the Rivière Neuve arm, including a lock overcoming the same difference in level at Chatou (185m by 18m). All locks are controlled by lights; enter behind the barges.

Draught

The channel is dredged to allow river-sea vessels drawing 4.00m to reach the port of Gennevilliers. Above here, and through Paris, the maximum authorised draught is 3.00m.

Headroom

Below Gennevilliers, all bridges offer a minimum headroom of 7.00m above the highest navigable water level. Above Gennevilliers, the minimum headroom is about 6.00m above normal water level, reduced to 3.70m above the highest navigable water level.

II – River Seine and routes north and east

Authority

- Grand port maritime de Rouen, 34 boulevard de Boisguilbert, 76000 Rouen,
  02 35 52 54 56 (PK 348-242)
- VNF Bassin de la Seine – UTI Boucles de la Seine
- 66 av. Jacques Chastellain, Île Lacroix, 76000 Rouen, 02 32 08 31 70 (PK 242-225)
- Subdivision d'Amfreville-sous-les-Monts: BP 8428, Pitres, 27108 Val de Reuil Cedex
  02 32 48 71 40 poses-amfreville.abs.sn-seine@developpement-durable.gouv.fr
  (PK 225-110)
- 65 quai de l'Écluse, BP 74, 95313 Cergy-Pontoise
  01 34 30 40 80 pontoise.abs.sn-seine@developpement-durable.gouv.fr (PK 110-51)
- 5bis, rue Nieuport, BP 84, 92153 Suresnes cedex
  01 46 25 04 40 (PK 51-10)
- quai de la Tournelle, 75005 Paris 01 44 41 16 80 (PK 10-0)

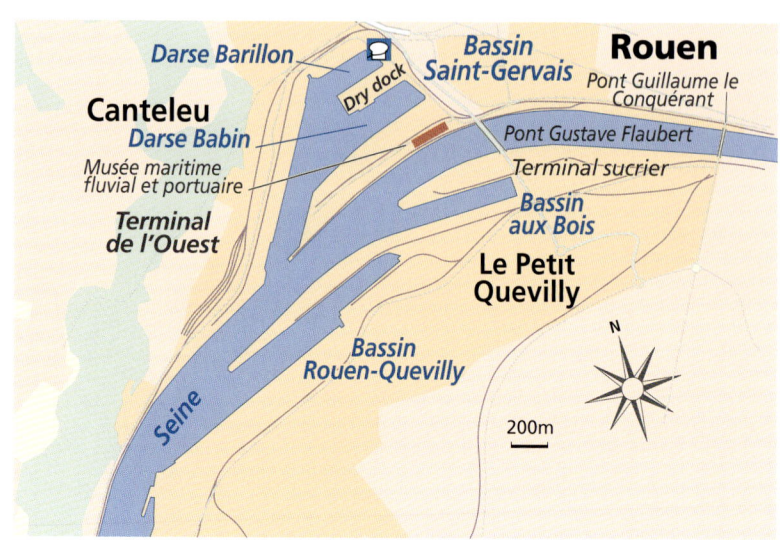

Route description

Established by the Vikings, Honfleur is steeped in maritime and cultural history. The port is linked with the foundation of Quebec and was remodelled – the Vieux Bassin – in 1681. In more recent times the town was associated with the painters Boudin, Courbet and Monet; and the composer Erik Satie. The Vieux Bassin must be one of the most picturesque harbours in Europe, but it is often crowded with both boats and tourists.

PK 355.7 Entrance to **Honfleur** harbour on south shore of estuary (described under 'Honfleur as entry port' in the introduction), night €31.50, water and electricity included, showers, wifi

PK 352.7 Pont de Normandie suspension bridge
PK 347.7 Official limit of river Seine
PK 345.9 Confluence of Risle, l/b

The Risle is a possible anchorage to wait for the tide. Just inside, a small stream enters from the right and beyond this a small stony reef appears near low water and runs half way across to about the middle of the river. This constrains the channel to opposite bank. It may not look dangerous, but it takes about 0.50m off the depth of the main channel.

PK 338.6 *Entrance to Canal du Havre à Tancarville* r/b (new lock)
PK 338.2 Tancarville suspension bridge
PK 338.2 *Entrance to Canal du Havre à Tancarville* r/b (old lock)
PK 331.8 **Quillebeuf-sur-Seine** ferry, town l/b opposite oil refinery
PK 324.5 Vieux-Port l/b
PK 323.3 Aizier l/b
PK 313.5 Villequier r/b
PK 309.6 **Caudebec-en-Caux** r/b, moorings (pontoons and buoys) r/b, 02 32 70 46 32, water, electricity, landing stage for trip boats

Historic village, known to the Vikings and historically famous as the place to watch the ferocious tidal bore or *mascaret*, now virtually extinct. There are two mooring pontoons; one may be in use by a river cruise ship, the inner side of the upstream pontoon is private. No services, free. There are also some mooring buoys a short distance downstream.

PK 308.2 Brotonne suspension bridge
PK 303.1 **La Mailleraye-sur-Seine** l/b
PK 301.2 Shipyard r/b (Le Trait)
PK 298.6 Ferry (Yainville), power station/factory d/s r/b
PK 295.2 Ferry (Jumièges)
PK 286.0 Ferry (le Mesnil-sous-Jumièges)
PK 278.0 **Duclair** ferry, visitor mooring r/b, 02 35 05 95 62, water, electricity, night €20, village r/b

The mooring barge is located by the ferry crossing. Boats should not attempt to moor on the inside, which is very shallow at LW.

PK 276.4 Yacht club r/b (l'Ânerie)
PK 260.1 D/s limit of port of Rouen
PK 259.7 **La Bouille** ferry, village l/b

Small floating pontoon between two piles. A possible brief stopping place, or under duress. This is the last place to moor bankside until Rouen (15km), as from here onwards it is prohibited. The approach to Rouen (one of France's most important ports) becomes increasingly industrial.

PK 252.9 Basin l/b (Petit Bassin)
PK 251.3 Basin l/b (dry docks, Lozai boatyard, 02 35 52 55 30)
PK 248.1 Ferry (Dieppedalle)
PK 246.7 Entrance to oil terminal (Bassin de Rouen-Quevilly) l/b
PK 245.5 **Rouen** entrance to Bassin Saint-Gervais r/b, managed by Rouen Port Authority, access to *port de plaisance*, 100 berths on pontoons, 10 visitor berths, night €18, water, electricity, shower, pump-out, rouen.portdeplaisance.fr

The city of Jeanne d'Arc and the cathedral of Monet is worth an extended stay. With the splendid new lift bridge in view (at 1400m), turn left into the sheltered Bassin Saint-Gervais, where the excellent marina is located, an easy and pleasant walk along the quayside into the centre. This part of Rouen, formerly commercial and industrial, is the subject of one of Europe's sustainable 'Future Cities' projects. There is a mast stepping/re-masting facility here, between the two *darses*. Yachtspeople need to be ready to prepare their mast stays, shrouds and equipment (including electronics connections) themselves. The facility is operated by the Lamanage Rouen-Dieppe Cooperative activiteplaisance@lamanage-rouen.fr. Cost €119 for the hour it normally takes, €49 per hour beyond that. Lift-out (subject to some wash from passing river traffic) and crane/travel hoist also available. For supporting timbers, there is a big BricoDepot about half way towards

Lower Seine

Lamanage Rouen-Dieppe's hoist in Rouen's Bassin Saint-Gervais. A mast-stepping facility is also available. © F-W

Rouen centre. For mast transport – **boat-loads.com** – or carry on board. The old *port de plaisance* is slightly closer to the centre at PK 242 but, being pontoons in the river itself, is subject to strong passing currents and everything (logs and branches) that floats down. It is next to the Villetard boatyard/chandlery. The local VNF office is also nearby.

PK **244.9** Entrance to Bassin aux Bois l/b
PK **244.3** Main road lift bridge (Pont Gustave Flaubert)

This impressive bridge is sadly a white elephant. It is only opened once every five years for the armada of historic ships.

The magnificent lift bridge (Gustave Flaubert) at PK 244 © F-W

PK **243.0** Bridge (Pont Guillaume le Conquérant)
End of maritime navigation
PK **242.4** **Rouen** bridge (Pont Jeanne d'Arc), tramway line M (also called 'Metro'), city centre r/b
PK **242.2** Bridge (Pont Boïeldieu), quays both banks
PK **242.0** D/s end of Île Lacroix, r/b arm (Pré au Loup) may only be entered on falling tide (against the current)
PK **241.9** Bridge (Pont Corneille)
PK **241.7** *Halte de plaisance*, alternative mooring for Rouen l/b (in Pré au Loup arm), 20 berths, night €24, water, electricity, showers, crane, repairs
PK **241.2** Bridge (Pont Mathilde)
PK **240.5** Railway viaduct (Eauplet)
PK **240.4** U/s end of Île Lacroix, r/b arm (Pré au Loup) may only be entered on rising tide (against the current)

PK **238.6** Fuelling station (barge) r/b

The fuel barge just upstream of Rouen is used by commercial traffic, and delays may be expected, but pleasure craft are also served.

PK **237.6** Amfreville/Saint-Étienne ferry
PK **235.9** D/s end of Île aux Bœufs (first island after Rouen), keep l/b side of all islands to PK 225
PK **235.7** Private quay l/b (iron foundry)
PK **233.4** Private quay l/b (paper mill)
PK **229.7** Road and railway bridges (Oissel)
PK **229.4** **Oissel** pontoon mooring l/b

Excellent mooring for attractive village

PK **228.0** Motorway bridge (A13)
PK **226.9** Submerged groyne between islands r/b
PK **225.2** U/s limit of Île Légarée, main channel l/b
PK **222.8** Commercial quay (Elbeuf) r/b
PK **221.4** Railway viaduct (Orival)
PK **219.4** Suspension bridge (Guynemer)
PK **218.9** **Elbeuf** bridge (Jean Jaurès), mooring d/s l/b
PK **218.2** Entrance to r/b arm leading to former locks (**Saint-Aubin-les-Elbeuf**), *port de plaisance* r/b, 02 35 78 42 78, 70 berths, 4 visitor moorings, night €14, fuel at service station, water, electricity (metered), showers €2, wifi, slipway, town l/b

Small quiet *port de plaisance* up a side channel (former lock). Access two hours each side of local HW.

Rouen moorings new (in the bassin Saint-Gervais) and old, in the 'Pré au Loup' river arm close to the city centre, at PK 242 © F-W

II – River Seine and routes north and east

PK **216.8** Confluence of Eure (unnavigable) l/b
PK **215.2** Entrance to Freneuse arm (unnavigable) r/b
PK **211.1** Motorway bridge (A13)
PK **207.9** Second confluence of Eure (unnavigable) l/b
PK **207.7** Pont-de-l'Arche bridge
PK **204.7** Railway bridge (Manoir)
PK **202.0** Locks (Amfreville), two chambers, footbridge, VHF 18, 02 32 40 04 41, weir l/b, **Poses** *halte* on quay u/s for 2 boats, free, water €2 for 10 min, electricity €2 per hour, shower

Two side by side chambers, call up on VHF 18 and watch the traffic lights. Potentially a deep lock at low tide, use the (widely-spaced) edge bollards and those set vertically and horizontally into the sheet piling sides.

Above the lock, this delightful quay offers a very pleasant mooring at Poses/Le Mesnil, but limited village facilities. © F-W

PK **200.8** U/s end of Grand Île, r/b arm leads to locks
PK **200.7** D/s end of Île d'Amfreville, l/b arm for u/s boats
PK **200.1** U/s end of Île d'Amfreville, r/b arm for d/s boats
PK **199.7** Minor channel l/b between Île du Noyer and Île du Trait
PK **198.9** U/s end of Île du Noyer, main channel r/b
PK **198.6** D/s end of Île de Tournedos, minor channel r/b
PK **198.3** Entrance to Poses lake l/b (recreational and water sports area), quay for sand barges d/s
PK **197.4** **Tournedos-sur-Seine** l/b
PK **196.7** D/s end of Île de Pampou, minor channel l/b
PK **196.3** U/s end of Île de Pampou
PK **195.4** D/s end of Île de Port Pinché, l/b arm for u/s boats
PK **194.3** R/b arm divides (Île de Connelle), minor channel r/b
PK **193.9** U/s end of Île de Port Pinché, r/b arm for d/s boats
PK **193.7** Porte-Joie l/b
PK **193.2** D/s end of Île du Moulin, main channel l/b
PK **192.2** Minor arm r/b between Île du Martinet and Île du Moulin
PK **191.8** Minor arm r/b between Île Brunel and Île du Martinet
PK **191.3** Minor arm r/b between Île du Bac and Île Brunel
PK **190.9** **Saint-Pierre-du-Vauvray** bridge, quay d/s l/b, for 6 boats, village l/b
PK **189.6** U/s end of Île du Héron, followed by Île du Bac, main channel l/b
PK **189.0** Piers of former railway bridge
PK **187.8** D/s end of Île de Lormais, main channel r/b
PK **186.1** Minor arm l/b between Île de la Cage and Île de Lormais
PK **184.1** U/s end of Île des Grands Bacs/Île de la Cage, main channel r/b

PK **184.0** **Venables** *port de plaisance* (Les Grèves du Lac) in former gravel pit l/b, 06 88 24 11 54, 150 berths, possible visitor moorings, night €18, water and electricity included, showers, wifi at *capitainerie*, crane, slipway, repairs **portdevenables.com**

Marina in a large flooded quarry.

PK **183.4** D/s end of Île du Port, ferry
PK **182.7** U/s end of Île du Port, channel l/b, **Muids** r/b

Small pontoon beside the very pleasant village with a small shop and the charming little Café de la Poste next door. Recommended.

PK **178.3** Small island (Île de la Motte) r/b, followed by Île de la Roque, minor channel r/b unnavigable
PK **175.7** Yacht harbour (Val Saint-Martin) r/b, 10 visitor berths, 02 32 21 00 67, **nautikhome.fr**, night €20, water, electricity, shower, crane 2t, slipway

The recommended small harbour at Val-Saint-Martin, ideal for visiting Les Andelys and Château Gaillard. GSV

PK **174.6** D/s end, Île du Château, l/b arm for u/s boats
PK **174.0** U/s end, Île du Château, l/b arm for d/s boats
PK **173.7** **Les Andelys** *halte* r/b, Château Gaillard and small town r/b, small boat harbour 100m upstream silted up and closed

A memorable location, with the beautiful ruined castle set on an overlooking crag of rock. It was built by Richard the Lionheart, as Duke of Normandy, to defend Normandy against the French.

PK **173.4** Bridge (Port Morin)
PK **170.9** D/s end of Île de la Tour, **Tosny** 500m up minor arm l/b
PK **168.3** U/s end of Île Bouret, minor arm l/b unnavigable
PK **167.4** D/s end of Île du Roule (extended by submerged dyke)
PK **165.0** U/s end of Île du Roule, main channel l/b
PK **164.0** **Courcelles-sur-Seine** bridge, industrial quay d/s l/b
PK **161.1** Locks (Notre-Dame-de-la-Garenne), four chambers, l/b, VHF 22
PK **160.1** U/s end of Île Falaise, channel l/b leads to locks, r/b channel leads to weir (may be passable during floods)

Lower Seine

This 'quay' at Tosny is in ruins, but overnight mooring may be attempted on a short and possibly private concrete jetty. © F-W

- PK **157.2** U/s end of Île aux Bœufs, Goulet arm l/b unnavigable
- PK **155.6** Minor arm r/b between Île Souquet and Île Emien
- PK **154.6** Minor arm r/b between Île Souveraine and Île Souquet
- PK **153.2** U/s end of Île Souveraine, main channel l/b
- PK **151.6** Industrial quays l/b
- PK **150.1** **Vernon** bridge (Clemenceau), *halte fluviale* (Les Tourelles) d/s r/b behind small islands, pontoon 60m for up to 8 boats, night €12, 06 52 74 08 09, fuel, water, electricity, showers, slipway, restaurant   info@yc-vernon.fr

Vernonnet is a popular and attractive place to moor, but there are shallows, so attention must be given to the small buoys and marks. Deeper draught craft may not get in. 3km distant, a pleasant bike ride, are Monet's house and the truly beautiful flower and water gardens at Giverny. The small town of Vernon is just across the bridge

Château des Tourelles and the old mill at Vernon, PK 150. © F-W

Monet's garden at Giverny © F-W

- PK **144.8** Disused lock chamber (Port-Villez) l/b, possible mooring but right beside the railway line
- PK **143.6** D/s end of Île de Merville, minor channel l/b forbidden to navigation
- PK **141.0** D/s end of Grande Île, u/s end of Île de la Flotte, minor channel l/b forbidden to navigation
- PK **139.8** **Bonnières-sur-Seine** bridge, industrial quays u/s l/b, 01 30 98 98 50, water, electricity, pump-out
- PK **138.8** U/s end of Île de Haute (followed by Grande Île), main channel l/b, Gloton arm r/b for access to **Bennecourt** *port de plaisance* (Port Saint-Nicolas), 06 09 80 69 73, 20 berths, 4 visitor moorings, night €20, electricity
- PK **132.0** D/s end of Île de Haute Isle, r/b arm navigable by small boats for access to Haute Isle
- PK **128.1** **Vétheuil** slipway r/b, u/s end of series of islands, small channels r/b unnavigable
- PK **128.0** D/s end, Île Saint-Martin, l/b arm for u/s boats
- PK **127.6** Private ferry in r/b arm
- PK **124.9** U/s end of Île Saint-Martin, r/b arm for d/s boats
- PK **120.7** Triple lock (Méricourt) l/b, VHF 18, weir
- PK **120.1** U/s end of Île de la Sablière, navigation l/b, port de plaisance (Port Ilon) in basin r/b, 06 50 64 22 95, 200 berths, 10 visitor moorings, night €13.50, fuel, water, electricity, wifi at *capitainerie*, pump-out, crane 12t, slipway, repairs   contact@port-ilon.com
  Guernes 2km, **Saint-Martin-la-Garenne** 5km

Port Ilon is a good marina set in an extensive, quiet and leafy flooded quarry. Anchoring is also possible. It includes lift-out and hardstanding facilities. Small chandlery, friendly and helpful. A possible over-wintering location. The nearest village, with shop and *boulangerie*, is Guernes, 2km.

Fuel and geraniums at Port Ilon, PK 120. © F-W

- PK **119.0** **Rolleboise** quay l/b
- PK **117.0** Châteaux de Sully l/b (Rosny-sur-Seine)
- PK **111.9** D/s end of Île l'Aumône, Limay arm r/b for access only
- PK **109.9** Access to Limay arm through short arm between Île aux Dames and Île aux Bœufs (headroom limited to 2.50m)

II – River Seine and routes north and east

PK **109.5** **Limay** port de plaisance on r/b of side-channel, 06 09 66 76 53, 30 berths, 4 visitor moorings, night €15, water, electricity, showers, wifi, slipway, repairs, town r/b

Accessed by the easily navigable, pretty side-channel, Limay has a ruined ancient bridge and a small village pontoon. The bridge features at the end of the François Truffaut film 'Jules et Jim', where Jim and Catherine drive off the end into the river. Just downstream from the bridge and pontoon, a small *halte* and boatyard 'La Marina'. Across the Île de Limay bridge lies the town of Mantes 'La Jolie' (the pretty), painted by Corot. This is where William the Conquerer (Guillaume le Bâtard) suffered a fatal accident falling from his horse.

PK **109.4** **Mantes-la-Jolie** bridge, town l/b
PK **108.5** Bridge (D983, Mantes bypass)
PK **108.2** Railway bridge (Mantes)
PK **107.1** U/s end of Île de Limay, main channel l/b
PK **106.8** Industrial port basin (Limay) r/b
PK **104.5** Porcheville thermal power station, quay r/b
PK **103.4** Île de Porcheville r/b and Île de l'État l/b, main channel between islands marked by stakes
PK **102.4** D/s end of Île de Rangiport, Blanc Soleil arm l/b for u/s boats
PK **101.3** **Gargenville** bridge
PK **100.8** U/s end of Île de Rangiport, Fermettes arm r/b for d/s xcboats
PK **99.7** Industrial quay r/b (cement works)
PK **98.6** D/s end of Île de Juziers, r/b arm small boats only
PK **97.5** Flins quay, car loading and unloading quays l/b (Renault)
PK **95.2** D/s entrance to former lock-cut l/b, keep to r/b side
PK **94.5** Entrance to former lock-cut l/b, keep to r/b side
PK **93.4** **Les Mureaux** bridge, industrial quay u/s l/b
PK **92.4** U/s end of Île du Fort, main channel in Mureaux arm l/b, Meulan arm r/b for access to **Meulan** municipal *halte* d/s of bridge r/b, 01 30 90 41 41, 2 visitor moorings, free (maximum 48 hours), water, electricity, slipway, restaurant

Another pretty side-channel leads to the town of Meulan, with excellent shops, markets and local produce. From upstream it is advisable to avoid the Meulan arm and its first bridge (the central arch seems forbiddingly small), and to use the Saint-Come arm which cuts in from just above Les Mureaux bridge.

Mooring at the charming old bridge over the Meulan arm. © F-W

PK **91.6** Industrial quay (EADS, Ariane V factory) l/b
PK **90.5** D/s end of Île de Vaux
PK **89.4** **Verneuil-sur-Seine** port de plaisance (Val de Seine) l/b, 01 39 28 16 20, 33 berths, 12 visitor moorings, night €25, water, electricity €4.80 per day, showers

Port de plaisance in a basin off the Seine.

PK **88.1** U/s end of Île de Vaux, Vaux arm r/b for small boats only
PK **87.2** **Vaux-sur-Seine** port de plaisance r/b (West Marina), pontoon for 10 boats, 06 10 72 09 57, one night free, water, electricity, showers, crane 15t, slipway, haul-out trailer 47t, repairs
PK **85.8** Yacht club moorings l/b
PK **85.4** **Triel-sur-Seine** boatyard l/b (Chantier Nautique Mallard, 01 39 65 60 73), 30m pontoon, mooring by request, water, electricity, slipway, repairs
PK **85.1** Bridge (Triel-sur-Seine)
PK **84.4** D/s end of Île d'Hernière, Médan arm l/b for u/s boats
PK **84.2** Industrial quay l/b
PK **84.0** Bridge (D1)
PK **83.2** Small arm (Couleuvre) between Île de Médan and Île d'Hernière, impracticable
PK **82.5** **Médan** l/b (on Médan arm)
PK **82.0** Private ferry in Médan arm, l/b
PK **81.7** U/s end of Île de Médan, Mottes arm r/b for downstream boats (except the biggest barges and push-tows)
PK **81.1** **Carrières-sous-Poissy** port de plaisance (Port-Saint-Louis) in former gravel pit r/b, 300 berths, 20 visitor moorings, night €13, water and electricity included, fuel, showers, crane 10t, slipway, repairs, restaurant **nouvellemarinaportsaintlouis.fr**

Large *port de plaisance* off the main river, also workshops. Fuel is available at a reasonable price.

PK **79.0** Boat moorings, quay 200m, slipways
PK **78.9** D/s end of Îlot Blanc
PK **78.1** U/s ends of Île du Grand Motteaux and Îlot Blanc, navigation in central arm, l/b arm navigable for access to Jet Sept Performances, Villennes, PK 80, 01 39 75 84 90, 17 berths, no overnight mooring, water, shower, slipway, repairs
PK **77.8** **Poissy** bridge

Small town with the remains of a 37-arch medieval bridge, a Peugeot factory and a visitor pontoon by the modern bridge (tucked behind the dolphin mooring for passenger boats).

PK **77.2** D/s end of Île de Carrières, pipeline crossing
PK **77.1** Former car loading quay r/b (Peugeot-Citroën factory)
PK **76.4** U/s end of Île de Carrières, Saint-Louis arm l/b, main channel r/b
PK **76.3** D/s end of Île de la Dérivation, lock (Carrières) in cut, r/b (closed)
PK **75.0** Weir (Denouval) r/b in passage between Île d'en Bas and Île de la Dérivation

Lower Seine

PK **74.0** Commercial boatyards l/b, water, electricity

This large commercial boatyard on the left bank in Achères has slipways and dry docks for the biggest barges.

PK **72.7** Double lock (Andrésy) l/b, VHF 22, weir

PK **71.8** U/s end of Île de Nancy, navigation in Plafosse arm l/b, access to **Andrésy** municipal *relais nautique* Saint-Exupéry in r/b arm, pontoons for 25 boats, night €25 (weekend €35), water, electricity, showers, wifi (at tourist info point), pump-out, slipway

PK **71.3** Confluence of Oise, r/b, numerous barges moored

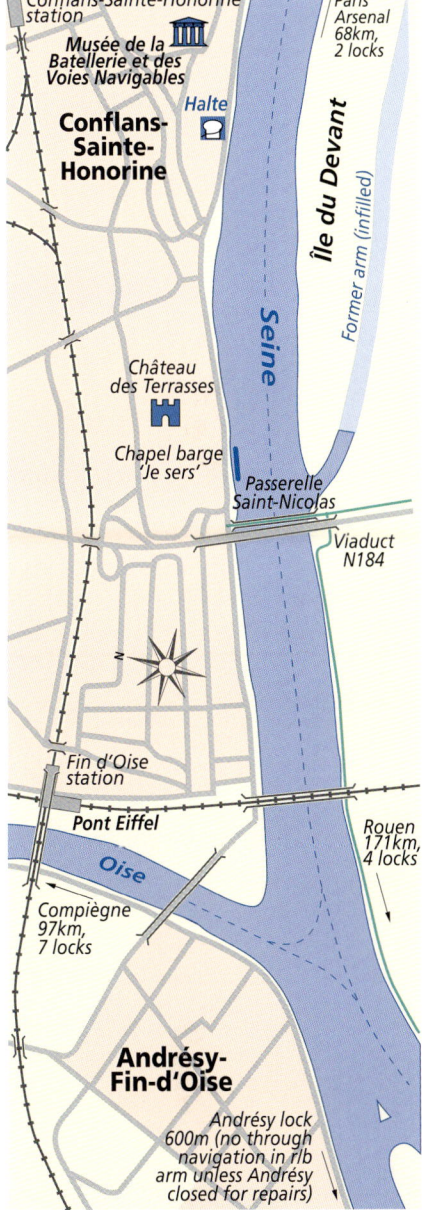

From the confluence, head north via the Oise to the Canal du Nord and to the English Channel ports: Saint-Valery-sur-Somme, Calais and Dunkerque.

PK **71.1** Railway bridge (Conflans)

PK **70.4** Viaduct (N184) and Passerelle Saint-Nicolas, barge moorings r/b

PK **70.3** D/s end of Île du Devant island, 'Je Sers' floating chapel

PK **69.6** **Conflans-Sainte-Honorine** municipal *halte de plaisance* r/b, managed by tourist office, pontoons for 10 boats up to 12m long, free (maximum 72 hours), water €1 per 250 litres, electricity €1 per 2 kWh

The barge capital of France offers this welcome little *halte de plaisance*, tucked in among the countless barges along the attractively landscaped quayside. A visit to the waterways museum, a short walk up the hill, is a rewarding experience, in the splendid Château du Prieuré

PK **68.9** U/s end of Île du Devant (small channel l/b infilled), Boat Paradise boat harbour, 100 berths, 5 visitor moorings, night €25, water, electricity charged, showers, slipway, repairs, restaurant 200m **boat.paradise@orange.fr**

The entrance is narrow and the depth is limited to 80cm, but for boats up to 10m length this boatyard and its services may be worth investigating.

PK **67.1** D/s end of island

PK **65.4** U/s end of Île d'Herblay, Garenne arm l/b for boats only

PK **64.8** **Herblay** r/b, ferry

PK **62.4** **La Frette-sur-Seine** boat moorings (*halte de plaisance*) r/b water, village and Auberge Au Fil de l'Eau, r/b

Village pontoon at La Frette, in attractive surroundings. The auberge 'Au Fil de l'Eau' is the half-timbered house behind the halte © F-W

PK **60.1** Industrial quay r/b (cement works)

PK **58.6** **Maisons-Laffitte** bridge, town l/b, **Sartrouville** r/b, slipway d/s

PK **58.3** D/s end of Île de la Commune, municipal boat moorings in entrance to Maisons-Laffitte arm l/b (draught 2.00m)

PK **57.9** Railway bridge (Maisons-Laffitte)

PK **56.1** U/s end of Île de la Borde, navigation r/b (Maisons-Laffite arm l/b, no access)

PK **55.1** Quay r/b

PK **54.5** Motorway bridge (A14)

PK **52.9** Island (Île Corbière), upstream take l/b arm

PK **52.7** Railway bridge (Pecq)

PK **52.4** Island (Île Corbière), downstream take r/b arm

PK **52.1** **Le Pecq** bridge (Georges Pompidou), quay u/s l/b, slipway u/s r/b

Quayside near supermarket (fuel). Railway station (RER into Paris.) close by.

PK **50.8** D/s end of Île de la Loge, Marly arm l/b unnavigable

II – River Seine and routes north and east

Marly arm via Bougival locks

The Marly arm of the Seine including the three side-by-side chambers of Bougival locks marks the entrance to Greater Paris area. This is the main route for navigation, while the alternative route via the Chatou arm is used by commercial navigation. Beside the bridge just upstream of the locks is a municipal *halte* that always seems very busy.

PK **48.7** Triple lock (Bougival) between Île de la Chaussée and Île de la Loge, VHF 22, Rivière-Neuve arm r/b to be used in time of flood

PK **48.2** **Bougival** bridge, municipal *halte* on 18m pontoon u/s r/b, 01 39 69 21 23, free (maximum 48 hours), water (token €2 for 240 litres), electricity (token €2 for 45 minutes), tokens from tourist office *tourisme-bougival.fr*

Between Bougival and Rueil, on the south bank by a white crane, there is a small (private) pontoon that might make a quiet overnight mooring.

PK **45.5** Railway bridge (Rueil)

PK **45.2** **Rueil-Malmaison** bridge, (Chatou) pontoon u/s l/b for 3 boats

An easy day's trip from the centre of Paris, this is a good pontoon (no services) adjoining a modern development. Lots of trees, shrubs and landscaping, walks along the river; with shops and other facilities (petrol station) within a short walk away, across the bridge in Chatou. Napoleon and Josephine lived at Rueil-Malmaison and it was later the subject for many of the Impressionist painters including Renoir, Manet and Monet.

Pontoon mooring at Rueil-Malmaison © F-W

PK **43.2** Entrance to port of Nanterre, l/b
PK **42.0** Motorway bridge (A14)
PK **41.8** Railway bridge (Carrières)
PK **40.9** Railway bridge (Nanterre), industrial quays l/b
PK **40.2** U/s end of Île de Chatou (or Île Fleurie), navigation in Marly arm, l/b, under normal conditions (navigation in Rivière Neuve arm, r/b, during floods only)

Châtou arm (Rivière-Neuve arm)

This is the alternative route for commercial traffic or during floods.

PK **48.1** Bougival bridge

PK **45.7** Railway bridge (Rueil)
PK **45.3** Bridge (Chatou)
PK **44.6** Lock (Chatou), l/b, VHF 18, weir
PK **42.0** Motorway bridge (A14)
PK **41.7** Railway bridge (Carrières)
PK **41.0** Railway bridge (Nanterre)
PK **40.2** U/s end of Île de Chatou (or Île Fleurie), Marly arm l/b

Back in the wide main river, commercial *péniches* transporting aggregates are often to be seen. After a short distance (PK35) there is the Port de Gennevilliers, the main commercial docks complex for Paris. Then one has the choice of taking one side or the other of the Île Saint-Denis; the southern channel is restricted to downstream traffic only, from the northern channel branches the Canal Saint-Denis (7 locks) that passes by the Stade de France and connects to the Canal Saint-Martin (5 locks and 2km tunnel) and hence the Arsenal basin, by-passing the long loop of the Seine in a direct line. At the southern tip of the island (PK25.5) there is a noteworthy hyperbolic paraboloid roofed sports centre.

PK **39.4** **Bezons** bridge (Boulloche), tramway line T2
PK **37.3** Bridge with aqueduct (Pont Neuf)
PK **35.8** **Argenteuil** bridge
PK **35.4** Railway bridge (Argenteuil)
PK **35.1** Entrance to port of Gennevilliers basins 1-4, l/b
PK **33.9** Entrance to port of Gennevilliers basins 5-6, l/b
PK **33.8** Motorway bridge (A15)
PK **32.8** D/s end of Île Saint-Denis
PK **32.2** Railway bridge
PK **31.8** **Épinay** bridge, slipway d/s r/b
PK **29.4** Industrial quay (Épinay-la-Briche) l/b
PK **29.0** **Villeneuve-la-Garenne** *port de plaisance* (Port Sisley) in Gennevilliers arm, 07 84 43 27 82, 22 berths, 4 visitor moorings, night €14, water and electricity charged, showers, restaurant 500m
PK **28.9** Junction with Canal Saint-Denis, r/b
PK **28.3** Bridge (Île Saint-Denis), tram line T1
PK **27.0** Motorway bridge (A86)
PK **26.8** New footbridge (projected)
PK **26.8** Projected boat harbour (pôle nautique) in Gennevilliers arm, new urban district on former industrial site
PK **26.1** Saint-Ouen bridge, industrial quays d/s r/b

Not a place for plaisanciers! One of the basins in the commercial port of Gennevilliers, PK34 - PK35

94

Lower Seine

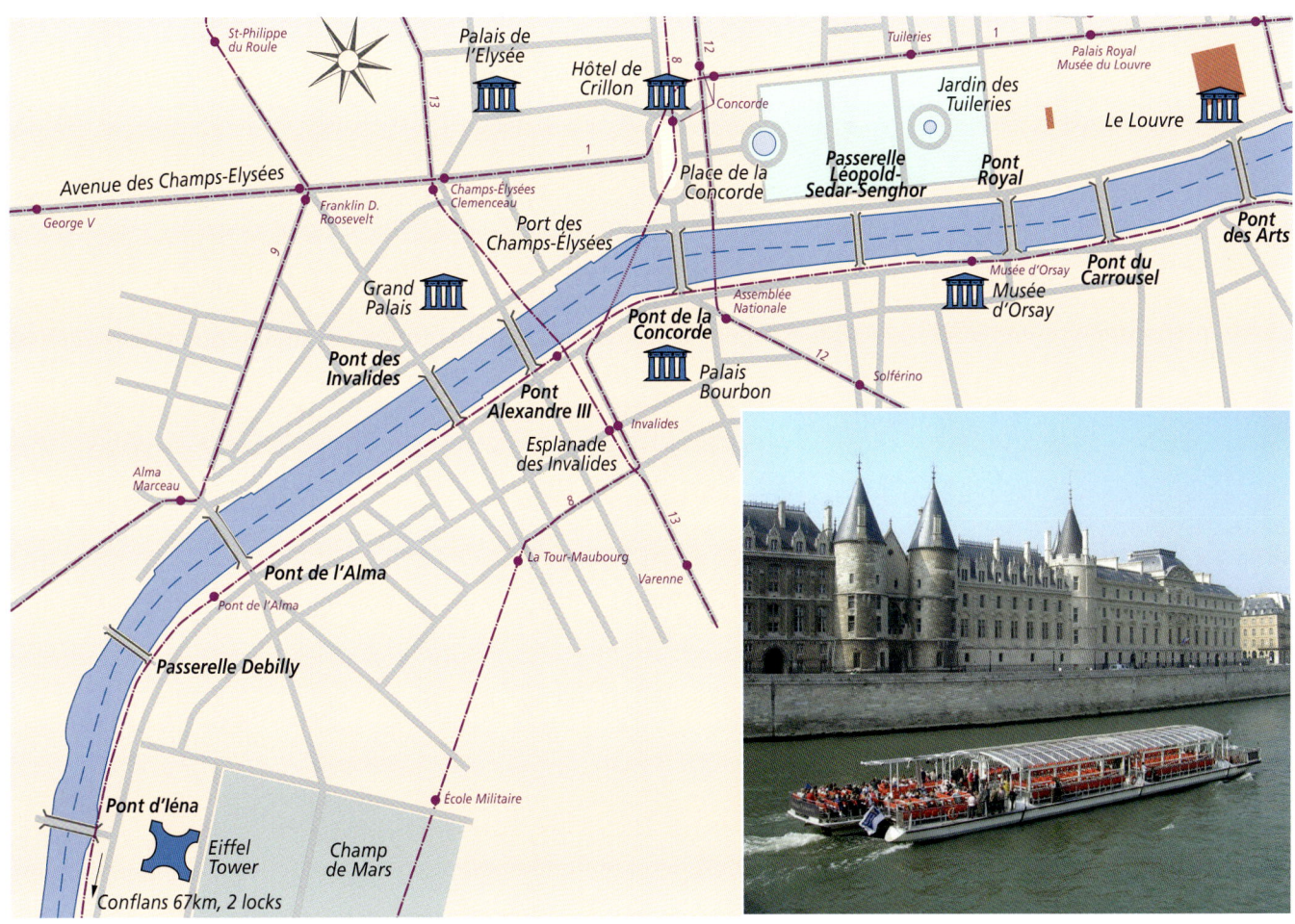

PK 25.5	U/s end of Île Saint-Denis, navigation continues in Saint-Ouen/Saint-Denis arm, r/b, l/b arm (Gennevilliers) navigable only for access to industrial quays (or for upstream vessels)
PK 25.1	Railway bridge
PK 24.6	Bridge (Gennevilliers), commercial quay (Asnières) u/s l/b, oil terminals d/s r/b
PK 24.0	**Asnières** *port de plaisance* (Port Van Gogh) l/b, 07 84 43 27 82, 100 berths, night €21, water, electricity, showers, wifi, pump-out, restaurant **fleuve-concept.fr**

From here the river is wide, with many houseboats (some are more like house-ships) lining the banks. Then along the arm by the Île de Puteaux, past the glittering brave new world office blocks of La Défense and through the Suresnes lock complex (three parallel chambers). Then past the Île Seguin (PK11), the site of the former Renault car factory, and, increasingly, past cement and aggregate and other industrial docks and terminals.

PK 23.6	Clichy bridge, Metro line 13
PK 22.7	**Asnières** bridge, slipway d/s l/b
PK 22.6	Railway bridge (Asnières)
PK 21.8	Levallois-Perret bridge and d/s end of Île de la Grande-Jatte
PK 20.7	Courbevoie bridge
PK 19.7	U/s end of Île de la Grande-Jatte, Neuilly arm r/b forbidden to navigation
PK 19.6	D/s end of Île de Puteaux
PK 19.3	**Neuilly** bridge, Métro line 1
PK 18.1	Puteaux bridge, slipway u/s l/b
PK 16.8	Triple lock (Suresnes) and weir in l/b arm, VHF 22, weir in r/b arm

Bateau-mouche heading downstream past the Conciergerie, the last remaining medieval building in Paris, PK1. [The map of central Paris is continued on the next page]

PK 16.4	**Suresnes** bridge
PK 14.8	Footbridge (Passerelle de l'Avre), *port de plaisance* (Port Suréna) d/s r/b, 06 60 69 06 14, 9 berths, €180/month, water, electricity **fleuve-concept.fr**
PK 14.2	Motorway bridge (A13)
PK 13.5	Bridge (Pont de Saint-Cloud)
PK 12.7	Private *port de plaisance* (Port Mazura) r/b, 17 boats, water, electricity, shower, slipway, repairs, wifi, night free but without services **mazura-marine.com**
PK 12.0	Bridge (Pont de Sèvres)
PK 11.9	D/s end of Île Seguin
PK 11.2	Bridge (Passerelle de l'Île Seguin)
PK 11.0	D/s end of Île Saint-Germain, Bras d'Issy-les-Moulineaux l/b
PK 10.9	U/s end of Île Seguin
PK 10.3	Bridge (Billancourt)
PK 9.6	Quay (Boulogne-Billancourt), r/b
PK 9.4	Bridge (Issy-les-Moulineaux)
PK 9.3	U/s end of Île Saint-Germain, navigation in Bras de Billancourt, r/b (l/b arm for rowing boats)
PK 8.8	D/s limit of City of Paris
PK 8.7	Motorway bridge (Boulevard Périphérique)
PK 8.2	Bridge (Pont du Garigliano)
PK 7.2	Bridge (Pont Mirabeau)

95

II – River Seine and routes north and east

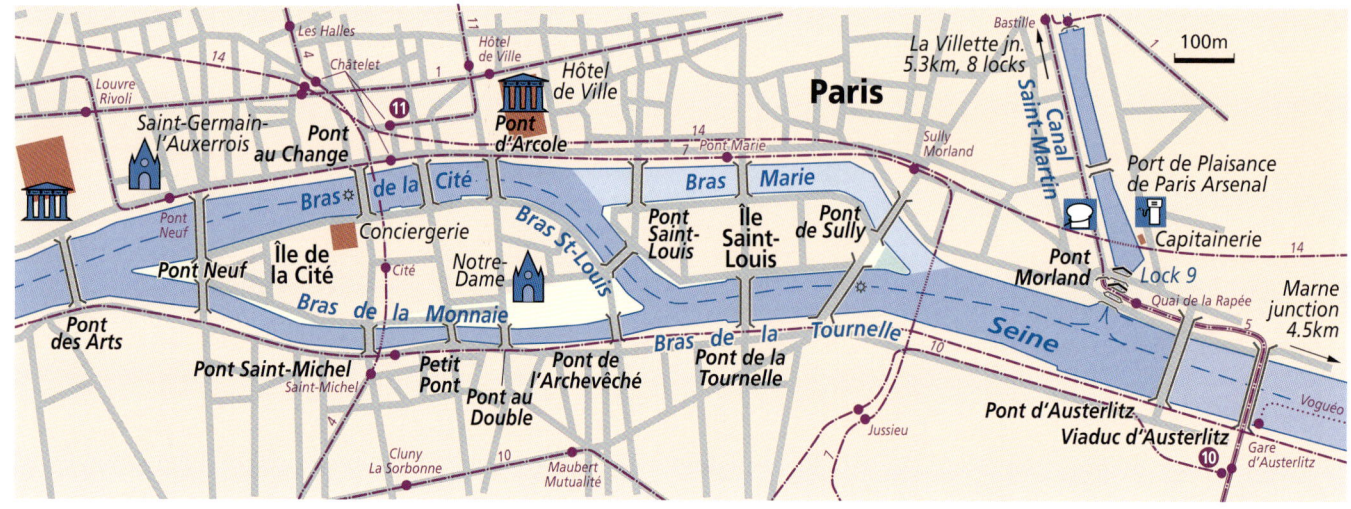

Bras de Grenelle (upstream only)

PK **6.7**	D/s end of Île des Cygnes, Bras de Passy r/b
PK **6.6**	Bridge (Pont de Grenelle)
PK **6.4**	Railway bridge (RER C)
PK **5.9**	Bridge (Pont de Bir-Hakeim) and Métro viaduct (line 6)
PK **5.8**	U/s end of Île des Cygnes
PK **5.3**	Bridge (Pont d'Iéna)

The Seine through Paris has been a challenge for visiting boats since closure of the seasonal moorings provided at Quai de Grenelle (just off the map above, downstream from the Pont d'Iéna). The Port des Champs-Élysées moorings have been unavailable to visiting boats for many years.

Cruising through the heart of one of the world's greatest cities is a unique privilege. Past the Statue of Liberty (small version), the Eiffel Tower, Les Invalides, the Grand Palais and the Tuileries, the Musée d'Orsay, the Louvre (but its pyramid not visible from the river, nor is the Opéra. Then the Île de la Cité, Notre Dame and the Île Saint-Louis, passing under innumerable historic bridges. The experience is unforgettable, but not relaxing for the person at the helm, who has to watch out, ahead and behind. The *bateaux-mouche* (flat, wide, long sightseeing boats) move very fast and do not make allowances, neither do the smaller waterbuses (*Batobus*). It is important to note the traffic flow, controlled by lights, around the two historic islands and the changes in left-bank/right-bank navigation.

PK **4.8**	Footbridge (Passerelle Debilly)
PK **4.4**	Bridge (Pont de l'Alma)
PK **3.7**	Bridge (Pont des Invalides)
PK **3.5**	Bridge (Pont Alexandre III)
PK **3.4**	**Paris** Port des Champs Élysées r/b, now operated by VNF exclusively for barges with professional/commercial activity, water, electricity, showers, slipway, restaurants
PK **3.0**	Bridge (Pont de la Concorde)
PK **2.6**	Footbridge (Passerelle Léopold-Sédar-Senghor)
PK **2.2**	Bridge (Pont Royal)
PK **1.9**	Bridge (Pont du Carrousel)
PK **1.6**	Footbridge (Pont des Arts)

Bras de la Cité

The Bras de la Monnaie on the left bank side is accessible to boats heading upstream, but is narrow and intensively used by bateaux-mouche and the Batobus services; it is much safer to keep the main arm, the Bras de la Cité.

PK **1.4**	D/s end of Île de la Cité, Bras de la Monnaie l/b
PK **1.3**	Bridge (Pont-Neuf)
PK **0.9**	Bridge (Pont au Change)
PK **0.7**	Bridge (Pont Notre-Dame)
PK **0.6**	Bridge (Pont d'Arcole)

Passing Notre Dame, before she lost her central spire, in a hotel barge: the magic of Paris enjoyed in the comfortable and intimate surroundings of one's own floating hotel © F-W

Bras Saint-Louis

PK **0.4**	D/s end of Île Saint-Louis, Bras Marie r/b
PK **0.3**	Bridge (Pont Saint-Louis)
PK **0.2**	U/s end of Île de la Cité, navigation enters Bras de la Tournelle
PK **0.0**	Bridge (Pont de la Tournelle), limit of Lower Seine, navigation continues in Haute-Seine

Just one kilometre upstream on the Upper river Seine (Seine amont) is the entrance to the Paris Canals (Canal Saint-Martin) and the popular *port de plaisance* in the Bassin de l'Arsenal (see 18. Paris Canals).

Lower Seine

17. Le Havre port and Canal du Havre à Tancarville

THE CANAL DU HAVRE À TANCARVILLE was built originally as a ship canal, and opened in 1887. It bypasses what was then still a difficult section of the Seine estuary over a distance of 27km from just below the Tancarville suspension bridge to the basins of the port of Le Havre. The Seine estuary is shallow, with strong tides and currents and an uncomfortable sea can kick up easily. It is also very prone to thick fog. The canal by-passes these potential hazards, but a few years ago the port of Le Havre decided to prohibit navigation to all recreational craft. The boatyard at Tancarville, equipped with a tall crane and travel-lift, a chandlery and a large hardstanding area, is now accessible only from the Seine, passing through the locks at Tancarville. The canal provided access to the charming village of Harfleur, once one of France's most important ports, associated with Agincourt and Henry V.

The canal was planned by Vauban, who built the 5km Harfleur canal between this little port and the main port of Le Havre. It was completed in 1887, with one 180m by 12m lock at Tancarville, wider (14m) in the chamber. A second lock was added in the 1980s, longer and wider (24m). The canal is linked to the sea by the Quinette de Rochemont lock, in the harbour, or the huge François 1er ship lock. A new lock was planned to connect the canal with the container terminal in the large outer basin, but this project was abandoned in favour of the 'Chatière' (cat-trap), a new 1.9km long breakwater to be completed by 2024, ensuring all-weather access for inland craft to the modern Bassin Hubert Raoul-Duval, at a cost of €125 million.

Le Havre as entry port

From the marina, the route is through the main inner harbour lock Sas Quinette into the large *Bassins* (docks) de l'Eure and Bellot. At the end of *Bassin Bellot* lies the large Sas Vétillart lock, the fall or rise depending on the tidal state, with a tall modern control tower next to it, followed by the *Bassin Vétillart*.

Navigation

Included here for completeness, the route inland on the canal from the Sas Vétillart is available only to commercial craft. It is forbidden to leisure craft. Skyscraping piles of containers mark the landscape to the first low concrete swing bridge. After a barge dock on the right comes a white lift-bridge (road/rail). At the end of a large wide dock lies a red lift-bridge (railway). From here the Canal Bossière branches off southwards, giving access to the large commercial docks and the Grand Canal du Havre. Then a green road and rail lift-bridge marks the start of the Tancarville Canal proper. The canal is generally quite calm. Lift-bridge 7 carries commercial vehicles to Le Havre's extensive industrial area south of the canal.

Locks

There are two locks within the port of Le Havre, the *Sas Vétillart* and *Sas Quinette de Rochemont*. The canal is then lock-free through to Tancarville. The two entrance locks accommodate push-tows up to 185m by 23m (new lock) or 14m (old lock). Travelling east for Rouen, the earliest one can exit the lock onto the river is HW-3 and this may not provide enough remaining upstream flow time to get to Rouen PK245. See under Lower Seine advice on intermediate moorings.

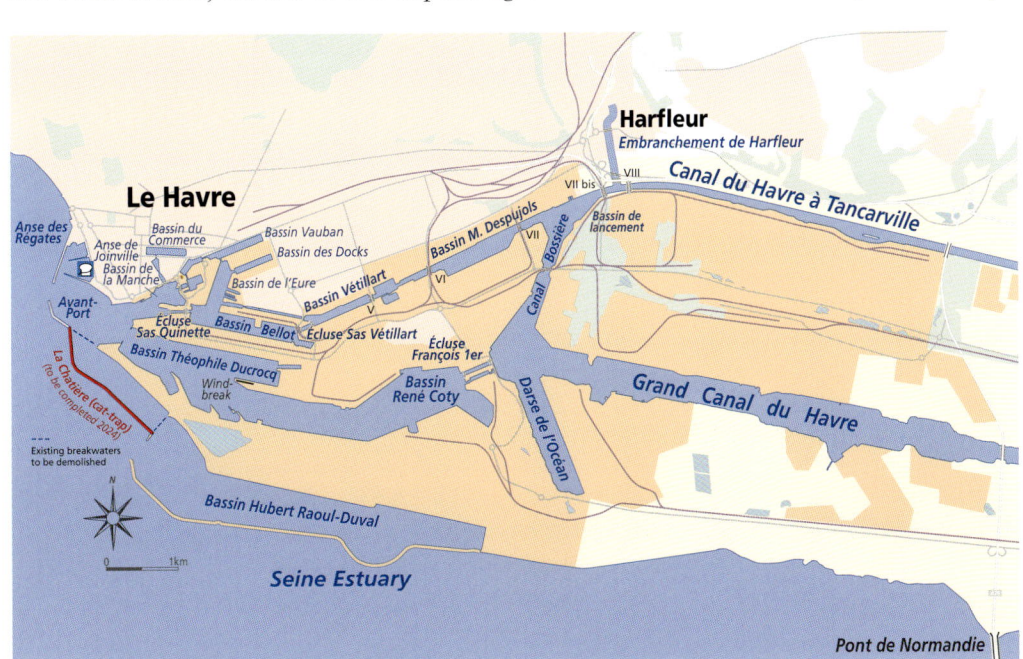

Draught

The maximum draught is 3.50m.

Headroom

The maximum authorised air draught is 55m. There are numerous movable bridges between Le Havre

II – River Seine and routes north and east

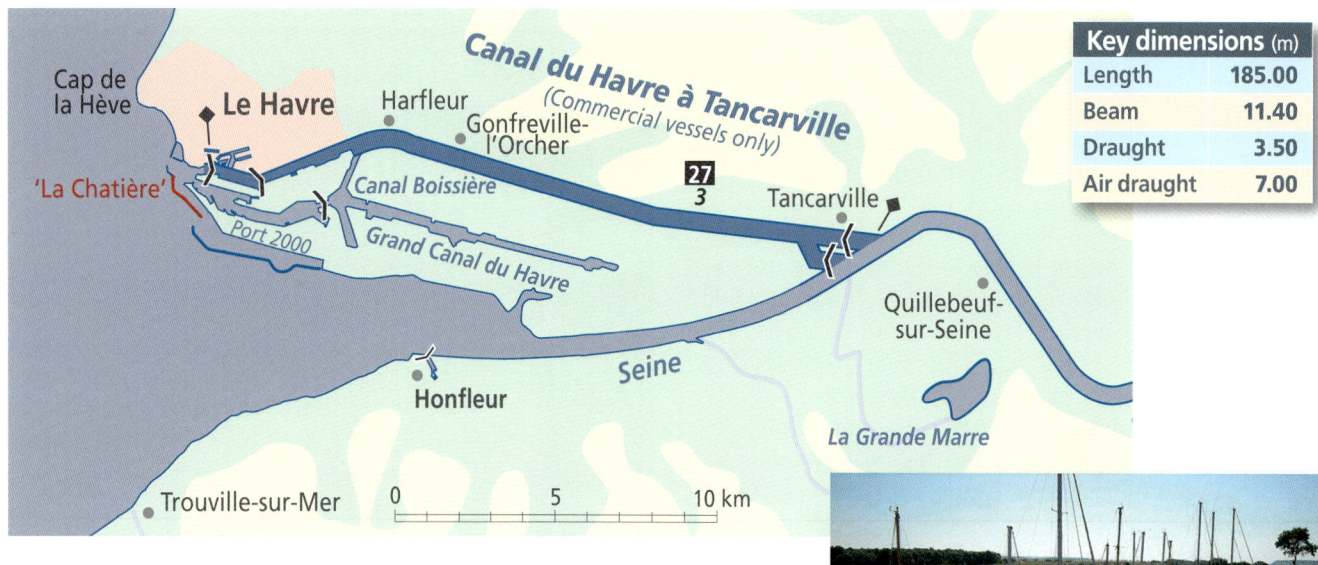

Key dimensions (m)	
Length	185.00
Beam	11.40
Draught	3.50
Air draught	7.00

and Harfleur, opened on demand by calling Le Havre bridge and lock control on VHF 12 or VHF 88. For craft higher than 7m the motorway bridge (PK 14) and the Pont du Hode (PK 8) have to be opened, the corresponding request being made by 1600 the day before passage (these bridges are not operated on Sundays and public holidays).

Authority
Grand port maritime du Havre
– Terre-plein de la Barre, BP 1413, 76067
Le Havre 02 32 74 74 00 *havre-port.fr*

Route description

PK 27.0	Inner basins of port of **Le Havre**
PK 25.8	Lock (sas Quinette de Rochemont)
PK 23.9	Lock (sas de Vétillart), moving bridges over both gates
PK 23.0	Bridge No V (Bassin Vétillart)
PK 22.1	Lift bridge No VI

This blue bridge serves the busy A29 motorway which crosses the Seine via the spectacular (and extremely high) Pont de Normandie. It is rarely operated, as commercial vessels, including the big car transport push-tows from the nearby Renault factory can pass underneath.

PK 20.8	Basin (Marcel Despujols) and industrial quays
PK 20.7	Lift bridge No VII
PK 20.0	Canal de Bossière (link south to Grand Canal du Havre)
PK 19.5	Bridge No VII bis
PK 19.3	**Harfleur** basin north bank, 600m long through foot-bridge (bridge No 9)

For six centuries Harfleur was the principal seaport of northwestern France. In 1415, it was captured by Henry V prior to the Battle of Agincourt. In the 16th century, the port began to dwindle in importance owing to the silting up of the Seine estuary and the rise of Le Havre. In 1887, the Tancarville canal restored waterborne access to the town from both the Seine and Le Havre. Turn off the canal and up the River Lézarte, under the two road bridges, but the river is reported to be heavily silted up. There are some excellent long-term *péniche* moorings along the river banks downstream of the historic village itself.

The Chantier Naval des Torpilleurs at Tancarville has pontoon moorings, a tall crane, travel-lift, large hardstanding area, chandlery and workshops. The facility may be useful, entering from the inland end only, as an intermediate stop between Le Havre and Rouen, depending on circumstances and timetables. © F-W

PK 19.1	Lift bridge No VIII
PK 16.0	Gonfreville oil refinery south bank
PK 14.4	Motorway lift bridge (D929 or A29)
PK 10.4	Conveyor bridge
PK 7.8	Swing bridge (Pont du Hode)
PK 1.1	Boatyard (Les Torpilleurs) r/b, 140 berths, 10 visitor moorings, water, electricity, shower, crane 12t *chantiernaval76.com*
PK 0.1	Entrance locks, VHF 18, bridge, moorings u/s

Tancarville (VHF 18) has two lock chambers side-by-side; how they are used depends on the tide, direction of passage and size and quantity of vessels. Boats need to be prepared to share with substantial barges and small ships, whether directed to the older lock (north) or the newer one to the south. Being the last in can be uncomfortable because all vessels tend to keep their props turning hard, so it can be very difficult to maintain direction and control when entering the lock and mooring up close behind them.

PK 0.0 *Junction with Seine*, d/s of Tancarville suspension bridge

Immediately outside the lock is the big Tancarville bridge and beyond that (north side) is a range of substantial steel pile dolphins (*ducs d'Albe*). This is where commercial vessels wait for the lock's operation. There is nowhere for pleasure craft to moor temporarily and the currents in this part of the river, close to the sea/estuary, are very strong indeed, in both directions. The guides say that yachts can moor between the piles and the bank. You may prefer to request (VHF 73) tying up to a waiting *péniche*.

18. Paris Canals

THE PARIS CANALS (*CANAUX DE LA VILLE DE PARIS*), opened in 1822, are increasingly popular for cruising and boat trips, while retaining their prime functions of water supply and commercial navigation in the industrial suburbs to the north of Paris. They are made up of the canalised river Ourcq and Canal de l'Ourcq, the Clignon branch canal, the Canal Saint-Denis and Canal Saint-Martin. Their combined length is 120km. The declining commercial traffic and parallel boom in pleasure cruising throughout France prompted the Paris city council to remove most of the earlier constraints and open up the entire system for recreational navigation in the 1980s. A small licence fee is charged for passage through the Canal Saint-Denis and Canal Saint-Martin:
– for boats of up to 15 m, €17.75,
– for boats longer than 15 m, €59.14.

These are very modest fees, especially as they cover the entire year. The licence gives access to the Canal de l'Ourcq, a unique and charming waterway, which passes through many places of historic interest, before reaching the former timber-loading quay at Port-aux-Perches and the equally remote location of La Commanderie at the end of the Clignon branch canal. Development of recreational navigation on these rural waterways has been handicapped by the narrow locks on the Canal de l'Ourcq above Les Pavillons-sous-Bois. These are being rebuilt to allow slightly broader-beam vessels to use the canal, but one narrow lock remains at Varreddes.

Among the earliest canalised rivers in Europe, the **Ourcq** *was surveyed by Leonardo da Vinci, and some works were undertaken in the 16th century. It then led directly to the Marne, through a series of flash locks and primitive locks. It was improved by Louis de Regemorte around 1750. The canal proper was built in 1822 after approval by Napoleon. The parallel locks were narrow and long (58.80m by 3.20m). The main aim of this canal is nowadays to provide water for cleaning the streets of Paris and feeding the other two canals. It is a free-flowing contour canal, a rare combination.*

The **Canal Saint-Martin** *was designed to by-pass Paris, when the Seine was not canalised and became dry in the summer. Napoleon also supported this project. Started in 1809, it was inaugurated only after his death in 1825. Locks are of the Marne size, 41.70m by 7.80m, all double staircase locks except for # 9 into the Seine. It was partly covered by a tunnel to facilitate army movement towards the insurrection-prone suburb of Saint-Antoine.*

The **Canal Saint-Denis** *is the other part of this intended short-cut, the Canal de l'Ourcq being the 'summit' level and link between the two canals. Started in 1805, it was inaugurated in 1826. Each site has two parallel locks, one Freycinet size, the other 62.50m by 8.10m. The depth is 3.20m. The upper lock has a fall of 10m, and incorporates a saving basin between the two chambers.*

Authority

Mairie de Paris (Direction de la Voirie et des Déplacements) – Service des Canaux
 – 62 quai de la Marne, 75019 Paris, 01 44 89 14 14
Circonscription des Canaux à Grand Gabarit
 – 5 quai de la Loire, 75019 Paris, 01 44 52 86 40 (the two canals in Paris and Ourcq to PK 11)
Circonscription de l'Ourcq Touristique
 – 6 avenue du Général Galliéni, 77100 Meaux,
 01 60 09 95 00 (rest of Canal de l'Ourcq)

Navigation

The licence issued by Canaux de Paris covers navigation all-year-round on the two canals within Paris.

A péniche enters lock No 4 on the Canal Saint-Denis
© CÉLINE PATIENT/VILLE DE PARIS

99

II – River Seine and routes north and east

There is no charge for use of the Canal de l'Ourcq. Access to the port of Paris-Arsenal through the first lock from the Seine is free of charge.

Canal Saint-Martin

The Canal Saint-Martin, opened to navigation three years after the Canal de l'Ourcq, in 1825, extends 4.5km from the Seine at the quai Henri IV, just upstream of the two islands in the heart of Paris, to the Bassin de la Villette, where it connects with the Canal de l'Ourcq. The canal has become an icon of Parisian charm, with its elegant iron footbridges, and trip-boats operate regular passenger services through the canal. Now it is also familiar to boat owners visiting Paris, thanks to the 180-berth marina in the Bassin de l'Arsenal, immediately beyond the entrance lock from the Seine. The marina is operated by Fayolle Marine

For almost half its length (2069m), the canal is in tunnel (in fact a succession of *voûtes* offering varying navigable widths) under two main boulevards and the Place de la Bastille. Vessels are not allowed to meet in the tunnel, and passage is controlled by lights.

Locks

There are 9 locks, of which the first, lock 9, gives access from the Seine to the marina. It is remote-controlled from the harbourmaster's office, which carefully monitors arrivals at the pontoon just outside the entrance. The other 8 locks are grouped in 4 double staircases. Their dimensions are 42 by 7.80m (authorised dimensions 40.70m by 7.70m).

Draught

The maximum authorised draught is 1.90m.

Headroom

The fixed bridges leave a minimum headroom of 4.37m. There are two swing bridges.

Towpath

The canal has a towpath throughout, but there is no public access to the towpaths in the tunnels.

Route description

There is a waiting pontoon just upstream from the entrance with a telephone to call up the harbourmaster on VHF 9 or 01 43 41 39 32. The lock is operated from 08:00 to 23:00. Mooring up can be tricky when the river current is strong and *péniches* or passenger boats are passing. The pontoon is a little unstable.

PK 4.6   Métro bridge (line 5) and bridge (voie Mazas), *junction with Seine* (Quai Henri IV) at PK 168

Paris Canals

PK **4.5** Lock 9, bridge (Morland), water
PK **4.3** **Paris**-Arsenal marina, 01 43 41 39 32, 06 88 93 55 63, 2180 berths, maximum length 25m, *fayollemarine.eu*, night €35, fuel, water, electricity, showers, wifi, pump-out, slipway, crane 7t, restaurant

The very popular *port de plaisance* in the large basin is attractively landscaped along the eastern quay, with a useful footbridge crossing it in the middle. Justly famed as 'the place to stay' (for a few days or for a long stay), it is very popular and booking or phoning ahead is strongly advised. Many passenger tourist boats pass through the basin on their way to La Villette or back to the Seine. The port is well run, safe and secure.

PK **4.2** Footbridge (Mornay)
PK **3.9** Metro bridge (Bastille, line 1), 17.60m wide passage, end of tunnel
PK **3.7** Voûte Bastille (length 180m, width 8.04m)
PK **2.2** End of voûte du Temple, beginning of voûte Richard-Lenoir (length 1510m, width 16m)
PK **1.9** Entrance to tunnel (voûte du Temple, length 276m, width 24.50m)
PK **1.8** Locks 7 and 8 (staircase, 01 42 03 44 32), water
PK **1.8** Footbridge (Rue de la Douane)
PK **1.6** Swing bridge (Rue Alibert/Rue Dieu)
PK **1.5** Footbridge (Richerand)
PK **1.4** Swing bridge (Rue de la Grange-aux-Belles)
PK **1.3** Locks 5 and 6 (staircase), footbridge u/s, water
PK **0.8** Bridge (Pont des Écluses Saint-Martin)
PK **0.7** Locks 3 and 4 (staircase), water
PK **0.5** Bridge (Louis Blanc), basin d/s
PK **0.4** Basin (Louis Blanc) with quays
PK **0.1** Tunnel (Voûte Lafayette), 103m long, 8.10m wide
PK **0.0** Junction with Canal de l'Ourcq (Bassin de la Villette), locks 1 and 2 (staircase), footbridge u/s, bridge, water

Canal Saint-Denis

The Canal Saint-Denis extends 6.6km from the junction with the Canal de l'Ourcq at the Bassin de la Villette to the Seine at Saint-Denis. It is the busiest of the three canals in Paris, passing through predominantly industrial suburbs, with numerous private quays used by commercial barges. For access to the Canal de l'Ourcq boaters may prefer to use the Canal Saint-Martin, entered 30km further upstream on the Seine, but the Canal Saint-Denis may be appreciated for its contrasting urban landscapes and imposing locks.

Locks
There are seven paired locks, overcoming a total difference in level of 24m. The large chamber is 62.50m long and 8.20m wide, while the small chamber is 38.90m by 5.20m. Maximum authorised dimensions are 60.50m by 8.00m.

Draught
The maximum authorised draught is 3.00m from the Seine to lock 3 and 2.60m in the remaining section to the Bassin de la Villette.

Headroom
The bridges leave a minimum headroom of 4.60m (maximum authorised air draught 4.44m).

Towpath
There is a towpath throughout.

Route description

PK **0.0** Junction with Canal de l'Ourcq, at PK 1.4, turning basin
PK **0.1** Lock 1, two chambers, water
PK **0.4** Bridge (Flandre), basin d/s l/b
PK **0.6** Railway bridge (main line Gare de l'Est)
PK **0.8** Bridge (Macdonald)
PK **0.9** Motorway bridge (*Boulevard Périphérique*)
PK **1.0** Private basin (*darse*) 500m long through footbridge l/b, **Aubervilliers** shopping centre

This basin has Aubervillier's extensive shopping centre 'Le Millénaire' on its north bank, which has a shuttle boat service running through to La Villette.

Aubervillers 'Le Millénaire' shuttle boat takes on passengers for the transfer to La Villette. © ICADE.FR

PK **1.3** Lock 2, two chambers, water
PK **1.8** Bridge (Stains), private quays d/s
PK **2.2** Lock 3, two chambers
PK **2.4** Footbridge (Aubervilliers), industrial quays d/s
PK **2.7** Bridge (Landy)
PK **3.0** Footbridge (Fraternité)
PK **3.2** Lock 4, two chambers, water
PK **3.3** Railway bridges (Soissons), RER line B
PK **3.4** Motorway bridge (A86)
PK **3.5** Bridge (Pailleux)
PK **3.9** Swing bridge and footbridge (Franc-Moisin)
PK **4.5** Footbridge (passerelle de l'Écluse)
PK **4.6** Lock 5, two chambers, motorway bridge (A1), water
PK **4.7** Bridge (avenue Président Wilson)
PK **4.9** **Saint-Denis** bridge (Pont de la Révolte), basin u/s, town centre and *basilique* 1km r/b
PK **5.3** Footbridge (Thiers)
PK **5.7** Lock 6, two chambers, water
PK **5.9** Footbridge (Gare de Saint-Denis)
PK **6.0** Bridge (Rue du Port), tramway line T1
PK **6.2** Bridge and railway bridge (main line Gare du Nord)

II – River Seine and routes north and east

PK **6.4** Projected marina l/b, as part of Saint-Denis 'gare-confluence' urban regeneration project
PK **6.5** Lock 7, two chambers, bridge (Briche), water
PK **6.6** Junction with lower river Seine (Seine aval) at PK 29

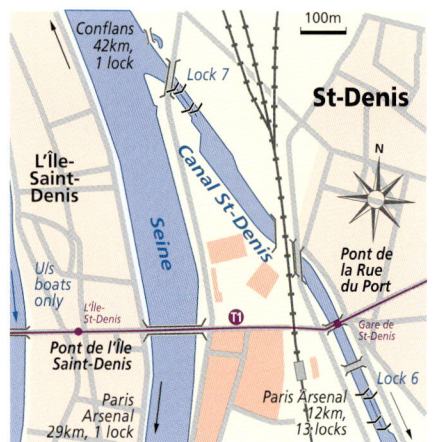

Canal de l'Ourcq

The Canal de l'Ourcq extends 108km from the Bassin de la Villette in Paris, where it joins the Canal Saint-Denis and Canal Saint-Martin, to the remote hamlet of Port-aux-Perches, on the edge of the Retz forest. The waterway is made up of three distinct sections:
- the widened section from La Villette to Les Pavillons-sous-Bois (11km),
- the 'narrow' canal from Les Pavillons-sous-Bois to Mareuil (86km),
- the canalised river Ourcq, over a distance of 11km from the diversion weir at Mareuil to Port-aux-Perches.

The widened section is navigable by Seine barges carrying up to 900 tonnes, but the rest of the waterway was historically used only by the narrow *flûte* or *demi-flûte d'Ourcq*, with a beam of only 3.20m. The available width is to be increased to 3.70m, by widening one of the two parallel chambers at each of the five narrow locks. These works were completed at four of the five locks on this section. This new beam is now sufficient for many boats and there is no reason why cruising should not develop on this system.

Pont de Crimée is lifted for a trip boat while pedestrians enjoy the view from the parallel footbridge.

Two matching warehouses stood at the end of La Villette basin. The one on the left was destroyed by fire and has been replaced by an attractive building including a hotel, while a new port de plaisance has been provided along the quay.

Alternative access may eventually be possible from the canalised river Marne at Lizy-sur-Ourcq, where a boat-lift has been projected to overcome the 13m difference in level.

No tolls are charged for use of the canal by boats, but a *laisser-passer* of limited duration must be obtained from the top locks of the Canal Saint-Denis or Canal Saint-Martin. Craft with an air draught of less than 1.90m are issued a straightforward *déclaration*.

The route description is given in the reverse direction, from La Villette to Port-aux-Perches, for the convenience of boats entering the canal from the Seine.

Navigation
Some commercial traffic may be encountered on the first section of the canal. Above Sevran it becomes much narrower and the current may be quite strong. Negotiating tight bends will require skilful handling, all the more so with longer craft.

Locks
There are 10 locks, overcoming a total difference in level of 13.80m. The first encountered when heading upstream from Paris is Sevran, 88m long and 8.10m wide. Then there are the five 'narrow' locks, originally 58.80m long and 3.20m wide. Four of these have in recent years been widened to 5.20m, thus increasing the maximum authorised beam to 3.70m (the canal is too narrow to accommodate broader-beam boats). It remains to widen the lock at Varreddes (or possibly to build a new parallel chamber, so that at least one of the original locks is preserved). No target date has been announced for completion of these works. The last four locks, on the canalised river Ourcq, are 63.00m by 5.20m.

Sevran lock is now automated like the others. A special key is supplied at the last locks of the two canals or at the office Quai de la Seine, for do-it-yourself operation of all the other locks, as well as the lift-bridges (free of charge, see below). A leaflet is also issued, giving all necessary instructions for lock operation, as well as for mooring on the canal, which is strictly controlled to prevent any attempts at residential mooring.

Draught

The maximum authorised draught is 2.60m on the widened section to Les Pavillons-sous-Bois (PK 11), and 0.80m throughout the rest of the waterway, although the available depth is 1.30m.

Headroom

The fixed bridges offer a minimum headroom of 4.09m on the widened section and 2.60m on the rest of the canal. There are two lift bridges, at Claye-Souilly (PK 27) and Congis (PK 71), which like the locks must be operated by the users and closed immediately after passage. At Claye-Souilly the bridge offers a headroom of 2.20m in the closed position.

Speed

The maximum authorised speed is 6km/h.

Towpath

There is a good towpath throughout.

Route description

PK 0.0	**Junction with Canal Saint-Martin**, Bassin de la Villette
PK 0.4	Footbridge (Moselle)
PK 0.7	**Paris** *port de plaisance* r/b

Lively pub terrace scene viewed from the Rue de Crimée lift-bridge
© JAMES LITTLEWOOD

This relatively recent Parisian *port de plaisance* is located in the vast basin reached at the end of the Canal Saint-Martin, and is administered by the Arsenal harbourmaster (charges are the same as at the Arsenal, see under Canal Saint-Martin).

PK 0.8	Lift bridge (Rue de Crimée) and footbridge, new *port de plaisance* r/b, end of basin
PK 1.1	Bridge (Rue de l'Ourcq)
PK 1.3	Railway bridge
PK 1.4	**Junction with Canal Saint-Denis**, r/b, turning basin

For 600m the canal runs through the elaborately landscaped Parc de la Villette, where the Service des Canaux has also established its headquarters in what used to be the offices of the slaughter yard (*Abattoirs*). This was historically the dominant feature in this poor part of the city.

PK 1.6	Footbridge (cycle path)
PK 1.9	Footbridge (cycle path)
PK 2.1	Bridge (Macdonald)
PK 2.2	Motorway bridge (*Boulevard Périphérique*), mooring basin d/s r/b
PK 2.6	Bridge (Mairie de Pantin)
PK 3.0	Footbridge
PK 3.3	Bridge (Delizy)
PK 3.7	Footbridge (Pantin)
PK 4.3	Bridge (Hippolyte Boyer)

PK 5.2	Railway bridge (through route Gare de l'Est)
PK 5.3	Railway bridge, industrial quays u/s
PK 5.7	Bridge (Folie)
PK 7.5	Railway bridge
PK 7.6	Motorway bridge (A86)
PK 7.9	Bridge (Bondy), tramway line T1, basin u/s
PK 8.1	Motorway bridge (A3)
PK 8.3	Footbridge
PK 8.7	Bridge (Aulnay-sous-Bois) and pipeline crossing

II – River Seine and routes north and east

PK 9.2	Footbridge	
PK 9.5	Bridge (de la Forêt)	
PK 9.8	Turning basin for barges up to 60m long	

This will be the limit of craft more than 3.20m in beam; beyond PK 11, the width of the canal is reduced dramatically from more than 20m (often 25m) to barely 10m.

PK 10.1	Footbridge
PK 10.6	Bridge (de l'Europe)
PK 11.2	Canal narrows, **Les Pavillons-sous-Bois** l/b
PK 11.4	Footbridge
PK 11.9	Bridge (de l'Union)
PK 12.5	Footbridge
PK 12.6	Tramway (line T4) and road bridges (Freinville)
PK 13.4	Lock (Sevran), basin u/s
PK 13.6	Footbridge
PK 14.0	Bridge
PK 14.1	**Sevran** bridge, town centre 300m r/b (Paris suburb)
PK 14.3	Pipeline crossing
PK 14.4	Footbridge
PK 15.1	Footbridge (long-distance footpath, Île-de-France)
PK 16.7	Footbridge
PK 16.8	Bridge (Villepinte), railway station (RER) r/b
PK 17.5	Basin (Moises) l/b
PK 18.3	Footbridge
PK 18.6	Private railway bridge (Lambert)
PK 19.3	Bridge (Mitry)
PK 19.6	New bridge (Mitry)
PK 20.3	Bridge
PK 21.1	Overhead power lines
PK 21.3	Motorway bridge (A104)
PK 24.0	Footbridge
PK 24.1	Bridge (Rosée), D212
PK 24.6	**Gressy** basin r/b, small village, château 600m r/b
PK 27.0	Main road bridge (N3, Claye-Souilly bypass)
PK 27.4	**Claye-Souilly** lift bridge, basin d/s l/b, slipway, village l/b
PK 28.2	Main road bridge (N3, Claye-Souilly bypass)
PK 29.1	Main road bridge (Marais), N3
PK 29.2	Railway bridge (TGV Est)
PK 29.9	Railway bridge (TGV interconnection)
PK 30.1	Railway bridge (junction between TGV Est and TGV interconnection)
PK 30.3	Bridge (Annet)
PK 31.9	**Fresnes-sur-Marne** bridge, village l/b
PK 32.9	Lock (Fresnes), two chambers, l/b, weir r/b
PK 34.9	Bridge (Précy)
PK 35.7	Bridge
PK 36.5	Bridge (Charmentray), basin u/s r/b
PK 38.0	Trilbardou pumping station (*usine élévatoire*) l/b (lifts water hydraulically from the Marne)
PK 38.5	Basin (Trilbardou) l/b
PK 38.8	Bridge (Parc)
PK 39.0	**Trilbardou** bridge, small village l/b
PK 40.2	Bridge (Vignely)
PK 40.4	Lock (Vignely), two chambers, l/b, weir r/b
PK 42.8	Bridge (Isles-les-Villenoy), D5
PK 43.5	Motorway bridge (A140)
PK 43.9	Pipeline crossing
PK 44.9	Pipeline crossing

Slipway at Claye-Souilly. Note the speed limit of 6km/h on this canal. WORLDWIDESTAR/PANORAMIO

PK 46.0	**Villenoy** bridge, village l/b
PK 47.0	Basin (Sucrerie) r/b
PK 47.3	Bridges (Ruellée)
PK 47.5	Lock (Villenoy), two chambers l/b, weir r/b
PK 48.2	**Meaux** bridge (Saint-Rémy), large basins u/s and d/s, town centre 800m l/b

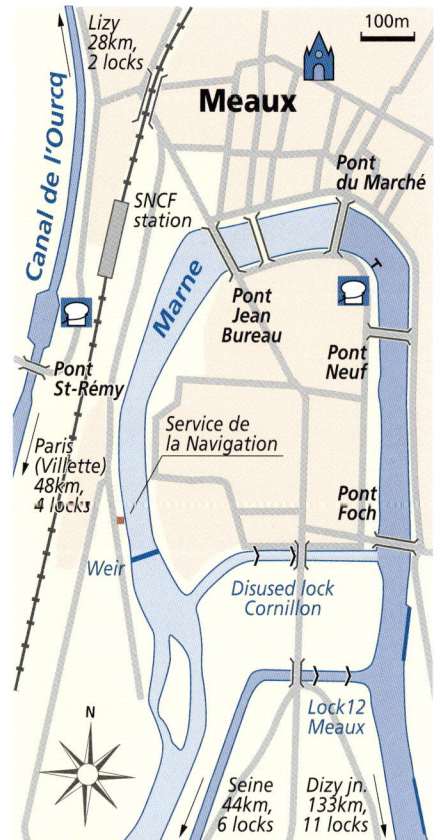

PK 48.8	Footbridge (Penchard)
PK 49.3	Skew road bridge (N330)
PK 50.4	**Crégy-lès-Meaux** bridge, village r/b
PK 52.1	Basin (Cordeliers) r/b
PK 53.1	Bridge
PK 53.5	Bridge (Justice), D405
PK 53.8	Railway bridge
PK 54.6	Bridge (Saint-Lazare), D603, basin u/s, Meaux town centre 1.5 km l/b

Paris Canals

PK 54.9	Lock (Saint-Lazare), two chambers, weir on bypass
PK 55.2	Bridge
PK 55.5	Bridge (George-Albert Bieth)
PK 55.7	Footbridge (Beauval)
PK 56.7	Bridge (avenue Henri Dunant)
PK 57.4	Upper station of former railway incline (used for transhipment between canal and river Marne below), moorings
PK 57.8	Bridge (Ferme de Beauval)
PK 58.6	Bridge (Beauval-Trilport), D603, basin d/s r/b
PK 59.0	Railway bridge
PK 60.1	**Poincy** bridge, village 400m l/b, boat moorings (original Saint-Line hire base) 900m on Marne
PK 60.7	Basin (Poincy) r/b
PK 64.1	Bridge (Voie Blanche, D405), basin u/s r/b
PK 64.7	Lock (Varreddes), two chambers, weir on bypass

Varreddes lock, the only lock on the Canal de l'Ourcq to retain its two original narrow chambers. © JACQUES HARPÉ DE LA GARDE

PK 64.9	Bridge (Bosse)
PK 66.4	**Varreddes** bridge (Maladrerie, D405), basin u/s r/b, village 700m l/b
PK 70.7	**Congis-sur-Thérouanne** lift bridge, basin u/s r/b, village 400m l/b
PK 71.5	Bridge (Congis)
PK 71.8	Bridge (Carreaux)
PK 73.5	Bridge (Villers-les-Rigault), turning point u/s
PK 74.1	Château de Villers r/b
PK 74.7	Basin (Confluent) r/b, site of projected boat lift connecting with river Marne below
PK 76.7	**Lizy-sur-Ourcq** bridge, basin d/s r/b, village l/b
PK 77.3	Bridge (Lizy amont), basins d/s r/b and u/s l/b
PK 79.8	Bridge (Vaches d'Echampeu)
PK 81.0	Railway viaduct (Ourcq), TGV Est
PK 82.0	Bridge (Vernelle), hamlet r/b
PK 83.2	Bridge (Marnoue-la-Poterie), basin u/s r/b
PK 85.4	Bridge (May-en-Multien)
PK 86.1	Basin (May) r/b
PK 87.2	Bridge (Ferme de Gesvres), château 700m l/b
PK 89.2	**Crouy-sur-Ourcq** bridge, large basin d/s, village 1.5km l/b
PK 90.2	Bridge (Varinfroy)
PK 90.9	Basin (Beauval) r/b
PK 91.5	Bridge (Beauval)
PK 92.6	**Neufchelles** bridge, basin u/s, village r/b
PK 93.6	*Junction with Canal du Clignon*, basin
PK 93.9	Railway bridge
PK 94.0	Basin (Collinance) r/b, former peat marshes
PK 96.1	Bridge (Vaches de Mareuil)
PK 96.8	**Mareuil-sur-Ourcq** bridge, large basin d/s r/b, weir on Ourcq l/b, navigation enters canalised river Ourcq, village r/b
PK 97.2	Lock (Mareuil) in short cut l/b, weir on river
PK 99.7	Lock (Queue d'Ham) l/b, weir stream r/b
PK 102.2	**Marolles** bridge, village 400m r/b
PK 102.4	Lock (Marolles) in short cut l/b, weir stream r/b
PK 102.9	Basin (Nimer) r/b
PK 103.8	Weir stream enters l/b
PK 104.1	**La Ferté-Milon** bridge, basin d/s r/b, village l/b
PK 104.3	Lock (La Ferté-Milon)
PK 104.4	Weir stream l/b
PK 105.2	Railway bridge
PK 106.8	Footbridge (Mosloy)
PK 107.7	Footbridge (Port-aux-Perches)
PK 108.1	**Port-aux-Perches** hamlet, head of navigation

Branch off Canal de l'Ourcq – Canal du Clignon

PK 0.0	*Junction with Canal de l'Ourcq* at PK 93.6, bridge (Clignon)

This canal is extremely narrow and shallow, definitely for light craft only.

PK 0.2	Railway bridge
PK 0.5	Aqueduct (Ourcq)
PK 1.2	**La Commanderie**, bridge, turning point, head of navigation

The narrow Canal du Clignon is delightful but accessible only to light craft. © DENIS BOUJUL/VILLE DE PARIS

II – River Seine and routes north and east

19. River Oise and Canal latéral à l'Oise

THE RIVER OISE EXTENDS 104KM from its confluence with the Seine at Conflans-Sainte-Honorine (Fin d'Oise) to the connection with the Canal latéral à l'Oise at Janville (commune of Longueil-Annel). It is extended by the Canal latéral à l'Oise from Janville to connect with the Canal de Saint-Quentin at Chauny, a distance of 34km. The overall route is therefore 138km long, and forms part of the important waterway route from the Seine to Northern France, Belgium and the Rhine. The Seine-Scheldt waterway is now to be upgraded to European Class Vb dimensions, with locks 185m by 12m, and the new Canal Seine-Nord Europe will replace the first section of the Canal latéral à l'Oise. A 2km length of the non-canalised river will remain navigable upstream of Janville to serve a boatyard.

Junctions are made with the Canal de l'Oise à l'Aisne (PK 3) and with the Canal du Nord (PK 18.6). Forming part of the busy 'north-south' route between the Seine basin and northern France and Belgium, the canal has seen large-scale improvement works, like the Oise further downstream. The lower section from the junction with the Canal du Nord is to be further widened or rebuilt on a parallel path as part of the Seine-Nord Europe Canal.

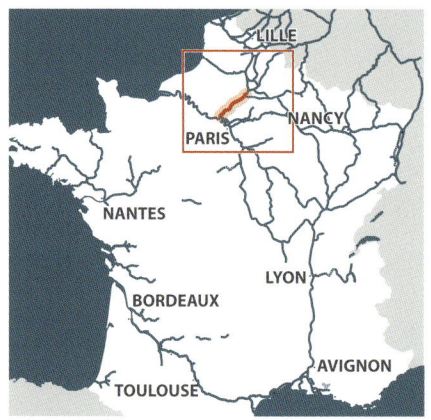

The river was navigated from the Middle Ages, but canalisation started only in 1835, with locks 41m by 6m or 46m by 8m. In 1910, a new set of locks 125m by 12m were built, with limited depth (2.50m, for a loading draught of 2.20m). Starting in 1965, after the deeper Canal du Nord was opened, new locks 185m by 12m were built, with a sill depth of 4m. Dredging in the river was not consistent throughout, and to prepare for the future Seine-Nord Europe Canal, all the weirs are being replaced, and a depth of 3.50m is to be provided throughout. The canal latéral was built in 1831 to provide a complete itinerary between the Canal de Saint-Quentin and the Seine, and to avoid the winding course of the river Oise in this section. Initially to Becquey dimensions, locks were later doubled and enlarged to 39m by 6m and 39m by 6.50m at each fall, with a depth of 2.50m. With the opening of the Canal du Nord, it was decided to further improve the canal downstream of the junction with this new canal. The canal was given 20cm more depth and 5m extra width, and two new locks 100m by 12m were built around 1970.

Navigation
This is mostly a *grand gabarit* waterway that is busy with large commercial barges and push-tows. The off-river ports de plaisance at Port-Cergy, L'Isle-Adam and Compiègne are all the more welcome.

Locks
There are seven locks on the river Oise, each with two large chambers side by side (185m by 12m and 125m by 12m) on a short diversion canal at the level of each weir. A mid-channel dividing wall extends out well beyond the lock, and binoculars are useful to check from a distance which lights on which chamber are giving the appropriate signals to wait or proceed. At Lock 1 (Venette) boats may be routed to the 125m chamber on the other side of the island; the lock-keepers have no direct view of this lock, but remote monitoring and control equipment has been installed. The small locks originally built adjacent to the weirs are disused. There are four electrically-operated locks on the Canal latéral. The two downstream of the junction with the Canal du Nord each have two parallel chambers, 100m by 12m and 39m by 6.50m. The two locks above the junction have two chambers of 39 by 6.50m.

Draught
The maximum authorised draught is 3.00m from the confluence with the Seine up to Creil (PK 75), 2.50m from Creil to the confluence of the river Aisne, and 2.40m through to the end of the Canal latéral à l'Oise. Under the current MAGEO programme (for *mise au gabarit européen de l'Oise*), dredging (and some realignment of bends) will increase the available draught to 3.50m up to the start of the Seine-Nord Europe Canal at (PK 98.7).

Oise and Canal latéral à l'Oise

Key dimensions (m)	
Length	39.00
Beam	6.00
Draught	2.40
Air draught	4.10

Dimensions apply to the upstream lateral canal (above Pont-l'Évêque). The river Oise has high-capacity barge dimensions, while the lateral canal between the river and Pont-l'Évêque has intermediate dimensions. This section will be replaced by the Seine-Nord Europe Canal, when opened.

Commercial activity at Fin d'Oise, which is part of the Conflans-Saint-Honorine site, the hub of inland water transport

Headroom
The headroom under the bridges is at least 5.00m above normal water levels, reduced to 4.10m above the highest navigable water level. The above-mentioned MAGEO project will increase the headroom on the high-capacity waterway to 7m. The maximum available headroom on the lateral canal is 4.10m.

Towpath
There is no continuous towpath.

Authority
VNF Bassin de la Seine, UTI Seine-Nord
- 65 quai de l'Écluse, BP 74, 95313 Cergy-Pontoise 01 34 30 40 80 (PK 0-28)
- 2 boulevard Gambetta, BP 20053, 60321 Compiègne cedex, 03 44 92 27 00, email *uti.seinenord@vnf.fr* (PK 28-138)

Route description

PK 0.0	**Confluence with river Seine** (see plan below)
PK 0.2	**Conflans-Sainte-Honorine** bridge, barge moorings, town centre 1.5 km l/b
PK 0.6	Railway bridge (Pont Eiffel)
PK 1.5	Conflans-Fin-d'Oise quay and boatyards r/b, moorings l/b
PK 2.3	Bridge (Neuville bypass)

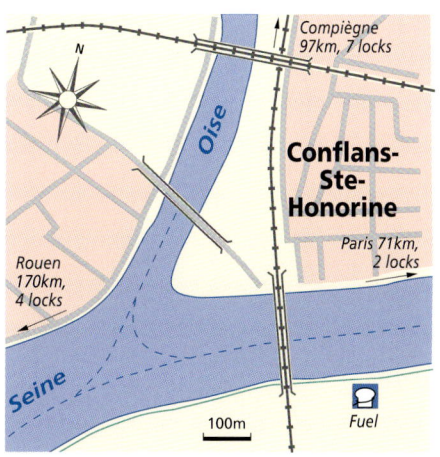

II – River Seine and routes north and east

- PK 3.4 **Neuville-sur-Oise** bridge, village l/b
- PK 5.0 **Jouy-le-Moutier** quay r/b, village 700m
- PK 6.7 Footbridge (Axe Majeur)
- PK 8.7 **Cergy-Pontoise** bridge, town centre r/b
- PK 8.8 **Port-Cergy** marina r/b, 01 34 24 11 77, 60 berths, night €19, water, pumpout, electricity, showers, slipway, repairs (on request) **portcergy.com**

A good mooring with metered water and electricity at L'Isle-Adam, in front of the restaurant L'Affiche. © SANCHALEX

Port Cergy © IRENE KRAVCHUK

- PK 9.4 Bridge (D203)
- PK 11.1 Skew railway bridge (RER regional metro)
- PK 11.5 **Éragny** pontoon l/b, 01 34 64 70 54, night €8, water, restaurant
- PK 12.8 Bridge (Éragny)
- PK 13.5 Motorway bridge (A15)
- PK 13.6 Lock 7 (Pontoise), VHF 18, parallel chambers, weir r/b
- PK 14.7 Railway bridge, barge moorings d/s r/b
- PK 14.8 **Pontoise** *halte* managed by tourist office/capitainerie, 01 34 41 70 60, pontoon 100m, 10 moorings, €12 per night including water and electricity, wifi, limited to 48 hours
- PK 14.9 Pontoise bridge
- PK 16.4 Industrial quays l/b
- PK 18.3 Railway bridge (Chaponval)
- PK 21.7 **Méry-Auvers** bridge, private quays l/b
- PK 24.4 **Mériel** road and railway bridge, village 400m l/b
- PK 27.7 **L'Isle-Adam** bridge, *halte* d/s l/b on pontoon, 24m, limited to 48 hours, water, electricity, slipway, small town 400m l/b, Parmain and railway station r/b
- PK 28.5 Lock 6 (Isle-Adam), VHF 22, parallel chambers, weir l/b
- PK 28.7 **L'Isle-Adam** marina l/b, through entrance lock, 06 69 02 43 14, new marina for 138 boats, visitor moorings in season €11 (6m) to €56 (25m) including water and electricity, pump-out, wifi, slipway

L'Isle-Adam has been a popular resort with its beach, open air swimming pool and park since 1900, and boaters have the choice between the serviced moorings close to the small town centre, downstream of the bridge on the left bank, or in the handsome new marina upstream of the locks, entered through a lock 30m by 6m.

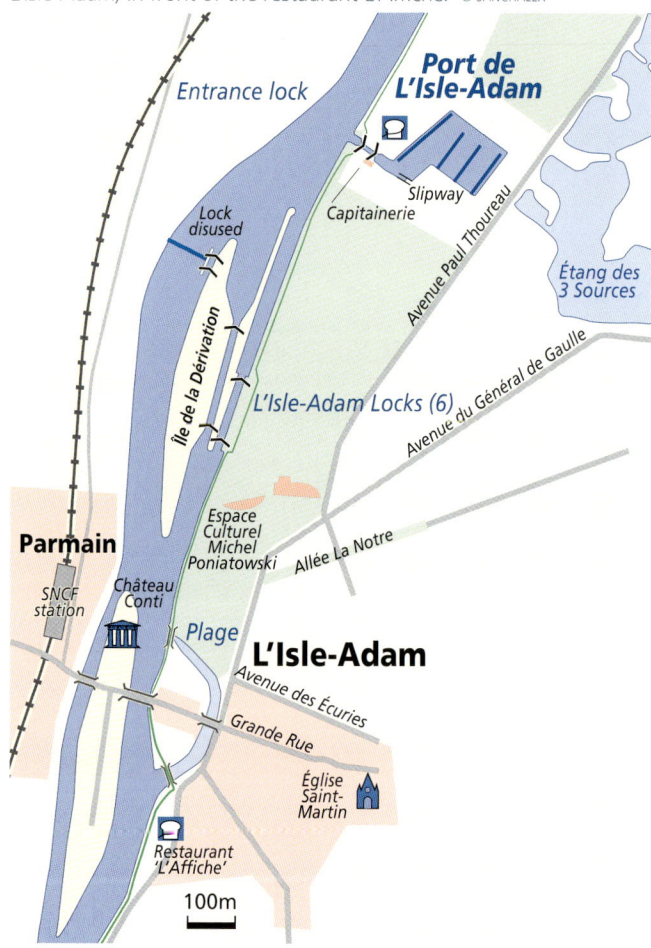

- PK 29.9 Island (Champagne), follow navigation signs
- PK 32.0 Motorway bridge (A16)
- PK 32.3 Bridge (D301 bypass)
- PK 33.6 Railway bridge
- PK 34.2 Industrial quays
- PK 34.9 **Beaumont-sur-Oise** bridge, quay u/s l/b, small town l/b
- PK 35.8 Bridge (D929 Beaumont bypass)
- PK 36.8 Industrial quays r/b
- PK 38.2 Entrance to cut bypassing river bend, l/b channel navigable (max draught 1.00m), **Noisy-sur-Oise** boat moorings on r/b of this arm between the two bridges
- PK 39.3 Bridge (Bruyères-sur-Oise) over new cut
- PK 39.9 End of new cut
- PK 41.7 Lock 5 (Boran), VHF 18, parallel chambers, weir l/b
- PK 43.7 **Boran-sur-Oise** suspension bridge, village 400m r/b
- PK 47.2 Public quay r/b

Oise and Canal latéral à l'Oise

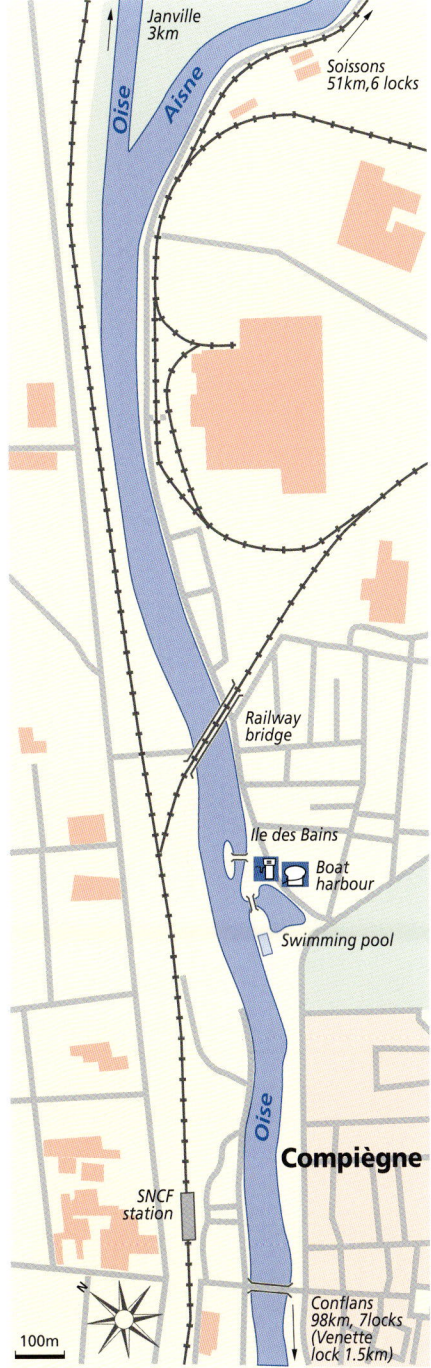

PK	
PK 48.0	**Précy-sur-Oise** suspension bridge, private quays u/s, village r/b
PK 50.2	Quay (Gouvieux) l/b
PK 52.1	**Saint-Leu-d'Esserent** suspension bridge, railway station and village 400m r/b
PK 54.7	Skew railway bridge (Laversine)
PK 56.3	Lock 4 (Creil), VHF 22, parallel chambers, weir l/b
PK 57.4	Bridge (D201 Creil bypass)
PK 58.3	Public quay (Long-Boyau) r/b, and industrial quays
PK 59.0	**Creil** bridge, town centre 500m l/b
PK 60.0	Bridge (D1016 Creil bypass), commercial quays u/s r/b
PK 62.5	**Verneuil-en-Halatte** suspension footbridge (Jean Biondi), quay d/s l/b for 2 boats, water, electricity, slipway, village 800m
PK 63.5	Industrial quays r/b (chemicals factory)
PK 64.6	**Rieux** quay r/b, village 400m beyond railway
PK 71.0	**Pont-Sainte-Maxence** bridge, small town l/b, commercial quays d/s
PK 72.4	Lock 3 (Sarron), bridge, VHF 18, parallel chambers, weir l/b, water
PK 76.2	Quay (Houdancourt) r/b
PK 79.5	Motorway bridge (A1)
PK 81.4	Railway viaduct (TGV Nord Europe)
PK 82.4	**Verberie** bridge, quay u/s l/b, village 500m
PK 83.4	Lock 2 (Verberie), VHF 22, parallel chambers, weir l/b
PK 84.3	Railway bridge, private quay d/s l/b
PK 88.3	**Lacroix-Saint-Ouen** suspension bridge, quay d/s r/b, village 1.5 km l/b
PK 89.2	Bridge (D200)
PK 92.2	**Jaux** footbridge, *port de plaisance* r/b, 06 27 24 11 17, 26 berths, 4 visitor moorings, night €12, water, electricity, showers €2.50, slipway, restaurant, village r/b
PK 94.1	Bridge (Compiègne bypass)
PK 95.0	Private quay r/b
PK 95.7	**Venette** quay r/b, village 400m
PK 95.9	Entrance to lock-cut r/b (navigation in both arms, new lock in main river)
PK 96.2	Lock 1 (Venette), VHF 18, in lock-cut (125m long chamber) or r/b side of main river (196m), weir l/b
PK 96.7	End of lock-cut, navigation re-enters river
PK 97.4	Boatyard (Guerdin) r/b, fuel
PK 97.7	Compiègne bridge, railway station r/b, town centre l/b
PK 98.5	**Compiègne** *port de plaisance* in basin l/b, Compiègne Yacht Club, 06 14 92 59 58, 70 berths, 5 visitor moorings, night €12, water and electricity included, showers, slipway, wifi **cyc.portdeplaisance@yahoo.fr**
PK 98.8	Railway bridge, commercial quays u/s r/b and d/s l/b
PK 98.7	Clairoix, start of sector I of the Canal Seine-Nord Europe under construction from 2023

From this point the description is given for the existing river Oise, while the new course of the Seine-Nord Europe Canal is described under that heading (in chapter I).

PK	
PK 99.5	**Confluence of canalised river Aisne**, l/b
PK 99.7	Bridge (N1031 Compiègne bypass)
PK 101.8	**Clairoix** bridge, private quay d/s r/b, village 1 km r/b
PK 103.0	Entrance to r/b branch, (navigable u/s 2km to Longueil-Annel *port de plaisance*, 12 berths, 03 44 76 02 19, water
PK 103.3	Entrance to l/b branch
PK 103.5	**Janville** bridge on r/b branch, village r/b beyond railway
PK 103.9	Two branches join
PK 104.4	**Connection with Canal latéral à l'Oise** (d/s of lock 4, Janville)

II – River Seine and routes north and east

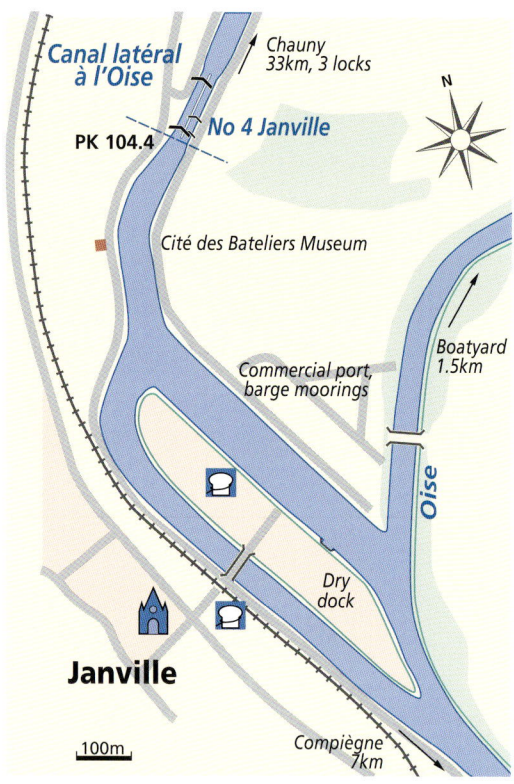

Longueil-Annel and the Cité des Bateliers viewed from the locks at Janville © JAMES LITTLEWOOD

Canal latéral à l'Oise

Navigation continues in the Canal latéral à l'Oise

- PK **104.4** Lock 4 (Janville), footbridge, VHF 22, parallel chambers
- PK **105.3** **Longueil-Annel** bridge, moorings d/s l/b, 03 44 96 24 06, water, electricity, village r/b
- PK **106.3** **Thourotte** bridge, quay u/s l/b, village r/b beyond railway
- PK **106.9** Boatyard l/b
- PK **107.6** **Montmacq** bridge, village 400m l/b

Montmacq is the site of the first lock on the new Seine-Nord Europe Canal. When completed, navigation will follow the river Oise and this length of the lateral canal will be closed to navigation.

- PK **109.9** Lock 3 (Bellerive), VHF 18, parallel chambers, basin d/s l/b
- PK **110.3** Bridge (Bellerive)
- PK **110.8** Basin (Ribécourt) r/b, private quay
- PK **111.6** **Ribécourt** bridge, quay u/s l/b, village 1 km r/b
- PK **112.7** Entrance to new cut bypassing bend in old canal
- PK **113.3** Bridge (Rouilly)
- PK **113.6** End of new cut
- PK **114.2** **Pimprez** bridge, village r/b
- PK **116.3** **Ourscamps** bridge, quay u/s l/b, abbey 800m l/b
- PK **117.7** **Chiry** bridge (Brûlé), village 1.5 km r/b
- PK **119.6** *Junction with Canal du Nord*, r/b

The above 15km of the canal will be replaced by the Seine-Nord Europe Canal, on a separate route mainly using the river Oise. The following 18km will remain intact as a canal for 38m *péniches*.

- PK **120.0** **Pont-l'Évêque** *halte nautique* in basin r/b through footbridge, 03 44 09 60 40, quays for 20 boats, 2 visitor moorings (maximum length 8m), €10 including water and electricity
- PK **120.1** Lock 2 (Sempigny), VHF 22, parallel chambers, quay d/s r/b
- PK **120.4** **Sempigny** bridge, quay u/s l/b, village 400m l/b
- PK **121.2** Basin (Pierrot), moorings
- PK **122.9** **Noyon** bridge (D934), basin and quays d/s, town centre 2.5 km r/b
- PK **124.0** Bridge
- PK **124.8** **Varesnes** bridge, quay u/s l/b, village 700m l/b
- PK **126.6** Basin r/b, moorings
- PK **127.2** Footbridge (Pont-à-la-Fosse)
- PK **127.8** **Babœuf** bridge, quay d/s l/b
- PK **129.2** Lock 1 (Saint-Hubert), VHF 18, parallel chambers
- PK **130.0** **Appilly** bridge, quay u/s l/b, village 700m r/b
- PK **131.6** **Quierzy** bridge, quays l/b, village 1 km l/b
- PK **133.3** **Manicamp** bridge, quay d/s l/b, village 1 km l/b
- PK **135.0** Bridge (Abbécourt)
- PK **135.4** *Junction with Canal de l'Oise à l'Aisne*, l/b
- PK **135.6** **Abbécourt** basin, moorings, boatyard, village 700m r/b
- PK **137.6** Pipeline crossing
- PK **138.0** **Chauny** municipal *halte* (Alfred Leroux) managed by association, 06 71 83 56 22, 12 visitor berths, night €8, water and electricity included, showers €2, crane 3.2 t, slipway, wifi, restaurant   *contact@portchauny.fr*
- PK **138.2** Chauny bridge, *connection with Canal de Saint-Quentin* quay d/s l/b, town centre 500m r/b

20. Canal de l'Oise à l'Aisne

THE CANAL DE L'OISE À L'AISNE, opened to navigation in 1890, forms an important link between the Canal latéral à l'Oise at Abbécourt basin (PK 3) and the Canal latéral à l'Aisne at Bourg-et-Comin (PK 38). This 48km junction canal still carries regular commercial traffic (up to 20 barges a day), but is also on one of the main routes used by boats heading south from Calais, Dunkerque or Belgium. Commercial traffic takes priority at the locks and at the tunnel. There are short aqueducts at each end of the canal, over the rivers Oise and Aisne. The summit level between the two valleys, at an altitude of 66m, includes a 2365m long tunnel at Braye-en-Laonnois. The tunnel's width at water level is 6.50m, and the free headroom at least 3.50m. All vessels proceed through the tunnel under their own power, respecting the lights at each entrance. There may be delays of up to one hour.

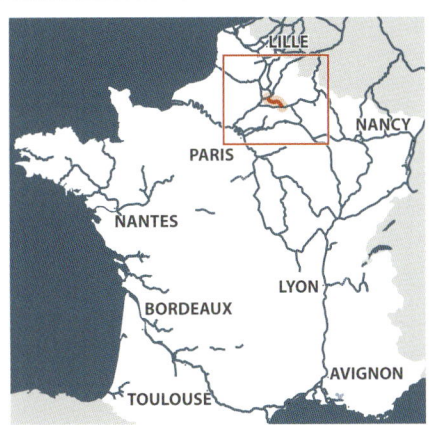

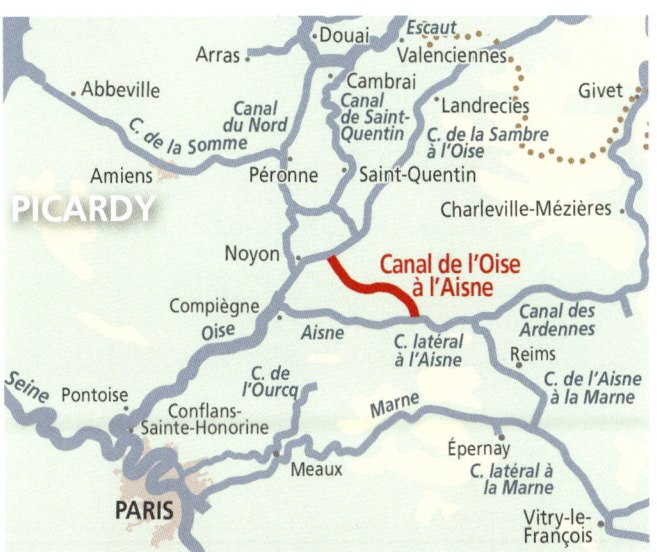

Part of the Freycinet plan, this link canal was one of the last to be built in France. It was opened in 1890, with locks 40.50m by 6m and a depth of 2.20m. These dimensions still apply today. The canal provides a short cut between Champagne and the Canal de Saint-Quentin, crossing the Oise on a fine aqueduct.

Navigation

The canal is very attractive, almost entirely rural, deep in the countryside away from towns and even villages. It ascends slowly to a plateau, then through the Braye-en-Laonnois tunnel, preceded by its imposing cutting. The canal descends quickly to Bourg-et-Comin.

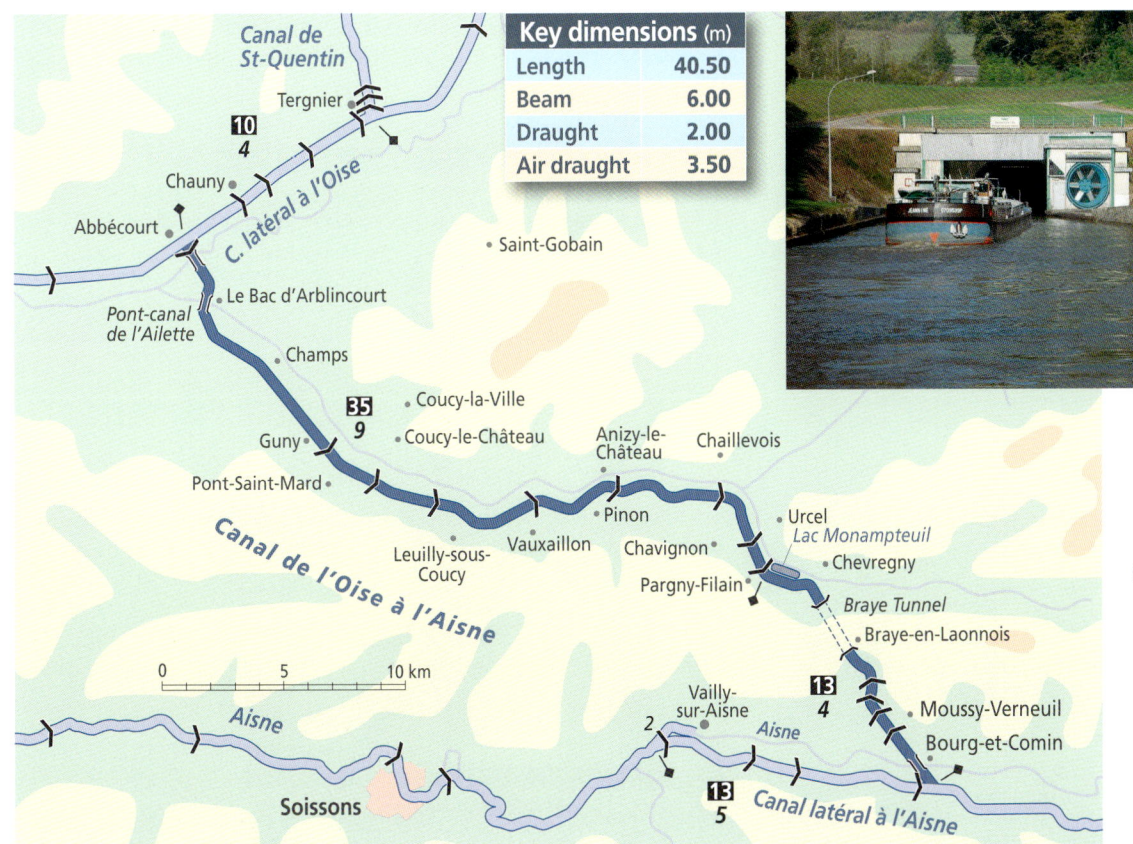

Key dimensions (m)	
Length	40.50
Beam	6.00
Draught	2.00
Air draught	3.50

Southern entrance to Braye-en-Laonnois tunnel, with its huge ventilator, and the tunnel-keeper's cabin
PK 41. © BINNENVAART IN BEELD

II – River Seine and routes north and east

Locks
There are 13 locks, of which 9 climb 24.96m from the Oise to the summit level, while 4 drop the 14.25m difference in level to the Aisne. They are of improved Freycinet dimensions, 40.50m by 6.00m.

Draught
The maximum authorised draught is 2.00m.

Headroom
The fixed bridges offer a headroom of not less than 3.50m.

Towpath
There is a good metalled towpath throughout.

Authority
VNF Bassin de la Seine, UTI Canaux de Picardie Champagne-Ardennes, 44 rue du Gouvernement, BP 616, 02321 Saint-Quentin Cedex, 03 23 05 78 00

Route description

PK	
PK 0.0	*Junction with Canal latéral à l'Oise* (PK 3), basin
PK 0.1	Bridge (Abbécourt)
PK 0.2	Lock 1 (Abbécourt)

This is the first of an easy sequence of nine locks ascending to Pargny-Filan.

PK	
PK 0.3	Oise aqueduct
PK 1.4	Bridge (Marizelle), quay u/s r/b
PK 2.8	Bridge (Bac)
PK 3.0	Ailette aqueduct
PK 3.4	Bridge (Manicamp)
PK 4.3	Bridge (Saint-Paul-aux-Bois), quay, turning basin d/s l/b
PK 7.7	**Champs** bridge, quay u/s l/b, small village 1200m r/b
PK 9.4	Bridge (Quincy)
PK 10.8	**Guny** bridge, quay d/s l/b, village 300m
PK 11.4	Bridge (Tempet)
PK 11.5	Lock 2 (Guny), water
PK 12.3	**Pont-Saint-Mard** bridge, quay and turning basin u/s l/b, village 1km
PK 14.1	Bridge (Crécy-au-Mont)
PK 14.2	Lock 3 (Crécy-au-Mont)
PK 16.0	Bridges (Béthancourt), D1 (two carriageways)
PK 16.1	Basin (Crécy-au-Mont), quay l/b, **Coucy-le-Château** 3km r/b
PK 17.1	Lock 4 (Leuilly)
PK 18.1	Bridge (Landricourt)
PK 19.3	Bridge (Courson), quay u/s l/b
PK 21.9	Railway bridge
PK 22.0	Lock 5 (Vauxaillon)
PK 22.4	**Vauxaillon** bridge, quay d/s l/b, village 2km
PK 24.4	Bridge (Locq)
PK 25.4	**Pinon** bridge, quay d/s and basin u/s l/b, village 1300m, **Anizy-le-Château** 500m r/b
PK 25.9	Railway bridge
PK 26.0	Lock 6 (Pinon), water
PK 31.0	Bridge
PK 31.1	Lock 7 (Chaillevois), quay u/s l/b
PK 33.2	Bridge (main road N2)
PK 33.4	**Chavignon** basin, quay l/b, village 1.5 km
PK 33.6	Bridge (D23)
PK 33.7	Lock 8 (Chavignon)
PK 34.9	Bridge (D15)
PK 35.0	Lock 9 (**Pargny-Filain**), municipal *halte* and turning basin u/s l/b, 03 23 21 68 59, night €7, water, electricity, beginning of summit level

Small village *halte* on pontoons, in a charming setting beside the Bassin de Monampteuil, a bathing and water sports lake, with a beach.

PK	
PK 37.8	**Chevregny** bridge, quay d/s r/b, village 1.5 km
PK 38.3	Braye tunnel, Oise portal

The tunnel is lluminated, ventilated and controlled by lights.

PK	
PK 40.7	Braye tunnel, Aisne portal
PK 40.9	**Braye-en-Laonnois** bridge, village 500m l/b
PK 41.4	Bridge (Épinettes)
PK 41.9	Bridge (Mont-Saint-Aubeu), quay d/s r/b
PK 42.6	Lock 10 (Moulin Brûlé), end of summit level
PK 43.3	Lock 11 (Metz)
PK 43.4	Bridge
PK 43.6	Quay (Moussy-Soupir) r/b
PK 43.9	Lock 12 (Moussy-Soupir)
PK 44.0	Bridge
PK 44.8	Lock 13 (Verneuil-Courtonne)
PK 45.4	Bridge (Verneuil)
PK 46.3	Bridge (Bourg, 9)
PK 46.7	Bridge (Bourg, 10)
PK 47.2	Aisne aqueduct
PK 47.5	**Bourg-et-Comin** bridge (11), quay d/s r/b, village 700m l/b

The location is close to the Chemin des Dames ridge where there were 430 000 French and German casualties (dead, wounded, unknown) during the second Battle of the Aisne in 1917

PK	
PK 47.8	*Junction with Canal latéral à l'Aisne* (PK 38)

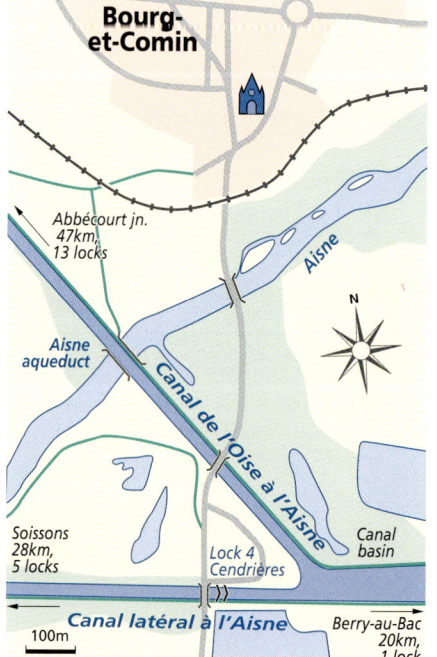

21. River Aisne and Canal latéral à l'Aisne

THE CANALISED RIVER AISNE EXTENDS 57km from the confluence with the Oise at Bouche d'Aisne, a short distance upstream of Compiègne, to the entrance to the Canal latéral à l'Aisne at Celles, 15km east of the historic town of Soissons. The route east continues on the Canal latéral à l'Aisne, connecting with the Canal des Ardennes at Vieux-lès-Asfeld, a distance of 51km. The total length is 108km. The lateral canal also connects with the Canal de l'Aisne à la Marne at Berry-au-Bac and with the Canal de l'Oise à l'Aisne at Bourg-et-Comin. This makes it an important hub in the waterway network, carrying both north-south and east-west traffic.

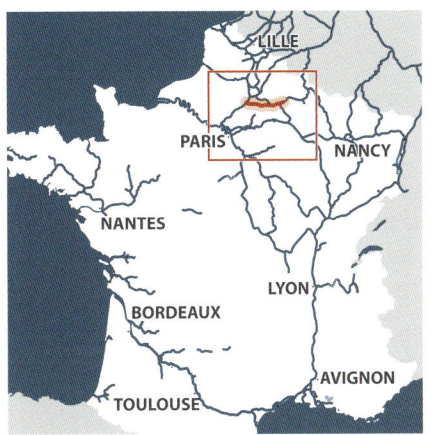

The river Aisne was a commercial navigation as early as the Gallo-Roman period, and the river was navigated by rafts from a long distance above the present limit of navigation at Vailly-sur-Aisne until the mid-19th century. The large-scale canalisation works were begun in 1836, at the same time as construction of the lateral canal. The canal was completed first in 1841, then two years later the river navigation. Commercial traffic in péniches carrying 220 tonnes is still several hundred thousand tonnes per year. Recreational traffic is mainly private boats. For many years there was discussion of the possibility of upgrading the river to high-capacity European standards, to serve the port of Reims or even as the first stage of a Seine-Moselle waterway.

Navigation
The river Aisne and the canal are well-maintained waterways, used by Freycinet barges with their 220-tonne loads. Well worth visiting on this route are the World War I armistice clearing at Rethondes, the historic town of Soissons and the 'canal junction' villages of Bourg-et-Comin and Berry-au-Bac. Boaters should be wary of encounters with laden barges in blind bends, bridge holes, junctions and during poor weather.

Locks
There are 7 locks on the river Aisne and 8 on the lateral canal. The locks on the river have dimensions larger than the Freycinet standard: 46m by 7.95m. Those on the lateral canal are the standard 38.90m by 5.20m. Celles is a

Key dimensions (m)	
Length	38.50
Beam	5.05
Draught	2.00
Air draught	3.50

double staircase lock. Locks are numbered 1 to 15, working downstream. The eight on the lateral canal are all equipped for automatic operation.

Draught
The maximum authorised draught is 2.00m at normal water level.

Headroom
On the river, all fixed bridges leave a clear headroom of 4.70m above normal water levels, reduced to 3.70m above the highest navigable water level. Bridges on the canal offer a clear headroom of 3.50m.

Towpath
There is a towpath throughout.

Authority
VNF Bassin de la Seine
UTI Seine-Nord Compiègne, 2 boulevard Gambetta, BP 20053, 60321 Compiègne cedex,
03 44 92 27 00, email *uti.seinenord@vnf.fr*

Route description

PK 108.3	**Confluence with Oise** (PK 38.3)
PK 106.7	Bridge (D66 Choisy by-pass)
PK 105.8	**Choisy-au-Bac** bridge, quay 50m long d/s r/b, village 200m
PK 104.9	Lock 15 (Carandeau) in short lock-cut l/b, VHF 18, water
PK 102.9	Bridge (Francport), quay d/s l/b, Armistice clearing and memorial 700m l/b
PK 99.4	**Rethondes** bridge, quay downstream l/b, village 300m r/b
PK 97.9	Lock 14 (Hérant) in lock-cut l/b, VHF 22, water
PK 93.6	**Berneuil-sur-Aisne** bridge, quay l/b, village 800m r/b
PK 92.2	Lock 13 (Couloisy) in lock-cut l/b, VHF 18, water
PK 90.6	**Attichy** bridge, quay d/s r/b, water, village 500m r/b
PK 89.0	**Jaulzy** l/b
PK 86.1	Quays l/b
PK 85.7	Lock 12 (Vic-sur-Aisne) in short lock-cut l/b, water, bridge
PK 85.4	**Vic-sur-Aisne** bridge, silo, municipal *halte* u/s r/b, 4 visitor berths, free for up to 48 hours, water and electricity free (in season only), showers, slipway, village r/b
PK 80.4	**Fontenoy** bridge, quay d/s l/b, village 1300m r/b
PK 78.6	Lock 11 (Fontenoy) in short lock-cut l/b, footbridge, water
PK 77.5	Quay (Osly-Courtil) r/b, commercial barges only
PK 75.5	Island, navigation in l/b arm
PK 75.0	Quay (Pernant) l/b, commercial barges only
PK 72.7	**Pommiers** bridge, quay d/s r/b, village 400m r/b
PK 69.7	Bridge (Pasly)
PK 68.3	Footbridge (Passerelle de Cuffies), pedestrian and cycle path
PK 68.2	Lock 10 (Vauxrot) in short lock-cut l/b, water
PK 67.9	Navigation re-enters river
PK 67.0	Bridge (Pont du Mail), public quay with services r/b, private quays l/b
PK 66.8	**Soissons** municipal *halte* r/b, 03 23 53 17 37, 8 berths on quay 200m long, free (up to 48 hours), town centre 400m l/b over bridge, water, electricity, showers €2, slipway
PK 66.6	Footbridge (Passerelle des Anglais)
PK 66.4	Bridge (Pont Gambetta)
PK 65.0	Railway bridge, private quays downstream l/b
PK 64.2	Entrance to lock-cut l/b, river navigable upstream 1.5 km to private quay r/b (Bucy arm)
PK 64.1	Lock 9 (Villeneuve-Saint-Germain), bridge, water
PK 63.5	End of lock-cut, navigation re-enters river
PK 62.9	Bridge (N2 Soissons bypass)
PK 61.1	Sand loading quay r/b
PK 59.1	**Vénizel** bridge, quay u/s r/b, village 300m l/b

A laden péniche *passes the delicately-shaded silos at Vénizel,* PK 59.
© JEAN PERRET

PK 58.0	Footbridge, paper mill quay l/b, mooring, water
PK 55.0	**Missy-sur-Aisne** bridge, quay d/s r/b, village 700m r/b
PK 52.8	Confluence of Vesle l/b
PK 52.0	**Condé-sur-Aisne** bridge, quay d/s l/b, village 500m r/b
PK 51.3	**Connection with Canal latéral à l'Aisne** (downstream of Celles double staircase lock)

The river Aisne is navigable 2km upstream from this point to the village of Vailly-sur-Aisne for boats with a maximum draught of 1m. This is a free municipal *halte*, with water, electricity, a slipway and services in the village: a worthwhile excursion for smaller craft.

Canal latéral à l'Aisne

- PK **51.3** *Entrance to canal from canalised river Aisne*, r/b
- PK **51.2** Double staircase lock 7/8 (Celles), bridge
- PK **49.9** Bridge (Chassemy)
- PK **48.9** **Vailly-sur-Aisne** bridge, pontoon mooring u/s l/b, small town 800m r/b
- PK **48.5** Downstream end of Vailly basin
- PK **48.2** Private quays l/b
- PK **47.4** Upstream end of Vailly basin
- PK **46.7** Lock 6 (Saint-Audebert), bridge, water
- PK **45.3** Presles-et-Boves bridge, village 200m l/b
- PK **44.5** Lock 5 (Cys-la-Commune), bridge, water
- PK **43.6** Bridge (Saint-Mard)
- PK **40.5** **Pont-Arcy** bridge, small village 300m r/b
- PK **38.5** Lock 4 (Cendrière), bridge, water, quay d/s l/b
- PK **38.4** **Bourg-et-Comin** municipal *halte* r/b, pontoon mooring for 3 boats, water, electricity, maximum 48 hours, village 800m r/b
- PK **38.3** *Junction with Canal de l'Oise à l'Aisne*, r/b
- PK **37.9** Bourg-et-Comin basin (500m long)

The basin at Berry-au-Bac viewed from the lock, PK 18. © GSV

- PK **18.7** Feeder enters r/b
- PK **18.5** Lock 3 (**Berry-au-Bac**), bridge, water, village 600m r/b
- PK **18.3** *Junction with Canal de l'Aisne à la Marne*, l/b
- PK **17.7** Upstream end of Berry-au-Bac basin, quays l/b, limited services

Good mooring to banks, but often windy.

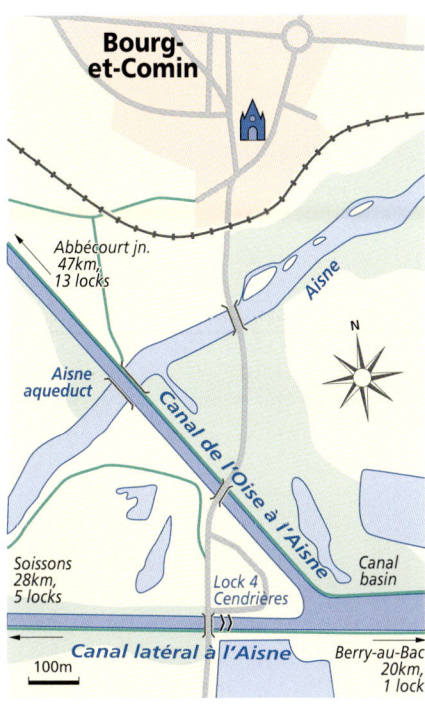

- PK **37.5** Bridge (Bourg)
- PK **36.7** Bridge (Moulin de Villers)
- PK **35.9** **Villers-en-Prayères** bridge, private quays u/s, village 1km l/b, Œuilly 1km r/b
- PK **34.5** Bridge (Aventure)
- PK **32.7** Bridge (Maizy)
- PK **32.1** **Maizy** *halte* l/b managed by VNF, 2 moorings (using own stakes), free, water, village and restaurant l/b
- PK **29.4** Accommodation bridge for farms
- PK **28.1** **Concevreux** bridge, quay u/s r/b, village l/b
- PK **25.8** Bridge (Canards)
- PK **24.6** Pontavert bridge, quay d/s r/b, village 700m r/b
- PK **23.4** Bridge (Cauries)
- PK **21.0** **Gernicourt** bridge, small village 400m l/b
- PK **19.0** Berry-au-Bac basin r/b
- PK **15.7** Bridge (A26 Autoroute des Anglais)
- PK **15.5** Bridge
- PK **13.9** Lock 2 (**Condé-sur-Suippe**), bridge, water, aqueduct u/s, village l/b, basin u/s for 300m
- PK **12.9** **Guignicourt** bridge, silo and loading quay u/s l/b, village 1km r/b
- PK **12.7** Railway bridge
- PK **11.8** Sand loading quay l/b
- PK **10.5** **Variscourt** bridge, quay and small village d/s l/b, mooring for 4 boats, water
- PK **7.2** **Pignicourt** quay, small village l/b
- PK **6.9** Lock 1 (Pignicourt), water, bridge
- PK **5.5** **Neufchâtel-sur-Aisne** bridge, quay u/s l/b, village 500m r/b
- PK **4.2** Quay (Évergnicourt) r/b
- PK **2.9** Bridge
- PK **0.0** *Junction with Canal des Ardennes* (d/s of Vieux-lès-Asfeld)

II – River Seine and routes north and east

22. Canal de l'Aisne à la Marne

THE CANAL DE L'AISNE À LA MARNE joins the Canal latéral à l'Aisne at Berry-au-Bac to the Canal latéral à la Marne at Condé-sur-Marne, a distance of 58km. The canal rises 40m through the cathedral city of Reims to a summit level at an altitude of 95.70m, including a tunnel 2302m long at Mont-de-Billy, and then drops down 23.80m towards the Marne. The maximum authorised dimensions for vessels passing through the tunnel are: draught 2.20m, beam 5.00m and air draught 3.70m. The towage service which used to operate in the tunnel was abandoned in the 1970s when the tunnel's ventilation system was installed.

*Hugues Cosnier, who designed the Canal de Briare, built the first canal between Reims and Sillery in the early 17th century. This was part of a grand plan to build canals by-passing Paris to the east. Work on this link followed those on the Aisne lateral, starting in 1841. The canal was opened in 1866. It was later planned to emulate Cosnier's idea of an orbital route from the Loire through to northern France. Only the north-south route was finally built, comprising this link and the Canal de l'Oise à l'Aisne. The route is still used by about 10 **péniches** per day, with grain as the principal traffic, while recreational traffic is mainly private boats in transit.*

Navigation
The canal is well-maintained and used by Freycinet barges loading and unloading in the port of Reims. The landscape is not outstanding, but Reims itself is a notable event, while Sillery is an attractive mooring place, followed by the impressive Mont-de-Billy tunnel shortly before Condé-sur-Marne. Boats proceed through the tunnel respecting the lights controlling the one-way traffic. The boat moorings in Reims are convenient but noisy.

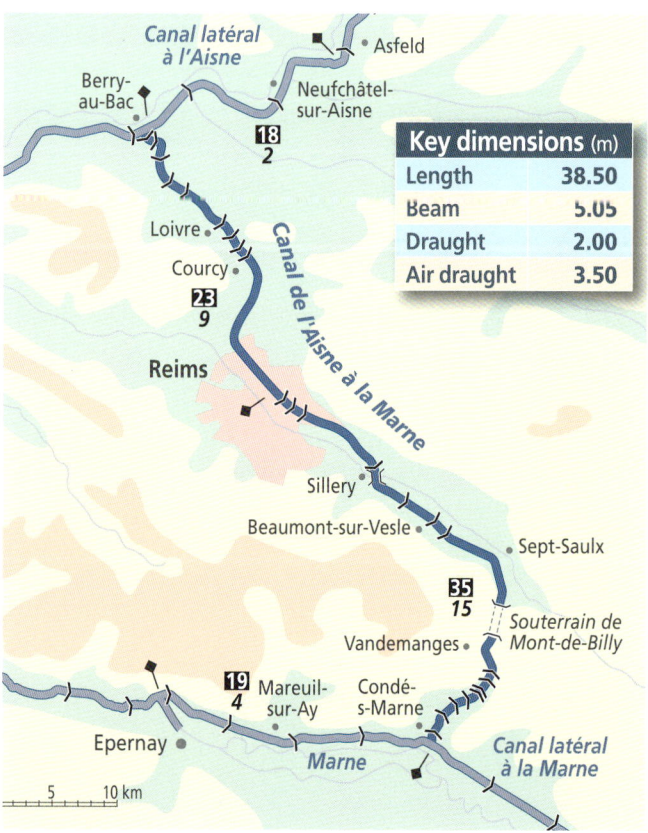

Key dimensions (m)	
Length	38.50
Beam	5.05
Draught	2.00
Air draught	3.50

Locks
There are 24 locks, 16 rising from the Aisne to the Mont-de-Billy summit, and 8 falling towards the Marne. All have effective dimensions of 38.50m by 5.20m, and are equipped for automatic operation. Control centres are at locks 1, 6, 10, at the Marne end of the tunnel and lock 24. At the approach to each unmanned lock at the start of a sequence, a suspended pole is to be manoeuvred (see *Introduction*). Locks 13 to 16 are operated independently.

Draught
The maximum authorised draught is 2.00m.

Headroom
The maximum authorised air draught is 3.50m.

Towpath
There is a good towpath throughout, except in the tunnel, where the rails of the old electric 'mules' are still in place, and access is forbidden to the public.

Canal de l'Aisne à la Marne

Authority
VNF Bassin de la Seine, UTI Seine-Nord – Chemin du Barrage, BP 30256, 51011 Châlons-en-Champagne 03 26 03 90 28

Route description

PK	
PK 0.0	*Junction with Canal latéral à l'Aisne* (Berry-au-Bac basin, PK 18.3), caution, basin often windy
PK 0.1	Lock 1 (Berry-au-Bac), start of regulated flight, bridge, quay u/s l/b
PK 1.2	Lock 2 (Moulin de Sapigneul)
PK 2.3	Lock 3 (Sapigneul), Côte 108 monument l/b
PK 3.8	Bridge (Neuville), quay u/s l/b, water, turning basin, Cormicy 2 km l/b
PK 4.7	Lock 4 (Alger)
PK 5.4	Le Gaudart, sugar beet loading quay l/b
PK 5.9	Lock 5 (Gaudart)
PK 6.8	Motorway bridge (A26)
PK 9.4	Lock 6 (Loivre), bridge, water, end of first regulated flight, moorings d/s l/b, village l/b
PK 10.1	Lock 7 (Fontaine), bridge, start of second regulated flight
PK 11.2	Lock 8 (Noue-Gouzaine)
PK 12.0	Lock 9 (Courcy), bridge, end of regulated flight
PK 12.5	Courcy bridge (Brimont), quay u/s l/b, water, moorings in turning basin, village 800m l/b
PK 14.5	Bridge (Bétheny)
PK 15.5	Quay l/b
PK 17.5	**La Neuvillette** bridge (D944), basin and quay d/s l/b, no services, centre r/b (suburb of Reims)
PK 18.6	Bridge (Reims ring road), shopping centre r/b
PK 18.8	Bridge (Saint-Thierry), commercial quay u/s r/b, canal silted l/b
PK 20.3	Bridge (Courcelles)
PK 20.4	Entrance to Reims basin (Port Colbert) r/b, 700m

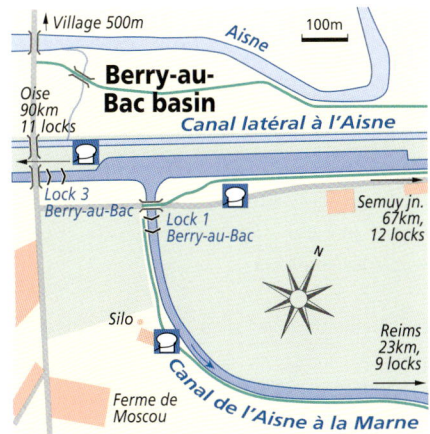

The decor is inviting enough, but in practice Reims is not a peaceful mooring. The football stadium on the other side of the canal generates noise on match evenings. © VILLE DE REIMS

The covered commercial port of Reims is still ready to handle péniche loads, especially grain

PK	
PK 21.0	Bridge (Saint-Brice), quay d/s r/b, quays u/s
PK 21.7	Footbridge (Saint-Charles)
PK 22.3	Skew railway bridge
PK 22.5	Railway bridge and footbridge (Bienfait)
PK 22.6	Bridge (Maréchaux)
PK 22.7	Congress hall r/b

II – River Seine and routes north and east

PK 22.9 Bridge (Pont de Vesle) over narrow section, tramway lines 1A, 1B
PK 23.3 Bridge (Pont de Gaulle)
PK 23.4 **Reims** basin (Vieux Port), *port de plaisance* u/s r/b, 03 26 88 55 36, pontoons and quays for vessels up to 38m, 16 berths, night €15, 3 nights €33, 5 nights €50, water, electricity, restaurant on barge, slipway, city centre 500m r/b *accueil@reims-tourisme.com*

Reims cathedral is spectacular and the city offers all imaginable facilities, but the *port de plaisance* can be very noisy.

PK 23.9 Bridge (Venise), good mooring to grassy bank u/s r/b, l/b heavily silted
PK 24.4 Lock 10 (Fléchambault), bridge, start of regulated flight, water, private quays u/s r/b
PK 25.2 Lock 11 (Château d'Eau), road bridge, private quays u/s r/b
PK 25.3 Bridge (Rouillat)
PK 25.8 Lock 12 (Huon), bridge, start of regulated flight, private quays u/s, emergency use only
PK 27.2 Bridge (Reims ring road)
PK 27.5 Bridge (Vrilly), industrial quays u/s r/b
PK 29.3 **Saint-Léonard** bridge, quay l/b, restaurant
PK 32.0 Bridge (Couraux)
PK 33.4 Lock 13 (Sillery), Vesle aqueduct u/s, quay d/s r/b
PK 33.6 **Sillery** bridge, *port de plaisance* in basin u/s managed by Reims, 03 26 07 57 24, 20 berths, night €15, 3 nights €33, 5 nights €50, water, electricity, showers €2, slipway €10, village 400m l/b *accueil@reims-tourisme.com*

Sillery is a port and village that gets excellent reviews, and is a good alternative to Reims. The facility is managed by Reims Tourisme.

PK 34.0 Bridge (Sillery)
PK 34.6 Bridge (Moulin de Sillery)
PK 34.8 Footbridge, pipeline crossing (sugar mill), quay u/s l/b
PK 35.4 Skew road bridge (D944, Sillery bypass)
PK 35.6 Lock 14 (Espérance), bridge
PK 36.5 Bridge (Prunay)

PK 38.4 Lock 15 (**Beaumont-sur-Vesle**), bridge, turning basin and quay u/s l/b, village 200m l/b
PK 39.5 Lock 16 (Wez), bridge, beginning of summit level
PK 40.6 **Courmelois** bridge, basin u/s, village 300m r/b
PK 43.3 **Sept-Saulx** bridge, basin d/s, no services, village 300m r/b
PK 44.4 Bridge (Issus)
PK 46.5 Northern entrance to Mont de Billy tunnel
PK 48.8 Southern entrance to Mont de Billy tunnel
PK 50.3 Bridge (Vaudemanges)
PK 50.9 **Vaudemanges** basin, quay l/b, slipway, village 800m r/b (over bridge)
PK 51.4 Lock 17 (Vaudemanges), bridge, end of summit level, start of regulated flight
PK 52.0 Lock 18 (Champ Bon-Garçon)
PK 52.5 Lock 19 (Longues-Raies)
PK 53.2 Lock 20 (Saint-Martin), bridge
PK 53.9 Lock 21 (Fosse-Rodé)
PK 54.1 Bridge
PK 54.6 Lock 22 (Isse)
PK 54.8 **Isse** bridge, small village 100m r/b
PK 55.9 Lock 23 (Coupé)
PK 57.7 Lock 24 (Condé-sur-Marne), bridge, water, end of flight
PK 57.9 **Condé-sur-Marne** basin, *halte* on quay r/b (managed by the *capitainerie* at Châlons-en-Champagne), 06 99 92 31 41, moorings for 12 boats, night €7, water, electricity, village r/b
PK 58.1 *Junction with Canal latéral à la Marne* (PK 48)

The port of Sillery, in its wide basin, is a favourite mooring on the canal.

Canal de l'Aisne à la Marne

The canal makes an impressive junction with the Canal latéral à la Marne at Condé-sur-Marne, where this drone view shows the convenient halte for the village, as well as the pumping station built in 1875 to supply the summit level with water from the river Marne.
© CLAUDE PARIS

CHAPTER III – CENTRAL FRANCE

Routes from Paris and Champagne through Burgundy to the river Saône

Leaving Paris, the *plaisancier* enters the 'core network' of French waterways, with three main routes up and over the Atlantic-Mediterranean watershed, as shown on the map below. For many, following in the footsteps of the founder of French waterway tourism Peter Zivy, or pioneer hotel barge operators Richard Parsons and John Liley, the central French canal system is the ultimate destination, ideal for a lifetime of cruising experiences and immersion in French culture, traditions and gastronomy. The author has always felt the same about the region, which includes one of his favourite waterways since his first visit in 1969 – the Canal du Nivernais. Time should be allowed to fully explore this 1600km network of navigable rivers and canals, to soak up and enjoy the best of rural France, and many delightful small and medium-sized towns, as well as the Burgundy region capital of Dijon, before heading on south on the Grande-Saône (covered in Chapter V Southeast France).

Including the whole of the 'Champagne' route means starting this region in Paris, where the left turn into the river Marne is just 5km upstream from the Paris-Arsenal *port de plaisance*. This route uses the Canal entre Champagne et Bourgogne, given this new name in the 1990s in an effort to increase its appeal, but it still sees nothing like the traffic it deserves... and needs, to help combat weed growth, which is now a menace on all little-used waterways.

The other itineraries follow the upper river Seine (also called the Petite Seine or Seine Amont) to the confluence towns of Saint-Mammès and Montereau respectively.

The Canal du Nivernais crosses from the Burgundy to the Bourbonnais route, also offering the shortest possible circular cruise in the region. At least four weeks should be allowed to complete this circuit, including time for visits. The excursion to Roanne can be recommended.

The Canal d'Orléans is sadly not available to private boats.

The Cher and Canal du Berry are included for reference, but are isolated from the main network.

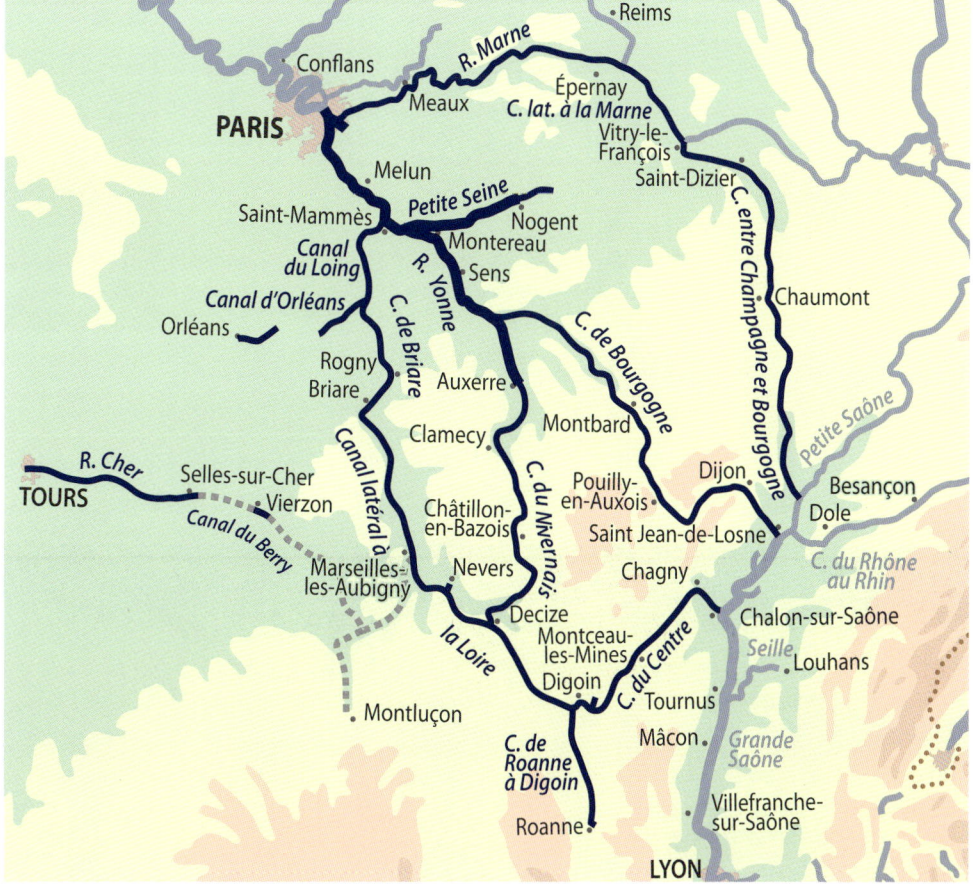

The hilltop medieval château of Châteauneuf-en-Auxois on the Canal de Bourgogne south of the summit level at Pouilly
© JOHN RIDDEL

III – Central France – routes to the Saône

23. Upper Seine

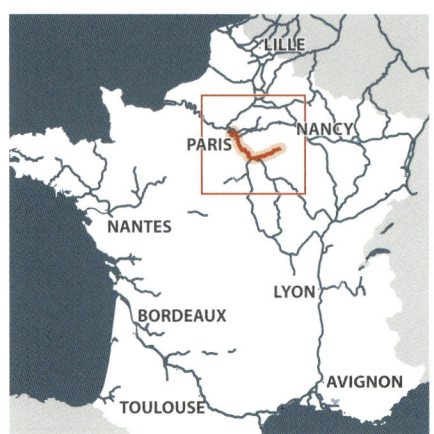

The upper seine officially starts at the Pont de la Tournelle, in the middle of the Île Saint-Louis in Paris, and is navigable for a total distance of 169 km up to the small town of Marcilly-sur-Seine (and the junction with the disused Canal de la Haute-Seine). Up to Nogent-sur-Seine (PK 20), it is a major transport artery, navigated by a substantial fleet of high-capacity barges, as well as the ubiquitous 38.50m *péniches*. The last section from Nogent to Marcilly, although a 'Freycinet' waterway, has long been abandoned by commercial traffic and sees very few boats.

The river winds gently and majestically through very attractive countryside, with many fascinating towns, villages and sites to discover, including the château at Fontainebleau. Cruise ships and hotel barges will be encountered. For the Seine from Le Havre to Pais, see under Lower Seine (Seine *Aval*).

The French conventional naming of the Upper Seine can be confusing. 'Upper' Seine corresponds to Seine *Amont*, which is a simplification, contrasting neatly with Lower Seine or Seine *Aval*. Historically the river has been called 'Haute Seine' from Paris to Montereau, then 'Petite Seine' over the last 68km to Marcilly. It is used by barges carrying 1000-tonne loads from the busy grain terminal at Nogent. This section, 29km long, is now to be upgraded to the European Class Va standards, for 2500 tonne barges, as part of the overall Seine-Scheldt project part funded by the European Union. This includes 10 km of new canal.

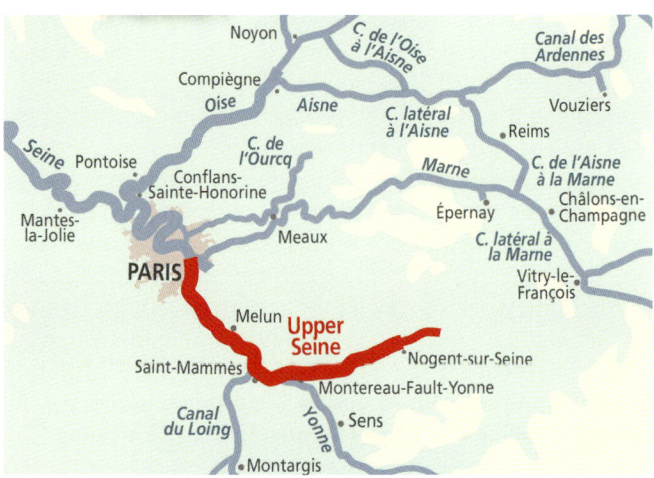

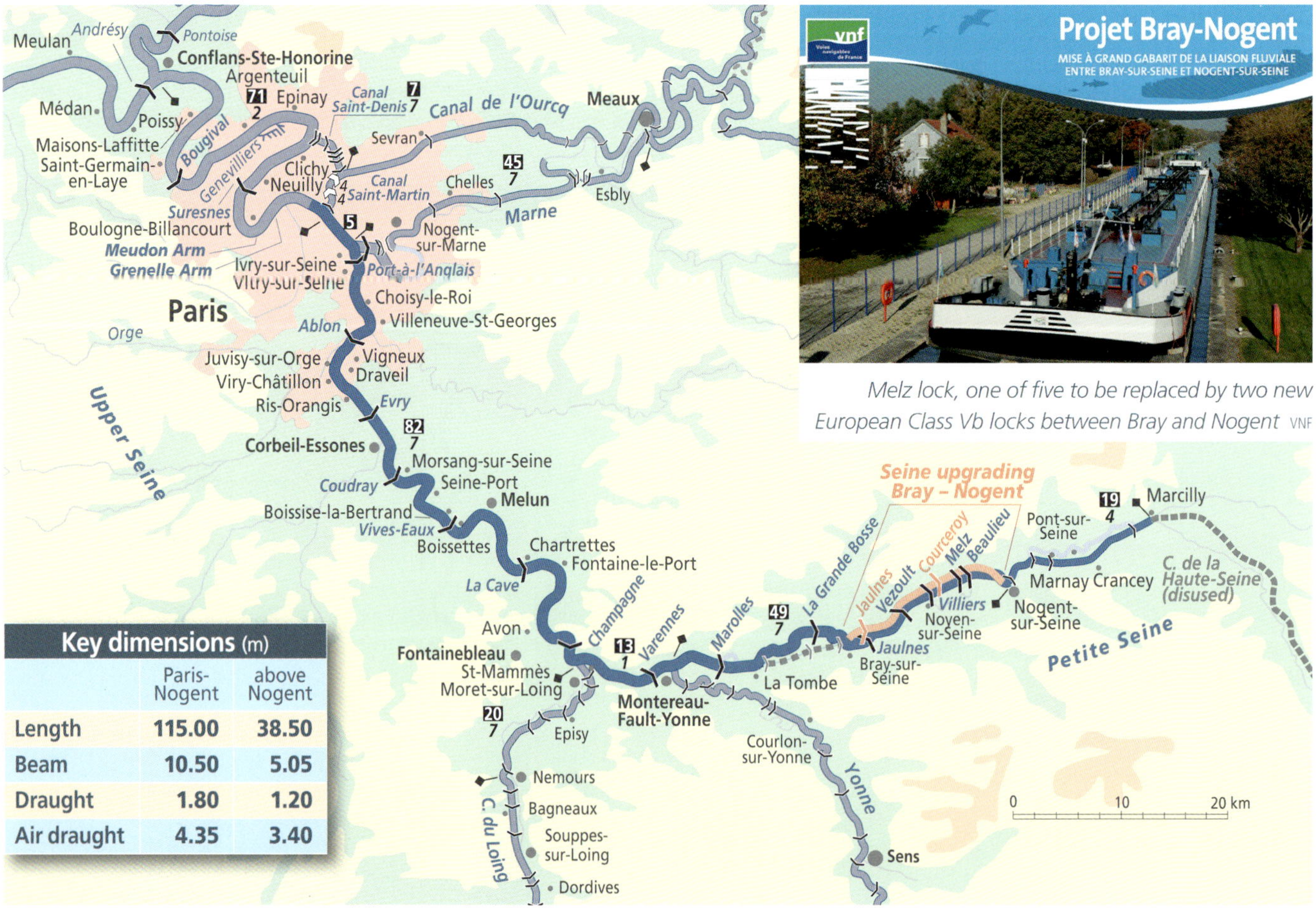

Melz lock, one of five to be replaced by two new European Class Vb locks between Bray and Nogent VNF

Key dimensions (m)	Paris-Nogent	above Nogent
Length	115.00	38.50
Beam	10.50	5.05
Draught	1.80	1.20
Air draught	4.35	3.40

122

Upper Seine

Connections are made with the Canal Saint-Martin (one of the Canaux de Paris) in Paris itself at PK 168, then with the canalised river Marne at Charenton (PK 163).

At Saint-Mammès (PK 81), the Seine connects with the important Bourbonnais route to the south, of which the first link is the Canal du Loing.

At Montereau (PK 68), the 'Haute' Seine becomes the 'Petite' Seine, and is joined by the canalised river Yonne on the left bank, forming part of the Burgundy route from Paris to the south of France.

The construction of weirs and locks on the Upper Seine followed logically after the works on the river up to Paris, using Poirée's movable weir technology, or that of Chanoine, with collapsing gates. Before then, the winding navigable channel of the Seine above Paris had a depth of under 0.90m for a third of the year, the banks were unprotected against floods and the towpaths were in poor shape. The Upper Seine was thus canalised between 1848 and 1899, with 13 locks (51.2 by 8.6m) and five canal sections in the Montereau-Marcilly section. This section was given the separate name of 'Petite Seine'. The navigation was extended in 1851 by the Canal de la Haute-Seine, 44km with 15 locks up the valley to Troyes. The Seine locks were improved and bigger chambers added in stages in the period 1912-1939. A new phase of improvements began after barge traffic restarted in 1944. The number of locks from Paris to Montereau was reduced to eight, and all now accommodate the biggest Rhine barges and 5000 tonne push-tows, 185m by 12m. The two new locks on the upgraded section from Montereau (Bray) to Nogent, to be built in the coming years as part of a major new investment by VNF, will be European Class Va, or 115m by 12.50m.

Despite the volume of commercial traffic, the Seine above Paris remains largely unspoilt and offers some of the most picturesque river scenery in France.

The limit between the Upper and Lower Seine is given as the Pont de la Tournelle, on the left bank arm of the Seine past the Île Saint-Louis, rather than the Pont Marie (the official zero point for the lower Seine) on the right bank arm, since navigation is obliged to follow the left bank arm. This is of little importance, however, since the two bridges are level with each other on either side of the island.

Navigation
Heading upstream beyond the Paris Arsenal *port de plaisance* one encounters a wide river busy with commercial traffic.

Locks
There are 19 locks on the Upper Seine above Paris, of which 8 in the section up to the Yonne confluence at Montereau (a difference in level of 20m), the other 11 on the 'dead-end' branch up to Nogent (a difference in level of 21m). In the first section all except Varennes have two chambers side by side, one on each side of the weir. All the weirs are of recent construction with movable gates, and when a certain flood stage is reached one of the gates is lowered to provide a navigable passage. The locks are electrically-operated and controlled by lights (lock staff now rarely give instructions over the loudspeakers). The seven locks on the 'Petite-Seine' from Montereau to Nogent will be whittled down to four in a few years, as two new locks 115m by 12.50m (European Class Va) are built above the first two, Marolles and La Grande Bosse, which were built in the 1970s to larger dimensions, 185m by 12m. The two new locks are at Jaulnes and Courceroy. The final four locks above Nogent are 38m long and 7.80m wide, although limited to barges of 5.05m beam.

Draught
The maximum authorised draught is 2.80m from Paris to Montereau, 2.20m from Montereau (PK 67) to Nogent bridge (PK 20), and 1.20m in the final section to Marcilly. However, until completion of the upgrading and new locks from Bray to Nogent the draught in this section is limited to 1.80m.

Headroom
The following table gives the minimum headroom offered by the fixed bridges in the successive sections:

	Normal water level	Highest navigable water level
Paris to La Grande Bosse	5.50	3.60
La Grande Bosse to Nogent	4.35	3.40
– after upgrading Class V	6.00	5.50
Nogent to Marcilly	3.40	2.80

Towpath
There is no towpath along the Seine.

Authority
VNF Bassin de la Seine
UTI Boucles de la Seine
– quai de la Tournelle, 75005 Paris 01 44 41 16 80 (PK 169-165)
– Avenue Pierre Mendès-France, 94340 Joinville-le-Pont 01 45 11 71 80 (PK 165-150)
– 26 quai Hippolyte Rossignol, 77000 Melun 01 64 83 50 00 (PK 150-68)
– Écluse du Pont Vert, B.P. 50, 10401 Nogent-sur-Seine 03 25 39 86 48

Working the locks, one has to be prepared to get lines – and hands – dirty. A characteristically slimey lock wall bollard. © F-W

III – Central France and routes to the Saône

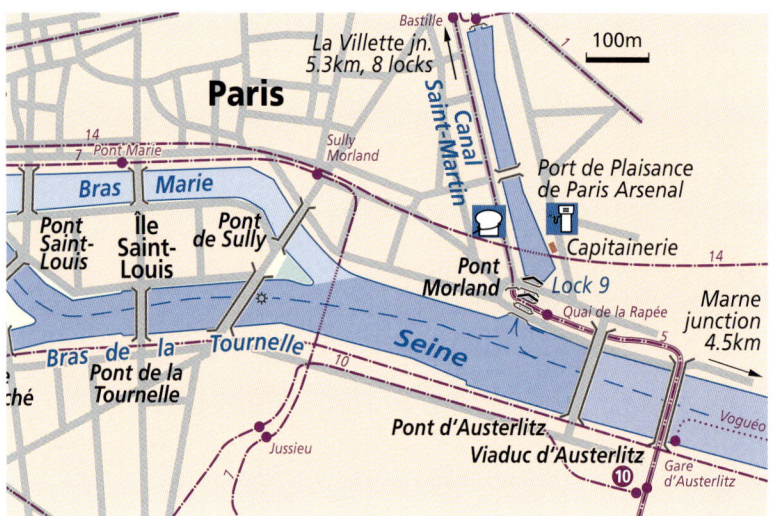

The Chinagora Hotel at the confluence of the Marne (left) and Seine (right)

Route description

For the first 500m navigation is in the Bras de la Tournelle, while the Bras Marie on the other side of the Île Saint-Louis is forbidden to recreational craft.

PK **169.1** Bridge (Pont de la Tournelle)
PK **168.7** Bridge (Pont de Sully)
PK **168.6** U/s tip of Île Saint-Louis, Bras Marie r/b forbidden

A slightly incongruous 19th century brick waterway engineer's office stands here on the left bank of the river, contrasting with the surrounding architecture.

PK **168.2** **Entrance to Canal Saint-Martin**, r/b, to enter canal (for Arsenal marina) moor at pontoon u/s or call on VHF 9, *capitainerie* 01 43 41 39 32, 230 berths, maximum length 25m, night €31, fuel, water, electricity, showers, crane 7t, restaurant, **fayollemarine.fr**

Justly famed as 'the place to stay' (for a few days or the entire winter), the Arsenal basin lies just upstream from the Île Saint-Louis, between the river and the Place de la Bastille. It belongs to the Canaux de Paris, but information is reproduced here as it is so important for boaters on the Seine. At the southern, river, end access is via a lock (open 08:00 to 23:00). There is a waiting pontoon just upstream from the entrance with a telephone to call up the harbourmaster on VHF 9 or 01 43 41 39 32. Mooring up can be tricky (the pontoon is a little wobbly) when the river current is strong and the passing *péniche* and river bus traffic can be hectic. The port is well run and surprisingly safe and secure. It is, however, very popular and booking or phoning ahead is strongly advised. **fayollemarine.fr**

PK **168.0** Bridge (Pont d'Austerlitz)
PK **167.8** Métro viaduct (Viaduc d'Austerlitz), line 5
PK **167.7** Bridge (Pont Charles De Gaulle)
PK **167.0** Bridge (Pont de Bercy), Métro viaduct (line 6)
PK **166.5** Footbridge (Passerelle Simone de Beauvoir)

The elegant footbridge leads from the Bercy gardens to the national library – Bibliothèque François Mitterrand – with its four book-end towers, a handsome addition to the left bank skyline in the 1990s. Works continue today on complete redevelopment of this area of the 13th *arrondissement*.

PK **166.2** Bridge (Pont de Tolbiac)
PK **165.6** Bridge (Pont National) and railway bridge
PK **165.3** Motorway bridge (Boulevard Périphérique), u/s limit of city of Paris
PK **164.3** Bridge
PK **164.2** Bridge (Nelson Mandela)
PK **163.7** **Charenton** footbridge and pipeline crossing (passerelle d'Ivry-Charenton), quay u/s r/b
PK **163.6** Ivry power station unloading quay l/b
PK **163.5** **Confluence of Marne**, r/b

The confluence has the distinctive landmark of the Huatian Chinagora Hotel and restaurant. The four-star hotel had a reprieve a few years ago, after Alfortville council gave notice of expropriation for redevelopment of the site. The hotel's managers plan to project 'startling light' on to the rivers Seine and Marne, from a new 400 m² extension on the waterfront (photo above).

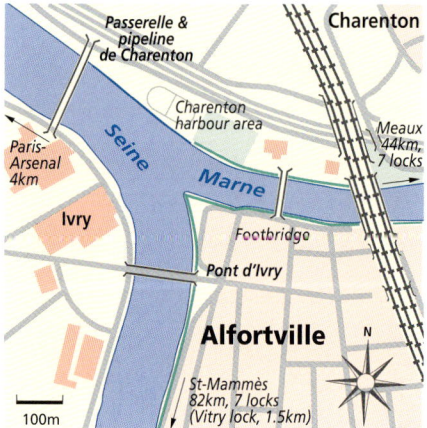

PK **163.3** **Ivry-sur-Seine** bridge
PK **162.3** Industrial quay r/b
PK **161.1** Lock 10 (Port-à-l'Anglais), chambers r/b and l/b, VHF 18, weir
PK **161.0** **Vitry-sur-Seine** suspension bridge
PK **159.9** **Alfortville** industrial quay r/b
PK **159.3** Footbridge and pipeline crossing
PK **158.8** Basin r/b (power station)
PK **158.6** Skew motorway bridge (A86)
PK **157.5** **Choisy-le-Roi** bridge, quay u/s l/b
PK **155.6** Railway bridge

124

Upper Seine

Port à l'Anglais lock on the Seine, downstream of the suspension bridge at Vitry-sur-Seine, PK 161. © PASCAL LEMAÎTRE/VNF

PK **154.6 Villeneuve-Saint-Georges** *port de plaisance* (Amicale des Navigateurs de Villeneuve Triage) r/b, 06 14 69 96 03, 50 berths, 5 visitor moorings, first night free, water and electricity charged, shower, slipway (2t), repairs

PK **152.4** Bridge (Villeneuve-Saint-Georges), town centre r/b

PK **150.0** Lock 9 (Ablon), chambers r/b and l/b, VHF 22, weir

PK **148.9** Confluence of Orge, l/b

PK **148.0** Railway bridge (Athis-Mons), industrial quays d/s l/b

PK **147.8 Vigneux** boat harbour (Port Premier Paris Sud) along public park r/b, 01 69 40 14 35, 40 berths, no overnight mooring, water, electricity, shower, pump-out

PK **146.4 Draveil** *port de plaisance* 'Port aux Cerises' in basin r/b, 106 berths (up to 24m), 01 69 83 46 60, night €25, water and electricity included (second night half price), shower, pump-out, slipway, restaurants *portauxcerises.fr*

PK **146.0 Juvisy-sur-Orge** bridge, town l/b, industrial quays d/s l/b

PK **145.0** Basin (Port Longuet) l/b

PK **144.3** Port of Viry-Châtillon, l/b, boat harbour r/b

PK **142.9** Port-aux-Malades boat Harbour, r/b

PK **141.8 Ris-Orangis** bridge, town 1 km l/b

PK **138.7** Lock 8 (Evry), l/b, two chambers, VHF 18, weir

PK **137.7 Evry** bridge, quay, boat moorings u/s l/b, station 400m l/b

PK **137.4** D/s tip of island, navigation in l/b arm

PK **136.6** U/s tip of island, navigation in l/b arm

PK **136.5** Commercial port of Corbeil-Essonnes l/b

PK **136.0** Motorway bridge (*La Francilienne*, N104)

PK **134.7** Confluence of Essonne, l/b

PK **134.4 Corbeil-Essonnes** bridge, quay u/s l/b, town centre l/b

PK **131.4** Commercial quay (Bas-Vignons) l/b

PK **131.2 Saintry-sur-Seine** *port de plaisance* r/b, 20 berths, 01 60 75 49 34, *portsaintry.com*, petrol, no overnight mooring, water, electricity, crane 4t, slipway, repairs

PK **129.7** Lock 7 (Coudray), chambers r/b and l/b, weir between, VHF 22, water, pipeline crossing

PK **128.8 Morsang-sur-Seine** boatyard (Chantier Klein), 01 60 75 01 09

PK **126.1** Bridge (Ponthierry)

PK **125.5 Saint-Fargeau-Ponthierry** *port de plaisance* in basin l/b (Port Seine École Loisirs), 06 03 95 00 51, 72 berths, pontoon for visiting boats, night €24, water, electricity, pump-out, slipway

Alluvial forest hides the important town of Évry, while barges of various sizes pass each other on the river above Évry lock, PK 139. © NORBERTO CRUZ

PK **123.4 Seine-Port** boat harbour (Cercle de Voile) r/b, village and restaurant 500m r/b

PK **122.6** Former lock (Citanguette) l/b

PK **119.4** Bridge (Sainte-Assise)

PK **116.0 Boissise-la-Bertrand** quay and village r/b

PK **115.8** Lock 4 (Vives-Eaux), l/b, two chambers, VHF 18, weir

PK **112.9** Boat club l/b

PK **111.8 Boissettes** boat harbour (Port Saint-Jacques) in small basin r/b, 06 08 17 83 53, 35 berths, no guaranteed visitor moorings, water, electricity, showers, pump-out, slipway *portsaintjacques.free.fr*

PK **111.0** Railway bridge (Mée), public quay u/s r/b, factories l/b

PK **110.2** D/s tip of Melun island, navigation in l/b arm (r/b arm for boat harbour, see above)

PK **110.0** Bridge (D606)

PK **109.7 Melun** bridge (Jeanne-d'Arc), *port de plaisance* d/s l/b, Tourist Office, 06 45 38 81 70, 14 visitor moorings, night €12, water, electricity, pump-out, restaurant d/s r/b, town centre 400m r/b

PK **109.6** Bridge (Maréchal de Lattre de Tassigny)

PK **109.2** U/s tip of Melun island, navigation in l/b arm, r/b arm for

PK **109.1** Boat harbour l/b (Brice la Plage), night €7, 01 64 37 00 21, electricity, restaurant

PK **107.3** Railway bridge (Pet-au-Diable), boat club u/s l/b

PK **102.0** Bridge (Chartrettes), village 1 km r/b

PK **101.1** Lock 3 (La Cave) l/b, two chambers, VHF 22, weir

PK **100.9 Chartrettes** boat club moorings in small basin r/b, 06 80 21 26 82, 38 berths, 4 visitor moorings, night €10, water and electricity included, wifi, restaurant 500m *cncssm@gmail.com*

PK **97.7** Bridge (Fontaine-le-Port)

PK **93.6 Samois-sur-Seine** municipal *halte* on pontoon for 3 boats l/b, 06 45 74 65 27, night €11, water and electricity included

The birthplace of Django Reinhardt has a renowned annual jazz festival.

III – Central France and routes to the Saône

Loing confluence, PK 81 in the foreground. The cruise ship stands out amongst the large number of péniches at this historic junction.
© GÉRARD DUBRECQ

PK **93.0** Samois island, navigation in r/b arm
PK **90.3** Bridge (Valvins), moorings, water, electricity
PK **89.8** **Avon** *port de plaisance* on quay l/b, Amicale des Marins du Pays de Fontainebleau, 06 49 95 62 63, 70 berths, 5 visitor moorings, night €15, water, electricity, showers, wifi *amf.amf@orange.fr*

This is the place to moor up to visit Fontainebleau, 4.5 km away.

PK **84.2** **Champagne-sur-Seine** bridge, **Thomery** boatyard Navire en Cale u/s l/b, 06 49 31 93 62, maintenance and repairs, crane 35t, dry dock 65m
PK **83.5** Lock 2 (Champagne) r/b, two chambers, VHF 18, weir, quay u/s r/b, moorings
PK **82.5** Voulzie Aqueduct (pipeline crossing)
PK **81.6** Fuelling station (BP) r/b
PK **81.5** Confluence of Loing (Canal du Loing) l/b
PK **81.1** **Saint-Mammès** bridge, *port de plaisance* d/s l/b for 16 boats, 06 47 68 79 51, night €9.50, water and electricity included, shower, wifi, fuel, town centre l/b

PK **79.7** Boat moorings
PK **76.6** Former lock (Madeleine) r/b, former Montereau thermal power station

There are many abandoned *péniches* in the old lock chamber.

PK **76.0** Overhead power lines

PK **75.4** Private basin r/b
PK **71.2** Lock 1 (Varennes) in short cut, r/b, VHF 22, bridge, water
PK **70.4** Railway bridge (Corbeil)
PK **67.1** Confluence of Yonne l/b

Petite-Seine

The Petite Seine is really worth exploring up to Marcilly, and in a few years maybe beyond on the Canal de la Haute-Seine to Méry-sur-Seine. This cul-de-sac waterway needs traffic to justify the investment. The excursion starts with the visit to the confluence town of Montereau, where it feels as though the Seine is the lesser of the two rivers. It is certainly a lot narrower than the Yonne at this point. Spare a thought for the Jean Sans Peur, the fearless Duke of Burgundy who during a meeting on this bridge with Charles VII was sliced into two vertically by one of the king's soldiers, Tanneguy du Châtel, in 1419.

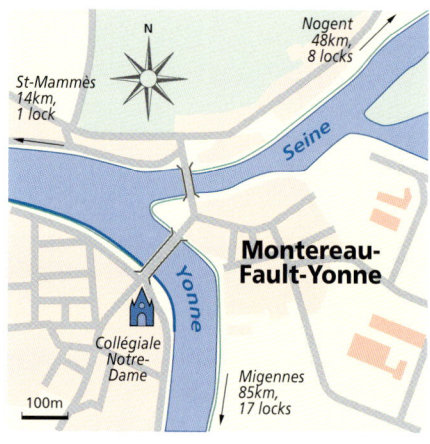

PK **67.0** **Montereau-Fault-Yonne** bridge (Seine), quays, town centre d/s l/b
PK **66.6** Industrial basin l/b
PK **66.4** Bridge (Saint-Martin), Montereau bypass
PK **65.4** Railway bridge (TGV Sud-Est Paris-Lyon)
PK **65.3** Motorway bridge (A5)
PK **63.7** Railway bridge
PK **61.1** End of lock-cut, navigation re-enters Seine
PK **60.8** Lock (Marolles), VHF 18, bridge
PK **60.7** **Marolles-sur-Seine** bridge, *halte* VNF u/s l/b on quay, 01 64 60 42 85, free for 72 hours, water, electricity, village l/b

Jaulnes lock and weir, PK 41 © P. LEMAÎTRE/DOC VNF

Upper Seine

PK 59.3	Entrance to Marolles lock-cut, l/b, weir r/b
PK 57.9	Conveyor bridge
PK 56.6	**La Tombe** bridge, quay u/s l/b, small village
PK 55.8	Former lock-cut entrance l/b (heading u/s, keep to Seine)
PK 51.5	Bridge (Roselle)
PK 47.8	Lock (Grande Bosse) l/b, VHF 22, weir, bridge
PK 44.3	Entrance to former Bray/La Tombe lock-cut, l/b, navigation continues in Seine
PK 43.8	**Bray-sur-Seine** bridge, municipal *halte* u/s l/b for 4 boats, 01 60 67 10 11, free, water, electricity, wifi (at campsite), slipway, small town l/b
PK 41.9	D/s tip of Jaulnes island, navigation in r/b arm
PK 41.3	U/s tip of Jaulnes island, navigation in r/b arm
PK 41.1	Lock 9 (Jaulnes), r/b, weir
PK 37.6	Conveyor bridge
PK 34.9	Lock 8 (Vezoult) l/b, weir r/b, water, fender piles
PK 34.2	Backwater, r/b, partly infilled
PK 33.7	U/s entrance to old arm, r/b
PK 33.1	**Noyen-sur-Seine** bridge, village 1km l/b, private moorings d/s r/b (Le Port Montain), water sports area in bypassed loop of river
PK 31.1	End of lock-cut, navigation re-enters Seine
PK 30.5	Lock 7 (Villiers-sur-Seine), bridge, basin u/s
PK 29.7	Bridge (Villiers-sur-Seine)
PK 27.7	Bridge (Courceroy)
PK 25.9	Lock 6 (Melz), bridge, water
PK 22.7	Bridge (Beaulieu)
PK 22.3	Basin, l/b
PK 22.2	Lock 5 (Beaulieu), flood lock, bridge, water, basin d/s l/b
PK 22.0	Entrance to Beaulieu/Villiers-sur-Seine lock-cut, r/b
PK 21.7	Main road bridge (D619, Nogent bypass)
PK 21.5	End of new cut
PK 21.0	Entrance to new meander cutoff, r/b
PK 20.5	Grain silos, quays l/b
PK 19.6	Nogent bridge (Pont Saint-Edme), quay d/s l/b beyond mill stream outfall
PK 18.7	Lock 4 (Nogent) in cut, r/b, water, Service Navigation
PK 18.5	**Nogent-sur-Seine** halte for 4 boats in mill stream (Bief des Moulins) l/b, 600m, 03 25 39 42 07, free for 72 hours, fuel (on request), water, electricity €4/day, attractive historic town centre

Approaching the moorings on the weir stream at Nogent-sur-Seine, after passing through the lock. © CALANDO

PK 16.6	Railway bridge
PK 16.5	End of lock-cut, navigation re-enters Seine
PK 16.3	Lock 3 (Bernières), sloping sides, bridge, water
PK 14.8	Bridge (des Ouitres)
PK 13.8	Lock 2 (**Marnay**), bridge, water, small village r/b
PK 11.8	Bridge (des Soupirs)
PK 11.0	**Pont-sur-Seine** lift bridge and footbridge, quay u/s r/b, village r/b

Failure of this lift-bridge at Pont-sur-Seine led to closure of the Petite-Seine above Nogent for several years, during which weed growth also posed serious problems. The bridge was restored in 2007, and this little-known and little-used waterway now deserves to be visited by many more boats than it used to see in the past. © ANDOSENN

PK 8.5	Bridge (Pâtures)
PK 8.2	Crancey aqueduct (length 26m, restricted width)
PK 7.9	Bridge (Maugis), **Crancey** 500m l/b
PK 4.1	Basin l/b (silted up)
PK 3.3	Lock 1 (Conflans), bridge, water
PK 3.2	Entrance to Conflans-Bernières lock-cut, l/b
PK 0.8	**Marcilly-sur-Seine** bridge, pontoon (20m) u/s l/b, slipway, village r/b
PK 0.4	Confluence of Aube and Seine
PK 0.0	**Junction with Canal de la Haute-Seine** (restoration in progress to Méry-sur-Seine)

III – Central France and routes to the Saône

24. River Marne

The river Marne is navigable upstream from its confluence with the Seine at Charenton to Épernay. It connects with the Canal latéral à la Marne at Dizy-Magenta, 5km before the head of navigation is reached at Épernay. This last section of the river from Dizy-Magenta up to Épernay is treated as a branch. From Charenton to Dizy, navigation extends over a distance of 178km, with 18 locks. The lower course of the river is bypassed in several places by lateral canals. The Canal Saint-Maur cuts off a long loop of the river between Maisons-Alfort and Joinville-le-Pont. It is 1.2km in length, the last 600m being in tunnel. The Canal de Chelles extends 9km from Neuilly-sur-Marne (PK 164) to Vaires-sur-Marne (PK 155), with a lock at each end. The Canal de Meaux à Chalifert is entered at Chalifert and rejoins the river at Meaux. It is 12km long and has three locks. Between the first two, near Chalifert, there is a 290m long tunnel.

The lower 5km of the loop bypassed by the Canal Saint-Maur is an important branch, giving access to the second biggest port in the Paris region at Bonneuil-sur-Marne. There is a large lock in this section.

In the section between the Canal Saint-Maur (PK 173) and Bry-sur-Marne (PK 168), the river twice divides into two navigable channels. Past the Île Fanac (PK 173) the left bank channel is for upstream-bound vessels and the right bank channel for downstream. However, when the river is in flood and the gates at Joinville weir are opened, vessels heading upstream are allowed to use the right bank channel. Past the Île des Loups and the Île d'Amour, the right bank channel is for upstream vessels and the left bank channel for those heading downstream (contrary to convention).

Navigation

Particular features of this (mainly) river navigation are the separate canal sections with their tunnels, and the many islands, which restrict the channel width on either side. No overtaking is the general rule in these channels, as well as when passing many of the other islands in the river. The conventional navigation signs indicate these restrictions.

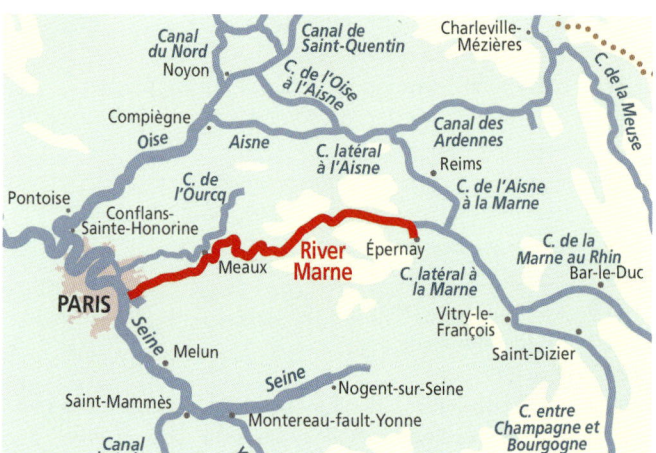

The Marne was a heavily navigated free-flowing river until the 19th century. However, it had one gated short cut, 500m long, the Canal de Cornillon in Meaux, which was built in 1235, possibly the oldest canal in France. The 'modern' canalisation was started in 1837, and completed up to Épernay in 1867. It included a number of canals bypassing the more extravagant meanders. Locks are wider than the Freycinet gauge, but shorter than those of the Canal Saint-Denis in Paris, of similar width. The Marne remains in the national VNF network as a commercial navigation.

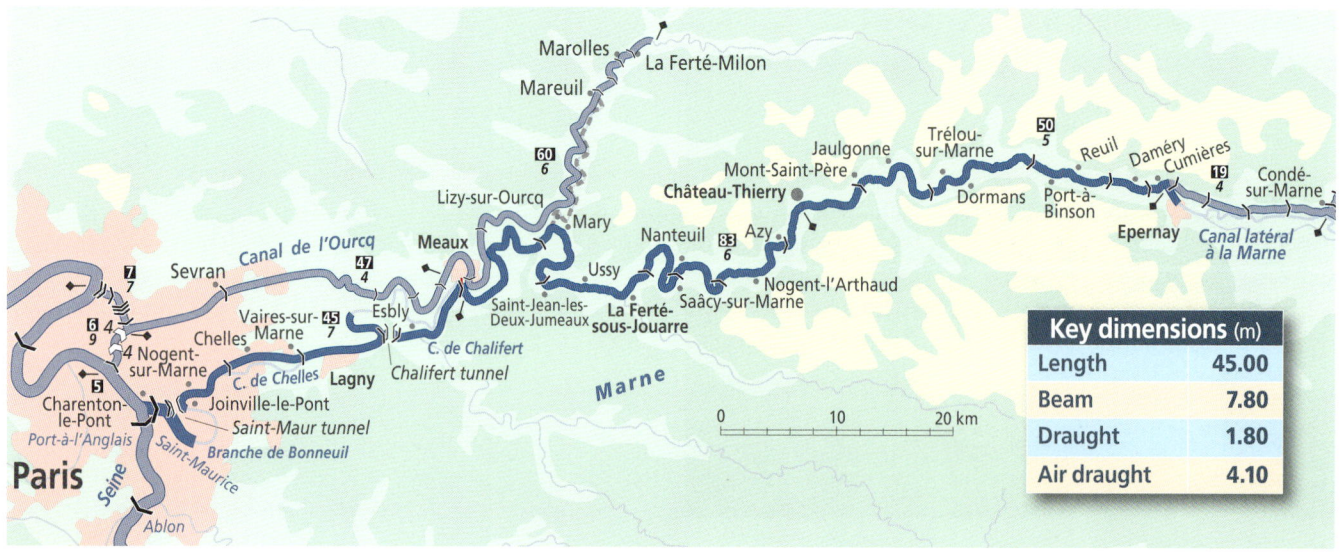

Key dimensions (m)	
Length	45.00
Beam	7.80
Draught	1.80
Air draught	4.10

Marne

The river is geneally lush, wide and gently-flowing; the scenery is leafy even close to Paris. Its character alters at Meaux where the Canal de Chalifert marks the end of the built-up outer suburban Paris region and the predominately rural Champagne. The river carries commercial traffic and is also a significant leisure water sports resource for eastern Paris, particularly at weekends. The river is also busy with péniches. Upstream of La Ferté-sous-Jouarre, by contrast, it is possible to cruise for hours without encountering a single vessel. Places to fuel immediately alongside the river are few, but there are service stations within easy walking distance. There are plentiful places to moor, from the simple to the well-resourced. The upper reaches above Meaux have many fallen trees and branches, on the banks and in the river itself. Some may be visible floating on the surface; there are also waterlogged ones just below. Keeping a good look-out is a good idea.

When the level of the river shows 35.32m (above sea level) on the gauge at Joinville bridge the lock at Saint-Maur functions as a flood outlet and is no longer available to navigation.

Locks

There are 18 locks, plus the lock at Créteil on the branch of the river leading to the port of Bonneuil. The first three are situated in short lock-cuts. Locks 4 to 11 are in the main river, set against one of the banks and level with the corresponding weir. The remaining locks are situated in the canals indicated above. The dimensions are 45.00m by 7.80m down to Neuilly-sur-Marne, while the last two locks (and the lock at Créteil) offer much larger dimensions: 125 by 12.00m. (It should be noted, however, that the available width in Saint-Maur tunnel is restricted to 8.60m).

Draught

The maximum authorised draught is 3.00m up to Neuilly-sur-Marne (PK 165) and on the branch to Bonneuil, then 1.80m throughout to Dizy and 1.50m on the branch to Épernay.

Headroom

The maximum authorised air draught is 4.40m from Épernay to Neuilly-sur-Marne, reduced to 4.10m above the highest navigable water level, and 6.40m on the remaining section, reduced to 4.70m above the highest navigable water level.

Towpath

There is no continuous towpath, but efforts are being made to develop a cycling itinerary throughout the valley, using the existing riverside paths and the towpaths in the lock-cuts as much as possible.

Authority

VNF du Bassin de la Seine
UTI Marne
- 17 route de Château-Thierry, 02400 Mont-Saint-Père
  ✆ 03 23 70 28 33 (PK 0-70)
- Barrage de Meaux, BP 176, 77108 Meaux, ✆ 01 60 24 76 76 (PK 70-160)

Route description

- PK **178.3** Confluence with Seine (PK 163.5)
- PK **178.0** Footbridge (Alfortville)
- PK **177.9** Railway bridge
- PK **177.7** Metro bridge (line 8)
- PK **177.6** **Charenton** bridge, town r/b, **Alfortville** l/b
- PK **177.2** Lock (Saint-Maurice) r/b, footbridge, VHF 22, water, telephone, weir
- PK **175.8** Footbridge (Charentonneau), **Maisons-Alfort** l/b
- PK **175.6** Two motorway interchange bridges (A4 west/A86)
- PK **175.2** Two motorway interchange bridges (A4 east/A86)
- PK **174.7** Entrance to Canal Saint-Maur, r/b junction with Bonneuil arm
- PK **174.5** Lock (Saint-Maur), VHF 18, water

Traffic through the short tunnel is controlled by lights. Look out for these when leaving the lock. And make sure your navigation lights are operational.

- PK **174.2** Saint-Maur tunnel, d/s entrance, basin r/b
- PK **173.6** End of tunnel and Canal Saint-Maur, navigation re-enters river Marne
- PK **173.4** **Joinville-le-Pont** bridge, town l/b, boat harbour on d/s tip of Île Fanac, 70 berths, 15 visitor berths, 01 48 83 35 10, night €16.10, water, electricity, showers €0.50, slipway, pump-out, wifi, *ville-joinville-le-pont.fr*

A small *port de plaisance* but with good facilities and an easy Métro ride into Paris.

The port de plaisance *at Joinville,* PK *174, where the Canal Saint-Maur re-enters the river.* © LUC GR

- PK **172.8** U/s tip of island (Île Fanac), follow navigation signs (u/s vessels keep to l/b, d/s vessels r/b)

Warning lights here inform boats heading downstream of the situation likely to be found at the upstream entrance to the Saint-Maur tunnel if navigating at normal speed. Green light only means 'at normal speed you will find the green light at the tunnel entrance'. Red and green (vertical) means 'prepare to stop upstream of the tunnel entrance'.

III – Central France and routes to the Saône

PK **172.4** Motorway bridge (A4, Autoroute de l'Est)

PK **170.8** **Nogent-sur-Marne** *port de plaisance* r/b, 90 berths, 10 visitor berths, second biggest boat harbour in region after Paris-Arsenal, night €18, 06 77 64 87 44, water, electricity, showers, slipway, pump-out, restaurant, wifi *fayolleplaisance.com*

This is a useful stopping place, about 12km from central Paris and the Paris-Arsenal *port de plaisance*. The port has good facilities, although getting to Nogent town centre involves a steep uphill walk.

PK **170.6** Nogent-sur-Marne bridge, d/s tip of islands, town r/b

PK **170.3** Nogent railway viaduct

PK **169.3** U/s tip of islands (Île d'Amour and Île aux Loups), follow navigation signs

PK **168.5** **Bry-sur-Marne** bridge, town centre l/b

PK **167.5** Footbridge (Bry)

PK **166.7** Railway viaduct (RER), commercial quays r/b, mooring possible but no services

PK **165.9** Railway viaduct

PK **165.3** Private bridge (water works), mooring d/s r/b

PK **165.1** Neuilly-sur-Marne bridge, town centre r/b

PK **164.9** Entrance to Canal de Chelles, r/b, **Neuilly-sur-Marne** boat harbour on r/b side of river just u/s (level with the lock), 06 82 98 74 79, 100 berths, 3 visitor berths, night €18, water, electricity, showers, slipway €15, restaurant

This port is congested, to one side of the deep lock on the river branch. Users have reported that it is shallow and subject to a strong downstream current passing through the pontoons, which are themselves difficult. Manoeuvring into and out of the stern-on moorings can be difficult.

PK **164.8** Lock 16 (Neuilly-sur-Marne), VHF 22, bridge, water

The quayside mooring with bollards above the lock may be preferred to the *port de plaisance*. East of Neuilly the Canal de Chelles is relatively narrow. Care should be taken when approaching the sides, with numerous instances of half-submerged and broken piling edges.

PK **163.6** Bridge (Ville-Évrard)

PK **162.6** Bridge

PK **162.3** Bridge (Chétivet)

PK **161.6** **Gournay-sur-Marne** bridge, quay d/s r/b, town centre l/b

PK **160.6** Bridge (Moulin), **Chelles** r/b

PK **159.9** Bridge (Chelles)

PK **158.8** Industrial basin and quay r/b

PK **158.1** Bridge

PK **156.6** **Vaires** bridge, small quay u/s r/b, town centre r/b

PK **155.9** Lock 15 (Vaires), VHF 17, bridge, water, navigation re-enters river Marne, navigable 2.3km d/s to **Noisiel**

PK **154.3** Motorway bridge (A104)

PK **151.8** Bridge (Joffre), mooring rings in wall r/b

PK **151.5** **Lagny-sur-Marne** bridge (Maunoury), *halte* managed by district, 01 64 02 15 15, 8 berths, free for 48 hours, water €3, electricity €3, *maisonfluviale@marneetgondoire.fr*, town centre l/b

Long (100m) pontoon by the bridge. The facility recently won an award, and is ideally located close to the 'Maison fluviale', shops and railway station.

PK **150.3** Boat club moorings l/b, 1 visitor berth, night €15.50, water and electricity included, wifi, 01 64 30 29 77, water, electricity, shower, crane 7 tonnes, slipway

PK **147.3** Footbridge (Dhuys)

PK **145.8** Navigation enters the Canal de Meaux à Chalifert, bypassed river Marne navigable u/s 6.6km to **Annet-sur-Marne**

Beware of shoals if proceeding upriver to Annet-sur-Marne. The 11km long Canal de Chalifert (1846) is leafy and picturesque. There are two locks at the west end, each side of the short tunnel. There are various opportunities to moor along its length, including to visit the nature reserve along the disused Grand Morin canal.

The slightly threatening sheet-piled edge of the otherwise charming Canal de Chelles above Neuilly lock, PK 165. The bollards are on the far bank. © COSTARMORICAINE

Popular mooring at Lagny-sur-Marne, PK 151 © JIPR

Marne

PK **145.7** Lock 14 (Chalifert), VHF 11, basin u/s
PK **145.6** Chalifert tunnel, d/s entrance

Passage is controlled by lights when heading downstream and by the lock-keeper at lock 14 when heading upstream.

PK **145.3** Chalifert tunnel, u/s entrance, one-way traffic, navigation re-enters river Marne
PK **145.2** Railway bridge (TGV)
PK **145.1** Lock 13 (Lesches), VHF 11
PK **143.9** **Coupvray** bridge, village 500m l/b
PK **143.5** Footbridge
PK **142.9** Railway bridge, quay d/s r/b
PK **142.4** **Esbly** bridge (2) and footbridge, quay d/s r/b, village r/b
PK **142.2** Canal latéral au Grand-Morin enters l/b (disused)
PK **141.9** Bridge (Esbly 1)
PK **141.8** Esbly aqueduct
PK **141.0** Condé aqueduct (one-way passage)
PK **140.8** **Condé-Sainte-Libiaire** bridge, village and château r/b
PK **139.0** Bridge (Roizes)
PK **138.0** Motorway bridge (A140)
PK **137.9** Bridge
PK **137.0** Bridge (Mareuil-les-Meaux 2)
PK **136.8** **Mareuil-les-Meaux** bridge (1), village 200m l/b
PK **133.6** Lock 12 (Meaux), VHF 14, bridge (Saints-Pères), water, mooring d/s l/b round corner
PK **133.5** Navigation re-enters river Marne, turn left for **Meaux** municipal *port de plaisance* l/b to embankment, 16 berths, free (maximum 48 hours), water, electricity, slipway, town centre r/b

Turn left (downstream) to reach the port after Meaux lock (12), passing through two bridges. There are also numerous moorings and boatyards around PK133. Meaux is the home of the 'Brie de Meaux' cheese.

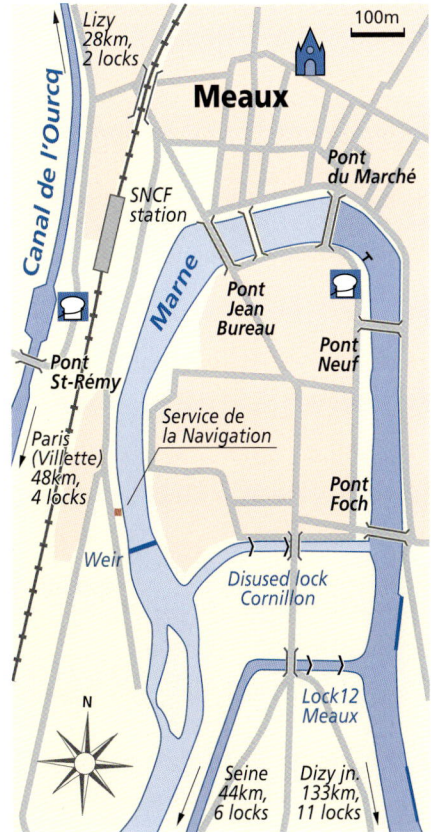

The port de plaisance *at Meaux*

PK **131.6** Sand unloading quay r/b
PK **128.7** Former lock (Basses-Fermes) l/b
PK **127.0** **Trilport** bridge, quay u/s l/b, village 200m l/b
PK **126.7** Railway bridge
PK **125.1** **Poincy** *port de plaisance* managed by Cercle Nautique du Port de Poincy in r/b arm, 06 50 46 22 75, 15 berths, 3 visitor moorings, night €12, water and electricity included, shower, village 400m *cnppoincy@orange.fr*

Sheltered pontoons with water and electricity, tucked behind a small island. This is the location of France's first hire boat base (Saint Line) in 1958.

PK **121.5** New road bridge
PK **121.2** **Germigny-l'Evêque** quay l/b, small village l/b
PK **115.5** Sand conveyor bridge and quay r/b
PK **113.4** Bridge (Congis)
PK **113.1** Lock 11 (Isles-les-Meldeuses) l/b, water, waiting quay u/s l/b, weir
PK **111.8** Island (Île de Cornille), follow navigation signs
PK **110.9** Railway bridge, quay d/s r/b
PK **110.6** **Mary-sur-Marne** bridge, village 300m r/b (mooring d/s of railway bridge)
PK **109.1** Sand unloading quay l/b
PK **108.7** Island
PK **102.8** Railway bridge (Armentières)
PK **100.6** Lock 10 (Saint-Jean), l/b, water, waiting quay u/s l/b, weir
PK **99.8** Island
PK **99.4** **Saint-Jean-les-Deux-Jumeaux** bridge, *halte* d/s l/b for 2 boats, water, electricity, pump-out, boat club moorings u/s r/b, village 400m l/b *contact@cpb-tourisme.fr*
PK **98.0** Island
PK **97.3** Motorway bridge (A4, Autoroute de l'Est), quays d/s both banks
PK **96.0** Island (Île de la Fosse-Tournille), channel in r/b arm, quay, water and electricity, draught 1.2m

III – Central France and routes to the Saône

PK 95.2   **Ussy-sur-Marne** bridge, village 300m r/b
PK 93.0   Grain loading quay r/b
PK 91.3   Bridge (Europe)
PK 90.4   **La Ferté-sous-Jouarre** bridge (Charles de Gaulle), *halte fluviale* on pontoons for 10 boats u/s r/b, water, electricity, slipway, town centre r/b   **contact@cpb-tourisme.fr**

The excellent *halte* managed by the local district (delightfully named Coulommiers-Pays de Brie!) is the ideal place to moor, but if preferred the town's quay is also a possible mooring beside the Leader supermarket, which is also near a service station. Nearby is the very large and salutary war memorial to 3000 unknown soldiers killed here in WWI. Approaching the *halte* watch for shallows immediately off the end of the island, indicated by buoys. The channel inside the island is fully navigable. The town, spread on both sides of the river, is worth exploring, with a fine Hôtel de Ville. Moorings and services may be charged, check via the above email address.

PK 87.1   Lock 9 (Courtaron), l/b, weir, very difficult access, no waiting quays
PK 85.7   Railway bridge (Saussoy)
PK 81.2   Railway bridge (Courcelles)
PK 80.1   **Luzancy** bridge, quay d/s l/b, village 300m l/b
PK 78.9   Private quay l/b (brick works)
PK 76.1   **Saâcy-sur-Marne** bridge, village 500m l/b
PK 75.7   Lock 8 (Méry) r/b, weir
PK 75.7   **Méry-sur-Marne** halte nautique r/b, water, electricity, village 500m rb
PK 74.7   Railway bridge
PK 74.2   **Nanteuil-sur-Marne**, bridge, *halte* u/s r/b for 2 boats, water, electricity, village r/b

Attractive pontoon mooring for two boats. *Boulangerie* and restaurant.

PK 69.0   Quay (Pisseloup) l/b
PK 66.6   Lock 7 (Charly) r/b, water, weir
PK 66.3   **Charly** bridge, extensive quay d/s r/b, water and electricity, village 1 km r/b
PK 63.3   **Nogent-l'Artaud** bridge, commercial quay and boat moorings u/s l/b, water, electricity, village 400m l/b
PK 62.3   Brick works, quay l/b
PK 56.8   **Azy-sur-Marne** bridge, moorings d/s r/b (campsite), slipway, village r/b

The river immediately above Azy is a favourite water sports place and can be busy, but the mooring itself is in a pleasant environment.

PK 56.2   Lock 6 (Azy), r/b, weir
PK 52.4   Bridge (D1003, Château-Thierry bypass)
PK 51.4   D/s entrance to Fausse Marne arm l/b
PK 50.4   **Château-Thierry** bridge, *halte* on pontoon d/s r/b, for up to 5 boats, night 5€ (maximum 72 hours), water €6 for 2 hours, electricity €4 per day (€2 for 12 hours), slipway, restaurant, town 300m r/b

A small town with a full range of facilities. In addition to the new *halte*, mooring is possible along the quay beside a narrow park 400m west of the bridge. It has room for many boats, but it is advisable to use the main *halte* managed by Château-Thierry Région (the district council). The park is popular and can become lively and noisy at weekends. There is a service station nearby.

Looking downstream from the bridge at Château-Thierry, PK 50. The former hire base used the sheds visible in the distance. A new halte has been provided along this quay.

Courcelles lock (# 4) and Marne valley landscape, PK 31   © F-W

The quay at Mont-Saint-Père, PK 41   © F-W

Marne

PK **49.8** Entrance to Fausse Marne arm l/b (forbidden to motor boats)

PK **42.5** Lock 5 (Mont-Saint-Père), r/b, weir, attractive holding quay u/s r/b

PK **42.2** Island (follow navigation signs)

PK **41.8** **Mont-Saint-Père** landing stage r/b, village 200m

Various bankside moorings, including the quay pictured left.

PK **41.5** Bridge (Mont-Saint-Père)

PK **41.1** **Mézy-Moulin** pontoon l/b, slipway, village 400m

PK **37.5** **Jaulgonne** bridge, municipal *halte* for 1 boat d/s r/b, night €5, water, electricity, slipway, restaurant with quay u/s r/b, village r/b

PK **32.1** Bridge (Passy)

PK **30.5** Lock 4 (Courcelles), r/b, weir

PK **28.5** Trélou-sur-Marne r/b

PK **26.3** **Dormans** bridge, *halte* on pontoons for 5 visiting boats run by campsite 'Sous le Clocher', 03 26 58 21 79, night €11, water and electricity included, showers at campsite, slipway, alternative mooring d/s at silo quay, village l/b

Excellent pontoons with services, but only during the high season for camping. Open without services from April to September.

PK **22.9** Bridge (Try), quay u/s r/b, **Verneuil** 1 km r/b

PK **17.7** Lock 3 (Vandières) sloping walls with pontoon, in short lock-cut, r/b

PK **15.2** Island (navigation in both arms)

PK **14.8** **Port-à-Binson** bridge, commercial quays u/s l/b, 3 floating pontoons, water, electricity, slipway, village l/b

PK **11.8** **Reuil** bridge, municipal *halte* on quay d/s r/b, moorings for 4 boats (unless a *péniche* is moored), water, electricity, slipway, village r/b

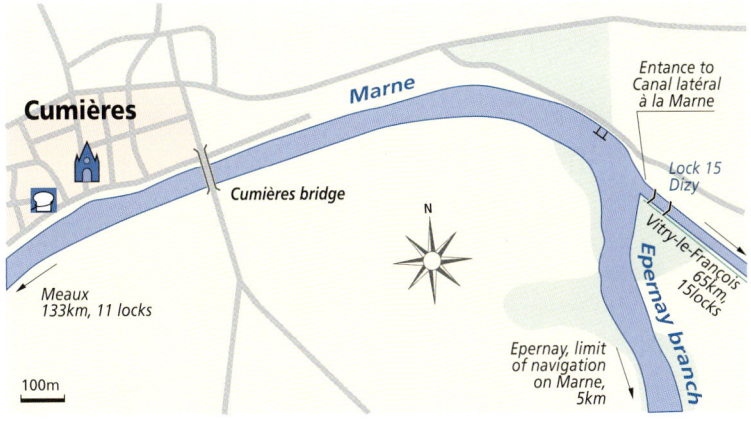

PK **8.3** End of lock cut

PK **8.2** Lock 2 (Damery), sloping walls with pontoon

PK **7.8** Bridge (Port aux Vins)

PK **6.6** Entrance to lock-cut, r/b, bridge

PK **5.4** **Damery** bridge, municipal *halte* on pontoon and quay for 5 boats u/s r/b, free (maximum 72 hours), water, electricity, slipway, village r/b

PK **3.3** End of lock-cut

PK **3.2** Lock 1 (Cumières), sloping walls with pontoon, bridge

PK **2.5** Entrance to Cumières lock-cut, r/b, bridge

PK **1.0** **Cumières** bridge, municipal *halte* for 2 boats, water and electricity, passenger boat, village d/s r/b

PK **0.0** Junction with Canal latéral à la Marne (d/s of Dizy lock) and junction with embranchement d'Épernay

The entrance to the Canal latéral à la Marne at Dizy lock. The Marne (right) is navigable up to the champagne town of Épernay.
© CLAUDE PARIS

III – Central France and routes to the Saône

Branches off the river Marne

Bonneuil Arm
PK 10.4	Junction with Canal Saint-Maur, r/b
PK 10.0	Bridge (Maisons-Alfort)
PK 9.0	Footbridge (Créteil)
PK 8.7	Quay (Saint-Maur-Créteil) r/b
PK 8.4	**Créteil** bridge, town l/b
PK 8.2	Lock (Créteil), l/b, VHF 18, weir, footbridge, water
PK 7.2	Footbridge (Passerelle de la Pie)
PK 6.9	Entrance to basins of port of Bonneuil, l/b

The port remains commercially active, although traffic has declined. There is little inerest in entering these basins.

PK 5.4	**Bonneuil** bridge, u/s limit of inland port of Bonneuil
PK 4.6	Railway bridge (RER)
PK 3.2	Bridge (Chennevières)
PK 3.1	D/s tip of Casenave island
PK 2.5	U/s tip of Casenave island, navigation in both arms
PK 0.5	Bridge (Champigny)
PK 0.0	Railway bridge, u/s limit of navigation

Herons are a delight to observe throughout the waterway system. The container terminal opposite is on the tip of land between the Bonneuil-sur-Marne port basins and the bypassed river Marne © STÉPHANE JEAN

Épernay Arm
PK 0.0	Junction with Canal latéral à la Marne, r/b, origin of canalised River Marne
PK 1.4	*Port de plaisance* in basin l/b

Blue Nautic basin and boat club moorings at the Épernay campsite, well equipped but somewhat out of town, 06 15 40 79 72 **bluenautic.fr**

PK 1.8	Bridge (D951)
PK 3.6	Épernay bridge, mooring (*halte nautique*) r/b, town centre 500m l/b
PK 4.2	**Épernay** *port de plaisance* l/b, 14 berths, 03 26 58 21 29, 06 21 89 13 90, night €20, water, electricity, shower, slipway, repairs, restaurant, wifi

Épernay, the capital of champagne (the product, not the region), has this excellent *port de plaisance*, pictured below, operated by the Société Nautique d'Épernay. It is secure and offers good services. It is close to the town centre and immediately adjacent to one of the Champagne houses, Castellane. It is a recommended detour from the main navigation route, and a visit to a Champagne house is enjoyable and educational. Quite apart from the large houses such as Mercier and Moët et Chandon, a really memorable experience can be had at one of the numerous small growers/makers at their village vineyard. An example is Domi Moreau, 03 26 59 45 85.

PK 5.0	Railway bridge, limit of navigation

The port de plaisance *at Épernay, in front of the impressive tower of the Castellane champagne house* © CLAUDE PARIS

25. Canal latéral à la Marne

THE CANAL LATÉRAL À LA MARNE extends from the navigable river Marne at Dizy to a junction with the Canal de la Marne au Rhin north-east of Vitry-le-François, a distance of 67km. At Condé-sur-Marne (PK 48) the canal connects with the Canal de l'Aisne à la Marne. The last 2km section of the canal is a cut built in the 1960s to bypass the town of Vitry-le-François. After that, part of the original line of the canal was infilled, from a three-way junction with the canals towards the Rhine and the Saône near the centre of Vitry-le-François. The short length which remains open is of little interest for pleasure cruising and the more convenient mooring for Vitry-le-François is on the Canal entre Champagne et Bourgogne.

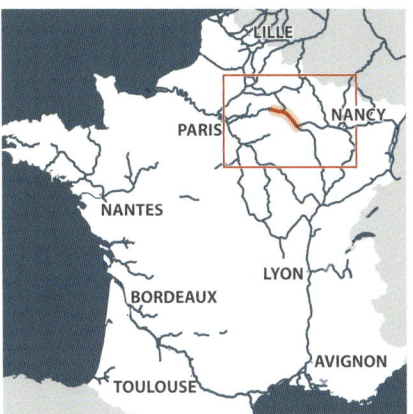

The canal was needed to bypass the river Marne, difficult to navigate upstream of Épernay. Works started in 1836 under the Becquey programme, and were completed in 1846. Lengthening of the locks to Freycinet dimensions was completed in the late 19th century. The first lock at Dizy has the same length as those of the Marne. The Vitry-le-François bypass was built in the 1960s.

Navigation

The canal is relatively short and is straight in parts but passes through some pretty villages most of which have opportunities to moor even if there is not a dedicated pontoon available. It also passes through one of the AOC Champagne areas, with the substantial town of Châlons-en-Champagne as its focus. The canal still carries some commercial traffic (about 10 *péniches* per day at each lock) that can be slow-moving and difficult to overtake; there is generally little point in trying, since *péniches* have priority at the locks and are allowed to start their day earlier than *plaisanciers*. It is better to slow down, leave a comfortable distance and enjoy. The advantage of there still being some commercial traffic is that it keeps the depth maintained. Speed limit 8km/h.

Locks

There are 15 locks, climbing from Dizy to Vitry-le-François, with a total difference in level of 34m. They are of standard dimensions, 38.50m by 5.20m.

All are mechanised, and all but two are operated by means of *perches* – rods that hang down over the water before the lock; twist to start the cycle. The other two have radar sensors. Opening hours during the season are 08:00 to 18:00.

Draught

The maximum authorised draught is 1.80m.

Headroom

The bridges leave a minimum clear headroom of 3.70m above normal water level.

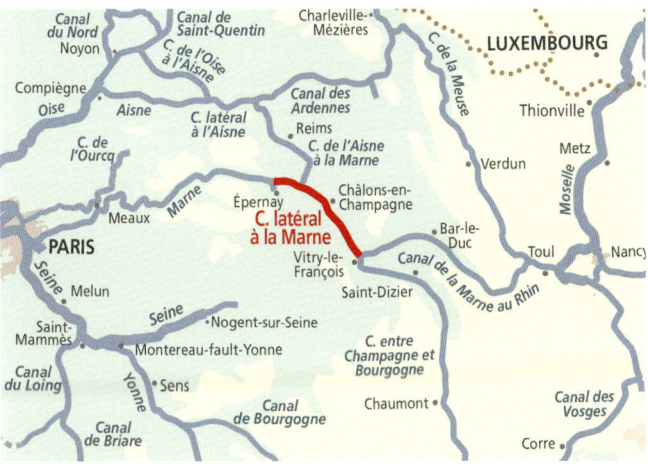

Towpath

There is a good towpath throughout.

Authority

VNF Bassin de la Seine, UTI Seine-Nord
– Chemin du Barrage, BP 256, 51011 Châlons-en Champagne
03 26 68 08 59

Route description

Épernay, the capital of Champagne, lies 5km upstream of this western end of the canal, on the river Marne.

PK 66.7	**Junction with navigable river Marne**
PK 66.6	Lock 15 (Dizy)
PK 66.1	Bridge (Hautvillers)
PK 65.3	Bridge (D951)
PK 64.7	**Dizy** bridge, quay u/s r/b, village 500m r/b
PK 62.6	Lock 14 (Ay), bridge, water
PK 61.7	**Aÿ** bridge (Villemoyer), quay d/s r/b, town r/b
PK 61.3	Railway bridge
PK 61.2	Bridge (Ruetz)
PK 60.2	Bridge (Cheminets)
PK 58.8	**Mareuil-sur-Ay** bridge, *relais nautique* d/s r/b, 03 26 56 69 24, 14 berths for vessels up to 20m, night €9.50, water and electricity included, shower, wifi, slipway, repairs, village with château r/b
PK 58.2	Basin d/s l/b (silted up)

III – Central France and routes to the Saône

PK 58.1 Lock 13 (Mareuil-sur-Ay)
PK 57.6 Bridge (D9, Mareuil bypass)
PK 55.3 **Bisseuil** swing bridge, village l/b

A very pleasant little village.

PK 55.1 Bridge (Bussin), former commercial quay d/s r/b
PK 53.0 Lock 12 (Tours-sur-Marne), bridge, private quay d/s l/b

PK 33.6 Châlons-en-Champagne industrial estate, quay r/b
PK 33.0 Footbridge
PK 32.4 Entrance to Canal de Junction (former commercial basin), r/b, turning basin
PK 32.2 Lock 9 (Châlons), permanently manned, bridge, water
PK 32.1 **Châlons-en-Champagne** quay and *relais nautique* pontoon, night €8 up to 10m, €10 including water and electricity, wifi, 03 26 26 17 98, close to town centre
relaisnautique@chalons-agglo.fr

The Blue Flag-rated *relais nautique* is at the Anse du Grand Jard, a basin behind the island immediately above lock 9. It consists of 12 finger pontoon berths and a few quayside moorings. The *capitainerie* has showers and a laundry. Châlons is the centre of the eastern AOC Champagne area. The city is historic and well-resourced. It is also possible to moor in the canal branch just below the lock and take a small dinghy (or a pleasure craft trip) from there along the rivers Nau and Mau.

Mooring at lock 9 in Châlons-en-Champagne
© CLAUDE PARIS

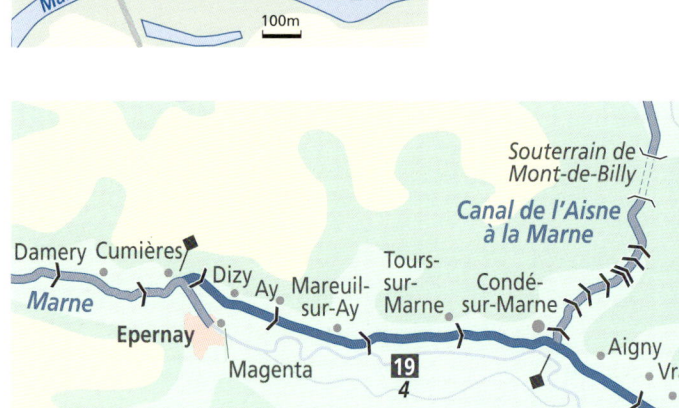

PK 52.9 **Tours-sur-Marne** village quay and mooring r/b

Pretty village and lock. Mooring on the village quay, no services

PK 48.7 **Condé-sur-Marne** bridges, quay u/s r/b, water, electricity, village r/b
PK 48.4 Junction with Canal de l'Aisne à la Marne, r/b, turning basin
PK 46.4 **Aigny** bridge, village 600m r/b
PK 44.3 Lock 11 (**Vraux**), bridge, water, village 1 km r/b
PK 42.6 **Juvigny** bridge, quay d/s r/b, village 1.5 km r/b
PK 40.8 Bridge
PK 39.3 Lock 10 (Juvigny)
PK 38.4 Motorway bridge (A26)
PK 37.2 **Récy** bridge, quay u/s r/b, village r/b
PK 36.2 Bridge (Therme-Brouard)
PK 35.8 Railway bridge
PK 35.4 Turning basin r/b
PK 34.8 **Saint-Martin** aqueduct and bridge, village r/b

Key dimensions (m)

Length	38.50
Beam	5.10
Draught	1.80
Air draught	3.70

Canal latéral à la Marne

The partially covered arms of the rivers Nau and Mau through Châlons-en-Champagne invite exploration in small craft. © EFFEL

PK 31.8 Island (Île du Jard), navigation l/b side only
PK 31.7 Footbridge (Passerelle du Jard)
PK 31.6 Aqueduct
PK 31.5 Bridge (Pont Louis XII), grain loading quay u/s r/b
PK 31.3 Bridge (D977)
PK 30.6 Bridge (Allées de Forêts)
PK 27.0 **Sarry** bridge, quay u/s r/b, village 500m r/b
PK 26.3 Lock 8 (Sarry)
PK 24.8 Bridge (Moncetz), quay d/s r/b
PK 23.7 **Chépy** bridge, quay u/s r/b
PK 21.8 Bridge (Saint-Germain-la-Ville)
PK 21.6 Lock 7 (Saint-Germain-la-Ville), water
PK 21.4 **Saint-Germain-la-Ville** quay r/b, village 500m r/b
PK 20.4 **Vésigneul-sur-Marne** bridge, small village r/b
PK 17.8 **Pogny** bridge, quay d/s r/b, village r/b
PK 17.1 Turning basin l/b
PK 16.9 Railway bridge
PK 16.6 **Omey** bridge, village r/b
PK 16.4 Pipeline crossing
PK 16.2 Private quay r/b
PK 15.1 Lock 6 (Chaussée-sur-Marne), water
PK 14.5 **La Chaussée-sur-Marne** bridge, quay u/s r/b, village r/b
PK 13.5 Bridge (Bois de Marne)
PK 12.0 **Ablancourt** bridge, quay u/s r/b, village r/b
PK 11.5 Lock 5 (Ablancourt)
PK 9.2   Lock 4 (Soulanges), bridge
PK 8.8   **Soulanges** basin, quay, village r/b

A quiet *halte* by grassland in this small village. No services or shops, but a pleasant overnight or lunchtime stop.

PK 8.0   Bridge (Bayarne)
PK 5.7   Private bridge
PK 5.5   Quay r/b (cement works)
PK 5.4   Bridge (Villers)
PK 4.8   Lock 3 (Couvrot), water
PK 4.4   Couvrot bridge, quay u/s r/b, village r/b
PK 3.7   Lock 2 (Ermite), bridge, water, turning basin d/s
PK 2.3   Lock 1 (Vitry-le-François), bridge, water
PK 2.2   Saulx aqueduct
PK 1.9   Junction with original line of canal through Vitry-le-François (entrance dammed, see plan)
PK 1.4   Bridge (N44)
PK 0.4   Bridge (D982)
PK 0.0   **Junction with Canal de la Marne au Rhin** (PK 0.9)

137

III – Central France and routes to the Saône

26. Canal entre Champagne et Bourgogne

THE CANAL ENTRE CHAMPAGNE ET BOURGOGNE (formerly Canal de la Marne à la Saône), taken with the canalised river Marne and the Canal latéral à la Marne, provides the first of the main waterway routes across central France between Paris and Lyon (followed by the Burgundy and Bourbonnais routes later in this chapter). Vitry is not in the official Champagne *appellation* area and Maxilly is not in Burgundy, but the canal does serve as a link between the two. The canal is also referred to by commercial barge operators (*mariniers*) as the 'Heuilley' canal.

It begins at Vitry-le-François, where it connects with the Canal de la Marne au Rhin (a short distance from the junction of the latter with the Canal latéral à la Marne) and crosses the Langres plateau before dropping down the Vingeanne valley to connect with the upper Saône at Heuilley-sur-Saône. The length of the canal is 224km. It rises 239m through 71 locks from Vitry up to Langres; and falls 156m through 43 locks from Langres down to Maxilly. On the summit level is the 5km long Balesmes tunnel.

The through route from Paris to Lyon using this canal is the longest of the three, but with the smallest number of locks, thanks mainly to its more recent construction and greater average lock depth than that of the older Canal du Centre and Canal de Bourgogne. It is also the most convenient route from northern France to the Saône. It remains little used except by boats in transit; annual traffic has been less than 100 boats in recent years.

The canal is very pleasant and well maintained, with interesting towns and villages along the route. The southern part is very rural, with practically no opportunities to fill up with either water or fuel. There are no canalside fuel pumps nor even canalside service stations there.

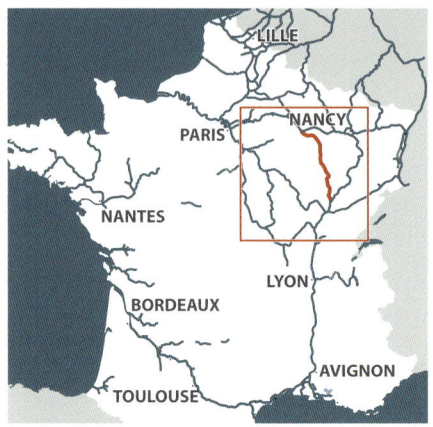

> *The Canal de la Marne à la Saône was one of the key projects under the Freycinet programme voted in 1879, which provided for 1400km of new waterways. At that time a 73km length with 31 locks had already been built (staring in 1862) under the name of Canal de la Haute-Marne. The planned budgets were regularly cut back in the following years, which made progress slow for the period, and the link was not completed until 1907. Commercial traffic survives on this route.*

Navigation

Navigating the canal should not present insurmountable difficulties to normal pleasure craft and it is one of the recommended routes from the Channel to the Mediterranean. It is usually reliably and well supplied with water. It still carries some commercial traffic, possibly two or three *péniches* per day at a lock. They can be slow-moving and difficult to overtake. There is little point in trying, since barges have priority at locks and are allowed to start their day earlier than *plaisanciers*. It is better to slow down, leave a comfortable distance and enjoy. The advantage of there still being some commercial traffic is that by 'ploughing' through they keep the depth maintained.

Check engine cooling water filter frequently: leaves and mud in the water and on the bed will get stirred up as you pass and especially as you go up or down in the lock.

PK 0 – Vitry-le-François ©F-W

Canal entre Champagne et Bourgogne

Approaching the Balesmes Tunnel entrance
© F-W

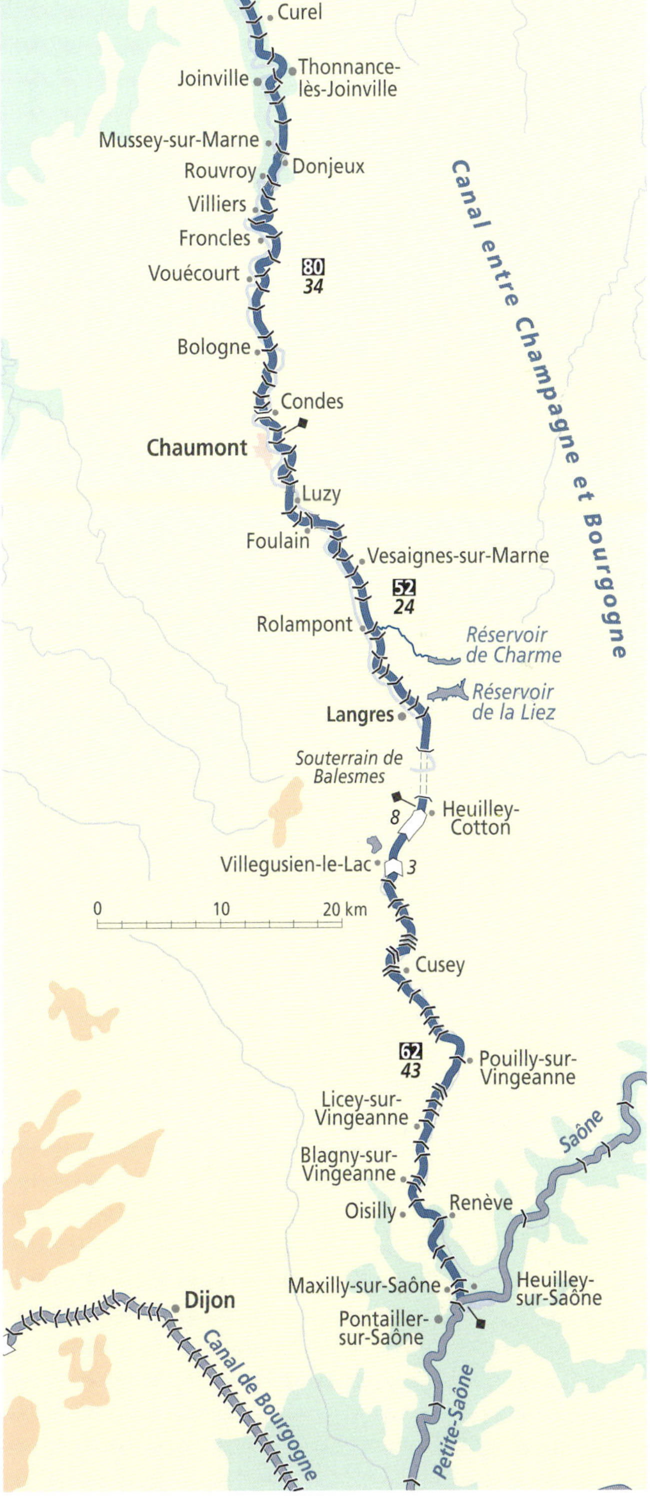

Key dimensions (m)	
Length	38.50
Beam	5.10
Draught	1.80
Air draught	3.45

Speed limit

The speed limit is 8 km/h. Estimate 3-4 km/h overall for a day's travel including locks, or count the locks separately, at 20 to 30 minutes per lock. Opening hours during the season are 08:00 to 19:00, the lock-keepers take lunch between 12:00 and 13:30, although the mechanised locks stay operational. Allow seven days for the passage.

Locks

There are 114 locks, of which 71 fall towards the Marne and 43 towards the Saône. They are 38.50m by 5.05m, and are nearly all equipped for automatic operation with remote control: locks 70 to 28 and 10 to 1 on the Marne side and all 43 on the Saône side. Lock 71 in Vitry is manned, as it is a local VNF office. Here a remote control will be supplied to proceed up the canal towards Langres. At the Saône end, lock 43 is always open and ready to operate a half cycle by raising the blue rod in the lock wall behind the ladder. When the lock is full, the gates remain closed until you have called the control centre. Once you have given your details, the control cabinet will be unlocked, and you will pick up a remote control unit. The lock cycle will then be completed by the operator. This ingenious system avoids the need to report before arriving on the canal at this southern end, which is far from the office at the bottom of the Heuilley-Cotton flight of locks.

Travelling lock-keepers accompany boats through the remaining manually-operated locks 27 to 11; they travel the towpath in a small car or on a moped, meet you at the lock (which they prepare), while boaters will usually assist in operating the lock, then they finish the cycle after you exit and travel on to meet you at the next lock. Working hours are strictly observed, including 1½ hours lunch-break. The lock-keepers are nearly always friendly and helpful. Other staff is available to take calls in case of operating difficulties at any of the other locks.

In some places, a radar detects the approach to the lock. Do not go too fast past the sensor or it will not detect you.

Going up the chain of deep locks on the Saône side approaching the tunnel can present the difficulty that it may not be possible to have crew 'at the top', which then means mooring near enough (this is dependent on bollard positions) to the rods 'at the bottom' to grab and push the blue rod up. This can sometimes be very tricky if it is covered with slimy algae. The rods are seemingly always opposite the ladder position, and the ladder is also slimy.

III – Central France and routes to the Saône

Many locks fill right to the brim and beyond; this means that protection is needed down at the waterline and into the water. Fenders must 'paddle' or fender boards be placed to prevent them from floating up.

Draught
The maximum authorised draught is 1.80m. This is the official value and may vary according to conditions.

Tunnels
The canal has a 10km long summit level south of Langres, at an altitude of 340m. This includes the Balesmes tunnel, 4820m in length, extended by narrow approaches to form a one-way only section 7.3 km long. Passage through the tunnel is controlled by the lock-keepers at each end of the summit level. It is therefore forbidden to moor in this pound. The Balesmes tunnel is lit. There is also a 308m long tunnel at Condes (PK 106), which is unique in being the only tunnel on the French waterway network (excluding the Paris canals) to allow simultaneous passage in both directions (the width being 18m). There are no special regulations regarding passage.

Headroom
The fixed bridges leave a minimum clear headroom of 3.45m.

Towpath
There is a good towpath throughout.

Authority
VNF Nord-Est, UTI Canal Champagne-Bourgogne
– 82 rue du Commandant Hugueny 52903 Chaumont, 03 25 30 79 51   *uti.ccb@vnf.fr*

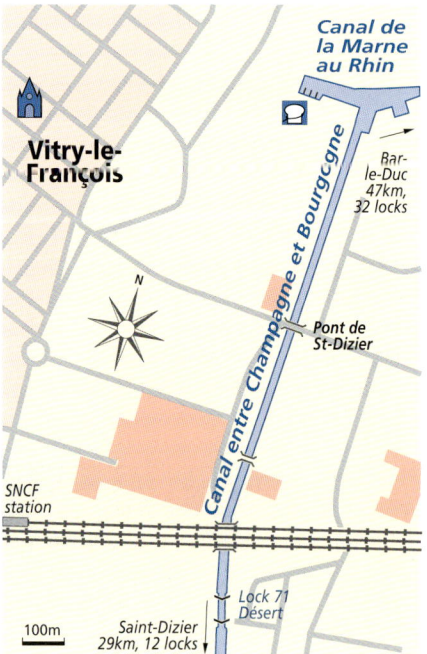

Route description

PK 0.0	**Connection with Canal de la Marne au Rhin**
PK 0.1	Quay (Citadelle) r/b, turning basin d/s
PK 0.5	**Vitry-le-François** bridge (Pont de Saint-Dizier), quay u/s l/b, 03 26 41 03 04, capacity 15 boats, night €11, water and electricity included, washing machine €4, crane, slipway, repairs, fuel 300m, town centre 700m l/b

This small *port de plaisance* lies on a bend, opposite a large *péniche* repair yard. It is relatively shallow. Helpful *capitaine* and staff. Possibility of dropping off sump oil in containers as well as recyclables and rubbish. Supermarket nearby, and pleasant town centre (rebuilt following wholesale destruction in WWII), markets Thursday and Saturday. It is also possible to moor along the canal bank opposite the basin, although the quay is not wide. The town also has a large Brico (DIY store).

PK 0.8	Private footbridge
PK 0.9	Railway bridge
PK 1.1	Lock 71 (Désert), footbridge, quay u/s l/b

Lock 71 features a lock wall edge that steps below water level. It is impossible not to rub against and difficult to stop lines slipping off the inset bollards.   © F-W

PK 1.4	Bridge
PK 2.3	Bridge (D396)
PK 2.7	**Frignicourt** quay l/b, village 800m l/b
PK 2.8	Lock 70 (Frignicourt), bridge
PK 5.4	Bridge
PK 6.1	Luxémont basin r/b, village 1 km r/b
PK 6.3	Lock 69 (Luxémont), bridge
PK 7.3	**Goncourt** bridge, basin u/s l/b (silted up), château 600m l/b
PK 8.9	Lock 68 (Ecriennes), bridge
PK 9.7	Bridge
PK 11.3	Lock 67 (Matignicourt), footbridge
PK 12.9	Bridge
PK 13.5	Lock 66 (**Orconte**), bridge, *halte* d/s l/b, 3 boats, night €9, water and electricity included, shower in season

A very attractive *halte*. Small village close by.

PK 13.8	Turning basin
PK 14.3	Bridge
PK 15.4	Lock 65 (Bruyères), bridge
PK 18.8	Lock 64 (Sapignicourt), bridge
PK 19.5	**Sapignicourt** bridge, small village 300m l/b
PK 20.2	Lock 63 (Perthes), bridge, quay d/s l/b, village 300m r/b
PK 20.7	Bridge

Canal entre Champagne et Bourgogne

PK 22.6	Lock 62 (Garenne), bridge
PK 24.1	Lock 61 (**Hallignicourt**), bridge, village l/b
PK 26.4	Lock 60 (Hoëricourt), bridge (airfield l/b)
PK 27.5	Main road bridge (N4, Saint-Dizier bypass)
PK 28.2	Lock 59 (Noue), right angle turn under bridge
PK 28.9	Bridge, private quay u/s r/b
PK 30.0	Bridge (Saint-Dizier)
PK 30.1	Lock 58 (Saint-Dizier)
PK 30.2	**Saint-Dizier** basin and municipal *port de plaisance* l/b, 03 25 05 31 84, 10 boats, free (maximum 72 hours), water, electricity, wifi, fuel delivery to order, town centre 400m l/b

Saint-Dizier is a small town with a full range of facilities. The extensive quayside has been developed as a *port de plaisance*. The town is famous for its art-deco iron balconies and for the Miko ice-cream factory, its landmark tower visible from the quayside.

PK 30.4	Bridge, private basin d/s r/b
PK 30.5	Footbridge
PK 30.8	Bridge
PK 31.3	Railway bridge
PK 31.4	Bridge (D384)
PK 32.0	Industrial quays l/b
PK 33.5	Railway swing bridge
PK 33.6	Lift bridge
PK 33.9	Main road bridge (N4, Saint-Dizier bypass)
PK 34.1	Lock 57 (Marnaval)
PK 35.5	Bridge
PK 36.1	Railway bridge (after right angle bend)
PK 36.3	Lock 56 (Guë)
PK 36.7	Bridge
PK 38.5	Bridge
PK 38.9	Chamouilley bridge, quay d/s r/b, village r/b
PK 39.4	Lock 55 (**Chamouilley**), municipal *halte* u/s r/b, timber pontoon moorings for 6 boats, free (maximum 5 days), water and electricity €8 for 16 hours, shower €1.40, pump-out

Charming *halte* beside the village. Small grocery/boulangerie. © F-W

PK 39.5	Railway bridge
PK 40.7	Lock 54 (Eurville)
PK 41.6	**Eurville** lift bridge (automatic), quay d/s r/b, village 300m l/b

Classic and modern canal landscapes in Saint-Dizier: the tree-lined canal in the suburb of La Noue, and (below) the bold architecture of the Centre Nautique. © LIONEL LEBRUN

This section of the canal has a number of lift bridges (*ponts levants*) and swing bridges (*ponts tournants*) bridges. Some are operated manually by lock-keepers and some operate automatically, an approaching boat being detected by radar. They must be approached at slow speed.

PK 43.0	Lock 53 (Bienville), footbridge, aqueduct u/s
PK 43.2	**Bienville** lift bridge (automatic), turning basin d/s, village 200m r/b
PK 43.6	Aqueduct
PK 45.9	Lock 52 (Bayard), aqueduct u/s
PK 46.3	**Bayard-sur-Marne** lift bridge (automatic), quay d/s l/b, village r/b

A small *halte* in a quiet location. Small supermarket nearby. Service station not far. Trains rumble past.

PK 47.2	Lift bridge
PK 48.2	Lock 51 (Fontaines), bridge, aqueduct u/s
PK 48.9	Lift bridge
PK 49.7	Railway bridge (disused)
PK 50.6	Lock 50 (**Chevillon**), bridge, quays u/s and d/s r/b, village 300m r/b
PK 52.8	Lock 49 (Breuil)
PK 54.6	Lock 48 (Curel), footbridge
PK 54.7	**Curel** lift bridge, quay u/s l/b, village 500m r/b
PK 55.6	Lift bridge (Autigny-le-Petit)
PK 56.5	**Autigny-le-Grand** lift bridge (automatic), small village r/b
PK 57.1	Lock 47 (Autigny-le-Grand), bridge
PK 58.3	Railway bridge
PK 59.3	Lock 46 (**Bussy**), bridge, quay u/s l/b

III – Central France and routes to the Saône

Unladen barge Poulbote *leaves Lock 24 Val des Choux, approaching the port of Chaumont La Maladière, PK 110*   CLAUDE PARIS

Small village *halte* in a quiet location. Just a quay and picnic table.

PK 60.3	**Thonnance-lès-Joinville** bridge, turning basin and quay u/s r/b, village 600m r/b
PK 61.1	Bridge (N67, Joinville bypass)
PK 61.2	Lock 45 (Rongeant), bridge, aqueduct u/s
PK 61.7	Private *halte* r/b at Hôtel-restaurant de la Vinaigrerie, 10 boats, night €8, water and electricity included, wifi
PK 62.5	**Joinville** bridge, quay u/s r/b, mooring for 10 boats, water €2 for 10 min, electricity €2 for 55 min, wifi, small town 300m l/b

A popular *halte* with water and electricity. The canal meanders through this very pretty village, which includes the Château du Grand Jardin, a restored 16th century manor house and park.

PK 63.2	Lock 44 (Joinville), bridge, water, quay u/s l/b

Public quayside and alternative mooring for Joinville.

PK 63.8	Bridge (N67, Joinville bypass), basin u/s
PK 66.0	Lock 43 (Bonneval), bridge
PK 67.6	Lock 42 (Saint-Urbain), bridge, quay d/s r/b, village 1200m r/b
PK 70.4	Lock 41 (Mussey), bridge, aqueduct u/s
PK 70.5	**Mussey-sur-Marne** lift bridge, village 1km l/b
PK 71.9	**Donjeux** bridge, turning basin and *halte* on quay for 4 boats d/s l/b, free, water, electricity, village 500m r/b
PK 73.2	Lock 40 (**Rouvroy**), bridge, aqueduct u/s, village 300m l/b
PK 74.0	Bridge
PK 76.0	Lock 39 (**Gudmont**), lift bridge u/s, quay u/s r/b, village 400m l/b
PK 77.2	Railway bridge
PK 77.9	**Villiers-sur-Marne** bridge, small village 400m l/b
PK 78.7	Lock 38 (Villiers), bridge
PK 79.6	Railway bridge
PK 81.2	Lock 37 (Provenchères), bridge, basin u/s l/b
PK 82.5	Railway bridge
PK 84.2	Lock 36 (Froncles), bridge
PK 84.4	**Froncles** *halte* l/b, 06 43 94 26 82, quay for up to 10 boats, night €3.05 (maximum 3 weeks), water €3.05, electricity €3.05, showers €2.55, pump-out, village 400m l/b

Excellent *halte* with all facilities, pretty little village and lovely scenery (the small supermarket is at the top end of the village).

PK 85.3	Turning basin
PK 85.6	**Buxières-lès-Froncles** bridge, quay u/s r/b, village l/b
PK 86.9	Lock 35 (Buxières), bridge
PK 88.6	Bridge
PK 89.7	Lock 34 (Vouécourt), bridge, quay d/s r/b, village l/b
PK 91.6	Lock 33 (Grandvaux), bridge
PK 93.2	**Viéville** lift bridge (automatic), *halte* u/s l/b, mooring for 8 boats, night €3.05 (maximum 3 weeks), water €3.05, electricity €3.05, village 300m r/b
PK 94.4	Lock 32 (Viéville), bridge
PK 96.4	Lock 31 (Roôcourt), bridge, turning basin u/s, small village r/b
PK 96.9	Railway bridge
PK 97.4	Lock 30 (Bologne), bridge, boat moorings d/s l/b, village 700m l/b
PK 97.7	Aqueduct
PK 98.0	Bridge, quay u/s r/b
PK 100.9	Lock 29 (Riaucourt), bridge, small village r/b

Short length of quayside by the pretty lock and adjacent buildings, a very pleasant location.

PK 102.7	Lock 28 (Mouillerys)
PK 104.0	Bridge
PK 104.5	Lift bridge
PK 104.6	Lock 27 (Brethenay)
PK 105.1	**Brethenay** quay and small village l/b
PK 105.5	Lock 26 (Condes), bridge (D200)

Canal entre Champagne et Bourgogne

Condes tunnel and the aqueduct over the Marne CLAUDE PARIS

PK 105.6 Condes tunnel, northern entrance
PK 105.9 Condes tunnel, southern entrance
PK 106.1 Aqueduct, lift bridge

The short tunnel at Condes, built in 1887, follows lock 26, and is itself followed by an aqueduct over the Marne and a small lift bridge (from which the above photo was taken), the ensemble making a fine example of late-19th century canal building.

PK 108.9 Lock 25 (Reclancourt), bridge, quay d/s r/b
PK 109.5 Turning basin
PK 110.0 **Chaumont** bridge (D674), quay (Port de la Maladière) d/s r/b, 03 25 31 61 09 (leave message), 10 boats, night €8.05, water €3.15, electricity €2.55 per day, shower €2.55, pump-out, wifi at *capitainerie*, town centre 2 km l/b

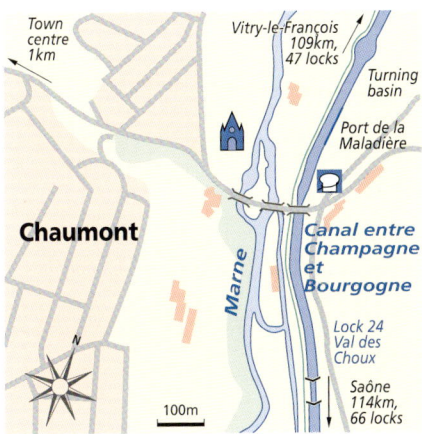

The *halte* at Chaumont (the capital of Haute Marne) is welcoming, with good facilities, and there is a large supermarket (E. Leclerc) just 1400m from the mooring, without having to climb up into the town (close to lock 25).

PK 110.4 Lock 24 (Val des Choux)
PK 111.9 Lock 23 (Choignes), bridge, quay u/s r/b
PK 113.0 Bridge
PK 114.9 Lock 22 (**Chamarandes**), bridge, quay u/s l/b, small village 300m l/b
PK 116.1 Lock 21 (Foulon de la Roche)
PK 117.0 Bridge
PK 117.6 Lock 20 (Val des Ecoliers), bridge
PK 118.0 Aqueduct
PK 118.7 **Verbiesles** bridge, small village 400m r/b

PK 119.6 Footbridge
PK 119.6 **Luzy-sur-Marne** lift bridge, quay u/s r/b, village 400m r/b

PK 120.5 Lock 19 (Luzy)
PK 122.2 Lock 18 (Pêcheux)
PK 122.8 Lock 17 (Foulain), bridge
PK 123.4 Aqueduct
PK 124.3 **Foulain** bridge, *halte* for 2 boats d/s r/b, water, village l/b

Two small timber pontoons by grass just below the bridge. There is water but the tap is beyond normal hose length away and does not have an attachment spout: jerrycans only. The village has a good service station not far from the mooring (across the bridge, over the level crossing, turn right).

PK 125.9 Lock 16 (Boichaulle), bridge, quay, turning basin d/s r/b
PK 127.2 Railway bridge
PK 127.3 Lock 15 (Pré-Roche)
PK 129.4 Bridge
PK 129.7 Railway bridge
PK 129.8 Lock 14 (Pommeraye), disused railway bridge
PK 131.0 **Marnay-sur-Marne** bridge, village 800m l/b
PK 131.1 Lock 13 (Marnay)
PK 132.6 **Vesaignes-sur-Marne** quay and village r/b
PK 132.9 Lock 12 (Vesaignes), bridge
PK 134.0 Bridge
PK 134.9 Lock 11 (Thivet), bridge
PK 136.5 Lock 10 (Prées), bridge
PK 138.8 **Rolampont** bridge, municipal *halte* for 3 boats d/s, free, water, electricity, restaurant, village l/b

A small quay, often occupied. Services may not be operational. However, the village is very pleasant with a basic range of facilities and there are other opportunities to moor bankside. A bike ride away (head north on the main village street) is the petrified waterfall and beautiful woodland scenery of La Tuffière, which is memorably unique and well worth visiting.

PK 139.2 Lock 9 (Rolampont), bridge
PK 140.4 Lock 8 (Saint-Menge), bridge

Halte at Rolampont (PK 139) and the nearby tuffières © F-W

III – Central France and routes to the Saône

Canal landscape in the Langres area © F-W

PK 140.6 Motorway bridge (A31)
PK 142.1 Lock 7 (Chanoy), bridge
PK 143.6 Lock 6 (Pouillot)
PK 144.4 Lock 5 (**Humes**), bridge, quay for 2 boats u/s r/b, water, village 500m l/b
PK 145.3 Bridge
PK 145.9 **Jorquenay** swing bridge, small village r/b
PK 146.3 Lock 4 (Jorquenay), bridge
PK 147.8 Railway bridge
PK 148.1 Lock 3 (Moulin-Rouge), bridge
PK 148.8 **Langres** bridge (D74), public *port de plaisance* d/s l/b, quay 70m long, water, electricity free for 1 hour morning, midday and evening, slipway, restaurant, town centre 2km l/b, turning basin d/s

The attractive port is close to Langres, a historic hilltop town with ramparts, a complete 2.5km curtain wall and fine buildings.

PK 149.8 Lock 2 (Moulin-Chapeau), bridge
PK 150.2 Bridge
PK 151.1 Bridge (**Champigny**)
PK 151.9 Skew railway bridge
PK 152.4 Bridge (N19)
PK 152.5 Lock 1 (Batailles), bridge, beginning of summit level
PK 154.9 Short tunnel under road (D17)
PK 155.4 Balesmes tunnel, northern entrance

Entry into the 5km tunnel is controlled from the locks at each end of the summit level; one way in each direction for a period of time. The control office for the tunnel and 12 locks is at Heuilley-Cotton, 03 25 88 42 02. The official speed limit of 4 km/h is extremely slow, and maintaining concentration and direction at that speed is a challenge. In practice, boats make it through the tunnel in about 1 hour, without incident. Avoid proceeding through the tunnel behind a *péniche*.

The tunnel is lit and most of the lights work (not all, there may be dark gaps) but a properly powerful torch or headlight is essential. Keep a close watch for logs and branches. A path runs the entire length, making the tunnel feel narrower than it actually is; there is plenty of headroom. Once through the tunnel and summit level it is downhill, and negotiating the locks becomes much easier.

PK 160.2 Balesmes tunnel, southern entrance

The canal's feel is very different each side of the tunnel. Emerging to be greeted by a view of the small village of Heuilley, the atmosphere is almost alpine. In the vicinity (PK 162 – PK 170) is a flight of 12 locks, some very close to one another and all between 4m and over 5m deep. Easy to descend, they are correspondingly difficult to ascend – even with crew waiting on the lockside, getting lines up to them whilst controlling the boat is tricky to say the least.

PK 161.7 **Heuilley-Cotton** bridge, basin d/s, village l/b
PK 162.1 Bridge
PK 162.6 Lock 1 (Versant Saône), bridge, water
PK 163.0 Lock 2
PK 163.5 Lock 3
PK 163.8 Lock 4, bridge (D241)
PK 164.2 Lock 5
PK 164.6 Lock 6
PK 165.1 Lock 7
PK 165.6 Lock 8 (bottom lock of Versant Saône flight), bridge (D67)
PK 166.4 Railway bridge
PK 167.1 Bridge
PK 167.5 **Villegusien-le-Lac** bridge, turning basin and quay u/s r/b, village 200m r/b

The village has a café-restaurant, and it is just a short walk to the lake, which is one of the reservoirs supplying the canal.

PK 167.8 Lock 9 (Villegusien), bridge, water
PK 168.2 Lock 10 (Pré-Meunier), footbridge
PK 168.7 Lock 11 (Château), bridge
PK 169.2 Piépape bridge, small village and castle r/b
PK 169.5 Lock 12 (Piépape), footbridge
PK 171.4 Vingeanne aqueduct
PK 171.6 Bridge (D128)
PK 171.9 Lock 13 (Bise l'Assaut)
PK 172.9 Lock 14 (Croix-Rouge), bridge
PK 173.5 Bridge
PK 173.7 Lock 15 (**Dommarien**), bridge, timber pontoon for 2 boats d/s l/b, water, turning basin, village 200m l/b

A small village *halte*. Pretty, but there are no facilities in the village.

PK 175.8 Footbridge
PK 176.4 Lock 16 (Choilley), bridge, quay d/s l/b, village 200m l/b
PK 177.0 Lock 17 (Foireuse), bridge
PK 177.7 Dardenay bridge (D128), small village l/b
PK 178.2 Lock 18 (Dardenay)
PK 178.9 Lock 19 (Grand-Côte), footbridge
PK 179.6 Lock 20 (Badin), bridge (D140)
PK 179.9 Aqueduct
PK 180.2 Lock 21 (Montrepelle)
PK 180.9 Lock 22 (Cusey), bridge, water

A new village *halte* with water and electricity.

PK 181.5 **Cusey** bridge, turning basin and quay d/s r/b, village 400m l/b
PK 183.5 Lock 23 (Bec), bridge

Canal entre Champagne et Bourgogne

PK 184.6 **Percey-sous-Montormentier** bridge, small village 500m l/b

PK 185.6 Lock 24 (Courchamp), bridge, turning basin and quay d/s r/b, village 400m r/b

Halte at Cusey, PK 180.9 © F-W

PK 186.6 Bridge
PK 187.6 Lock 25 (Romagne), bridge
PK 189.0 Lock 26 (**Saint-Maurice**), bridge, quay u/s l/b, village 1km l/b
PK 190.2 Lock 27 (Lavilleneuve), footbridge
PK 192.1 **La Villeneuve-sur-Vingeanne** bridge, turning basin, quay d/s r/b, small village r/b
PK 194.0 Lock 28 (Pouilly)
PK 194.8 Bridge
PK 195.1 **Pouilly-sur-Vingeanne** bridge, small village l/b
PK 196.7 Lock 29 (**Saint-Seine**), bridge, basin u/s r/b, village 1.5km l/b
PK 197.3 Lock 30 (Lalau)
PK 198.2 Lock 31 (Fontaine-Française)
PK 198.7 Bridge
PK 199.5 Lock 32 (Fontenelle), bridge
PK 200.4 Bridge
PK 201.8 Lock 33 (Licey), bridge
PK 202.7 **Licey-sur-Vingeanne** bridge, quay u/s r/b, village r/b
PK 204.1 **Dampierre-et-Flée** bridge, quay u/s r/b, small village 400m r/b
PK 204.4 Lock 34 (Dampierre), bridge
PK 205.2 Lock 35 (Beaumont), bridge, turning basin, quay d/s, r/b
PK 206.6 Bridge (Ramisse), private quay u/s r/b
PK 207.9 Lock 36 (Blagny), bridge
PK 208.5 **Blagny-sur-Vingeanne** quay and small village r/b
PK 208.6 Lock 37 (Rochette), bridge
PK 210.1 Railway viaduct
PK 210.5 Lock 38 (**Oisilly**), bridge, *halte*, small village r/b
PK 211.0 Bridge
PK 211.4 Quay r/b
PK 212.4 Bridge, quays d/s
PK 214.4 Lock 39 (Renève), bridge, turning basin and *halte* d/s r/b, village 500m l/b
PK 215.8 Lift bridge
PK 216.0 **Cheuge** bridge, *halte*, small village r/b
PK 217.4 Lock 40 (Cheuge)
PK 219.3 Lock 41 (Saint-Sauveur), bridge, quay d/s r/b, village 500m r/b
PK 220.0 Bridge
PK 221.1 Bridge (D25)

PK 222.7 Lock 42 (**Maxilly**), bridge, *halte* u/s r/b, quay 90m long, water and electricity (€3 per token), village 400m r/b

The last (or first) pair of locks, shortly before the canal joins the River Saône. The contrast between the narrow parallel-sided canal and the broad river is striking.

PK 222.9 Bridge
PK 223.0 Lock 43 (Chemin de fer), railway bridge
PK 223.5 Bridge
PK 224.2 **Junction with river Saône** (Heuilley lock-cut, PK 127), footbridge

Lock at Maxilly, PK 222.7 © F-W

Looking up the canal from the junction just above Heuilley lock on the Saône © F-W

145

III – Central France and routes to the Saône

27. River Yonne

THE NAVIGABLE RIVER YONNE extends from its confluence with the Seine at Montereau-Fault-Yonne (see Upper Seine) to Auxerre, where it joins the Canal du Nivernais, a distance of 108km. Over the first 65km, up to the junction with the Canal de Bourgogne, it is common to the Burgundy and Nivernais routes through central France. The last 23 km section upstream from the junction at Migennes forms part of a cross link between the Burgundy and Bourbonnais routes from Paris to Lyon. The Yonne is an attractive cruising river, with huge locks but little commercial traffic (except below Pont-sur-Yonne, where some of the gravel pits are still active). The meandering river is bypassed by lock-cuts at three places: Courlon, Joigny and Gurgy.

> *The river was a free-flow navigation through the ages, until Poirée successfully tested in 1834 (near Clamecy) his design for a needle weir. The design was improved by Thenard five years later, and the Government then approved works to canalise many rivers on this basis. One weir and lock were built on the Yonne after 1840, but most of the works were conducted from 1861. The locks were enlarged to Freycinet standards in the late 19th century, then again to their current dimensions after World War II.*

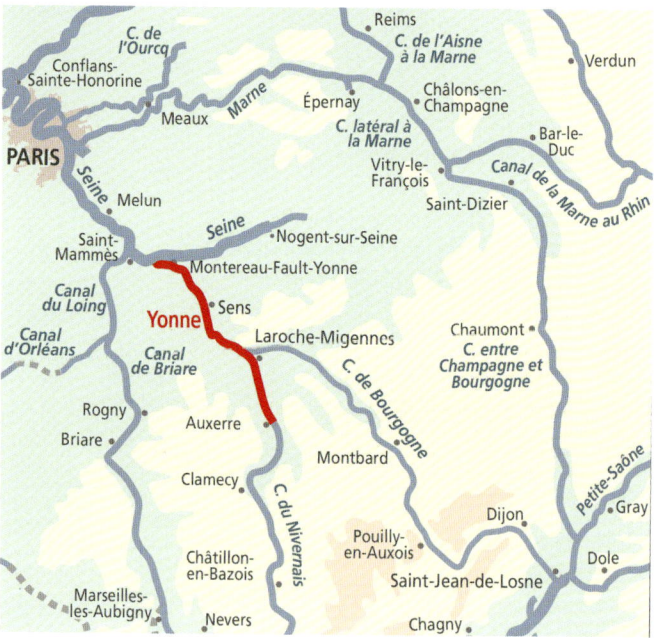

Navigation
Except during floods, when navigation becomes difficult long before the highest navigable water level is reached, the majestic river Yonne and its contrasting narrow lock-cuts make an ideal cruising waterway, in a broad valley dotted with sand and gravel pits and woodlands. The main difficulty is caused by the sloping-sided locks, although many of these have been equipped with pontoons for recreational craft to tie up to. Some commercial traffic will be encountered, especially in the lower reaches below Migennes, where extensive gravel workings off to the side are a significant feature.

Locks
There are 26 locks. The first three from the Seine are 96m long and 10.50m wide, followed by 14 locks, from Port-Renard up to Laroche-Migennes (junction with Canal de Bourgogne) that are slightly narrower (8.30m). The last nine locks between Laroche-Migennes and Auxerre are 93m long and 8.30m wide. Many of the locks had sloping sides, which were particularly awkward for boats proceeding downstream until pontoons were installed. Lock-keepers are present at all locks.

Draught
The maximum authorised draught is 1.80m.

Headroom
The lowest bridges are the Pont de la Tournelle in Auxerre and Courlon bridge (PK 87). The first offers a headroom of 4.40m above normal water level, reduced to 4.20m above the highest navigable water level (over the navigable width of 8.30m). The corresponding dimensions at Courlon are 4.80 and 4.40m. The headroom on the Yonne has recently made the national news after a new bridge was built at Pont-sur-Yonne. Its headroom was consistent with these ruling dimensions, but 30cm lower than that of the bridge it replaced, which put an end to a benefit enjoyed by barge operators on the lower section of the river.

Towpath
There is a good crushed gravel service road (former towpath) throughout.

Authority
VNF du Bassin de la Seine
UTI Yonne
– 60 quai de la Fausse-Rivière, 89100 Sens
03 86 83 16 32   uti.yonne@vnf.fr

Yonne

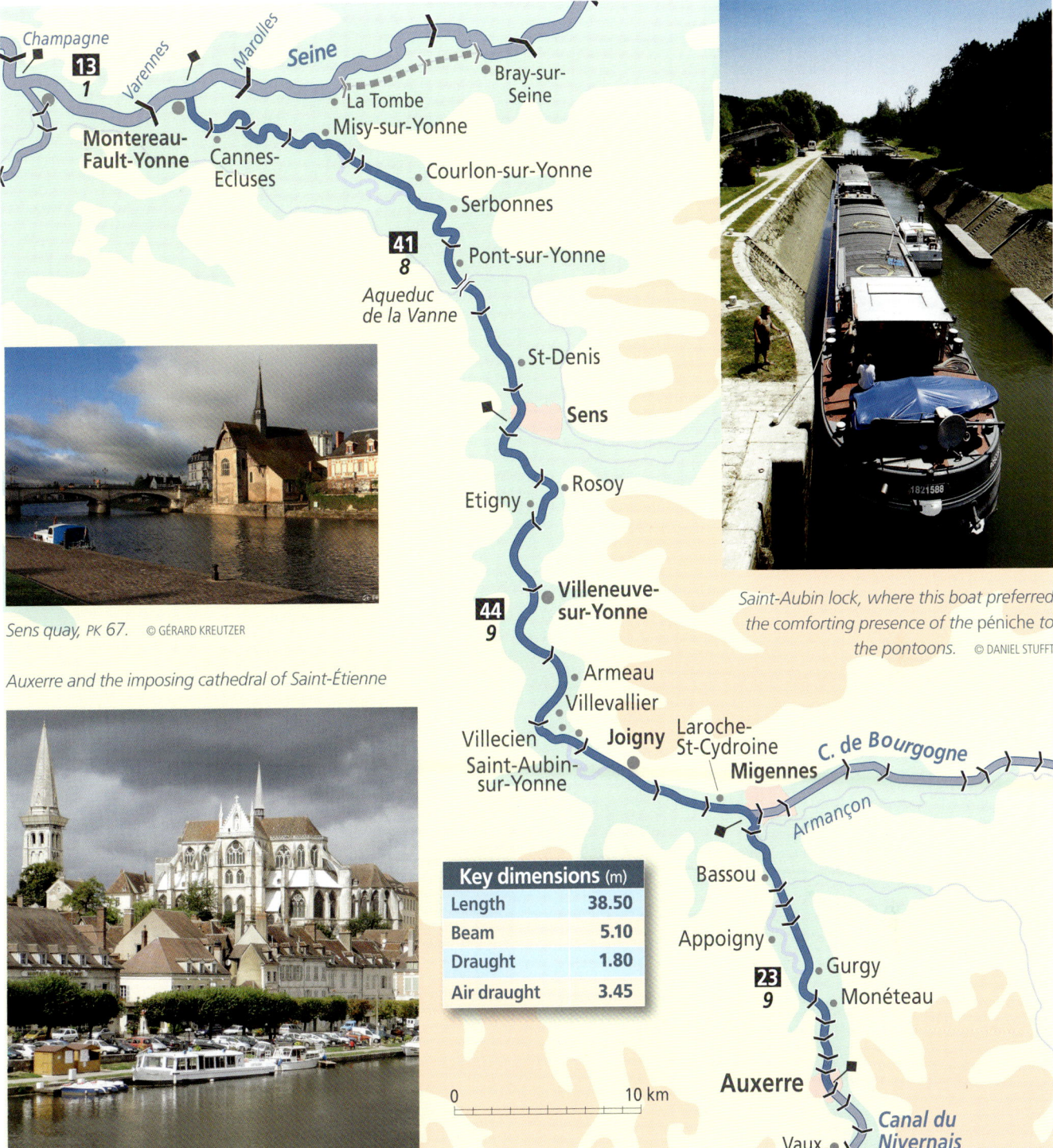

Sens quay, PK 67. © GÉRARD KREUTZER

Auxerre and the imposing cathedral of Saint-Étienne

Saint-Aubin lock, where this boat preferred the comforting presence of the péniche to the pontoons. © DANIEL STUFFT

Key dimensions (m)	
Length	38.50
Beam	5.10
Draught	1.80
Air draught	3.45

Route description

PK 108.0 *Confluence with Seine* (PK 68)

PK 107.9 **Montereau-Fault-Yonne** bridge (Pont de l'Yonne), moorings for 22 boats, 01 64 70 44 00, night €12, water, electricity, slipway

Attractive small town nestled in the sweeping bend of river. The Seine is noticeably narrower than the Yonne.

PK 107.1 Skew road bridge (Pont Georges Pompidou), D605

PK 104.7 Lock 17 (Cannes), sloping sides, r/b, weir

At this lock and the two that follow, there is no pontoon to moor to within the lock chamber.

PK 104.4 **Cannes-Écluses** bridge, quay for boats u/s l/b, village 200m

PK 100.6 Lock 16 (La Brosse), sloping sides, r/b, weir

PK 98.0 Footbridge

PK 97.6 Sand barge quays

PK 96.2 Lock 15 (Barbey), sloping sides, r/b, weir

PK 93.8 **Misy-sur-Yonne** bridge, mooring d/s r/b, village 300m

III – Central France and routes to the Saône

PK 91.8 Lock 14 (Port-Renard) r/b, beginning of lock-cut
PK 90.3 Lock 13 (Vinneuf), sloping sides, bridge

Pontoon to tie up to within the lock chamber. The same applies to all the sloping-sided locks up to Saint-Aubin.

PK 89.2 Bridge (Gain)
PK 88.6 Bridge (Morlaix)
PK 87.3 Bridge (Courlon) and flood gate
PK 87.2 End of Courlon lock-cut, navigation re-enters Yonne
PK 87.0 **Courlon-sur-Yonne** r/b
PK 84.0 **Serbonnes** r/b
PK 83.4 Serbonnes château r/b
PK 80.4 Lock 12 (Champfleury), r/b, weir
PK 79.1 **Pont-sur-Yonne** *halte* l/b, two 60m pontoon moorings, village 100m

All services in this small town, its most distinctive feature being the three surviving arches of the old bridge built under Louis XIV.

PK 78.8 Bridge (Nouveau Pont, Pont-sur-Yonne)
PK 76.1 Vanne aqueduct (Paris water supply)
PK 74.7 Hotel (Le Manoir de l'Onde) l/b
PK 74.5 Lock 11 (Villeperrot), sloping sides, r/b, weir
PK 71.9 Motorway bridge (A19)
PK 71.0 **Saint-Denis** quay and village r/b
PK 69.5 Lock 10 (Saint-Martin), r/b, weir
PK 68.0 Commercial quays r/b
PK 67.6 Road bridge (Pont Neuf)
PK 67.3 (Boats heading u/s) river divides, navigation in r/b arm
PK 66.8 **Sens** bridge, municipal *halte* on concrete quay with widely-spaced bollards d/s r/b, 10-15 boats, free (maximum 48 hours), water, electricity, slipway, town centre, restaurants r/b

Sens is a charming town and the Saint-Étienne cathedral is well worth visiting.

PK 66.5 River divides, navigation in r/b arm
PK 65.3 Lock 9 (Saint-Bond), sloping sides, r/b, weir
PK 62.6 Bridge (D1060, Sens bypass)
PK 60.5 Lock 8 (Rosoy), sloping sides, r/b, weir
PK 59.5 Quay (Rosoy) r/b
PK 57.0 **Étigny** bridge, village 400m l/b
PK 56.0 Lock 7 (Étigny) with sloping sides, r/b, weir
PK 54.1 Quay (Passy) r/b, private quay l/b
PK 50.5 Lock 6 (Villeneuve-sur-Yonne) with sloping sides, r/b, weir
PK 50.0 **Villeneuve-sur-Yonne** bridge, municipal *halte* d/s l/b, 35 boats, 06 68 18 30 57, night €10, water €5 (800 litres), electricity €5 for 12 hours, showers €2, slipway, repairs, crane on request, small town and hotel/ restaurant r/b, *flipper.nautic@gmail.com*

A favourite mooring on the Yonne, with vestiges of medieval fortifications and a recommended quayside restaurant.

PK 44.9 Lock 5 (Armeau) with sloping sides, r/b, weir
PK 41.8 **Villevallier** bridge, mooring r/b
PK 40.3 Lock 4 (Villevallier), r/b, weir

PK 37.4 Bridge (D606)
PK 37.0 Villecien r/b
PK 36.1 **Saint-Aubin-sur-Yonne** quay and village r/b
PK 36.0 End of lock-cut, navigation re-enters Yonne
PK 35.4 Lock 3 (Saint-Aubin) with sloping sides, bridge
PK 32.7 Bridge (Épizy) and flood gate
PK 32.6 Entrance to Joigny lock-cut, r/b
PK 32.0 Short quay r/b for restaurant La Côte-Saint-Jacques (three-star)
PK 31.6 **Joigny** *port de plaisance* l/b (Port des Maillotins), Locaboat hire base, 03 86 62 06 14, 28 berths, 4 visitor moorings, night €20, water and electricity included, showers €3, slipway, repairs, restaurant 100m

As often at boat hire bases, the possibility of mooring and using the available services depends on how busy the base is with its clients. Principal changeover days (especially Saturdays) are to be avoided. It is advisable to call the base in advance, to be sure of being able to moor. Just downstream from the Locaboat pontoons are two good stretches of quay on the same bank. Boats also moor immediately downstream and upstream of Joigny bridge, and there is another quay at about PK30.7 on the left bank. Joigny is a bustling, historic market town with lots of facilities (supermarkets, brico) within easy reach.

PK 31.1 Joigny bridge, town centre r/b
PK 28.7 Lock 2 (Pêchoir), l/b, weir
PK 24.8 Lock 1 (Épineau), l/b, weir, boat club with slipway d/s r/b

Entering lock 1 Épineau, PK 25 © ROUFINAK

PK 23.8 **Laroche-Saint-Cydroine** bridge, municipal *halte* on pontoon d/s r/b, night €5, water, electricity, village r/b
PK 22.9 Quay (Coches), r/b, **Migennes** 500m

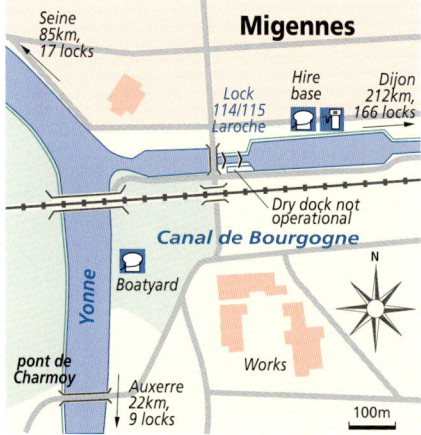

Yonne

PK 22.7	*Junction with Canal de Bourgogne*, r/b
PK 22.6	Railway bridge (Laroche)
PK 22.3	Boatyard (Evans Marine International), 03 86 92 93 13

A long-established and well-respected boatyard founded by the late John Parfitt, offering extensive facilities and services, including standing space for undertaking one's own repairs.

PK 22.2	Bridge (Charmoy)
PK 21.8	Bridge (Migennes)
PK 21.4	Confluence of Armançon, r/b
PK 21.1	Lock 9 (Gravière), l/b, weir
PK 17.9	**Bassou** bridge, village 400m l/b, **Bonnard** r/b, free mooring for 4 boats, 03 86 73 25 55, showers at camp site €2.20
PK 17.0	Lock 8 (Bassou), r/b, weir
PK 15.6	End of Gurgy lock-cut, navigation re-enters Yonne
PK 15.4	Lock 7 (Raveuse), bridge d/s
PK 14.0	Lock 6 (Néron), bridge d/s
PK 12.9	**Appoigny** bridge (skew), commercial quay u/s l/b, village 1.5km l/b
PK 12.0	Bridge (Chaumes)
PK 10.6	Bridge (Gurgy) and flood gate
PK 10.5	Entrance to Gurgy lock-cut, r/b
PK 10.1	**Gurgy** quay r/b, municipal *halte*, pontoon for up to 8 boats, 07 89 27 74 67, free, water €6 (800 litres), electricity €6 for 12 hours, wifi
PK 8.9	Motorway bridge (A6, Autoroute du Soleil)
PK 7.5	Lock 5 (Monéteau), r/b, weir
PK 6.8	**Monéteau** bridge, mooring r/b
PK 5.9	Lock 4 (Boisseaux), l/b, weir
PK 4.3	Lock 3 (Dumonts), l/b, weir
PK 3.2	Bridge (D606 Auxerre bypass)
PK 2.5	Lock 2 (Île Brûlée), l/b, weir
PK 1.0	Lock 1 (Chaînette), l/b, weir
PK 0.8	Bridge (Pont de la Tournelle)
PK 0.7	Bridge (Jean Moreau), hotel boat and trip boat moorings u/s l/b
PK 0.3	**Auxerre** footbridge, Aquarelle *port de plaisance* r/b, 90 berths, 30 visitor berths, *aquarelle-france.fr*, 03 86 46 96 77, night €12.50, fuel, water, electricity, showers €2, gantry 30t, slipway and winch, pump-out, storage, repairs, wifi, city centre and cathedral l/b

The hotel barge Luciole moored in Auxerre. The author passes on his bicycle (with the white helmet). © BOB NAYLOR/WATERMARX

Situated on the River Yonne, Auxerre originally became prosperous as an active port on the wine route. Today the town is the capital of the Yonne *département*. With 40 000 inhabitants, the it has a gentle, relaxed atmosphere with interesting shops and lots of casual restaurants. The medieval old town starts right behind the quay. From there, steep narrow cobbled streets with half-timbered houses lead up to the magnificently restored Saint-Étienne Cathedral. Moorings on west bank quayside, which has been improved by the town in recent years, but more for hotel barges and passenger boats than smaller craft, or at the *port de plaisance* opposite, but can be very popular, with boats often rafting up two or three deep. Supermarket nearby.

PK 0.0	*Connection with Canal du Nivernais* (Pont Paul-Bert in Auxerre)

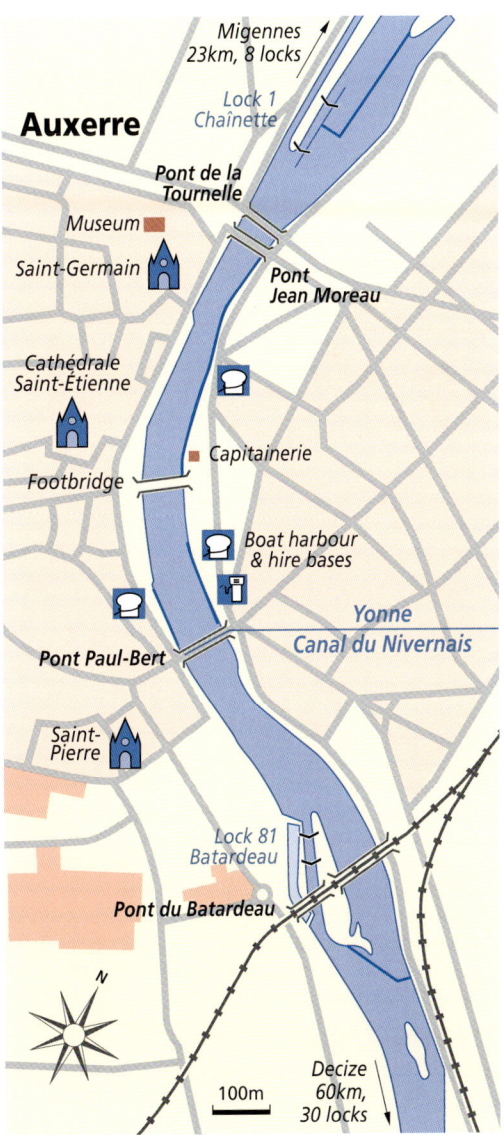

III – Central France and routes to the Saône

28. Canal de Bourgogne

THE CANAL DE BOURGOGNE CONNECTS the river Yonne at Laroche-Migennes with the river Saône at Saint-Jean-de-Losne, a distance of 242km. It provides the most spectacular and heavily-locked route between the Seine and the Mediterranean, rising to a summit level at an altitude of 378m, the highest in France. This pound includes a tunnel at Pouilly-en-Auxois, 3337m in length, extended by narrow cuttings on either side. A towage service used to operate with an electrically-powered tug and a ballasted caisson, for barges with an air draught greater than 3.10m, but this little-used and costly service was withdrawn in the 1970s. Boats proceed through the tunnel under their own power, provided that they have suitable lights, a klaxon and/or horn, and lifejackets sufficient for all on board. Authorisation must be requested at lock 1Y (Pouilly-en-Auxois) for boats arriving from the Yonne and at lock 1S (Escommes) for boats arriving from the Saône. When the tunnel-keeper has ensured that the pound is clear, he will give the go-ahead. Proceed at 6 km/h, without stopping, so as to clear the summit level quickly. If preferred, short lengths of log, which are normally to be found stacked outside the lock-keeper's cottage at either end, can be lashed fore and aft, possibly passing through your bollards. Extending about 30cm, they will assist in keeping the vessel in the middle of the channel as they scrape along the walls.

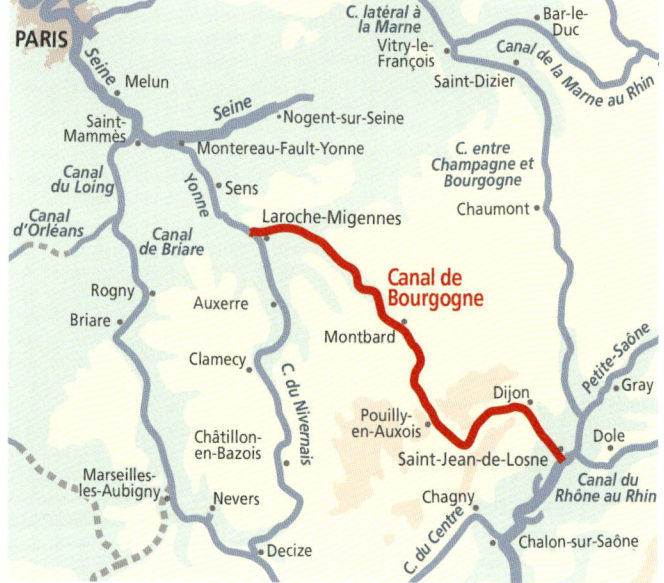

A canal on this route from the Saône to the Seine was envisaged in the early 17th century during the reign of Henri IV. The route was the subject of intense debate, reflected in a number of published works in the 17th and 18th centuries. Works began in 1774, and Dijon was reached from the Saône in 1808. It was another 24 years before the canal was opened throughout, in 1832. The locks were lengthened to the Freycinet standard in 1882, but the tunnel remained a bottleneck, even after the 1867 steam tug was replaced by an electric tug in 1893. The canal was experimentally taken over by the Région Bourgogne in 2010, but after two years returned to VNF's management. It carries very little traffic, and the region baulked at the rehabilitation expenditure to be committed.

Key dimensions (m)	
Length	38.50
Beam	5.10
Draught*	1.40
Air draught	3.50

* The available draught should be 1.80m, but in the absence of commercial traffic siltation at lock entrances has occurred in many locations, and the available depth is limited to 1.60m until further notice.

There is no longer any commercial traffic on the Canal de Bourgogne, except for the occasional mini-pushtow which enters from the Yonne, turns in the basin and then reverses up through one more lock to load grain at the silo. This beautiful waterway is a popular route for hotel barges, mainly on the eastern side of the summit. For *plaisanciers*, there is ample compensation for the large number of locks in the splendid scenery, with numerous sites of tourist interest to visit on or near the canal.

Navigation

The canal has the greatest density of locks of all the central French canals, and this makes it quite a challenge. The gradient is shallower and the locks are therefore further apart in the lower sections, roughly from the Yonne to Montbard and from Pont d'Ouche down to Saint-Jean-de-Losne. There is relatively sustained traffic in these sections during the high season, but there are very few boats crossing the summit. A consequence is that the *plaisancier* has to be accompanied by a mobile VNF lock-keeper to work through all the locks, and this takes some of the carefree spontaneity out of the day's cruising in the fabulous Burgundy countryside.

Users have reported differing states of maintenance of the canal, with problems resulting from weed growth, trees encroaching on the canal cross-section, lock gates blocked by dense packs of floating weed and lock walls bulging and leaking. At Tonnerre, several hundred metres of concrete piling is bulging and could seemingly collapse without warning. The section from Tonnerre to Venarey-les-Laumes is in relatively good condition; this is the section that has the heaviest traffic in hire boats. Bulging and leaking locks are a cause of concern on the flights of locks from Venarey

Canal de Bourgogne

up to the summit. From the summit level to the Saône the canal is regularly navigated by hotel barges, and is in a much better condition than on the Yonne side. Overall, these reservations should not dissuade the boater from cruising through this canal, which is consistently inspiring through its engineering, the landscapes, the châteaux and all the other heritage sites dotted along the route.

The maximum authorised speed is 6km/h for all boats throughout the canal.

Locks
There are 189 locks, of which 113 fall towards the Yonne and 76 towards the Saône. Lock dimensions are 39.00m by 5.20m. Two of the locks on the Yonne side have double numbers (106/107 and 114/115). These were originally built as staircase locks, but were replaced by single deep locks when the canal was upgraded to Freycinet standard. A lock-keeper is present at most of the locks up to lock 55Y and at all the locks on the Saône side, except at the start of the season when travelling lock-keepers are assigned to boats entering the canal. From lock 55Y to lock 16Y, the locks are operated throughout the season by travelling lock-keepers who manage sets or *chaînes* of locks. Advance notice is to be given at lock 55Y for the long climb to the summit level: between 9:00 and 11:00 to start in the afternoon, or between 13:30 and 17:00 for a start the following morning. Nineteen locks on the Yonne side (84Y to 81Y and 15Y to 1Y) and two on the Saône side (53S and 63S) have been equipped for automatic operation.

Draught
The maximum authorised draught is at present 1.40m (reduced from the official 1.80m on account of siltation).

Headroom
There are many fixed bridges, about half of them sited at locks. They all leave a clear headroom of 3.40m above normal water level.

Towpath
There is a good towpath throughout, except along the summit level and through the tunnel.

Authority
VNF Centre-Bourgogne,
  UTI, CEMI Armançon
– avenue Alfred Grevin, 89700 Tonnerre,
  03 86 54 82 70 (PK 0-94)
CEMI Auxois
– 11 rue du port, 21320 Pouilly-en-Auxois,
  03 80 90 85 98 serge.begat@vnf.fr (PK 94-173)
CEMI de l'Ouche
– 10 rue du port, 21600 Longvic,
  03 80 48 09 59 eric.mougenot@vnf.fr (PK 173-242)

Route description

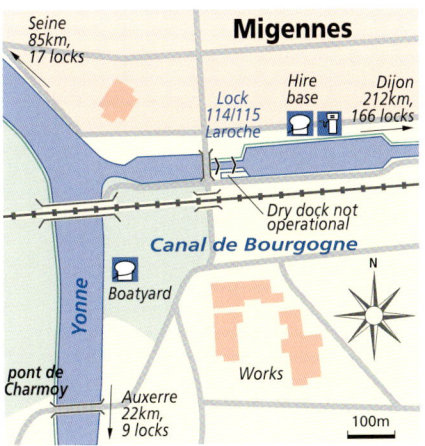

PK 0.0	Junction with canalised river Yonne (PK 23)	
PK 0.2	Bridge (Migennes)	
PK 0.3	Deep lock 114/115Y (Laroche), VHF 18, height 5.13m	
PK 0.5	**Migennes** basin, moorings, Le Boat hire base, 03 86 80 08 60, 12 visitor berths, night €10.60, water and electricity included, diesel, showers €3, wifi, slipway, restaurant, town centre 400m migennes@leboat.fr	
PK 0.8	Footbridge (access to station)	
PK 1.7	Lock 113Y (Cheny), mechanised, bridge, basin d/s r/b, silo u/s l/b	
PK 6.5	**Esnon** bridge, quay d/s r/b	
PK 7.9	Lock 112Y (Moulin-Neuf), quay d/s r/b	
PK 9.2	**Brienon-sur-Armançon** bridge, quay in basin d/s, Tourisme Fluvial du Centre hire base, 06 04 51 19 73, night €10, water and electricity included, showers €2.50, wifi, village r/b, brienonmarine.fr	
PK 9.6	Brienon sugar refinery, quay l/b	
PK 10.2	Lock 111Y (Boutoir), bridge, Créanton aqueduct u/s	
PK 12.5	Bridge (Crécy), quay d/s r/b	
PK 14.1	Railway bridge (Avrolles), TGV Sud-Est line	
PK 15.1	Lock 110Y (Duchy), bridge, quays d/s r/b	
PK 17.2	Lock 109Y (Maladrerie), bridge, quay d/s r/b	
PK 18.6	Lock 108Y (Saint-Florentin), bridge, Armance aqueduct	
PK 18.8	**Saint-Florentin** basin and boat harbour r/b, mooring for 45 boats, 15 visitor berths, night €10, water, electricity (metered), showers, slipway, pump-out, repairs, wifi, moorings for large vessels l/b (no services), town centre 700m r/b portdeplaisance89600@gmail.com	

Saint-Florentin is one of the most popular *ports de plaisance* in Burgundy.

PK 19.1	Bridge (Saint-Florentin, N77) and railway bridge	
PK 19.3	Quay r/b, Gruc	
PK 20.9	Footbridge	
PK 21.8	Lock 106/107Y (**Germigny**), VHF 20, bridge, quays u/s and d/s r/b, village 1km r/b	
PK 23.4	Lock 105Y (Egrevin), bridge	
PK 25.2	**Butteaux** bridge, quay u/s r/b, village 700m	
PK 26.8	Lock 104Y (Percey), bridge	
PK 27.5	**Percey** quay r/b, small village 300m	
PK 27.8	Lock 103Y (Chailley), bridge	
PK 29.4	Lock 102Y (Villiers-Vineux)	
PK 30.5	Lock 101Y (Flogny)	

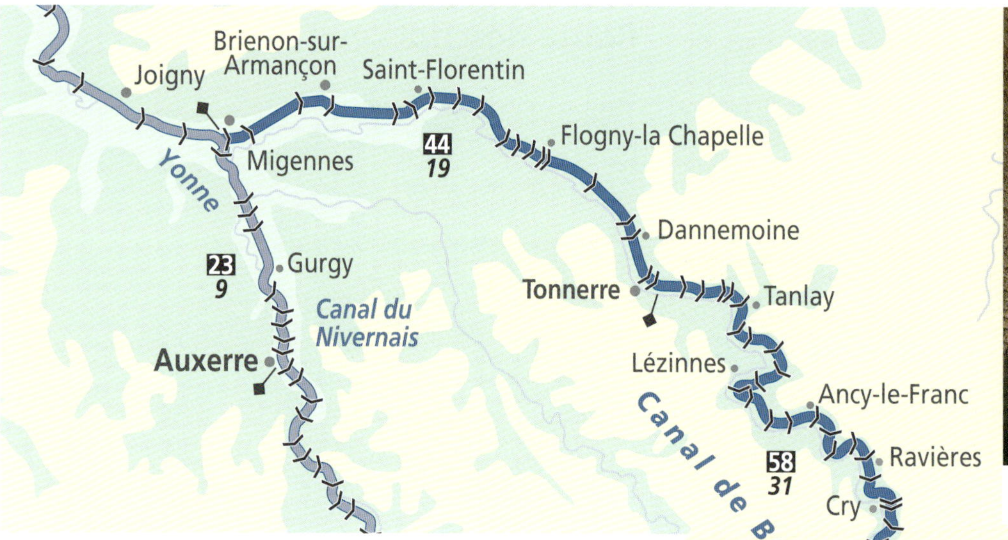

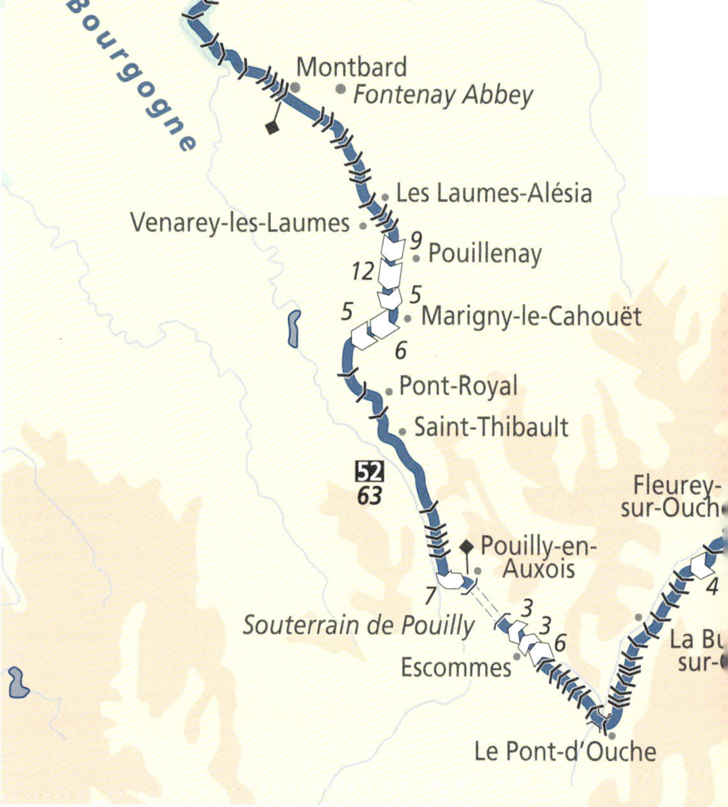

III – Central France and routes to the Saône

Church in Fontenay Abbey

PK 30.9	Lock 100Y (Flogny), basin d/s	
PK 31.4	**Flogny** bridge, boat moorings d/s r/b, water, electricity, village 500m	
PK 32.8	**La Chapelle** bridge, quay d/s r/b, village 900m	
PK 34.9	Lock 99Y (Charrey), bridge, quay d/s r/b	
PK 37.9	**Tronchoy** bridge, village r/b	
PK 39.1	Lock 98Y (Cheney), bridge	
PK 40.0	**Dannemoine** quay r/b, village 400m	
PK 40.3	Lock 97Y (Dannemoine), bridge, water	
PK 42.8	Footbridge (Épineuil)	
PK 44.1	Lock 96Y (Tonnerre), bridge	
PK 44.3	**Tonnerre** basin and boat harbour, France Afloat hire base, mooring for 25 boats, night €9 up to 5 persons on board, €17 for 6 or more, water and electricity included, showers (€2.50), town centre 1 km l/b	
PK 44.6	Lock 95Y (Tonnerre), VHF 22, bridge	
PK 45.1	Bridge (D905)	
PK 46.5	Lock 94Y (Arcot), bridge	
PK 48.7	Lock 93Y (Arthe)	
PK 49.9	Bridge (Arthe)	
PK 50.4	Lock 92Y (Saint-Martin)	
PK 50.8	Lock 91Y (Commissey), bridge	
PK 51.6	**Commissey** bridge, small village r/b	
PK 52.7	Lock 90Y (Tanlay), VHF 18	

Lock 90Y, Tanlay

Pouilly basin and the summit viewed from Lock 1Y

Canal de Bourgogne

The splendid renaissance château at Tanlay

PK **53.0** **Tanlay** basin r/b, municipal *halte*, 5 berths for boats, 2 moorings for hotel barges, night €8 water and electricity included, village with château r/b

PK **53.2** Bridge (Tanlay)
PK **54.6** Overhead power lines
PK **55.2** Lock 89Y (Moulin de Saint-Vinnemer), bridge
PK **56.4** **Saint-Vinnemer** bridge, quay u/s r/b, village r/b
PK **56.7** Lock 88Y (Saint-Vinnemer)
PK **59.6** Lock 87Y (**Argentenay**), bridge, village 300m l/b
PK **61.4** Lock 86Y (**Ancy-le-Libre**), bridge, village 400m
PK **63.0** Railway bridge (main line Paris-Dijon)
PK **63.4** Lock 85Y (Lézinnes), bridge, water, basin u/s r/b, village 600m l/b
PK **65.1** Lock 84Y (Batilley), mechanised, cement works quay u/s
PK **66.3** Lock 83Y (Pacy), mechanised

PK **66.9** Quay (Pacy-Varennes) r/b
PK **67.5** Bridge (Pacy)
PK **69.7** Lock 82Y (Argenteuil), mechanised, bridge
PK **70.2** Railway bridge (through route Paris-Dijon)
PK **71.2** Lock 81Y (Rapille), mechanised, bridge
PK **73.7** Bridge (Cusy)
PK **73.8** **Ancy-le-Franc** basin, municipal *halte* r/b, up to 10 berths, night €8, water and electricity included, village with château 800m r/b
PK **74.4** Lock 80Y (Ancy-le-Franc), VHF 22, bridge
PK **75.4** Lock 79Y (**Chassignelles**), bridge, village r/b
PK **77.1** **Fulvy** bridge, basin d/s, small village 700m l/b
PK **77.8** Lock 78Y (Fulvy)
PK **80.1** Lock 77Y (Papeterie), bridge (Chassignelles)
PK **81.8** Lock 76Y (Huilerie), bridge (Ravières)
PK **82.1** Railway bridge
PK **82.3** Bridge (Ravières)
PK **82.6** **Ravières** basin, *port de plaisance*, 03 86 55 70 68, free mooring for 6-10 boats (€20 for barges), water, electricity, showers, winter base of hotel barges of European Waterways Ltd, village 150m r/b
PK **82.9** **Nuits-sur-Armançon** bridge, quay u/s r/b
PK **83.2** Bridge
PK **84.1** Lock 75Y (Nuits), bridge
PK **86.5** Lock 74Y (Arlot), bridge
PK **87.2** Lock 73Y (**Cry**), bridge, municipal *halte* d/s r/b, up to 3 boats, free, water, village 400m l/b
PK **89.3** Lock 72Y (Perrigny), bridge
PK **91.5** Lock 71Y (Forge d'Aisy), bridge, basin u/s
PK **91.8** Bridge (D905, Aisy by-pass)
PK **92.4** **Aisy-sur-Armançon** bridge, quay u/s l/b, village 400m
PK **93.0** Bridge (Rougemont)
PK **94.0** Lock 70Y (Rougemont), bridge
PK **95.0** Lock 69Y (Buffon)
PK **95.5** Bridge (Grande-Forge), mooring possible u/s r/b

Moor here to visit the fascinating ironworks, inspired by Buffon's work, using hydraulic power to activate all the machines. The canal was built through a cutting to bypass the site, which was already in full production when the canal was being designed.

PK **96.4** **Buffon** bridge, small village r/b
PK **96.9** Former bridge (Petite-Forge), restricted passage

The canal narrows past the historic Buffon forge

III – Central France and routes to the Saône

PK **97.6** Lock 68Y (Buffon)
PK **98.5** **Saint-Rémy** bridge, quay u/s l/b, village 300m, château opposite
PK **99.3** Lock 67Y (Saint-Rémy), bridge
PK **100.6** Lock 66Y (Fontenay)
PK **101.4** Lock 65Y (Montbard), aqueduct u/s, bridge (D980)
PK **101.7** **Montbard** lower basin, marina r/b, pontoons for 8 boats, 03 80 92 69 50, night €10, water, electricity, showers, slipway, restaurant, town centre 300m
PK **102.2** Lock 64Y (Montbard), bridge, water
PK **102.3** Bridge (Gare)
PK **102.5** **Montbard** upper basin l/b, 03 80 92 01 34, mooring for 20 boats, night €10 including water/electricity (€8 from fifth night), showers, restaurant, slipway

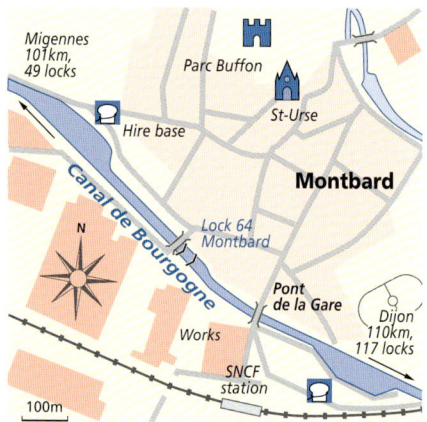

Montbard is a must for shopping (no further possibilities before Pouilly-en-Auxois) and for the museum dedicated to the early 19th century scientist and inventor Buffon. Montbard is a lively town, proud of its heritage and that of the nearby Fontenay abbey, a UNESCO World Heritage site.

PK **102.8** Railway bridge (through route Paris-Dijon)
PK **105.3** Lock 63Y (Nogent)
PK **106.0** **Nogent** bridge, quay d/s l/b, small village
PK **106.3** Lock 62Y (Moulin de Nogent)
PK **108.2** Lock 61Y (**Courcelles**), bridge, water, small village l/b
PK **109.3** Lock 60Y (Benoisey)
PK **109.9** Bridge (Benoisey)
PK **111.1** Lock 59Y (Seigny)
PK **111.4** Bridge (Grignon)
PK **112.2** Lock 58Y (Grignon)
PK **112.8** Lock 57Y (Granges), bridge
PK **113.2** **Les Granges-sous-Grignon** bridge, village l/b
PK **114.5** Lock 56Y (Venarey)
PK **115.3** **Venarey-les-Laumes** bridge, quay d/s l/b, Nicols hire base, moorings, 03 80 92 30 05, up to 12 boats, night €8.50, water €3.50, electricity €3.50, showers, slipway, restaurant, village 400m l/b, remains of Gallo-Roman town 5km r/b *venarey@nicols.com*

The quay beside the basin and one of the large workshops are used by French Country Waterways hotel barges, for maintenance and repairs, as well as being their headquarters.

Arrange here to meet lock-keeper who accompanies boats for the next day and a half (minimum) while locking through from 55Y to 16Y.

Venarey-les-Laumes © AEROPIX DIJON

PK **116.0** Lock 55Y (Venarey)
PK **116.3** Bridge (Venarey)
PK **116.6** Lock 54Y (Venarey)
PK **116.9** Lock 53Y (Mussy)
PK **117.5** Lock 52Y (Mussy), bridge
PK **118.2** Lock 51Y (Pouillenay)
PK **118.6** Lock 50Y (Pouillenay)
PK **118.9** Lock 49Y (Pouillenay), basin u/s
PK **119.1** Lock 48Y (Pouillenay)
PK **119.3** Lock 47Y (Pouillenay)
PK **119.6** Lock 46Y (Pouillenay)
PK **119.7** **Pouillenay** bridge, basin u/s l/b, village 800m r/b
PK **119.9** Lock 45Y (Pouillenay)
PK **120.2** Lock 44Y (Pouillenay), basin u/s l/b
PK **120.4** Lock 43Y (Pouillenay)
PK **120.7** Lock 42Y (Pouillenay)
PK **121.0** Lock 41Y (Pouillenay), bridge
PK **121.3** Lock 40Y (Pouillenay)
PK **121.5** Lock 39Y (Pouillenay)
PK **121.8** Lock 38Y (Pouillenay)
PK **122.1** Lock 37Y (Pouillenay), basin u/s
PK **122.3** Lock 36Y (Chassey 6)
PK **122.7** Lock 35Y (Chassey 5), bridge
PK **122.9** Lock 34Y (Chassey 4), large basin u/s, overnight mooring
PK **123.3** Lock 33Y (Chassey 3)
PK **123.4** **Chassey** bridge, small village 700m l/b
PK **123.6** Lock 32Y (Chassey 2), basin u/s l/b
PK **123.9** Railway bridge
PK **124.0** Lock 31Y (Chassey 1), bridge
PK **124.4** Lock 30Y (Marigny)
PK **124.7** Lock 29Y (Marigny)
PK **125.1** Lock 28Y (Marigny)
PK **125.4** **Marigny-le-Carouët** lock 27Y, bridge, municipal *halte* u/s, free, water €1.50
PK **125.8** Lock 26Y (Marigny), basin u/s l/b
PK **126.0** Lock 25Y (Marigny)
PK **126.4** Lock 24Y (Marigny), bridge
PK **127.0** Lock 23Y (Marigny), bridge
PK **127.3** Lock 22Y (Marigny)
PK **127.7** Lock 21Y (Marigny)
PK **128.4** Lock 20Y (Marigny), bridge
PK **128.8** Lock 19Y (Marigny)
PK **129.2** Lock 18Y (Marigny)
PK **129.5** Lock 17Y (Charigny)

Canal de Bourgogne

PK **129.9** Lock 16Y (Charigny), bridge

This is the last of the series of lock operated by accompanying lock-keeper. The locks from here up to Pouilly are automatic.

PK **131.0** Bridge (Villeneuve-sous-Charigny)
PK **132.3** Lock 15Y (Braux), bridge
PK **132.6** Cutting (La Croisée), one-way traffic for 470m
PK **134.0** **Braux** bridge, basin d/s r/b, village 700m r/b
PK **134.8** Bridge (Pierre-My)
PK **135.3** Lock 14Y (Braux)
PK **135.5** Cutting (Saucy), one-way traffic for 280m
PK **136.3** Bridge (Saucy)
PK **137.1** **Pont-Royal** bridge, basin d/s r/b managed by La Maison du Canal, 8 boats, free, water, electricity, showers, wifi (all services charged), slipway, small village, restaurant

Another way of enjoying the canal at Pont-Royal

A sleepy hamlet built around what was once a bustling canal basin, but is now a haven of tranquillity and *joie de vivre*, symbolised by the Maison du Canal B&B in the former toll house, also offering a comfortable motor yacht moored in the basin, for overnight stays. Vitteaux is a small town just 8km east, useful for supplies, while the medieval fortress of Thil is just a little further away in the opposite direction (west), and is well worth visiting. Unfortunately the adjoining Sainte-Trinité collegiate church is privately owned and cannot be visited.

PK **137.5** Lock 13Y (Pont Royal)
PK **137.8** Beginning of Creuzot cutting (1130m in length), one-way traffic only (with passing bays) PK **138.5** Bridge (D970)
PK **138.6** Bridge (Creuzot)
PK **139.0** End of cutting
PK **140.0** **Saint-Thibault** bridge, basin u/s r/b, village 600m r/b (shop)
PK **141.0** Cutting (Saint-Thibault) 145m long, bridge
PK **142.9** Bridge (D970)
PK **143.8** **Beurizot** bridge, basin with quay d/s r/b, village 400m r/b
PK **145.9** Bridge (D970), basin d/s r/b
PK **146.5** Bridge (Gissey-le-Vieil)
PK **147.9** Lock 12Y (Gissey-le-Vieil), bridge
PK **148.1** Basin (Grandchamp)
PK **148.9** Bridge (Garreau)
PK **149.4** Bridge (Éguilly), castle l/b
PK **149.7** Lock 11Y (Éguilly), start of regulated flight (one or two lock-keepers on duty from here to the summit level)

Part of the Creuzot cutting, viewed from the widening in the middle

PK **150.5** Lock 10Y (Croix-Rouge)
PK **151.3** Lock 9Y (Morons)
PK **151.7** Lock 8Y (Carrons)
PK **152.6** Lock 7Y (Chailly), bridge
PK **153.1** Lock 6Y (Argilas)
PK **153.4** Lock 5Y (Pelleson)
PK **153.7** Lock 4Y (Cercey), bridge
PK **154.0** Lock 3Y (Champ-Roger)
PK **154.3** Lock 2Y (Lochère)
PK **154.6** Lock 1Y (Pouilly), bridge, beginning of summit level

The lock-keeper here checks that your boat has a suitable light for proceeding through the Pouilly tunnel, and also lends a VHF radio for communication if necessary.

PK **154.7** **Pouilly-en-Auxois** basin r/b, 03 80 90 77 36, mooring for 12 boats, free, water €4/1000 litres, electricity €5/day, shower, slipway, wifi, *cap-canal.fr*, former tunnel tug in dry dock, restaurant, village 1.5km with all shops

Pouilly sits proudly on top of the canal tunnel and has a good choice of shops, a supermarket and other services. It owes its relative prosperity much more to the nearby motorway junction than to the canal, which sees very little traffic. The local trip-boat *Billebaude* offers excursions through the tunnel.

PK **155.1** Beginning of Pouilly cutting (narrow)
PK **155.8** Footbridge
PK **156.0** Pouilly tunnel, northern entrance
PK **159.4** Pouilly tunnel, southern entrance
PK **160.1** Bridge (Lochère)
PK **160.3** End of cutting
PK **160.4** **Escommes** basin l/b, moorings, water and electricity
PK **160.7** Lock 1S (Escommes), end of summit level, dry lock r/b

Northbound, the lock-keeper here checks that your boat has a suitable light for proceeding through the Pouilly tunnel, and also lends a VHF radio for communication if necessary.

III – Central France and routes to the Saône

The passenger boat Billebaude *exits Pouilly tunnel southbound.*

PK **161.1** Lock 2S (Sermaize), bridge
PK **161.4** Lock 3S (Rambourg)
PK **161.7** Lock 4S (Grand-Pré)
PK **162.1** Lock 5S (Chevrotte)
PK **162.4** Lock 6S (Chaume)
PK **162.7** Lock 7S (Vachey)
PK **163.1** Lock 8S (Vandenesse), bridge
PK **163.2 Vandenesse-en-Auxois** *halte* l/b, quay 150m long, 06 07 26 54 02, water €4/day, electricity €6/day, village r/b, restaurants **communedevandenesse.com**

A spectacular location, overlooked by the medieval château at Châteauneuf.

PK **163.5** Lock 9S (Fourneau), moorings u/s
PK **163.9** Lock 10S (Mine)
PK **164.2 Châteauneuf** bridge, village with hilltop castle 1200m l/b
PK **164.4** Lock 11S (Rêpe)
PK **165.1** Lock 12S (Révin), bridge
PK **165.4** Motorway bridge (A6)
PK **165.9** Lock 13S (Sainte-Sabine)
PK **166.4** Bridge (Sainte-Sabine), quay d/s r/b
PK **167.6** Lock 14S (Bouhey), bridge
PK **168.4** Lock 15S (Fontenis)
PK **169.2** Lock 16S (Crugey)
PK **169.5 Crugey** bridge, basin d/s r/b, small village r/b
PK **169.7** Motorway bridge (A6)
PK **170.1** Lock 17S (Rempart)
PK **171.4** Lock 18S (Roche-aux-Fées), bridge
PK **172.0** Lock 19S (Sarrée), bridge
PK **172.5** Bridge (Froideville)
PK **172.6 Pont d'Ouche** basin and private *port de plaisance*, managed by Le Bistrot du Port, 06 80 02 17 38, 18 berths, night €7.50, water and electricity included, showers €3, wifi, wintering possible, small village, restaurant

This is the only port between Pouilly and Dijon.

PK **172.8** Ouche aqueduct
PK **173.1** Lock 20S (Pont d'Ouche)
PK **173.8** Lock 21S (Baugey)
PK **175.1** Lock 22S (Veuvey)
PK **175.7 Veuvey-sur-Ouche** bridge, water, quay u/s r/b, village l/b
PK **176.5** Lock 23S (Antheuil)
PK **177.4** Lock 24S (Angles)
PK **179.1** Lock 25S (Forge), bridge
PK **179.6** Lock 26S (Bussière), bridge, water, basin u/s l/b, **La Bussière-sur-Ouche** 300m l/b
PK **180.2** Lock 27S (Bouchot)
PK **181.3** Lock 28S (Chaume)
PK **182.5** Lock 29S (Saint-Victor), bridge, **Saint-Victor-sur-Ouche** 200m r/b
PK **183.9** Lock 30S (Dennevy)
PK **184.5** Bridge
PK **185.0** Lock 31S (Barbirey)
PK **186.2** Lock 32S (Gissey-sur-Ouche)
PK **186.5 Gissey-sur-Ouche** bridge, moorings in basin u/s r/b, 06 48 23 47 72, night €3.50, water €0.75/100 litres, electricity €5.50/day, shower, small village l/b
PK **187.5** Lock 33S (Saint-Eau)
PK **189.0** Lock 34S (Moulin Banet)
PK **189.8** Lock 35S (Champagne)
PK **190.5** Lock 36S (**Sainte-Marie**), bridge, village 300m l/b
PK **192.1** Lock 37S (Roche-Canot), moorings d/s l/b
PK **193.5** Lock 38S (Pont-de-Pany), bridge, basin, moorings d/s r/b
PK **194.0** Skew motorway bridge (A38)
PK **194.7** Lock 39S (Chassagne)
PK **195.4** Lock 40S (Morcoeuil)
PK **196.3** Lock 41S (Potet), turning basin d/s r/b
PK **197.4 Fleurey-sur-Ouche** bridge, moorings u/s r/b, village r/b
PK **198.0** Lock 42S (Fleurey)
PK **198.7** Disused railway bridge
PK **199.6** Lock 43S (Creux-Suzon)
PK **200.6** Lock 44S (Combe-de-Fain)
PK **201.7** Lock 45S (Velars), bridge
PK **201.8 Velars** quay r/b, water and electricity, village l/b over bridge, all services
PK **202.6** Lock 46S (Verrerie)
PK **203.8** Lock 47S (Crucifix)
PK **205.0** Lock 48S (Neuvon)
PK **205.9** Lock 49S (Craie)
PK **206.9 Plombières-lès-Dijon** basin l/b, *halte* on 80m long quay, 06 66 37 20 24, night €13 (up to 20m), water and electricity by tokens, slipway, village 400m l/b
PK **207.0** Lock 50S (Plombières), bridge
PK **208.0** Motorway bridge (A38)
PK **208.4** Lock 51S (Bruant), mooring d/s l/b for Lac Kir

The lake named after the Chanoine Kir (who gave his name to the popular apéritif mixing blackcurrant liqueur and white wine) is a popular park that can become crowded at week-ends.

PK **210.2** Lock 52S (Carrières Blanches), bridge
PK **210.5** Lock 53S (Marcs-d'Or), automatic
PK **210.8** Bridge
PK **211.2** Bridge
PK **211.3** Lock 54S (Larrey), footbridge and bridges
PK **212.3** Bridge

Canal de Bourgogne

PK **212.4 Dijon** basin, *port de plaisance*, mooring for 30 boats managed by VNF, 03 45 34 13 50, night €11, water, electricity, shower €2, town centre 1km l/b (good tram service)

It can be a squeeze to moor in the large basin, which has many residential barges, but the illustrious capital of Burgundy is a place to stay and enjoy for a week or more. Some passing boats moor on the quay on the towpath side, but this is a big city, and all due precautions should be taken.

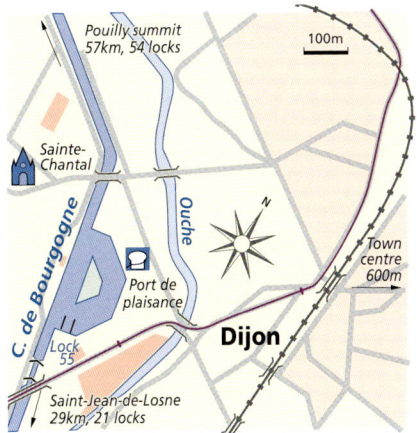

PK **212.7** Lock 55S (Dijon), bridge
PK **213.3** Bridge (Dijon ring road), former basin d/s r/b
PK **213.5** Railway bridge (main line Dijon-Lyon)
PK **214.1** Footbridge (access to railway yard)
PK **214.9** Lock 56S (Colombière), bridge
PK **215.0** Railway bridge, basin and quay d/s r/b
PK **215.9** Lock 57S (Romelet), new road bridge
PK **216.3** Bridge (N274 motorway spur)
PK **216.7 Longvic** bridge, village (Dijon suburb) 500m l/b
PK **217.0** Lock 58S (Longvic)
PK **217.5** Lock 59S (Beauregard), bridge
PK **218.4** Lock 60S (Préville), quay u/s r/b
PK **219.3** Lock 61S (Grand-Ouges), bridge, quay d/s r/b
PK **220.7** Lock 62S (Petit-Ouges), bridge
PK **221.4** Lock 63S (Vernois), automatic
PK **222.0** Motorway bridge (A31)
PK **222.6** Lock 64S (Époisses), bridge, moorings d/s r/b, turning basin l/b
PK **223.6** Lock 65S (Bretenières), bridge
PK **225.2** Lock 66S (Rouvres), VHF 20, bridge
PK **226.3** Lock 67S (**Thorey**), bridge, small village r/b, bakery, little shops, supermarket
PK **227.1** Lock 68S (Combe)
PK **228.2** Lock 69S (Longecourt), VHF 22, bridge, mooring u/s l/b
PK **228.3 Longecourt-en-Plaine** basin, silo and quay l/b, village r/b

Fine château in the village 700m from the lock.

PK **229.9** Lock 70S (Potangey)
PK **230.6** Bridge (Potangey), mooring d/s l/b
PK **231.8** Lock 71S (Aiserey), VHF 18, bridge
PK **233.1** Lock 72S (Bièrtre)
PK **235.1** Lock 73S (Pont-Hémery), bridge, quay d/s r/b
PK **236.3** Bridge (Chapelle)
PK **236.9** Lock 74S (Brazey). private quay u/s r/b (old sugar mill)

PK **237.4 Brazey-en-Plaine** bridge (Pont de Montot), basin d/s r/b, village 500m r/b
PK **239.6** Lock 75S (Viranne), mechanised, bridge
PK **239.7** Bridge (D968)
PK **240.2** Railway bridge
PK **241.5 Saint-Usage** bridge, canal basin with moorings d/s, night €10, dry dock, shipchandler, all services, village 250m l/b
PK **242.0** Lock 76S (Saint-Jean-de-Losne), VHF 20, bridge
PK **242.1 Saint-Jean-de-Losne**, *junction with Saône* and entrance to canal basin (Gare d'Eau), Le Boat hire base, H2O port de plaisance 03 80 39 08 08, 250 berths, 10 visitor moorings, night €10, water, electricity €2, Blanquart-Yachting 06 07 74 82 30, 80 berths, 8 visitor moorings, night €10, water, electricity, shower, crane, slipway, pump-out, repairs, chandlery, restaurant, wifi, Atelier Fluvial boatyard and dry dock, all repairs and maintenance, 03 80 27 03 00, town centre 500m

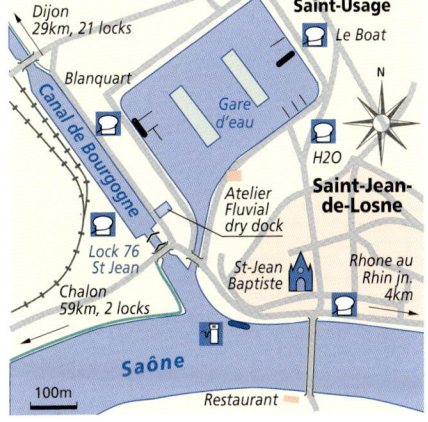

The Gare d'eau at Saint-Jean-de-Losne

III – Central France and routes to the Saône

29. Canal du Nivernais

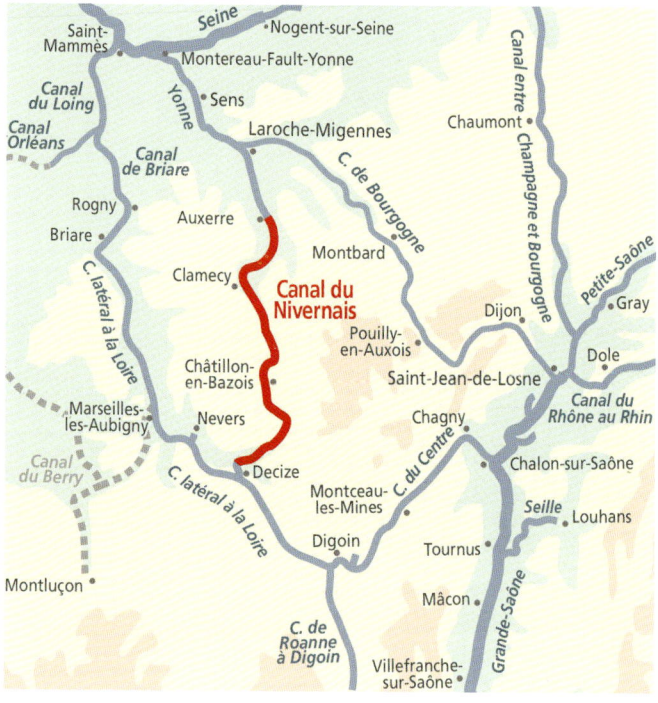

The Canal du Nivernais is a jewel of the French waterway network, passing through pretty woodlands, green tunnels of foliage and charming villages, with banksides planted with fruit and nut trees. It provides an alternative to the main north-south routes from the Seine basin to the Saône and Rhône, connecting the Yonne at Auxerre (upstream from the junction with the Canal de Bourgogne) to the Loire at Decize, a distance of 174 km. Across the Loire from Saint-Léger-des-Vignes is the entrance to the Decize branch of the Canal latéral à la Loire, while the Yonne gives access to the Canal de Bourgogne at Migennes. The Nivernais thus forms a cross link between the Bourbonnais and Bourgogne routes from Paris to Lyon.

The 58km central section of the canal from Sardy (PK 73, on the Yonne side) to Cercy-la-Tour (PK 15, on the Loire side) was built with 'sub-standard' locks 30m long, thus precluding its use as a through route by 38.50m barges. This was the main reason for its commercial decline, consequent lack of maintenance and its rapidly deteriorating condition in the 1960s. Thanks to the interest aroused by the Saint Line hire base, established on the canal's summit level in 1964, closure was avoided, and the central section was conceded by the State to the department of Nièvre in 1972. Rehabilitation works financed by the *département* with State and regional contributions secured the canal's future.

At the same time mooring and service facilities for pleasure boats were set up throughout the canal. Hire bases have come and gone but presently there are five companies offering well over 100 boats for cruising on the canal. It is also regularly navigated by a few hotel barges, which cruise primarily between Auxerre and Clamecy. The Nivernais was the home to *Palinurus*, the first hotel barge, in the late 1960s, and is still the preferred route of John and Penny Liley's hotel barge *Luciole*.

The 4.5km summit level, at an altitude of 262m, connects with the Étang de Baye, a large reservoir which becomes a hive of dinghy sailing and other recreational activity during the summer.

There is one branch, extending 3.9km from the *râcle* (a local word for *bief* or reach) du Maunoir (PK 154) to the town of Vermenton on the river Cure.

> The Canal du Nivernais was not originally designed as a through route but as a feeder waterway to float firewood from the Morvan to the already established log-floating route on the Yonne and Seine, to serve the needs of Paris. The works begun in 1784 were interrupted by the Revolution. When they were resumed in the 1820s, the project had evolved to a regular navigation for horse-drawn barges connecting the Loire at Saint-Léger-des-Vignes (near Decize) to the canalised river Yonne at Auxerre, a distance of 174km. The canal was opened as such in 1841 but suffered almost immediately from railway competition and was never a commercial success. However, it has become one of the most popular cruising waterways of the Burgundy network over the last 40 years.

Navigation

The canal incorporates numerous river sections or *râcles* in the the Yonne valley. In these reaches the channel is maintained over a width of only 20m from the bank on the towpath side and care should be taken to keep within this limit. At Basseville (PK 118.5) the canal crosses the Yonne on the level and at right angles. Previously, during high water, a cable and winch system was used to assist in the crossing. The fixed weir has now been replaced by a hydraulic gated weir, adjustable at short notice. Although the crossing must be completed cautiously, it is no longer a reason for concern. An unusual hazard is the intermittent presence of small platforms to allow animals that have fallen into the canal to climb out. These plates of metal jut out from the bank just under the surface of the water.

The summit level includes three tunnels, La Collancelle (758m), Mouas (268m) and Les Breuilles (212m), separated by deep cuttings. The minimum headroom is 3.75m and the minimum width 5.60m. One-way traffic is enforced and controlled by lights.

The speed limit is 8 km/h, reduced to 3 km/h when passing moored boats.

Canal du Nivernais

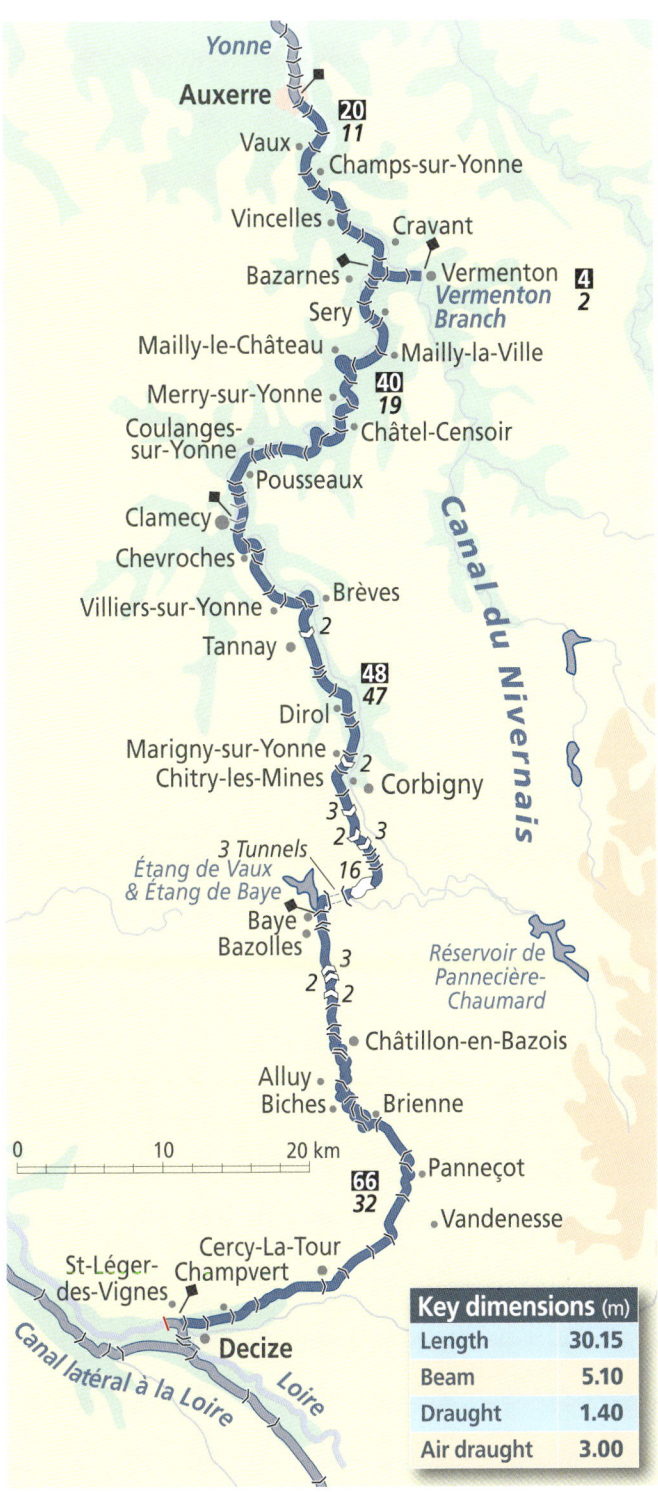

Key dimensions (m)	
Length	30.15
Beam	5.10
Draught	1.40
Air draught	3.00

In recent years the canal's water supply system has been improved, so that stoppages due to drought are rare.

Locks

There are 112 locks, including 4 stop locks. From the summit level to the Loire there are 32 locks and 3 stop locks, while on the Yonne side there are 76 locks and one stop lock. In addition there are five sets of flood gates numbered as locks. There are several double staircase locks and one triple staircase. There were originally 114 locks, but stop lock 47 bis and lock 48 at Clamecy were closed, and navigation here follows the River Yonne instead of the former lock-cut. From Auxerre to Sardy-lès-Épiry and from Cercy-la-Tour to Saint-Léger-des-Vignes (as well as on the Vermenton branch), the lock dimensions are 38.50m by 5.30m. The locks on the central section have reduced dimensions of 30.15m by 5.10m.

Draught

For the first 3km from Saint-Léger and from Clamecy down to Auxerre, including the Vermenton branch, the maximum permissible draught is 1.70m. The central section is open to vessels with a maximum draught of 1.20m only. A 10-year dredging campaign should be completed by 2025, restoring an authorised draught of 1.40m, with a regular depth of 1.60m. This involves extracting a total of 285 000m³ of sediments, or an average of 40 cm over the 7m wide channel throughout the shallow section of the canal. Water levels above Clamecy and over the summit to Cercy-la-Tour have been a problem in the past but now difficulties only arise in periods of extreme and prolonged drought.

Headroom

From Saint-Léger to La Copine basin (PK 3) the minimum headroom is 3.70m. Onwards, the headroom under the fixed bridges at normal water level is 2.70m as far as Sardy (this restricted headroom applies to two bridges, at Cercy-La-Tour and upstream of Vandenesse. From Sardy to Auxerre, the headroom is 3.10m, reduced to 2.97m under the bridge at Picampoix (lock 21) and to about 3.00m under the bridge at Mailly-la-Ville (PK 146). The fixed bridges on the Vermenton branch leave a minimum headroom of 3.35m.

Towpath

There is a good towpath throughout the length of the canal section from Saint-Léger to Clamecy. Along the river sections between Clamecy and Auxerre the official right-of-way is only occasionally practicable, or flanked by a local road.

Authority

VNF Centre-Bourgogne, UTI Nivernais
– rue au Loup, 58800 Corbigny   03 86 20 27 05
uti.nivernais@vnf.fr

The first lock (Batardeau) entering the Canal du Nivernais from the Yonne in Auxerre. © BINNENVAART IN BEELD

III – Central France and routes to the Saône

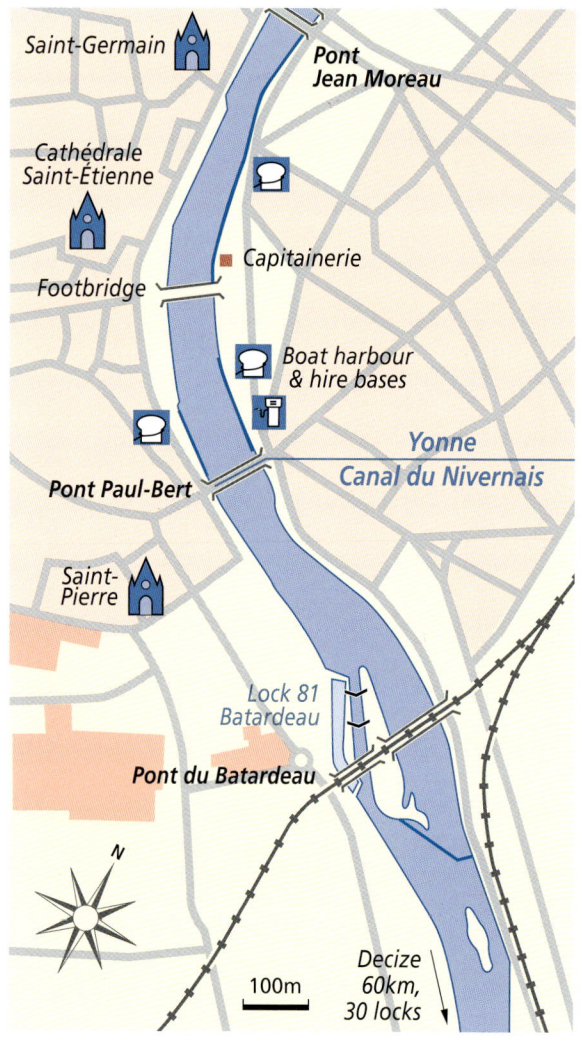

Route description

PK **174.1** **Auxerre** bridge (Paul-Bert), large town with all shops and services, junction with canalised river Yonne, quays d/s (see under Yonne)

The town of Auxerre and its fine *port de plaisance* belong to the River Yonne. See the description on p. 153.

PK **173.8** Lock 81 (Batardeau) in short lock-cut l/b
PK **173.7** Railway bridge (Batardeau)
PK **172.5** Lock 80 (Preuilly) in lock-cut l/b
PK **170.6** Lock 79 (Augy) in 320m lock-cut l/b
PK **168.6** Lock 78 (Vaux) in 450m lock-cut l/b
PK **167.9** **Vaux** bridge, village and restaurant l/b

Short-term mooring possible above and below the bridge, to a sloping masonry quay.

PK **166.2** Lock 77 (Toussac), in lock-cut

Lock-cut separated from the river by a stone wall.

PK **165.0** Lock 76 (Bélombre), bridge (D606), **Champs-sur-Yonne** 300m
PK **163.6** Railway bridge (Bazine)
PK **163.4** Lock 75 (Bailly) in lock-cut l/b
PK **162.9** Navigation re-enters Yonne (râcle de Bailly)
PK **162.4** **Bailly** quay r/b, water, electricity

Mooring quay, water (might be cut off). The former underground stone quarries are now used by the Bailly-Lapierre wine cooperative. Their speciality is the sparkling Crémant de Bourgogne.

PK **161.2** Lock 74 (Vincelottes) in lock-cut l/b
PK **160.6** **Vincelottes** bridge, village and restaurant 400m r/b
PK **160.4** Navigation joins Yonne for 900m (râcle de Vincelles)
PK **160.1** **Vincelles** quay l/b, water, electricity, shower, slipway, village l/b

Good mooring by the small village, water.

PK **159.5** Lock 73 (Vincelles), bridge, navigation enters 5.1km long canal section
PK **158.2** Lock 72 (Rivottes), bridge
PK **156.6** Bridge (Colombier)
PK **156.4** Former branch with disused lock, r/b
PK **155.9** **Cravant** bridge (D606), *halte* u/s r/b, night €8, water and electricity included, wifi, shop in village 500m
PK **154.4** Lock 71 (Maunoir)
PK **154.1** Junction Vermenton Branch, r/b

The small town of Vermenton and the village of Accolay are both well worth the detour. See below the description of the branch.

PK **154.0** Railway bridge (Maunoir)
PK **153.7** Lock 70 (Saint-Aignan), navigation enters Yonne (râcle du Maunoir)
PK **153.0** Bridge (Croix-Minet), quay d/s l/b, **Bazarnes** 1 km
PK **152.4** Lock 69 (Sainte-Pallaye)
PK **151.9** **Sainte-Pallaye** bridge (Romains), village r/b
PK **151.5** Bridge (Parc de Sainte-Pallaye)
PK **151.1** Flood gate 68 (Prégilbert)
PK **151.0** **Prégilbert** bridge, village r/b
PK **150.1** Lock 67 (Dames), lift bridge d/s, navigation enters Yonne
PK **149.9** Railway bridge (Dames)
PK **148.6** Lock 66 (Saint-Maur), navigation joins Yonne for 640m (râcle des Dames)
PK **147.6** **Sery** bridge, small village r/b
PK **147.5** Lock 65 (Sery), bridge
PK **146.1** Quay l/b, boatyard, long-term moorings and dry-land storage, repairs

Hire boat enters the lock-cut at Mailly-la-Ville, PK 146.
© ALAIN DOIRE - BOURGOGNE TOURISME

Canal du Nivernais

The spectacular Saussois cliffs, PK 137. © HAL STUFFT

Delightful landscape where the canal runs alongside the river Yonne, here in Merry-sur-Yonne, PK 135 © F-W

PK **146.0** Flood gate 64 (Mailly-la-Ville), bridge

Take care when the Yonne is running high, reducing headroom on the canal.

PK **145.7** **Mailly-la-Ville** r/b, municipal *halte* on pontoons r/b, 03 86 81 42 14, water, electricity, wifi, slipway, all shops
PK **145.4** Lock 63 (Mailly-la-Ville), navigation enters Yonne
PK **145.2** Bridge (Mailly-la-Ville)

Beware, this is one of the lowest bridges on the canal.

PK **142.8** Lock 62 (Parc), navigation joins Yonne for 600m (*râcle du Bouchet*)
PK **142.4** Railway bridge (Parc)
PK **141.7** **Mailly-le-Château** bridge, municipal *halte* in small basin 30m d/s l/b, village 1 km up hill
PK **141.2** Canal narrows for 350m
PK **140.9** Railway bridge
PK **140.8** Flood gate 61 (Mailly-le-Château), entrance to lock-cut
PK **139.4** Lock 60 (Ravereau), navigation enters Yonne (*râcle de Mailly-le-Château*)
PK **139.0** Bridge (Graves)
PK **138.0** Flood gate 59a (Saussois), bridge, quay l/b, **Merry-sur-Yonne** 500m l/b
PK **137.7** Entrance to lock-cut, one-way traffic only
PK **136.5** Lock 59 (Réchimet), navigation enters Yonne (*râcle du Saussois*), keep close to towpath on outside of bend, restaurant, mooring to bollards possible but awkward
PK **136.1** Bridge (Terres Rouges)
PK **135.9** Railway bridge (Terres Rouges)
PK **135.0** Canal narrows for 235m
PK **134.5** Lock 58 (Magny), bridge
PK **133.1** Bridge (Gade)
PK **132.6** Lock 57 (Châtel-Censoir), bridge
PK **132.5** **Châtel-Censoir** basin and municipal *halte* l/b, 35 berths, 3 barge moorings, night €11, day €6, water and electricity included, shower, slipway, village over bridge

A charming small town, proudly sitting on a bluff overlooking the canal and the river Yonne, with all shops and services.

PK **130.2** Lock 56 (La Place), bridge

PK **128.7** Railway bridge (La Place)
PK **127.9** Bridge (Gué Saint-Martin)
PK **127.1** Lock 55 (Lucy-sur-Yonne)
PK **126.1** **Lucy-sur-Yonne**, bridge, village r/b
PK **125.1** Lock 54 (Bèze), bridge
PK **124.1** Flood gate 53a (Bèze), bridge
PK **123.7** Lock 53 (Crain), canal joins Yonne for 34m
PK **122.8** **Coulanges-sur-Yonne**, lock 52, bridge, Canalous hire base and quay u/s r/b, water, shower, village 1 km over bridge
PK **121.5** Lift bridge (Pousseaux)
PK **121.1** **Pousseaux** bridge, quay u/s r/b, water, village 200m, **Surgy** 1 km over bridge
PK **120.7** Canal narrows, one-way traffic (with one passing place)
PK **120.0** End of narrow section
PK **119.3** Bridge (Basseville)
PK **118.7** Stop lock 51 (Basseville)

Going upstream, wait at the open stop lock until Basseville lock (50) has opened. Then, keeping away from the weir, go straight into the lock without slowing down while crossing the river.

The approach to Clamecy viewed from the lock, with the port de plaisance basin off to the right, PK 114. The quay shown here offers additional moorings if the port is full. © THOMAS KREIG

161

III – Central France and routes to the Saône

PK **118.5** Lock 50 (Basseville), navigation crosses Yonne on the level, towpath bridge r/b, weir l/b
PK **117.7** Bridge (Envilliers)
PK **117.1** Lock 49 (Garenne)
PK **116.6** Bridge (Presles)
PK **116.1** Bridge (N151, Clamecy bypass)
PK **116.0** Flood gates (Forêt) l/b, navigation re-enters canal (boats heading u/s, turn left through these gates)
PK **115.9** Small island, pass on l/b side
PK **114.5** Entrance to former lock-cut, l/b (lock 47b Clamecy-Saint-Roch), disused, navigation follows Yonne
PK **113.9** Bridge (Bethléem), moorings along quay l/b for Clamecy
PK **113.7** Lock 47 (Les Jeux), swing bridge u/s, navigation enters Yonne
PK **113.6** **Clamecy**, *port de plaisance* u/s of lock in basin l/b, 06 10 02 97 17, night €12, water and electricity included, shower, small town l/b

Clamecy is the emblematic capital of the historic timber-floating trade, before the canal was built. The river Yonne, swollen here by the Beuvron, was readily *flottable*. meaning that it could bear timber rafts. The museum dedicated to the rafting business is well worth a visit, as well as the town for all its facilities, and attractive quarters around the various arms and mill-streams of the Beuvron. *clamecyhautnivernais-tourisme.fr* (for this *halte* and those at Chevroches and Villiers-sur-Yonne)

PK **112.9** Bridge (Picot)
PK **112.0** Flood gate r/b, connection with Yonne (not navigable)
PK **111.7** Lock 46 (Maladrerie), bridge
PK **111.6** Basin l/b
PK **110.6** Lock 45 (Armes)
PK **110.1** **Chevroches** bridge, *halte* d/s l/b on quay, 06 10 02 97 17, free, mooring for restaurant, water and electricity may be available
PK **109.3** Lock 44 (Chantenot), bridge
PK **107.2** Bridge (Cuncy), quay with bollards l/b, picnic, overnight
PK **106.5** Lock 43 (Cuncy), bridge
PK **105.7** Swinging footbridge (Villiers), abandoned, permanently open
PK **104.8** **Villiers-sur-Yonne** bridge, village l/b, *halte* d/s r/b on 100m long quay, 06 16 02 97 17, water and electricity may be available
PK **104.6** Lock 42 (Villiers)
PK **103.7** Canal narrows, one-way traffic for 200m
PK **102.8** Lock 41 (Esselier)
PK **102.5** **Brèves** bridge, village 300m, turning basin
PK **102.3** Lock 40 (Brèves)
PK **100.2** **Asnois** bridge, village 200m
PK **99.2** Lift bridge (de l'Âne), mooring with bollards d/s r/b, picnic area
PK **98.1** Double staircase lock 38/39 (Tannay), bridge
PK **96.8** Bridge (Gravelot)
PK **95.8** **Flez-Cuzy** bridge, quay u/s l/b, moorings both banks, restaurant, village 400m, Le Boat hire base (Tannay), 03 86 29 35 52, 24 berths (subject to availability), night €12, water and electricity included, shower, **Tannay** 1.5 km (all shops, wine cellar)

The best mooring for visiting Tannay. Mooring possible on opposite bank if the quay extending the hire boat base is occupied.

PK **95.5** Lift bridge (Curiot)
PK **94.5** Lift bridge (Saint-Didier)
PK **93.5** Lock 37 (Moulin Brûlé)
PK **93.2** Lock 36 (Laporte), bridge, quay d/s l/b
PK **92.2** Lock 35 (Châtillon)
PK **92.0** End of one-way section
PK **90.7** **Monceaux-le-Comte** bridge, quay u/s r/b, village 1 km
PK **90.0** Canal narrows, one-way traffic for 2 km (with passing places)
PK **89.6** Lift bridge (Marais)
PK **89.6** **Dirol** quay l/b, water
PK **89.4** Lift bridge (Thoury)
PK **89.0** Lock 34 (Dirol), bridge
PK **88.5** Lock 33 (Mont), bridge
PK **88.0** Canal narrows for 100m, no passing
PK **86.3** Lift bridge (Chazel)
PK **86.1** Railway bridge (Mortes)
PK **85.9** Lock 32 (Mortes)
PK **85.5** Turning basin
PK **84.9** Quay, r/b, mooring possible both sides, no services
PK **84.6** Lock 31 (Gravier), bridge
PK **84.4** **Marigny**, l/b
PK **84.2** Lock 30 (Marigny), bridge
PK **83.2** Lock 29 (Chitry)
PK **82.5** Lift bridge (Germehay)
PK **82.1** **Chaumot** basin, l/b, moorings, 06 30 93 05 26, night €12.50, water and electricity included, shower, slipway, restaurant, camp site
PK **82.0** Bridge (Chitry), D977bis
PK **81.9** **Chitry-les-Mines** basin r/b, Marine Diesel boatyard, 03 86 26 94 99, 45 berths, night €5, *marine-diesel.fr*, water €2, electricity €3.50/day, shower, fuel supplied on demand, village 300m (no services), preferred mooring for access to **Corbigny** 3 km

The author had his boat in the Chaumot basin many years ago, and Chitry-les-Mines is still as charming as ever, with its *château* uncharacteristically down in the plain and not on the hill, and friendly service for all kinds of mechanical repairs and parts replacement by John Johnson, the son of founder Ted Johnson. Ted was trained as the Peter Zivy's mechanic in the early days of Saint-Line at Baye, from 1965.

Halte with welcoming reception building and snack bar at Chitry-les-Mines, PK 82. © DOMINIQUE INIESTA

Canal du Nivernais

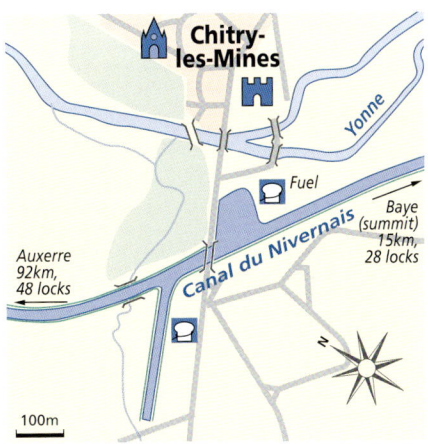

Locks 2, 3 and 4 on the picturesque (but challenging) flight of 16 locks at Sardy-lès-Épiry, PK 71. © S. JEAN-BAPTISTE, CONSEIL DÉPARTEMENTAL DE LA NIÈVRE

La Collancelle tunnel, the first (and longest) of the three tunnels on the summit level at Baye, PK 68. © DAVE BALLINGER

PK 81.3 Lock 28 (Chaumot)
PK 80.7 Marcy basin
PK 80.2 Lock 27 (Marcy), bridge
PK 79.8 Double staircase lock 25/26 (Eugny)
PK 79.6 Basin r/b, moorings, water, electricity
PK 79.5 End of cutting
PK 79.3 Bridge (Eugny), D958, **Corbigny** 2.5 km
PK 78.8 Bridge (Chaise)
PK 78.6 High bridge (Chaise)
PK 78.2 Beginning of La Chaise cutting, one-way traffic, Yonne feeder with flood gates, r/b
PK 77.6 Lock 24 (Yonne), bridge, basin d/s r/b, Locaboat hire base, pontoon moorings, 03 86 20 07 29, 16 berths, night €15, water and electricity included, shower €2.50, washing machine €5, slipway, pump-out, repairs
PK 77.1 Lock 23 (Pré Colas), quay d/s l/b
PK 76.6 Lock 22 (Surpaillis)
PK 76.3 Lock 21 (Picampoix), bridge (reduced headroom 2.97m) **Marcilly** 2 km
PK 76.2 Picampoix quarries, bridge, former loading quay r/b
PK 76.0 Lock 20 (Bois des Taureaux)
PK 75.4 Lock 19 (Petite Corvée)
PK 74.8 Lock 18 (Creuzet), bridge
PK 74.4 Lock 17 (Champ du Chêne)
PK 73.8 **Sardy-les Épiry**, basin l/b, swimming pool, village 500m over bridge
PK 73.6 Lock 16 (Sardy), bridge, spring water
PK 73.4 Lock 15 (Champ Cadoux), last of the 30m locks
PK 73.0 Lock 14 (Pré Ardent)
PK 72.7 Lock 13 (Doyen)
PK 72.6 Lock 12 (Pré Doyen)
PK 72.2 Lock 11 (Bellevue)
PK 71.9 Lock 10 (Patureau-Volain), basin d/s
PK 71.7 Lock 9 (Fussy), moorings d/s r/b
PK 71.5 Lock 8 (Mondain)
PK 71.3 Lock 7 (Gros Bouillon)
PK 71.1 Lock 6 (Planche de Belin), bridge
PK 70.9 Lock 5 (Demain)
PK 70.8 Lock 4 (Roche)
PK 70.7 Lock 3 (Patureau)
PK 70.6 Lock 2 (Crain)
PK 70.4 Lock 1 (Port-Brûlé), end of summit level
PK 70.2 Bridge (Port-Brûlé)
PK 69.3 Bridge (Breuilles)
PK 68.6 Tunnel (Breuilles), 212m long

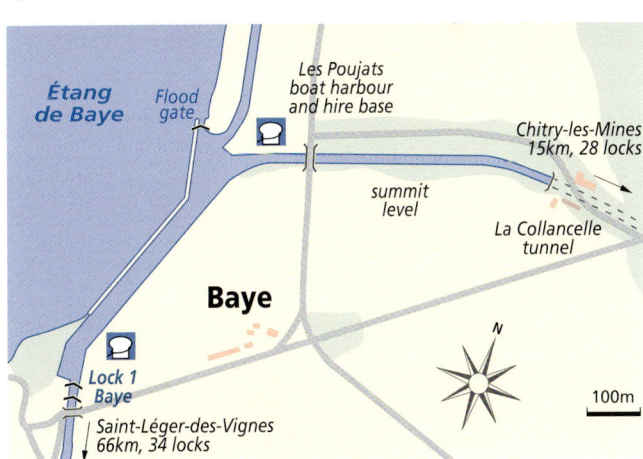

PK 68.2 Tunnel (Mouas), 268m long
PK 67.2 Tunnel (La Collancelle), 758m long
PK 66.6 Bridge (Les Poujats), canal narrows, one-way traffic
PK 66.5 Quay (Poujats), Aqua Fluvial hire base, 03 86 38 90 70, 40 berths, night €10, water and electricity included, shower, crane 14t, slipway, pump-out, repairs *aquafluvial.fr*

This boatyard was created by Peter Zivy nearly 60 years ago. Moorings and services in an extremely picturesque location beside the Étang de Baye.

III – Central France and routes to the Saône

PK **66.0** Lock 1 (**Baye**), bridge, beginning of summit level, village 200m, restaurant
PK **63.8** Lock 2 (Bazolles)
PK **63.6** Lock 3 (Bazolles), bridge, moorings u/s and d/s r/b, **Bazolles** 500m (bar/tabac, baker, small shop)
PK **61.8** Bridge (Mougny)
PK **59.7** Triple staircase lock 6/5/4 (Chavance), bridge
PK **59.5** Basin (Chavance) r/b, mooring bollards
PK **59.4** Double staircase lock 8/7 (Chavance)
PK **57.1** Double staircase lock 10/9 (Mont-et-Marré), bridge, moorings u/s, restaurant and swimming pool l/b
PK **56.1** Lock 11 (Orgue)
PK **54.6** Lock 12 (Orgue), bridge
PK **53.9** Lock 13 (Mingot), bridge (very low), Aron aqueduct u/s
PK **53.8** Bridge (Mingot), warning, very tight curve
PK **51.2** **Châtillon-en-Bazois** bridge, municipal *halte* l/b, 3 boats, free, water, electricity, slipway, château r/b
PK **51.0** Lock 14 (Châtillon-en-Bazois)
PK **50.6** Lock 15 (Châtillon-en-Bazois), bridge, municipal *halte* and Canalous Plaisance hire base u/s r/b, night free, water, electricity, navigation enters river Aron, keep to towpath side, r/b
PK **49.1** Stop lock 16 (Cœuillon), bridge, navigation leaves river
PK **47.5** Bridge (Pont), follow channel on outside of bend, **Alluy** 1.5 km
PK **46.3** Bridge (Éguilly)
PK **45.9** Lock 17 (Éguilly)
PK **42.7** Lock 18 (Meulot), bridge
PK **41.9** Bridge (Cray), **Biches** 500m
PK **41.3** Bridge (Romenay)
PK **40.8** Lock 19 (Villard), bridge
PK **38.8** Lock 20 (Brienne)
PK **38.1** Lock 21 (Fleury), *halte* u/s l/b managed by local association, 06 19 54 28 53, free, water €1.50/100 litres, electricity €5/day, shower €2, restaurant r/b, campsite with swimming pool and picnic area, **Brienne** 1 km
PK **36.4** Lock 22 (Bernay), bridge
PK **35.0** Bridge (Prairie)
PK **33.6** Bridge (Magny), quay r/b
PK **32.1** Lock 23 (Saigne), bridge
PK **31.2** Bridge (Anizy)
PK **31.0** Lock 24 (Anizy), navigation leaves river, mooring basin

PK **29.7** **Pannecot** municipal *halte* l/b, suitable for smaller vessels only, 03 86 84 32 70 (campsite), 20 berths, night €9, water, and electricity at campsite in season, shower, slipway
PK **29.6** Stop lock 25 (Pannecot), bridge, navigation enters river Aron
PK **29.5** **Pannecot**, mooring l/b d/s of lock, village over bridge
PK **27.7** Lock 26 (Sauzay), bridge
PK **26.0** Bridge (Hâtes de Scia), basin l/b
PK **24.6** Bridge (Baudin)

Beware, this is one of very low bridges on the canal.

PK **23.6** Lock 27 (Moulin d'Isenay), bridge
PK **23.2** Moulin d'Isenay basin, l/b, **Vandenesse** (village and château) 3 km
PK **22.6** Former lift bridge
PK **21.6** Lock 28 (Isenay), bridge
PK **21.5** Isenay quay, l/b
PK **20.9** Lift bridge (Tremblay)
PK **20.1** Bridge (Saint-Gratien)
PK **18.6** Lock 29 (Chaumigny), bridge
PK **17.1** Bridge (Martigny), overnight/picnic mooring l/b
PK **15.9** Lock 30 (Cercy-la-Tour), bridge, basin u/s r/b, navigation enters river Aron
PK **15.6** **Cercy-la-Tour** municipal *halte* on quay r/b, 03 86 50 89 01, night free, water, electricity, showers at camp site on opposite bank of river Aron, slipway

Comfortable pontoon mooring in the large basin where the water of the canal mingles with that of the river Aron. Ideally located beside the small town.

PK **15.4** Stop lock 31 (Cercy-la-Tour), bridge, navigation leaves river

Beware, this is another of the lowest bridges.

PK **13.7** Bridge (Coulangette)
PK **12.6** Bridge (Vernizy)
PK **9.9** Saint-Gervais bridge and basin, l/b, **Verneuil** 2 km
PK **8.7** Bridge (Roche)
PK **8.2** Lock 32 (Roche), Andarge aqueduct u/s
PK **7.5** Bridge (Marcou)
PK **6.5** Site of a former footbridge
PK **4.9** Lock 33 (Champvert), bridge
PK **4.7** **Champvert**, quay r/b
PK **3.7** Bridge (du Port)
PK **3.1** **La Copine** basin, r/b, Centre Technique Fluvial, 06 42 38 22 87, repairs, crane 17t, dry dock (up to 24m)
PK **3.0** Railway bridge
PK **2.9** Bridge (Copine)
PK **1.9** Lock 34 (Vauzelles), bridge
PK **1.4** Bridge (Saint-Thibault), quays above and below, r/b, 03 86 25 09 76, night €10, water, electricity, pump-out, **Decize** 1 km
PK **0.9** Lock 35 (Loire)
PK **0.0** **Saint-Léger-des-Vignes**, junction with the Loire and the Canal latéral à la Loire, quay r/b

Pontoon halte at Cercy-la-Tour, PK 15. © MARTIN DUDLE-AMMANN

Canal du Nivernais

Vermenton branch

PK 0.0	**Junction with main canal** (râcle du Maunoir, PK 154.1)
PK 0.7	Lock (Noue), bridge
PK 2.2	Bridge (Moulin Jacquot)
PK 2.5	**Accolay** bridge, quay u/s l/b, 03 86 81 56 87, capacity 10 boats, night €12.50, water, electricity, shower at camp site, slipway, village l/b

Very good quayside moorings at a pleasant village, with an active water-jousting centre (using slipways downstream of the bridge) and formerly an art pottery centre.

PK	
PK 3.0	Lock (Accolay), bridge
PK 3.8	Flood gate (Vermenton), bridge
PK 3.9	**Vermenton** municipal *port de plaisance* managed by France Fluviale hire base, 03 86 81 54 55, 20 berths, night €10, diesel, water and electricity €4, wifi, repairs, village 500m *francefluviale.com*

Attractive village, station for trains to Paris and Avallon. This is one of the many places on the French waterways that have always been operated by expatriates from the UK and other English-speaking countries.

Connection to Canal latéral à la Loire

via river Loire and Decize branch

The branch belongs to the Canal latéral à la Loire, but the route is described here for convenience (the PK given here are not official).

PK	
PK 0.0	**Canal du Nivernais** enters the river Loire

Turn left (upstream) on river Loire.

PK	
PK 0.3	Quay r/b, just above the confluence of the river Aron
PK 1.1	**Decize** *halte*, r/b, concrete quay with timber edge and bollards, 90m long, town centre 400m

A welcome development allowing boats to moor on the broad river and visit and shop in Decize, a small town but with a good range of services. Market on Friday.

PK	
PK 1.3	Bridge (Decize)
PK 1.8	**Entrance to Decize branch of Canal latéral à la Loire**
PK 1.8	Lock 16ter (Decize), lift up to 4.00m, bridge
PK 2.1	**Decize** basin, length 380m, Le Boat hire base, 03 73 15 00 00, 80 berths, night €9, water, electricity, showers, slipway, restaurant, wifi

Good new *port de plaisance* in the large canal basin. Intermarché supermarket close by with fuel.

PK	
PK 2.3	Lock 16bis (Saint-Maurice), lift 2.50m, bridge

Water available at the lock (as an alternative to the port).

PK	
PK 2.4	**Junction with Canal latéral à la Loire** through route (PK 68)

The 'town' quay for mooring in Decize, but with no services. © RUDI S.

30. Canal du Loing

THE CANAL DU LOING, ONE of the series of waterways forming the 'Bourbonnais' route from Paris to Lyon, is entered from the Seine at Saint-Mammès, a town popular with barge-owning families, and follows the river Loing southwards to connect with the Canal de Briare below Buges lock, north of Montargis. In its length of 49km, it twice enters the bed of the river for a short length. The valley is wooded and pleasant throughout, with lakes resulting from former gravel pits. Commercial traffic has declined significantly, but the canal remains open all year round to accommodate barges, mostly carrying grain for export.

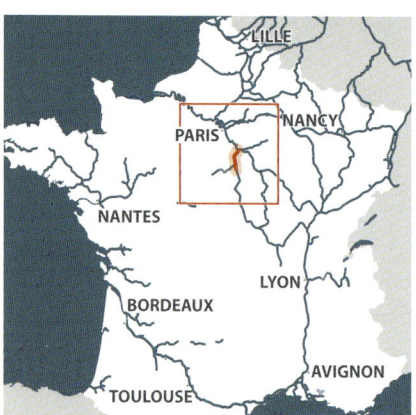

Navigation
Navigation on this well-maintained canal is straightforward, with no particular difficulty to be expected.

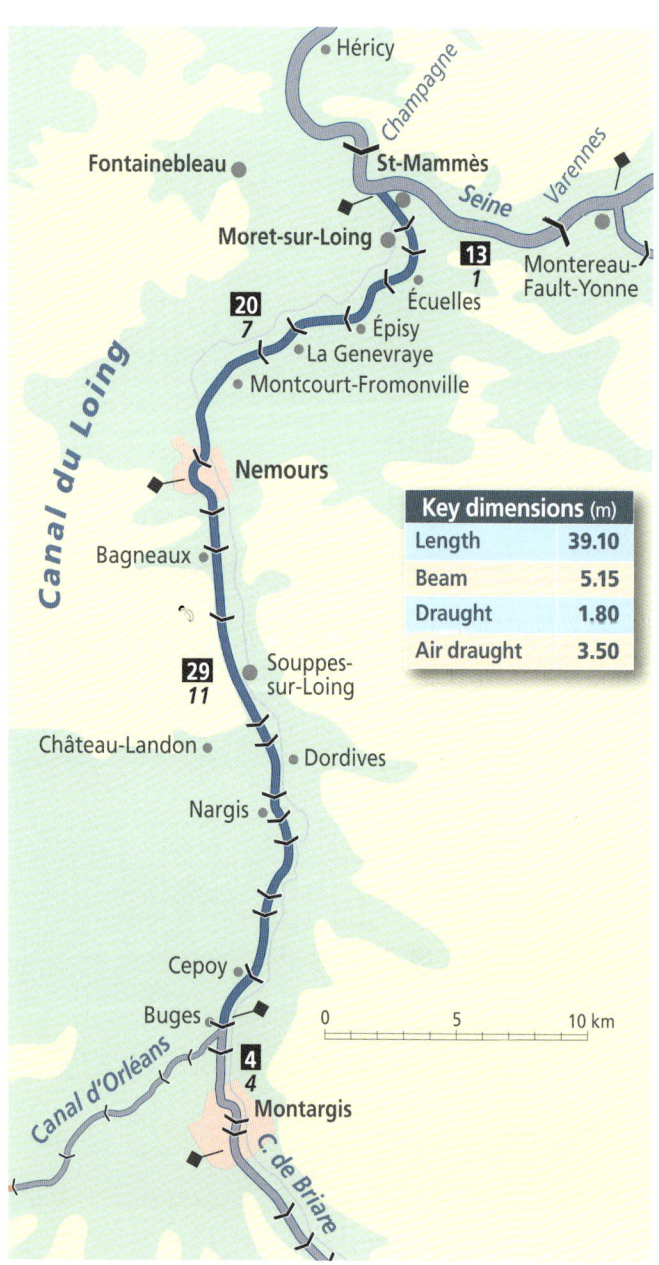

Key dimensions (m)	
Length	39.10
Beam	5.15
Draught	1.80
Air draught	3.50

With the canals from Briare and Orléans completed respectively in 1641 and 1693, merchants started complaining about the poor navigability of the river Loing. The Duc d'Orléans ordered a survey and designs for the navigation as built – part-river and part-canal – were submitted to Royal assent and approved in 1720. Work started immediately, and the canal was completed in 1723, with some improvements made the following year. The first lock, Cepoy, dates from 1680 since it was part of the Canal d'Orléans. Modernisation to Freycinet dimensions was completed in the late 19th century.

Locks
There are 18 locks, with uniform dimensions of 39.10m by 5.20m, plus a flood lock at Fromonville (No. 13), which is normally open. The original lock 20 at Saint-Mammès was made redundant and the adjacent weir demolished when the Champagne weir and locks were built on the Upper river Seine. All the locks have been equipped for automatic operation.

Draught
The maximum authorised draught is 1.80m.

Headroom
All bridges leave a minimum headroom of 3.50m above the normal water level.

Canal du Loing

Towpath
There is a good towpath throughout, taken over by local roads in the sections through Montargis, Nemours and Saint-Mammès.

Authority
VNF Centre-Bourgogne, CEMI Briare
– 14, bld des Belles Manières, 45200 Montargis 02 38 95 09 20
subdi.montargis@vnf.fr

Route description

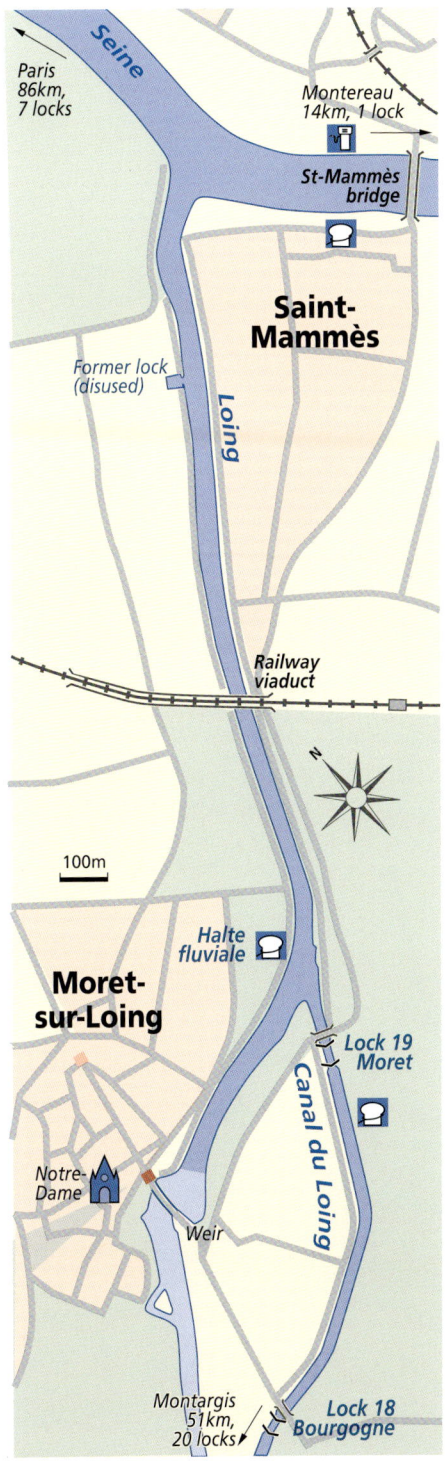

PK **49.4** **Saint-Mammès**, *confluence with Seine*

Saint-Mammès is a community of retired *péniche* owners and operators, and they line the banks along the lower reaches of the river Loing. Some still active *péniches* may also be moored here awaiting cargo. See under the Upper Seine details of the pontoon moorings 450m u/s of confluence.

PK **49.1** Boatyard and slipway, l/b
PK **48.4** Railway viaduct
PK **47.9** **Moret-sur-Loing** *halte* on pontoons l/b, 06 47 68 79 51, moorings for 12 boats, night €12, water and electricity included, showers €2, wifi at *capitainerie*

Ideal mooring in the enchanting environment that inspired the impressionist painter Alfred Sisley, among many other artists. Moret is a pretty medieval town and gateway to Burgundy.

PK **47.7** Lock 19 (Moret), bridge
PK **46.9** Lock 18 (Bourgogne), automated, bridge (D302), Moret-sur-Loing town centre 600m
PK **46.6** Aqueduct crosses canal
PK **46.4** Road bridge (D606, Moret-sur-Loing bypass)
PK **45.6** Quays r/b, no services
PK **44.8** Écuelles r/b
PK **44.1** Lock 17 (Ecuelles), bridge
PK **41.8** Quay l/b
PK **41.2** Lock 16 (**Épisy**), bridge, quay u/s l/b, village, restaurant r/b
PK **40.9** Private quay l/b
PK **39.6** Quay (Launay) r/b
PK **38.7** Lock 15 (Berville)
PK **38.1** **La Genevraye** bridge, quay d/s l/b, village r/b
PK **36.4** Lock 14 (Bordes)
PK **34.7** **Montcourt-Fromonville** bridge, village r/b, quay d/s r/b
PK **32.6** Flood lock 13 (Fromonville), footbridge, navigation enters river Loing
PK **31.7** Motorway bridge (A6 Paris-Lyon)
PK **30.8** Bridge (Hochart), D240, Nemours bypass
PK **30.7** Private commercial quays l/b, private long-term moorings r/b
PK **30.2** Navigation leaves river Loing, entering canal l/b

Saint-Mammès is a favourite residence for retired barge owners, while hot air ballooning is a favourite excursion for hotel barges. © GÉRARD DURBECQ

167

III – Central France and routes to the Saône

PK **30.1** Lock 12 (Buttes), bridge
PK **29.8** **Nemours** municipal *halte* along quay l/b, for 8 boats, night €9, water, electricity

Before entering lock 12 to tie up at this practical *halte*, it is worth proceeding up the bypassed river Loing (checking carefully for the available depth) for superb views of the town, its riverside houses on the right bank and a succession of historic buildings on the town side, culminating in the 12th century château. Smaller boats will find attractive alternative moorings for Nemours on the river.

Nemours château on the bypassed river Loing, PK 29 ©DANIEL PELLETIER

PK **29.4** Bridge (Paris)
PK **28.8** Bridge (Récollets), town centre r/b

Quayside moorings with water and electricity along the narrow curved route around the town, but there may be little space.

PK **28.2** Quay (Fontaines), l/b
PK **27.4** Lock 11 (Chaintreauville), bridge
PK **26.0** Quay (Fromonceau) l/b
PK **25.7** Lock 10 (Bagneaux), bridge
PK **25.2** Quay for Pyrex factory, l/b
PK **24.4** **Bagneaux-sur-Loing** bridge, village 600m l/b
PK **22.4** Bridge (Glandelles), quay d/s l/b
PK **21.3** Lock 9 (Beaumoulin), bridge, quay d/s l/b
PK **20.7** Railway bridge
PK **20.4** Turning basin r/b
PK **19.1** Pipeline crossing
PK **18.8** **Souppes-sur-Loing** bridge, municipal *halte* along quay d/s l/b for 3 boats, night €6, water, electricity, town 900m r/b

Comfortable *halte*

PK **18.3** Railway bridge
PK **17.0** Lock 8 (Egreville), bridge, basin d/s l/b, restaurant, shops
PK **15.9** Lock 7 (Néronville), bridge, water available
PK **14.9** Motorway bridge (A77)
PK **14.3** **Dordives** bridge, quay u/s l/b, village r/b 1 km
PK **12.8** Bridge (Toury)
PK **11.1** Lock 6 (Brisebarre)

PK **10.5** **Nargis** quay and village with shops l/b

Another pleasant *halte* and village

PK **10.4** Lock 5 (Nargis), bridge
PK **8.9** Lock 4 (Retourné)
PK **8.1** Bridge (Vaux)
PK **5.9** Lock 3 (Montabon)
PK **5.3** Bridge (Les Vallées)
PK **5.1** Lock 2 (Les Vallées), water
PK **4.3** Motorway viaduct (Viaduc du Loing), A19
PK **3.0** **Cepoy** municipal *halte*, quayside mooring for up to 8 boats, free (maximum 7 days), water and electricity (metered), village with shops l/b

Cepoy is an attractive village, well worth stopping at to enjoy the village atmosphere and way of life, before the bustle of Montargis just a few kilometres to the south.

PK **2.3** Bridge (Cepoy)
PK **2.2** Lock 1 (Cepoy)
PK **0.5** Railway bridge
PK **0.0** **Junction with Canal de Briare** (d/s of lock 36, Buges)

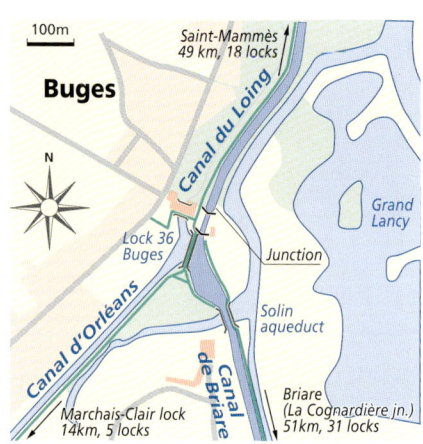

31. Canal de Briare

THE CANAL DE BRIARE WAS THE FIRST major 'watershed' canal to be built in Europe. It was completed in 1642, 40 years before the more famous Canal du Midi. It linked the river Loing north of Montargis with the river Loire in Briare. For centuries it was a lifeline for Paris, food and fuel (wood and coal) being brought to the capital by barge from the upper Loire and Allier valleys. When the Canal latéral à la Loire was enlarged, with its famous aqueduct crossing the Loire at Briare, the connection was made at La Cognardière, 2.6km and four locks from its junction with the Loire. The bypassed section of the canal was initially retained as a branch, then abandoned after commercial traffic ceased. It was restored in the 1980s to give boats access through three locks down to the canal basin in the middle of the town, now among the biggest and most popular *ports de plaisance* in France. The canal extends 57km from its connection with the Canal du Loing at Buges lock, north of Montargis, to the original lock down into the river Loire. Connection is made with the Canal latéral à la Loire at PK 2.6 (La Cognardière, north of Briare). The canal is part of the 'Bourbonnais' route from Paris to Lyon.

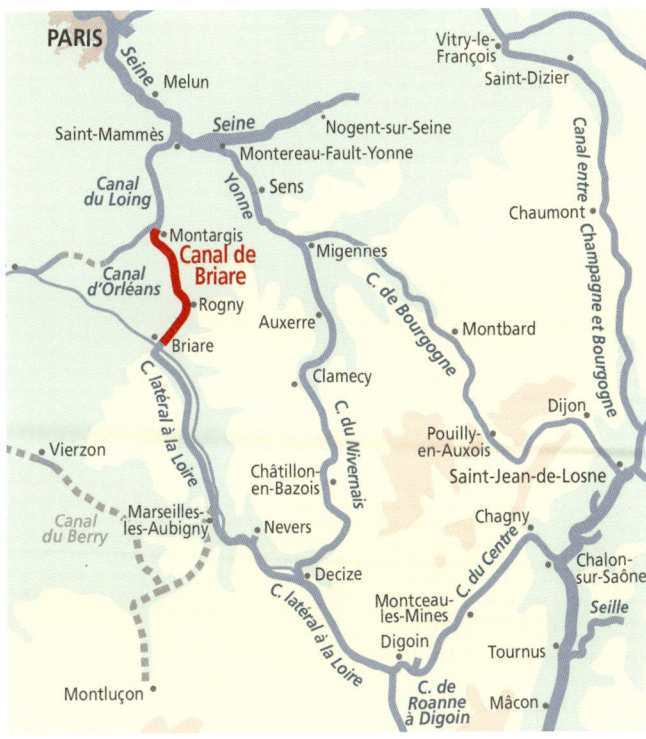

Europe's first major watershed canal was started under Henri IV in 1604, as part of the public works programme initiated by his minister Sully. The works were in hand by contractor Hugues Cosnier when the king was assassinated in 1610. The project was revived in 1638 with new contractors Guillaume Bouteroue and Jean Guyon and completed in 1642 at a cost of 6.5 million francs. The canal was enlarged under the Becquey programme in 1830-37. The Freycinet modernisation involved practically rebuilding the canal, with a new route bypassing the staircase locks at Rogny and at several other locations.

Navigation
Navigation is straightforward in this well-maintained canal. A major breach occurred in June 2016, but was quickly repaired, and VNF has carried out preventive measures to avoid future breaches.

Locks
There are 35 locks, of which 24 rise from the Loing to the summit level at an altitude of 165m, the remaining 11 falling towards the river Loire (of which eight on the through route of navigation and three on the branch down into Briare). Dimensions of the locks on the through route are 39.00m by 5.20m. Those on the branch to Briare are 30.40m by 5.20m. Locks 35 to 31 and 26 to 19 rising from the Loing are manually operated, while the Montcresson flight (30 to 27) and all locks from the summit level down to Briare are automatic. These are worked in three sets: 18-13, 12-8 and 7-2. Transition from one to the next may be effected by the user or by the staff member advising the colleague responsible for the next set. Report to the waterway manager at La Cognardière for access to Briare via the old canal. This VNF staff member will start the sequence for the three locks down to the canal basin in Briare N.B. At La Cognardière there is also an open stop lock for access to the Canal latéral à la Loire).

Draught
The maximum authorised draught is 1.80m (1.20m on the branch).

Headroom
All the fixed bridges leave a minimum headroom of 3.50m above the normal water level. There are several lift bridges in the flight of locks between La Cognardière and the summit level.

Towpath
There is a metalled towpath throughout, except on the branch to Briare harbour (crushed stone).

Authority
VNF Centre-Bourgogne, CEMI Briare
– 17, rue du Pont Canal, 45250 Briare, 02 38 31 26 20

III – Central France and routes to the Saône

Key dimensions (m)	
Length	30.40
Beam	5.05
Draught*	1.20
Air draught	3.50

*1.80m on the through route used by commercial traffic

Mooring under the church at Montbouy, PK 32. © HAL STUFFT

Route description

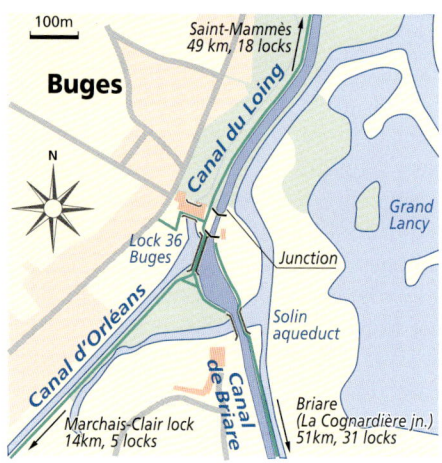

Halte with pontoons. Site of the first paper mill to print notes for the Bank of France (1804), a long paper manufacturing history. Here is the (blocked off) entrance to the 79km long Canal d'Orléans, abandoned in 1954, but currently in the process of restoration.

PK 54.1	Lock 36 (Buges), bridge, junction with Canal du Loing and with Canal d'Orléans, u/s of lock l/b
K 53.9	Aqueduct (Solin)
PK 53.4	Lock 35 (Langlée), bridge
PK 53.1	Railway bridge, basin d/s (commercial quays)
PK 52.0	Bridges
PK 52.0	Bridges
PK 51.1	Private commercial quays l/b, mooring possible
PK 50.8	Bridge (Québec), Montargis commercial quays d/s r/b, moorings l/b, no services
PK 50.6	Footbridge
PK 50.5	Bridge (Saint Nicolas)
PK 50.2	Bridge (Loing)
PK 50.1	Lock 34 (Reinette), bridge
PK 49.8	**Montargis** footbridge, town centre l/b

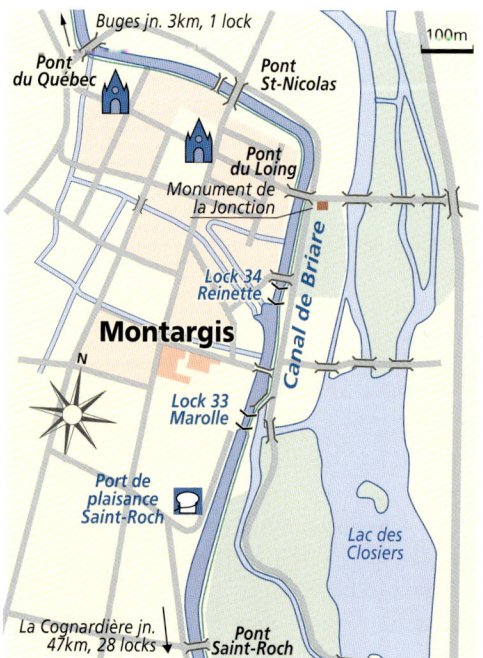

Canal de Briare

PK **49.7**	Lock 33 (Marolle), water, dry dock u/s l/b	
PK **49.5**	**Montargis** *port de plaisance* Saint-Roch for 35 boats, 06 70 03 38 44, night €10.50, water and electricity included, fuel delivered to order, slipway	

Montargis is a popular *port de plaisance* in a delightful setting. The historic town – a second 'gateway to Burgundy' after Moret-sur-Loing – is also called the 'Venice of the Gatinais' because of the network of mill streams (shown on the plan opposite).

PK **49.2**	Bridge (Saint-Roch)
PK **48.0**	Bridge (D60 Montargis bypass)
PK **47.8**	Pipe bridge
PK **47.7**	Bridge (Moulin Bardin)
PK **46.8**	Railway bridge
PK **45.4**	Lock 32 (Tuilerie), bridge, turning basin d/s l/b, restaurant
PK **43.4**	Lock 31 (Sablonnière), bridge, **Conflans-sur-Loing** 800m
PK **41.5**	Lock 30 (Souffre-Douleur)
PK **41.0**	Lock 29 (Moulin de Tours), bridge
PK **40.6**	Lock 28 (Chesnoy)
PK **40.2**	Lock 27 (Montambert), locks 27-30 automated
PK **37.6**	**Montcresson** bridge, quay, turning basin u/s, village 400m

Another pleasant *halte*.

PK **34.7**	Bridge (Salles), quay d/s l/b, water and electricity
PK **34.3**	Footbridge

It is worth attempting an informal mooring here to see the Chenevières château and gallo-roman ruins.

PK **33.1**	Footbridge
PK **31.9**	**Montbouy** bridge, municipal *halte* along quay d/s l/b for 3 boats, water, electricity €4 (4 hours), restaurant, wifi

Historic village with a fine church (Notre Dame Saint-Blaise)

PK **31.7**	Lock 26 (Montbouy)
PK **30.6**	Bridge (Brangers)
PK **29.4**	Lock 25 (Lépinoy), bridge
PK **27.8**	Footbridge (Ronce)
PK **26.9**	Bridge
PK **26.3**	**Châtillon-Coligny** bridge, *halte* along quay for 15 boats u/s r/b, 02 38 92 55 51 free (maximum 48 hours), water, electricity, shower €2, slipway, pump-out, restaurant, 12th century castle in village
PK **25.8**	Lock 24 (Châtillon)
PK **25.3**	Turning basin r/b
PK **25.0**	Lock 23 (Gazon)
PK **24.5**	Lock 22 (Briquemault), lift bridge
PK **21.8**	Lock 21 (Moulin Brûlé), bridge
PK **21.2**	Lock 20 (Picardie)
PK **20.7**	Lock 19 (Dammarie-sur-Loing)
PK **20.5**	**Dammarie-sur-Loing** bridge, municipal *halte* on quay u/s r/b, for 4 boats, draught 1m, free (maximum 72 hours), water, electricity
PK **19.5**	Bridge (Bruxelles)
PK **18.1**	Turning basin and moorings r/b
PK **16.6**	**Rogny-les-Sept-Écluses** basin r/b (Quai Sully), managed by Tourisme Fluvial du Centre hire base at PK 16.2, 03 86 74 56 34, 15 visitor moorings, night €11, water and electricity included, shower, wifi at tourist office, slipway, shops, quayside restaurant

This is the first of two possible moorings in the historic location of Rogny-les-Sept-Écluses. The village is noted for the old staircase lock, replaced more than a century ago by a flight of Freycinet-gauge locks and now a memorable attraction in the parkland landscape. The second mooring is in a side basin at Port des Lancières, PK 16.2.

Mooring at Rogny-les-Sept-Écluses, PK 16 © PATRICE LAFONTAINE

PK **16.4**	Bridge (Rogny, rue Léon Jupitre)
PK **16.2**	Basin r/b (Port des Lancières), Tourisme Fluvial du Centre hire base, 03 86 74 56 34, 10 visitor moorings, night €11, water and electricity included, wifi
PK **16.1**	Lock 18 (Sainte Barbe), bridge, mooring u/s l/b
PK **15.8**	Lock 17 (Rogny), bridge, original 17th century flight of seven (staircase) locks, r/b
PK **15.5**	Lock 16 (Chantepinot)
PK **15.2**	Lock 15 (Saint Joseph)
PK **14.9**	Lock 14 (Racault), bridge
PK **14.4**	Lock 13 (Javacière), end of summit level
PK **13.7**	Bridge (Noue)
PK **12.7**	Bridge (Rondeau), grain loading quay
PK **9.8**	Lock 12 (Gazonne), lift bridge, beginning of summit level
PK **8.8**	Lock 11 (Petit Chaloy), lift bridge, turning basin, quay u/s l/b
PK **8.4**	Lock 10 (Notre-Dame)
PK **8.1**	Lock 9 (Fées), lift bridge, quay u/s r/b
PK **7.6**	**Ouzouër-sur-Trézée** bridge, municipal halte d/s r/b, 07 78 42 11 77, quayside mooring for 8 boats, free (maximum 48 hours), water, electricity, shower, village r/b
PK **7.1**	Lock 8 (Moulin Neuf), lift bridge, quay u/s r/b
PK **6.6**	Feeder crosses canal on aqueduct
PK **6.1**	Turning basin
PK **5.9**	Lock 6 (Courenvaux), lift bridge, quay d/s r/b
PK **5.3**	Lock 7 (Ouzouer-sur-Trézée), locks 7-18 automated, quay u/s l/b
PK **4.7**	Lock 5 (Venon), lift bridge
PK **4.5**	Former quay (Petit Moulin) r/b
PK **2.8**	Former quay (Belleau) r/b

171

III – Central France and routes to the Saône

The spectacular staircase at Rogny, built during the reign of Henri IV, PK 16.
© CAMPING DES LANCIÈRES

PK **2.7**	Bridge (A77 motorway)	
PK **2.6**	Lock 4 (La Cognardière), footbridge	
PK **2.6**	Junction with Canal latéral à la Loire, see map next page	
PK **1.8**	Bridge (D7)	
PK **1.6**	Lock 3 (La Place), bridge	
PK **1.0**	Railway bridge	
PK **0.7**	Lock 2 (Briare), bridge	
PK **0.3**	**Briare** basin, *port de plaisance* along quay l/b, 85 moorings, visitor moorings if available, 06 08 95 03 20, VHF 12, depth 1.20m, night €13, fuel, water, electricity, shower, slipway, pump-out, wifi, trip boats, town centre 400m	

This is the popular *port de plaisance* in the town centre on the old canal. The other is on the Canal latéral à la Loire at **PK194**. (See also under this canal for the famous Briare aqueduct.) The *capitaine* may direct you to moorings upstream or (mainly) downstream of lock 2 Rochereau and the main road bridge. Friendly and helpful over-wintering community For on-line reservation: ***contact.briare@marinov.fr***.

PK **0.2**	Locaboat hire base in Gare d'eau r/b (see plan opposite),
PK **0.1**	Bridge (Baraban)
PK **0.0**	Lock 1 (Baraban) junction with river Loire

The lock has been restored but is impracticable except when the Loire is relatively high, hence not easy to navigate. This is unfortunate, because the site is superb and some mixing of canal craft and traditional vessels on the Loire in Briare would make the site even more appealing.

Baraban lock and the river Loire. Access impracticable most of the year, and then with a serious air draught restriction under the bridge over the tail of the lock. © IVANOHE76

Canal de Briare

Rochereau lock is adorned with flowers and sculptures. © F-W

Locaboat Holidays hire base in the Gare d'Eau © F-W

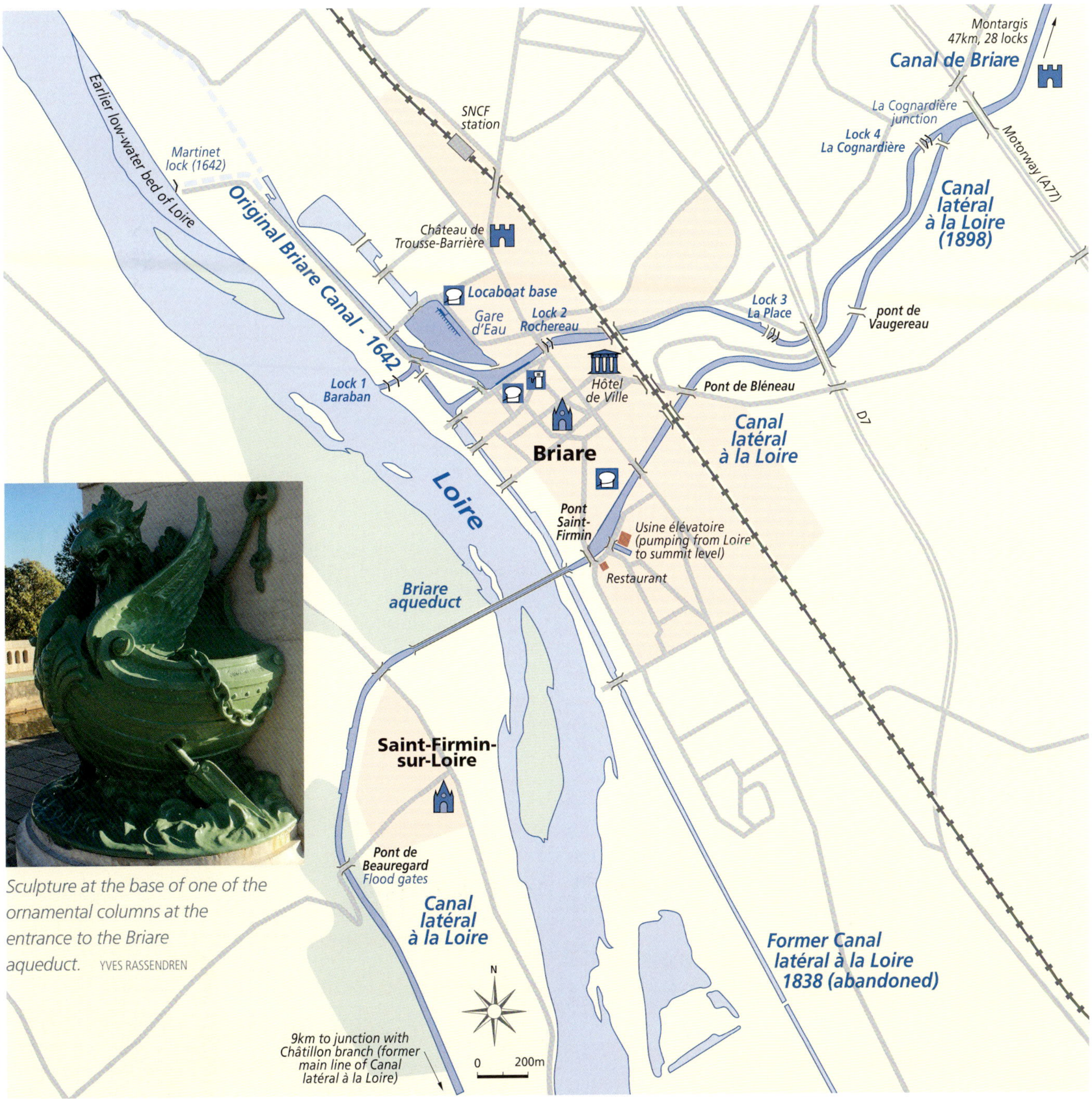

Sculpture at the base of one of the ornamental columns at the entrance to the Briare aqueduct. YVES RASSENDREN

III – Central France and routes to the Saône

32. Canal latéral à la Loire

The canal latéral à la loire follows the course of the river Loire from Briare, where it connects with the Canal de Briare, to Digoin, where it connects with the Canal du Centre, a distance of 196km. It is an important waterway, forming part of the least heavily-locked route from the Seine to the Saône, but it passes through an essentially rural region of central France, with little to suggest its history as an industrial lifeline. Large-scale maintenance works were carried out in the 1990s to restore the original navigable standards, as well as consolidating the fragile banks. Connections are made with the Canal du Nivernais via the branch to Decize and a channel dredged across the river Loire (PK 68) and with the Canal de Roanne à Digoin at PK 6. The canal also used to connect with the remarkable Canal du Berry system, sadly closed since 1955, at Marseilles-les-Aubigny (PK 125).

The canal was opened in 1838. As originally built, the canal included a treacherous crossing of the Loire near the downstream end, improved by a system of breakwaters but nevertheless prone to stoppages during high or low water. A bypass was thus opened in 1896, including the spectacular aqueduct over the Loire at Briare, continuing up the Trézée valley to connect with the Canal de Briare at La Cognardière.

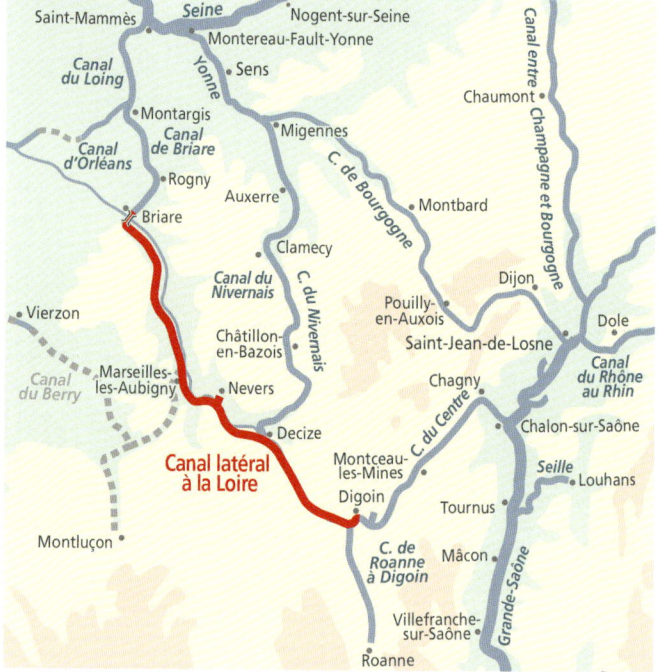

Six branches remain open to navigation. The **Châtillon** branch (PK 187), length 4.6km with 3 locks, leads to Les Mantelots basin. This was the former through route of the canal down to the Loire crossing. The branch is open on weekends only during the summer for access to the vast Mantelots basin, but may be almost choked with weed and silted up to a large extent; restoration of the Loire crossing and the right bank canal through to the port of Briare is a remote prospect. The **Saint-Thibault** branch (PK 160), length 0.7km, leads to a lock down to the Loire, which is closed to navigation. The **Givry-Fourchambault** branch (PK 119), length 2.4km with 2 locks, links with the Loire. For both these branches, 24 hours' notice must be given to the Saint-Satur subdivisional engineer for passage. The **Nevers** branch (PK 100), length 2.8km with 2 locks, leads to Nevers. Here a third lock leading down to the Loire was long used as part of a swimming pool. The **Decize** branch (PK 68), length 0.5km and 2 locks, links with the Loire and the Canal du Nivernais, and includes the extensive basin at Decize, which also has a hire base. These latter branches have automatic locks. The **Dompierre** branch (PK 29), length 2.7km with no locks, leads to the small town of Dompierre-sur-Besbre, which has a hire base. It is very narrow.

The Apremont branch (PK 112), which serves as a feeder canal from the Allier, is no longer open to navigation.

Navigation

Navigating the canal should not present any difficulty for pleasure craft, and the 'Bourbonnais' route is sometimes recommended as the easiest option for crossing France from the Channel to the Mediterranean. It is usually reliably and well supplied with water, but this may alter during and after long hot summers, when the route is then not as dependable as the eastern (Champagne) route.

The speed limit 8km/h. Estimate 3 to 4km/h overall for a day's travel including locks, or count the locks and add about 20 minutes for each. Unlike many canals, the latéral à la Loire has lock-keepers to work all the locks on the through route, although when traffic is light one lock-keeper may be assigned to accompany a boat through a series of locks. Traffic is monitored efficiently, and it would be exceptional to find nobody at a lock and to have to call up VNF.

Some locks fill right 'to the brim' and beyond and this means that boats must be protected down at the waterline and into the water. Fenders must drop below the water and/or use fender boards to prevent them from floating up.

The engine cooling water filter should be checked frequently; weed, leaves and mud in the water and on the bottom can get stirred up, and this also happens while in a lock, emptying or filling.

Canal latéral à la Loire

Locks

There are 37 locks, including one double staircase lock (21/22) at Le Guétin. The original lock 23 was eliminated, which is why the locks are numbered 1 to 38. They are of standard Freycinet dimensions, 38.50m by 5.17m, with the exception of Lock 11 (Gailloux), where the chamber is slightly narrower (5.14 m). The locks rise from Briare towards Digoin, overcoming a difference in level of 98m.

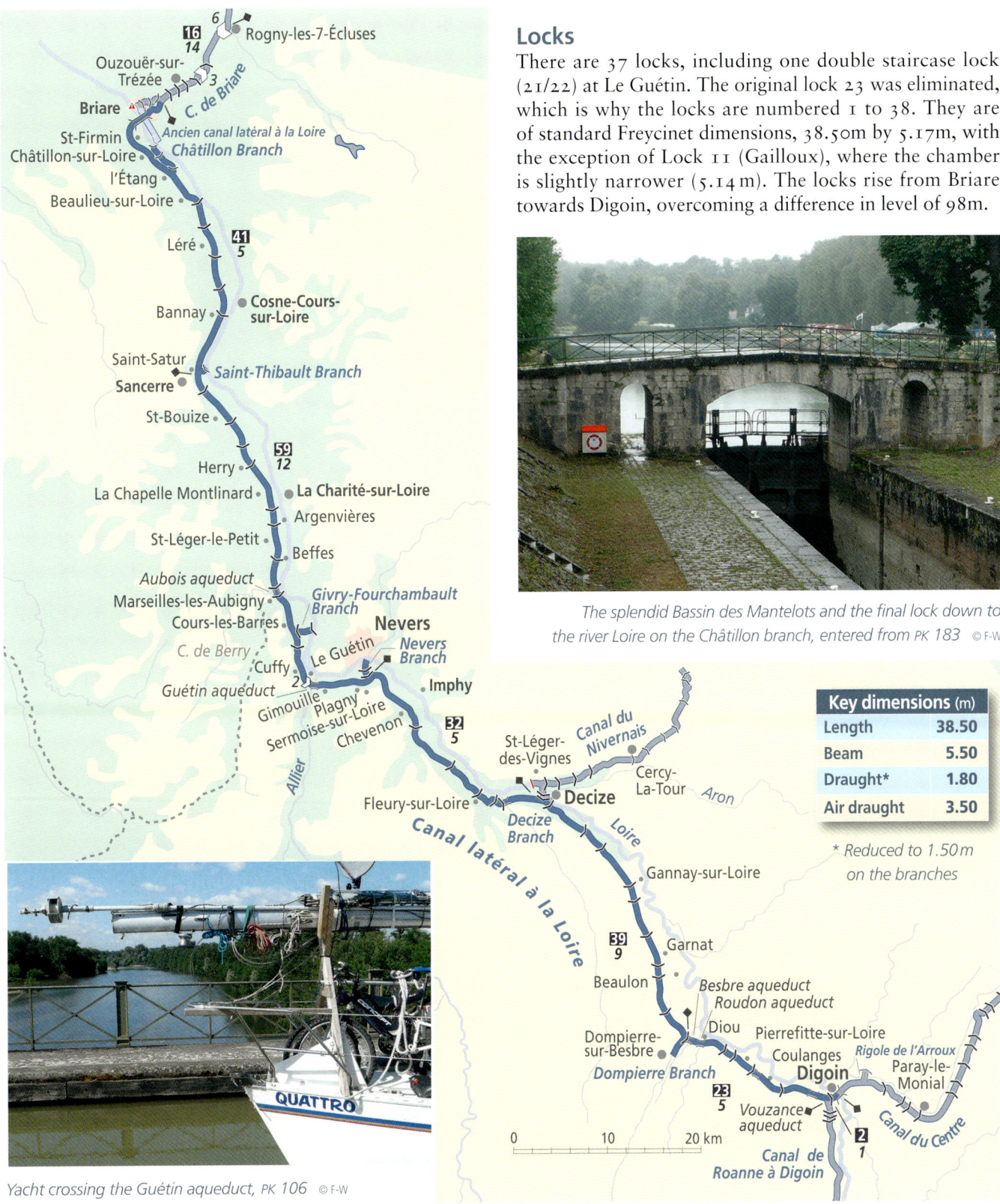

The splendid Bassin des Mantelots and the final lock down to the river Loire on the Châtillon branch, entered from PK 183 © F-W

Key dimensions (m)	
Length	38.50
Beam	5.50
Draught*	1.80
Air draught	3.50

Reduced to 1.50m on the branches

Yacht crossing the Guétin aqueduct, PK 106 © F-W

The canal has three fine aqueducts, situated at Digoin (240m, over the Loire), Le Guétin (334m, over the Allier) and Briare (660m, over the Loire). Navigation is one-way across all these aqueducts. At Digoin and Briare, the first vessel to reach either end of the aqueduct has priority. At Le Guétin, the lights controlling passage through the double staircase lock also control passage across the aqueduct.

Draught

The maximum authorised draught is 1.80m.

Headroom

Bridges leave a minimum clear headroom of 3.50m.

Towpath

There is a towpath throughout the length of the canal, forming part of the European cycle route Nantes-Budapest.

III – Central France and routes to the Saône

Authority
VNF Centre-Bourgogne.
CEMI Saint-Satur
– Port de Saint-Thibault, 18300 Saint-Satur, 02 48 54 06 98
  cemi-decize@vnf.fr (PK 110-200)
CEMI Decize
– 1 quai de la Jonction, 58300 Decize, 03 86 77 39 40
  cemi-decize@vnf.fr (PK 29-110)
CEMI Digoin
– 2 rue Guilleminot, 71160 Digoin, 03 85 53 01 89
  cemi.montceau-les-mines.dt.centrebourgogne@vnf.fr (PK 4-29)

Route description

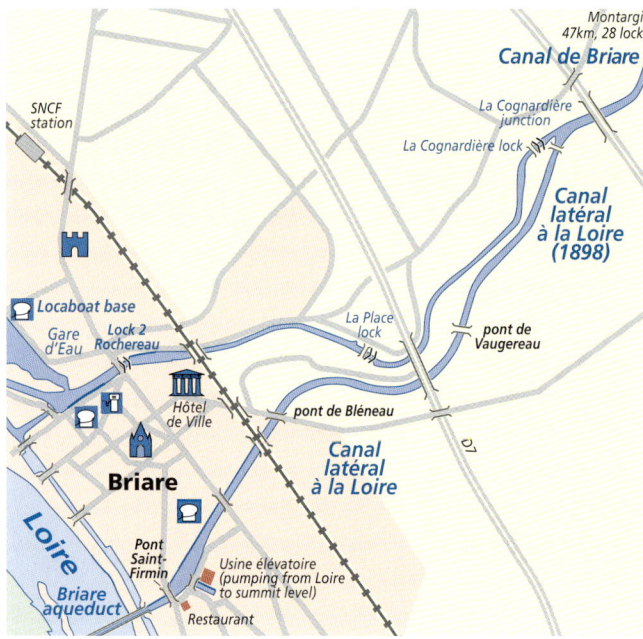

The most emblematic monument on French waterways, the famous Briare aqueduct completed in 1996, PK 197 © LOIRE À VÉLO

- PK **199.9** Footbridge (Cognardière), flood gate
- PK **199.8** Aqueduct (Cognardière)
- PK **199.1** Bridge (Vaugereau)
- PK **198.8** Road bridge (D7, Briare bypass)
- PK **198.3** Bridge (Bléneau)
- PK **198.2** Railway bridge
- PK **198.0** Briare bridge (D957)
- PK **197.7** **Briare** basin, moorings west bank for up to 8 boats depending on length, 06 08 95 03 20, night €13, water and electricity included, slipway, repairs, town centre 300m, restaurant with private moorings east bank

This bustling harbour is managed independently from the extremely popular *port de plaisance* in the town centre on the 'dead end' section of the Canal de Briare. See under that canal for the whole picture. Boats in transit north to south may prefer this comfortable harbour and boat hire base, with all facilities and its spectacular location just a few steps from the famous aqueduct, but the main *port de plaisance* on the Canal de Briare is not to be missed.

- PK **197.6** Beginning of Briare aqueduct (663m long), bridge (Saint-Firmin)
- PK **196.9** End of Briare aqueduct

Icon of the French canals, the aqueduct was designed by the canal engineer Abel Mazoyer and the fourteen masonry supports were constructed by the Eiffel company. The paired obelisks at each end reflect the same feature on the Pont Alexandre on the Seine in Paris and the aqueduct is lit by a chain of Art Nouveau style lamp standards. It followed the introduction of the nationwide Freycinet gauge for canal peniches and replaced a crossing over the River Loire that was susceptible to flooding, currents and droughts. Until recently it was the longest canal aqueduct in the world. The short by-passed canal sections on either side of the river are still navigable, however there are significant draught and headroom restrictions, particularly on the southern/western branch.

Briare basin close to the famous aqueduct, PK 198. The boatyard does repairs and has a large slipway.

- PK **196.7** Canal on embankment crosses D951
- PK **196.2** Saint-Firmin basin l/b
- PK **195.9** Bridge (Beauregard), flood gate
- PK **194.9** Bridge (Motte), castle r/b
- PK **193.7** Bridge (Chailloux)
- PK **192.5** Bridge (Hautes-Rives)
- PK **192.1** Aqueduct
- PK **192.0** Bridge (Châtillon)
- PK **191.5** **Châtillon-sur-Loire** basin and *port de plaisance* l/b, 40 boats, 10 visitor moorings, 06 32 08 15 80, night €9.50, water included, electricity, shower €2, crane 6t, slipway, repairs (*chatillonplaisance.fr*), restaurant, village 300m
  capitaineriechatillon@orange.fr

Canal latéral à la Loire

The port de plaisance *at Châtillon, PK 192, is justifiably popular. It is also a Le Boat hire base.* © GSV

A popular mooring and attractive historic village.

PK **191.4** Footbridge (Mantelot)
PK **190.7** Bridge (Rabuteloires), flood gates
PK **189.1** Bridge (La Folie)
PK **188.1** Bridge (Gannes)
PK **186.7** L'Étang bridge, flood gates, moorings d/s l/b, no services
PK **186.6** Junction with former through route (Châtillon branch) r/b (see separate table below)
PK **184.3** **Beaulieu** bridge, basin and municipal *halte* village d/s l/b, moorings along campsite embankment for 10 boats, free (maximum 48 hours), water, electricity, showers €3, wifi at tourist office, slipway
PK **183.1** Bridge (Plessis)
PK **182.3** Lock 38 (Maimbray), aqueduct, bridge d/s
PK **184.7** Bridge (Chenevières)
PK **179.5** **Belleville-sur-Loire** bridge, mooring for 24 boats above and below lock 37, tourist office 02 48 72 54 96, free, water, electricity, showers, slipway, wifi, village, supermarket and restaurant l/b

This *port de plaisance* is an especially good stop. Access to free water and electricity is by means of an adapter obtainable from the tourist office, which also has wifi and is immediately adjacent to excellent, tree-shaded moorings lying below the lock. The key to immaculately maintained services, including hot shower, is held by the lock-keeper.

Hire boat moored at Belleville-sur-Loire, PK 179. © J WELSCH

PK **179.2** Lock 37 (Belleville), quays u/s and d/s l/b
PK **178.7** Bridge (Rue)
PK **178.4** New road bridge
PK **176.8** **Sury-près-Léré** bridge, municipal *halte* d/s l/b, for 5 boats, night €5 (free first two nights), water, electricity, wifi, village l/b village l/b
PK **175.3** **Léré** bridge, basin and municipal *halte* d/s l/b, for 9 boats, free, water, electricity, wifi, village l/b

Free *halte*, a good small silo mooring.

PK **173.6** New road bridge
PK **173.5** Lock 36 (Houards), bridge
PK **171.4** Bridge (Ménétreau)
PK **170.4** Bridge (Gravereau)
PK **169.6** Lock 35 (Peseau)
PK **169.0** Bridge (Giraude)
PK **168.0** Bridge (Fouchards), quay and basin d/s l/b, château 600m
PK **167.2** Bridge (Bussy)
PK **165.8** Railway bridge
PK **165.6** Lock 34 (Bannay), bridge
PK **165.3** **Bannay** l/b

This is a very picturesque section of the canal.

PK **164.3** Bridge (Île), quay u/s l/b
PK **163.1** Bridge (Beaufroy)
PK **160.9** Bridge (Mivoie)
PK **159.5** Junction with Saint-Thibault branch r/b, see under branch for details of boat harbour
PK **159.4** **Saint-Satur** bridge and basin, *port de plaisance* for vessels up to 23m long, 02 48 72 10 88, 50 boats, 10 visitor moorings, night €10.50, water €4, electricity €4/day, showers, wifi

Saint-Satur basin on the Saint-Thibault branch, PK 155, is ideally situated for visiting the spectacular village of Sancerre © PETER VICKERY

PK **156.9** **Ménétréol-sous-Sancerre** bridge, basin and municipal *halte* d/s l/b, for up to 12 boats, water €4.50, electricity €4.50/day, showers €2.50, wifi (all from restaurant Le Floraine), village l/b, preferred mooring for visiting **Sancerre** 2.5 km on hilltop
PK **156.1** Lock 33 (Thauvenay), bridge
PK **154.5** Bridge (Rousseaux)
PK **152.7** **Saint-Bouize** bridge, basin u/s l/b, village 1 km
PK **151.9** Moule aqueduct
PK **150.9** Lock 32 (Grange), bridge, castle 1 km
PK **150.3** Basin (Guillons) l/b, no services
PK **148.4** Bridge (Champalay)
PK **145.9** Lock 31 (Prée), bridge

III – Central France and routes to the Saône

PK **144.9** Bridge (Sarrée)
PK **143.4** Basin
PK **142.9** Lock 30 (**Herry**), bridge, municipal *halte* d/s l/b, quay 80m long, free, water €0.50 per 100 litres
PK **140.9** Bridge (Châtillon)
PK **139.7** Bridge (Charreau)
PK **138.4** Bridge (Nambault)
PK **137.1** **La Chapelle-Montlinard** bridge, basin and *halte*, free, water, electricity, slipway, mooring for **La Charité** 2 km on r/b of Loire

Former boatyard with dry dock. Possible excursion to La Charité-sur-Loire with its Cluniac monastery, a UNESCO World Heritage site on the pilgrimage route to Santiago de Compestela in northern Spain.

PK **135.6** Lock 29 (Rousseaux), bridge
PK **134.9** Quay (Charnaye) l/b
PK **134.4** Quays (Comillons)
PK **133.9** Bridge (D45e)
PK **133.5** **Argenvières** basin, village r/b
PK **132.1** Lock 28 (Argenvières), bridge
PK **131.5** **Saint-Léger-le-Petit** bridge, village l/b
PK **130.1** Bridge (Radis)
PK **128.9** Basin l/b
PK **128.4** Lock 27 (**Beffes**), bridge d/s, municipal *halte* d/s, for 12 boats and 1 *péniche*, free (24 hours), water, electricity, showers, pump-out, village r/b

Pleasant bankside mooring.

PK **127.6** Footbridge
PK **126.0** Turning basin l/b
PK **125.6** Lock 26 (Aubois), bridge d/s, freight office
PK **125.4** Aubois aqueduct and basin l/b
PK **125.3** Lock 25 (Aubigny), bridge d/s
PK **124.7** Former junction with Canal de Berry l/b

Constructed in 1840 and 141km long, the canal was closed in 1954 because of water limitations and the restricted gabarit. Built with narrow locks on the British model, the canal was never upgraded to the Freycinet standard. Some sections have been restored.

PK **124.5** **Marseilles-les-Aubigny** basin and municipal port de plaisance l/b, 02 48 76 44 99, 2 visitor moorings, night €8, water and electricity included, shower €2.50, additional moorings r/b, boat repair yard Chantier Naval Evezard, 06 78 10 60 80, crane 50t, small town l/b

A large, quiet basin offering both quayside mooring and pontoons.

PK **124.0** Bridge (Poids de Fer)
PK **121.6** Bridge (Dompierre)
PK **120.0** **Cours-les-Barres** bridge, municipal *halte* on quayside for 7 boats, free, water, electricity, restaurant, village l/b
PK **119.2** Bridge (Crille)
PK **118.5** Junction with Givry-Fourchambault Branch r/b, basin

Advance notice must be given to VNF at Saint-Satur to enter the branch.

PK **118.4** Bridge (Mahauts), quay r/b

PK **116.2** Bridge (L'Aubray)
PK **116.0** Lock 24 (L'Aubray)
PK **113.7** Bridge (Presle), castle
PK **112.6** **Cuffy** footbridge, village l/b
PK **111.8** Bridge (Colombier)
PK **111.5** Junction with Apremont branch (Allier feeder canal), closed to navigation

The disused branch is worth exploring on foot or by bike, to visit the remarkable 'Écluse des Lorrains'.

The circular lock enabled péniches coming from the branch (seen 'head on') having entered the lock, to be lowered to river level and rotated so as to exit onto the river Allier below the weir. © GORDON KNIGHT

PK **111.4** Bridge (Caillettes)
PK **110.4** Double staircase lock 21/22 (Guétin), bridge, basin d/s, l/b, quay with bollards, bar/tabac/épicerie r/b

The impressive double staircase lock at the end of the Guétin aqueduct © YVES RASSENDREN

PK **110.0** Guétin aqueduct (over river Allier), access controlled by lights
PK **109.6** Bridge (Sampanges), Gimouille basin u/s l/b, overnight mooring permitted
PK **108.8** **Gimouille** bridge, very tight, proceed with caution, village l/b
PK **107.9** Bridge (Colombier), D976, castle 200m
PK **106.8** Bridge (Marais)

Canal latéral à la Loire

PK **104.3** Bridge (Seuilly)
PK **103.6** Railway bridge
PK **103.4** Bridge (Pavillon), **Challuy** 500m
PK **102.6** **Plagny** bridge, D907, boat moorings in basin u/s l/b, Tourisme Fluvial du Centre hire base, 03 86 74 56 34, no overnight moorings, services for hire boats only, crane 5t, restaurant
PK **101.8** Motorway Bridge (N7)
PK **101.4** Bridge (Peuilly)
PK **101.0** Bridge (D907a)
PK **100.4** Junction with Nevers Branch, r/b, see details below
PK **100.2** Bridge, **Sermoise-sur-Loire** 1km
PK **98.7** Bridge (Crot de Savigny)
PK **97.3** Bridge (Forêt de Sermoise)
PK **94.0** Bridge (Crezancy)
PK **93.4** **Chevenon** bridge, village and château 800m l/b
PK **91.3** Bridge (Atelier)
PK **89.7** Lock 20 (Jaugenay), bridge d/s
PK **88.5** Bridge (Planches)
PK **86.3** Bridge (Chamond), basin d/s l/b
PK **85.8** Lock 19 (Uxeloup)
PK **85.2** Bridge (Uxeloup)
PK **83.9** Bridge (Vèvre)
PK **81.9** Bridge (Motte-Farchat), basin u/s l/b, château 1km
PK **80.7** Lock 18 (Fleury)
PK **80.4** **Fleury-sur-Loire** bridge, *halte nautique* for 10 boats, night €9, water and electricity included, showers €2, wifi, small village l/b
PK **78.9** Bridge (Perrière)
PK **76.8** **Avril-sur-Loire** bridge, small village r/b
PK **76.0** Lock 17 (Abron), Abron aqueduct u/s, basin d/s
PK **75.6** Bridge (Forge-Neuve)
PK **74.9** Lock 16 (Acolin), Acolin aqueduct u/s
PK **74.2** Bridge (Réau)
PK **71.4** Bridge (Beaugy), basin d/s l/b
PK **70.9** Bridge (Châlons)
PK **70.0** Bridge (Vaux)
PK **68.7** **Germancy** bridge, basin d/s l/b, small quay u/s r/b, water, **Decize** 1400m
PK **68.4** Junction with Decize branch and Canal du Nivernais, r/b, see under branch for details of Decize *port de plaisance*
PK **67.2** Bridge (Saulx)
PK **66.8** Lock 15 (Saulx)
PK **64.2** Bridge (Croix-des-Feuillats)
PK **61.4** Bridge (Motte)
PK **60.9** Lock 14 (Motte)
PK **59.6** Cornats bridge, basin u/s l/b
PK **58.2** Lock 13 (Huilerie)
PK **57.4** Bridge (Nogent)
PK **54.8** Bridge (Rue des Gués)
PK **52.5** Lock 12 (Vanneaux), bridge d/s
PK **52.2** **Gannay-sur-Loire** *port de plaisance* in basin l/b (Les Vanneaux), 04 70 42 57 32, 18 boats, night €15, water, electricity, showers, slipway, restaurant, tourist office, Entente Marine boatyard and wintering, village 1km r/b
PK **50.7** Bridge (Viviers)
PK **49.3** Lock 11 (Gailloux), bridge d/s
PK **47.8** Bridge (Boise)
PK **46.3** Bridge (Rozière)

Rope to be pulled at the entrance to the Nevers branch, to work the first of the two locks. © F-W

PK **45.3** Lock 10 (Rozière)
PK **44.5** Bridge (Saint-Martin), **Paray-le-Frésil** 2km, l/b
PK **42.6** Bridge (Huilerie)
PK **40.6** **Garnat-sur-Engièvre** bridge, municipal *halte* for 6 boats on pontoon u/s l/b, free, water, slipway, restaurant in village r/b
PK **39.6** Lock 9 (Clos du May), bridge d/s
PK **37.7** **Beaulon** bridge, municipal *halte* for 10 boats d/s l/b, free, water, electricity, village 1km
PK **37.6** Lock 8 (Beaulon)
PK **36.7** Bridge (Petrot)
PK **35.0** Bridge (Thiel)
PK **32.7** Lock 7 (Bessais), bridge d/s
PK **31.2** Skew bridge (Taillis)
PK **30.0** Bridge (Abbaye de Sept-Fons), moorings u/s r/b
PK **29.2** Junction with Besbre feeder canal, embranchement de Dompierre, l/b, see p.181 details of port
PK **29.1** Lock 6 (Besbre), bridge d/s
PK **28.9** Besbre aqueduct, length 86m
PK **27.2** Bridge (Ternat)
PK **26.9** Roudon aqueduct
PK **26.8** Bridge (Prats)
PK **25.8** Bridge (Saligny), Diou 300m
PK **25.4** **Diou** bridge, municipal *halte* for 5 boats d/s l/b, free, water, electricity, restaurant, village 400m
PK **20.2** Railway bridge
PK **23.5** Bridge (Cluzeau)
PK **22.6** Lock 5 (Putay), bridge d/s
PK **21.2** Bridge (Theil)

Digoin aqueduct © HAL STUFFT

III – Central France and routes to the Saône

PK 6.1	Junction with Canal de Roanne à Digoin l/b

This canal leads to the popular *port de plaisance* at Roanne.

PK 5.3	Chassenard basin, 830m long
PK 5.0	Lock 1 (Digoin), bridge
PK 4.7	Digoin aqueduct over river Loire, 240m long
PK 4.6	Bridge (Perruts)
PK 4.4	Bridge (Charolles), convenient moorings on both banks, no services, town centre 150m
PK 4.1	Footbridge
PK 4.0	**Digoin**, junction with Canal de Centre, *port de plaisance* and Canalous-Plaisance hire base u/s on Canal du Centre, 03 85 88 97 26, 45 berths, night €6.20, fuel, water €2, electricity €3.20, showers €1.70, crane 35t, slipway, repairs, town centre 800m

The port is on the Canal du Centre. It accepts boats up to 12m only, longer boats moor short of this facility, on the canal latéral (see map left).

Branches off Canal latéral à la Loire

Châtillon Branch *(former through route)*

PK 0.0	Junction with through route (PK 187)
PK 0.0	Lock 39 (L'Étang), bridge
PK 1.5	Bridge (Gannes)
PK 2.3	Lock 40 (La Folie), bridge, municipal gîtes in lock cottage
PK 3.9	Bridge
PK 4.3	Lock 51 (Les Mantelots), bridge, basin u/s
PK 4.3	Junction with the river Loire

Saint-Thibault (Saint-Satur) Branch

PK 0.0	Junction with through route (PK 159.5), stop gate, bridge
PK 0.1	**Saint-Thibault** basin and boat harbour (Port de Saint-Satur-Saint-Thibault), 50 berths, night €6.50, 02 48 54 14 17, water, electricity, showers, crane 6t, repairs, restaurants
PK 0.6	Lock 33ter (closed to navigation)
PK 0.7	Former junction with the river Loire

Givry-Fourchambault Branch

PK 0.0	Junction with through route (PK 118.5)
PK 0.1	Lock 24bis (Crille), lift 1.20m, bridge, basin d/s
PK 2.3	**Givry** bridge, basin and moorings u/s r/b
PK 2.4	Lock 24ter (Givry), lift variable
PK 2.4	Junction with the river Loire

Nevers Branch

PK 0.0	Junction with through route (PK 100)
PK 0.1	Lock 22 (Verville), lift 3.00m, bridge
PK 0.5	Motorway bridge (A77)
PK 0.8	Lock 23 (Rombois) PK 2.2 Skew bridge (D13)
PK 2.8	**Nevers**, *port de plaisance* with pontoons r/b under trees, 06 74 54 81 77, 62 berths, 25 visitor moorings, night €11, water €2/500 litres, electricity €3/night, showers €2, fuel on request, pump-out, restaurant l/b, town centre 1 km

Good moorings and possible overwintering. Nevers itself lies on the other side of the Loire within walking distance. There is also an excellent bus service from Plagny, on the canal, which is just as quick. Tourist Office.

PK 20.6	Lock 4 (Theil)
PK 19.6	Bridge (Enfer), D779
PK 19.0	**Pierrefitte-sur-Loire** bridge, municipal *halte* for up to 8 boats d/s l/b, free, water, village r/b
PK 18.2	Bridge (Oddins)
PK 16.6	Lock 3 (Oddes), aqueduct u/s
PK 16.3	Bridge (Vesvres)
PK 14.8	**Coulanges** bridge, *halte* for 5 boats, free, water/electricity €2 by tokens purchased by credit card, small village
PK 14.3	Basin (Coulanges) l/b
PK 13.5	Lock 2 (Thaleine), bridge
PK 12.0	Bridge (Mortillon), D779
PK 10.4	Bridge (Micaudière)
PK 8.5	Bridge (Péage)
PK 8.0	Vouzance aqueduct
PK 7.9	Quay (Fontaine-Saint-Martin) l/b, water
PK 7.7	Bridge (Donjon), D994
PK 6.7	Basin (La Broche), r/b
PK 6.2	Bridge (Chassenard)

Canal latéral à la Loire

Decize branch

PK 0.0	*Junction with through route* (PK 68)	
PK 0.1	Lock 16bis (Saint-Maurice), lift 2.50m, bridge	
PK 0.2	**Decize** basin, length 380m, Le Boat hire base, 03 73 15 00 00, 80 berths, 16 visitor berths, night €10, water, electricity, showers (€2), pump-out (€5), diesel, slipway, restaurant, wifi	

Good *port de plaisance* in the branch off the canal, through one lock. Intermarché supermarket close by with fuel. Water also at the lock.

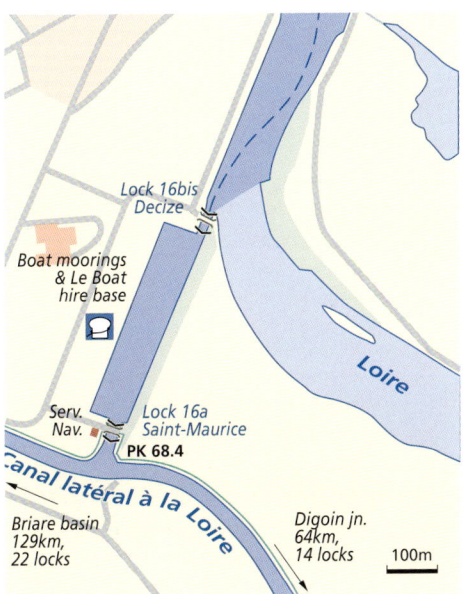

PK 0.5	Lock 16ter (Decize), lift up to 4.00m, bridge
PK 0.5	*Junction with navigable length of the Loire* (for access to the Canal du Nivernais)

For the complete connection via the navigable length of the river Loire in Decize, see under the Canal du Nivernais, p.165.

Dompierre branch

PK 0.0	*Junction with through route* (PK 29), bridge
PK 0.3	Bridge (N79)
PK 0.6	Railway bridge
PK 0.7	Overhead power lines
PK 1.1	Canal narrows

Care required in this very narrow section, 600m long, with shallow, rocky sides. Meeting other craft may be tricky.

PK 1.6	Accommodation bridge
PK 2.1	Bridge (the lowest on this branch)
PK 2.4	**Dompierre-sur-Besbre** basin, head of navigation, Locaboat hire base (caution: low bridge), 30 berths, 15 visitor moorings, 04 70 48 27 27, night €15, diesel, water, electricity, shower (during office hours), small slipway, pump-out

The Locaboat Holidays hire base in Dompierre-sur-Besbre © F-W

The port de plaisance at Decize. © VILLE DE DECIZE

III – Central France and routes to the Saône

33. Canal du Centre

THE CANAL DU CENTRE, THE SECOND RIVER-TO-RIVER link to be built in central France, was opened to navigation in 1790. It rises gently from the Loire valley at Digoin, where it connects with the Canal latéral à la Loire, to a summit level at an altitude of just over 300m in the former coal-mining and industrial basin of Le Creusot/Montceau-les-Mines, and then drops more steeply to the Saône at Chalon-sur-Saône, a distance of 112km. The original cut through Chalon, entering the Saône at the Port de la Chambre de Commerce, was infilled in the 1950s and obliterated by a modern boulevard, and replaced by a new cut to the north of the town. This cut is 2.1km shorter than the original line, which explains why the route description (using the original KP markers) ends at PK 2.1. A 3km length of the old line was retained as a branch serving the Saint-Gobain factory, but is no longer accessible. It connects with the through route at PK 5.7.

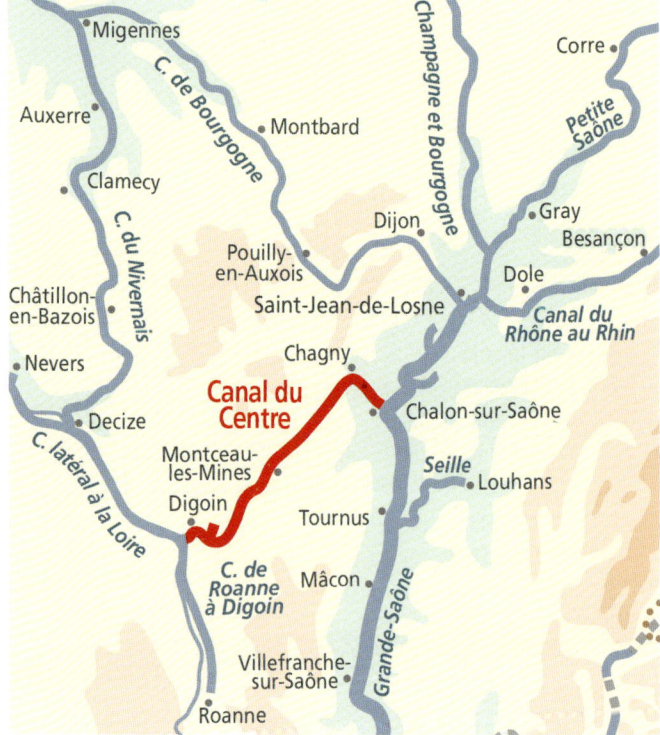

The Canal du Centre, one of the technical wonders of its times, was built by the engineer Gauthey concurrently with the Canal de Bourgogne. Started in 1784, it was inaugurated in 1793, 40 years before the Canal de Bourgogne was completed, and was the first link between the Loire (leading to the Seine through the Canal de Briare) and the Saône. Its locks were 28 by 4.75m. It was first enlarged in 1830 to Becquey dimensions (30m by 5.2m), then again to reach the present Freycinet size (38.5 by 5.2m) around 1890.

Navigation
There is very little commercial traffic and the canal, which is winding and passes through some thickly wooded countryside, has parts that are very beautiful, and is constantly interesting, with excellent *ports de plaisance* and *haltes* along the route. The main difficulty could be water supply, which is notoriously inadequate when severe drought sets in, as has frequently been the case in recent years.

Locks
There are 61 locks, of which 35 (numbered 1 to 35M for Mediterranean) fall towards Chalon and 26 (numbered 1 to 26O for Océan) fall towards Digoin. Dimensions are 39.00m by 5.20m, except for lock 34b on the new cut at Chalon, which is 40.00m by 6.00m. This lock replaces three on the original line, hence its exceptional depth of 10.76m.

All the locks on the Saône side are equipped for automatic operation, with the lock entrance controlled by lights and the actual locking cycle actuated by pulling on the blue cord set in a steel pillar at the lock side. Many of these locks are deep, with central floating bollards, and operated by a pull-cord at the far end of the lock. If an accompanying *éclusier* is not present to pull the cord it can be tricky to bring the boat forward in the lock, pull the cord and then reverse to pick up the (probably single) bollard before the lock starts filling and life becomes exciting. Some locks fill 'to the brim', which makes fendering difficult. In case of emergency, the cycle is interrupted by pulling on the red cord (see also the section on automatic locks in the Introduction). Some automatic locks recognise the exit of a first boat when there are actually two in the lock, leaving only a short period of time for the second to exit before the gates start to close – be on your guard in these circumstances.

Draught
The maximum authorised draught is 1.80m.

Headroom
The bridges leave a nominal minimum headroom of 3.50m, but boats approaching this height must pay particular attention at Saint-Léger-sur-Dheune bridge (PK 31), which is reported to offer a few centimetres less headroom.

Canal du Centre

Lift bridge over the entrance to the Arroux feeder canal, PK 112
© YVES RASSENDREN

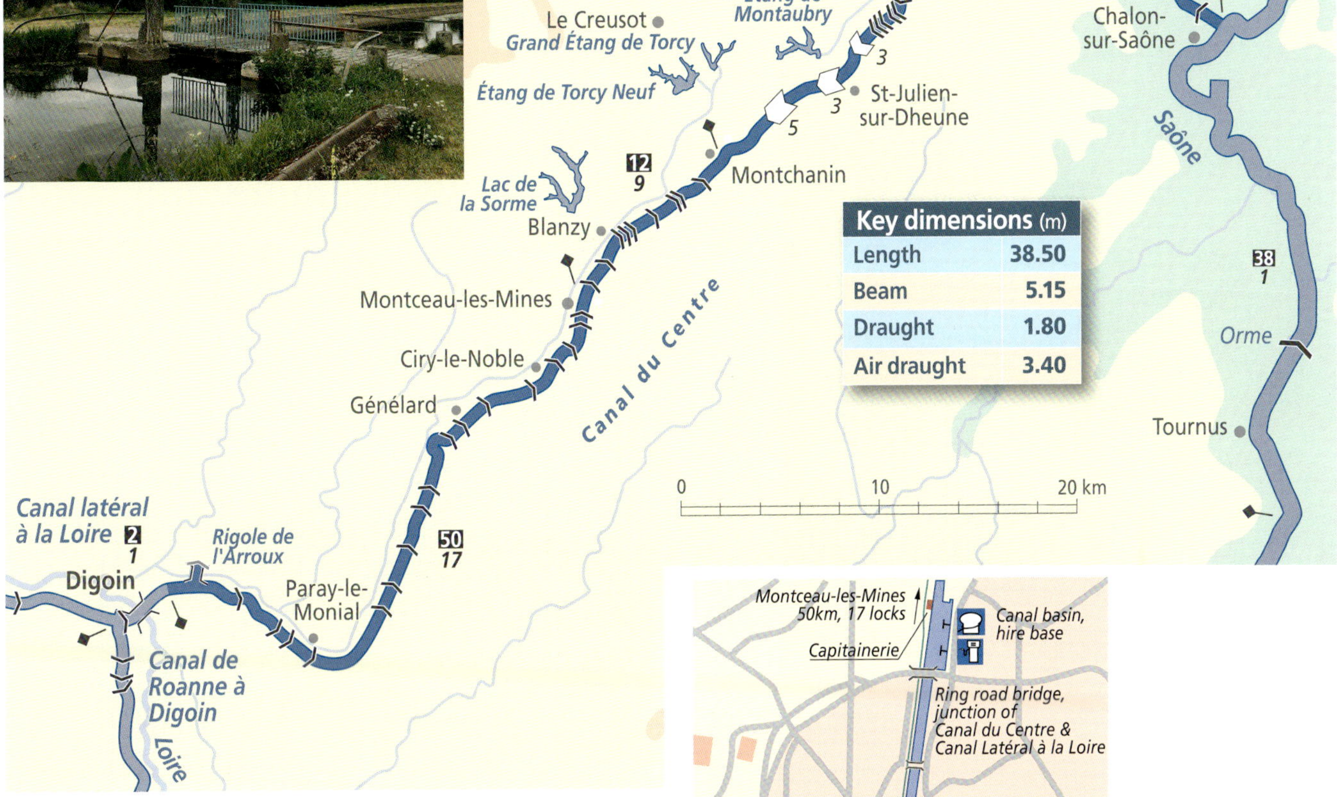

Key dimensions (m)
Length	38.50
Beam	5.15
Draught	1.80
Air draught	3.40

Towpath
There is a metalled towpath throughout, serving as a public road (D974) between Paray-le-Monial and Saint-Léger-sur-Dheune. Elsewhere, the towpath is in good condition.

Authority
VNF Centre-Bourgogne, CEMI de Montceau
– 9ème écluse Océan, 71300 Montceau-les-Mines,
03 85 67 90 50
cemi.montceau-les-mines.dt.centrebourgogne@vnf.fr

Route description

PK **114.2** Bridge (Digoin ring road D979), *junction with Canal latéral à la Loire*, see plan of Digoin right

PK **114.1** **Digoin** basin, moorings r/b, *port de plaisance* and Canalous Plaisance hire base l/b, 50 berths, 20 visitor moorings, 03 85 88 97 26, night €6.20, fuel, water €2.10, electricity €3.20, showers €1.70, crane 8t, slipway, repairs, town centre 800m

The municipal port only accepts boats up to 12m; longer boats moor south of the main road bridge, on the Canal latéral à la Loire.

PK **113.1** Railway bridge
PK **112.5** Bridge (Blattiers)

Port de plaisance and Canalous hire base in Digoin, PK 114 © F-W

III – Central France and routes to the Saône

PK 111.7 Junction with Arroux feeder canal (rigole de l'Arroux), formerly navigable 13km to Gueugnon (abandoned)

The feeder canal and the industrial town of Gueugnon make a fascinating side trip. A cycle path has been laid out along the feeder's towpath. The canal was formerly navigable for *berrichon* barges, 27.50m by 2.70m, and has a working lift bridge carrying the towpath across the entrance.

PK 110.3 Bridge (Paradis)

Charming canal landscape from the bridge at PK 110 looking towards Paray-le-Monial. © YVES RASSENDREN

PK 107.7 Lock 26 (Bessons)
PK 105.0 Bridge (Colaillot)
PK 104.6 Colaillot quay l/b (commercial)
PK 104.8 Bridges (N79)
PK 104.5 Lock 25 (Mont)
PK 102.9 Lock 24 (Quarrés), water
PK 102.4 Bridge (Quarrés)
PK 102.1 Bridge (Quatre-Chemins)
PK 100.8 Bridge (Faubourg), service station l/b, water
PK 101.8 **Paray-le-Monial** quays, turning basin and municipal *halte* r/b, 06 83 81 33 31, moorings for 10 boats, night €10, water and electricity included, wifi, town centre 400m

Halte with water and electricity, noisy road nearby but attractive historic village with impressive Catholic basilica by the canal, a site visited by countless pilgrims on the route to St James of Compostella.

PK 101.5 Lock 23 (L'Hyron), water
PK 99.9 Bridge (Romay)
PK 99.5 Railway bridge
PK 98.1 Bridge (Bord), basin d/s r/b

PK 96.9 Bridge (N79)
PK 95.9 Lock 22 (Volesvres)
PK 95.8 Volesvres bridge, village 600m r/b
PK 94.5 Lock 21 (Haillers), bridge
PK 91.7 Lock 20 (Gravoine)
PK 91.4 Bridge (Gravoine), quay u/s l/b
PK 89.9 Bridge (Montceau)
PK 88.5 Bridge
PK 88.3 Lock 19 (Digoine), bridge, basin d/s l/b, moorings d/s r/b, auberge, Digoine château 1.5 km
PK 86.8 Lock 18 (Thiellay)
PK 86.0 Bridge (Corbary)
PK 85.2 Palinges bridge, quay u/s l/b, village l/b
PK 83.6 Bridge (Montet)
PK 82.6 Lock 17 (Montet), water
PK 81.7 **Génelard** bridge, basin and *halte* d/s l/b, moorings for 12 boats, free (maximum 1 week), water, electricity, showers, village centre 400m

Excellent mooring. The shops in this little industrial town are on the other side of the level crossing. The site is remarkable for the deep masonry-lined cutting that winds round the village just before reaching lock 16.

PK 81.6 Lock 16 (Génelard), moorings u/s l/b
PK 81.0 Bridge (over entrance to Génelard cutting), one-way traffic
PK 80.9 Quay l/b (Vernizy), service station r/b
PK 78.9 Lock 15 (Civry), bridge
PK 75.7 Lock 14 (Ciry), bridge, quay d/s r/b
PK 74.9 **Ciry-le-Noble** bridge, basin d/s l/b, village r/b
PK 73.7 Lock 13 (Azy)
PK 72.7 Bridge (Four)
PK 72.1 Lock 12 (Four)
PK 71.4 Bridge (Pont des Vernes)
PK 70.2 Bridge (Maison Morin)
PK 68.7 Bridge (Galuzot), restaurant, service station d/s r/b
PK 68.3 Railway bridge
PK 67.8 Lock 11 (Vernois), turning basin d/s
PK 67.3 Lock 10 (Chavannes)
PK 67.2 Bridge (Chavannes)
PK 66.5 Railway bridge
PK 66.2 Bridge, service station r/b, basin d/s l/b
PK 64.7 Lift bridge II
PK 64.5 Lift bridge I and parallel footbridge, quay d/s r/b
PK 64.3 Pedestrian lift bridge
PK 64.2 **Montceau-les-Mines** basin, *port de plaisance* r/b, 06 07 54 70 08, 37 berths, night €11, water and electricity included, shower, wifi, pump-out €2, restaurant, large town l/b   *mbouillet@montceaulesmines.fr*

A thoroughly business-like former mining town, Montceau-les-Mines has an attractive pedestrian street for shopping very close to the port. The partial infilling of the canal basin to create a car park in the late 1970s was disappointing, but more recent development and landscaping, and the addition of the elegant blue footbridge, have given the port a certain charm.

PK 64.1 Footbridge
PK 63.9 Lock 9 (Montceau), bridge, freight office, water
PK 62.1 Lock 8 (Mireaux)
PK 61.1 **Blanzy** bridge, municipal *halte* u/s r/b, for 5 boats, free,

Canal du Centre

water, electricity, village r/b

Port de plaisance in Montceau-des-Mines, PK 64 © F-W

PK 60.1 Railway bridge
PK 59.4 Lock 7 (Roche), bridge (Saint-Gelin)
PK 58.5 Lock 6 (Brûlard)
PK 57.9 Lock 5 (Planche-Calard), bridge
PK 55.5 Lock 4 (Parizenot), bridge
PK 53.9 Lock 3 (Favée)
PK 53.7 Turning basin
PK 53.5 Lock 2 (Brenots), bridge, private quay d/s l/b, auberge
PK 52.4 Lock 1 (Océan), beginning of summit level
PK 52.2 Boat moorings on short branch, east bank
PK 51.9 **Montchanin** bridge (D28), short quay d/s l/b, moorings to bank u/s, café-restaurant 400m, town centre 1800m
PK 49.7 Bridge (D18)
PK 49.4 Old railway bridge
PK 49.3 Overhead power lines
PK 49.7 Road bridge (N80)
PK 48.9 Railway viaduct (TGV Paris-Lyon)
PK 48.7 Lock 1 (Méditerranée), bridge, quay d/s r/b, beginning of summit level
PK 48.5 Lock 2 (Charmois)
PK 48.2 Lock 3 (Fourneau)
PK 47.8 Lock 4 (Ravin), bridge
PK 47.3 Lock 5 (Forge), bridge, Ecuisses, 1.5 km r/b
PK 45.8 Lock 6 (Motte)
PK 45.5 Lock 7 (Rocher)
PK 45.2 Lock 8 (Abbaye)
PK 45.0 **Saint-Julien-sur-Dheune** bridge, municipal *halte* d/s r/b, for 5 boats, water, electricity, restaurant
PK 44.2 Lock 9 (Moulin de Saint-Julien), shallow basin d/s r/b
PK 43.7 Lock 10 (Chez-le-Roi), bridge
PK 43.2 Lock 11 (Villeneuve)
PK 41.1 Lock 12, bridge
PK 40.4 Lock 13
PK 39.7 Lock 14, quay d/s l/b, Perreuil 1.5 km
PK 38.7 Bridge (Motte)
PK 38.4 Lock 15
PK 38.0 Lock 16
PK 37.0 Lock 17, bridge, turning basin u/s, Saint-Bérain-sur-Dheune r/b
PK 35.8 Lock 18, bridge, quay u/s l/b
PK 34.6 Bridge (Lochères)
PK 33.8 Lock 19
PK 33.0 **Saint-Léger-sur-Dheune** *port de plaisance* and Locaboat hire base in basin r/b, 03 85 98 03 03, mooring for 22 boats, night €17, water and electricity included, shower during office hours, restaurants, village r/b

Port de plaisance operated by Locaboat. The inner harbour is shallow (possibly less than 1m) and space may be limited. Pleasant village. Au P'tit Kir restaurant by the canal is recommended.

Saint-Léger-sur-Dheune

PK 32.9 Bridge (Saint-Léger-sur-Dheune), caution low bridge
PK 32.8 Footbridge
PK 32.1 Lock 20
PK 31.8 Bridge (Planche-Tapois, D148)
PK 30.7 Lock 21
PK 30.3 **Dennevy** bridge, quay l/b, village r/b
PK 29.3 Lock 22
PK 28.8 Lock 23
PK 28.5 **Saint-Gilles** bridge, quay and village r/b
PK 26.4 **Cheilly-lès-Maranges** bridge, municipal *halte* for 5 boats u/s l/b, water, restaurant, village 1 km
PK 25.0 Bridge (Corchanut)
PK 24.7 **Santenay** municipal *halte* for 4 boats l/b, free, water, village 1 km

Halte, water only. Many opportunities to taste and buy excellent Pinot Noir

185

III – Central France and routes to the Saône

Burgundy wines.

PK 23.6	Bridges (Fontaine Beaunoise and D974)
PK 22.5	**Remigny** bridge, village below canal
PK 20.1	Bridge (Bouzeron), L'Escarg'eau hire base and mooring for 4 boats d/s l/b, 06 98 58 85 90, night €4.60, water, electricity
PK 19.5	Bridge (Chagny) and aqueduct over main-line railway
PK 19.4	**Chagny** basin and municipal *halte* l/b, mooring for 11 boats, night €15, two nights €22, water, electricity, showers, *capitainerie*, town and station l/b

Excellent secure pontoon moorings s short walk from the small town centre with all shops and services. The narrow cutting beyond the basin has been dredged.

PK 17.8	Lock 24
PK 17.2	Lock 25
PK 16.6	Lock 26, bridge, **Rully** municipal *halte* d/s r/b, free, water, village 2 km

Rully has some of the most reputed wines from this area.

PK 16.2	Lock 27
PK 15.7	Lock 28
PK 15.2	Lock 29
PK 14.5	Lock 30
PK 13.8	Lock 31 (2.50m) bridge (Gué de Niffette)
PK 12.9	**Fontaine** bridge, quay d/s l/b, village 2 km
PK 11.4	Lock 32 (5.12m) the first of many equipped with floating bollards
PK 11.3	Bridge (Gauchard), trunk road N6
PK 9.6	Lock 33 (3.17m) bridge, La Loyère l/b
PK 8.6	Motorway bridge (A6)
PK 8.2	Lock 34 (1.83m) bridge, water
PK 7.8	**Fragnes** municipal *halte* l/b, quay for 20 boats, 03 85 45 97 65, night €10.50, water, electricity, shower €2, cycle service station, restaurant, wifi, shops

Well serviced moorings beside a small village shopping arcade.

PK 6.6	Quay l/b, industrial zone, no services
PK 5.8	Junction with Saint Gobain factory branch (former through route, heavily silted, no access)
PK 5.3	Bridge (D19), mooring
PK 4.5	Bridge (D5)

The restaurant L'Embarcadère spans the canal just downstream of this bridge. Fuel from the adjacent Centre Leclerc, but jerrycans are required.

PK 4.4	Supermarket cafeteria built across the canal, potential mooring for provisions
PK 4.2	Railway bridge
PK 3.8	Bridge
PK 3.7	Lock 34bis (10.76m), floating bollards
PK 3.4	Turning basin and industrial quays
PK 2.1	**Chalon-sur-Saône** *junction with Saône*

Continue downstream on the Saône to the excellent *port de plaisance* in the Gélise arm of the river on the left bank (see under Grande Saône).

Mooring at Fragnes, PK 8 © F-W

Approaching the deep lock in Chalon, PK 4

34. Canal de Roanne à Digoin

THE CANAL DE ROANNE À DIGOIN BEGINS close to the latter town, on the Canal latéral à la Loire, and runs south along the Loire valley to terminate in a large basin in Roanne. The basin is connected with a short navigable (but disused) length of the river Loire, through which the canal receives its water supply. The distance from Digoin to the Roanne basin, historically a coal terminal but now developed as a large and well-equipped *port de plaisance*, is 55.6km. The canal is ideal for pleasure cruising, passing through the unspoilt countryside of the upper Loire valley, although some local representatives and an association – Roanne Fluvial – are campaigning for a revival of commercial traffic.

> *This canal was needed to bypass the Loire, which offered navigable conditions that were inadequate for the industrial era, at the same time serving as a feeder to the Canal latéral à la Loire. The canal was conceded to the Compagnie Franco-Suisse, founded in 1827, and designed by engineer De Varaigne. Works started in 1831 and the canal was inaugurated in 1838. Modernisation to Freycinet standards was designed by engineer Léonce-Abel Mazoyer after the State bought back the canal from the concessionary in 1863.*

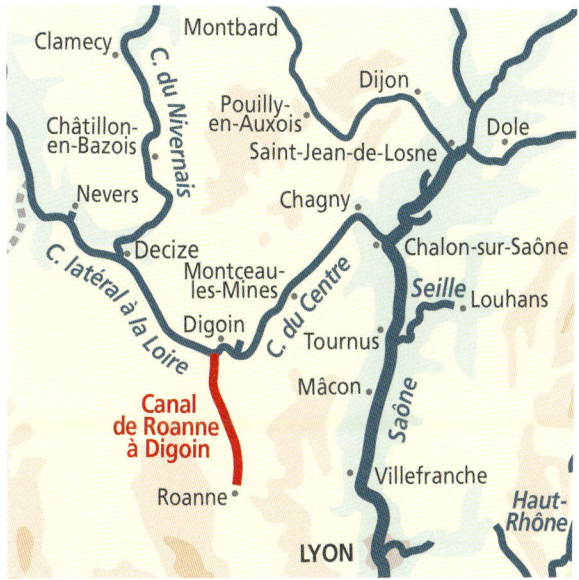

Navigation

The canal has earned the nickname of the *canal tranquille* for its peaceful atmosphere, passing through unspoilt rural areas and sleepy villages, contrasting with the constant bustle and animation of the terminal basin in Roanne, a fair-sized town with all imaginable services. This means that little traffic will be encountered, and virtually no commercial traffic.

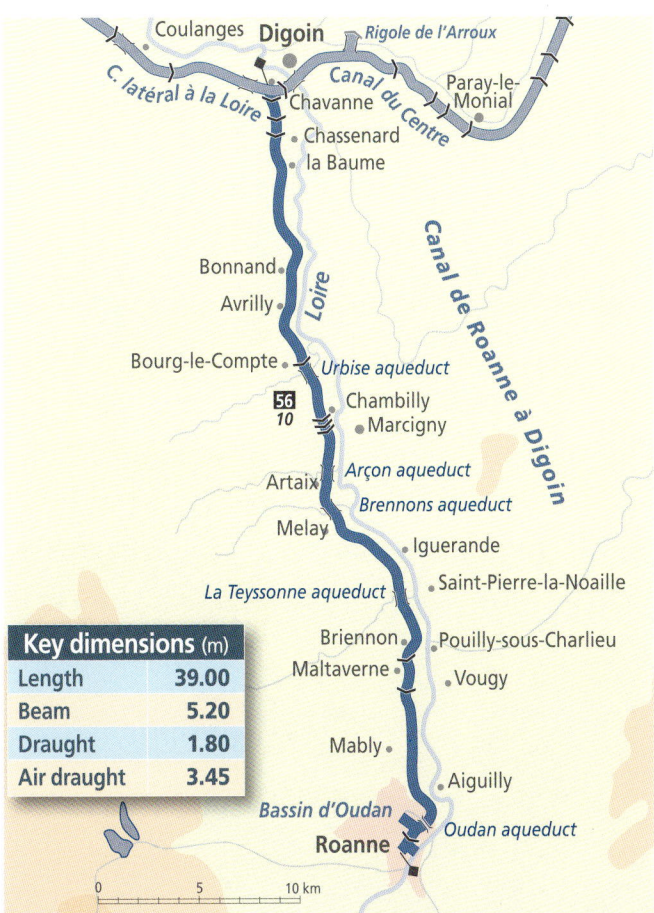

Locks

There are 10 locks of standard dimensions 39 by 5.20m. The total rise from Digoin to Roanne is 37m. Locks 4, 7 and 8 are among the deepest on the Freycinet network, 6.00 and 7.19m respectively. From 1st November to 31st March, lock operating times are 0900-1200 and 1300-1730, but notice of passage has to be given to the canal engineer's office before 1600 the previous day. In season locks are operated every day of the week, to 1900.

Draught

The maximum draught is 1.80m.

Headroom

The minimum headroom is 3.45m above normal water level.

III – Central France and routes to the Saône

Towpath
There is a good towpath throughout.

Authority
VNF Centre-Bourgogne, CEMI de Montceau-les-Mines – 9ème écluse Océan, 71300 Montceau-les-Mines, 03 85 67 90 50
email *cemi.montceau-les-mines.dt.centrebourgogne@vnf.fr*

Route description

PK 55.6	Junction with Canal latéral à Loire, **Digoin** 2 km
PK 55.2	Bridge (Bretons)
PK 54.7	Lock 10 (Bretons)
PK 54.3	Main road bridge (N79)
PK 53.4	Lock 9 (Beugnets), bridge
PK 52.3	Lock 8 (Chassenard)
PK 51.7	Bridge (Blancs)
PK 50.9	Bridge (Saint-Léger)
PK 49.7	Bridge (Séez)
PK 48.9	Bridge (Croix-Rouge), **Chassenard** municipal *halte* u/s l/b, moorings for 3 boats, free, water and electricity by tokens, €2
PK 48.2	Bridge (Beaume)
PK 46.5	Bridge (Giverdon)
PK 44.9	Bridge (Lurcy)
PK 42.4	Bridge (**Bonnand**), *halte* u/s r/b, for 6 boats, free, water €2, electricity €2 per 4 hours, payment by credit card

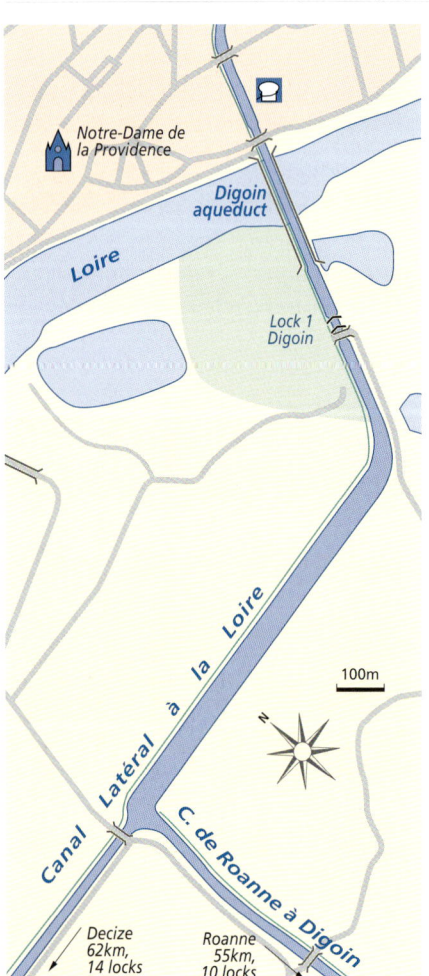

PK 40.7	Bridge (Morgat)
PK 40.3	**Avrilly**, quay l/b, small village l/b
PK 39.2	Bridge (Thynet)
PK 38.7	Bridge (Bouillets)
PK 37.3	Bridge (Bas-de-Bouis)
PK 36.6	Lock 7 (Bourg-le-Comte)
PK 36.5	Bridge (Bourg-le-Comte)
PK 36.0	Bridge (Gallay)
PK 35.7	**Bourg-le-Comte** quay, *halte*, and Urbise aqueduct, village 300m l/b
PK 35.5	Bridge (Meillerands)
PK 34.9	Bridge (Biscot)
PK 34.5	Bridge (Diens)
PK 33.3	Bridge (Croix-Valentin)
PK 33.0	**Chambilly**, basin r/b, water and electricity paid in units by credit card, **Marcigny** 2.5 km

Good moorings in the basin, 100m long quay with bollards. Chambilly has limited possibilities, but the nearby market town of Marcigny has all services. Market day is Monday.

PK 32.8	Lock 6 (Chambilly), bridge
PK 32.3	Lock 5 (Montgrailloux), bridge
PK 31.8	Lock 4 (Artaix)
PK 30.8	Bridge (Narbot)
PK 30.3	Bridge (Augers)
PK 29.8	Bridge (Artaix 2) and basin d/s l/b, *halte* and camp site, water (€2 per 20 minutes), electricity (€2 per 4 hours), slipway

Delightful rural moorings in the basin or along the bank just outside it, as may be preferred by deeper-draught vessels, as the basin is liable to silt up.

PK 29.6	Arçon aqueduct
PK 29.1	Bridge (Artaix 1)
PK 29.0	**Artaix**, quay l/b
PK 28.2	Bridge (Fanges)
PK 27.4	Bridge (Arcelles)
PK 26.3	Brennons aqueduct
PK 26.1	Bridge (Melay)
PK 26.0	**Melay-sur-Loire**, *halte* l/b, 03 85 84 04 84, water and electricity paid in units by credit card (in season only), shower, village 1.5 km, turning basin
PK 25.5	Bridge (Corrètes)
PK 24.8	Bridge (Bagnots)

Peaceful mooring on the canal beside at Artaix, PK 30 © BERNARD THIRY

Canal de Roanne à Digoin

PK **23.9**	Bridge (Gallands)	
PK **23.3**	Bridge (Putenat)	
PK **22.8**	Bridge (Brivet)	
PK **21.2**	**Iguerande**, quay l/b, water, electricity, village 1.5 km on r/b of Loire	
PK **21.1**	Bridge (Duplan)	
PK **20.2**	Bridge (Valendru)	
PK **19.6**	Bridge (Ray)	
PK **18.6**	Bridge (Teyssonne)	
PK **18.5**	Teyssonne aqueduct	
PK **16.0**	Bridge (Boutasson)	
PK **15.0**	Bridge (Briennon), D4, **Pouilly-sous-Charlieu** 2 km and **Charlieu** 7000m	
PK **14.7**	**Briennon** *port de plaisance*, Les Marins d'Eau Douce, 04 77 69 92 92, 20 berths, €7, diesel, water €3, electricity €4, showers €3, crane on request, slipway, restaurant barges, village l/b, *lesmarinsdeaudouce.fr*	

The most appealing mooring place on the canal, in a large basin beside the *Parc des Canaux*, where finding a place may be a challenge in high season. There is always the possibility of mooring to the bank beyond the serviced moorings, to visit the village, the restaurant barge and take on provisions.

PK **13.6**	Lock 3 (Briennon), bridge
PK **12.9**	Bridge (Rate)
PK **12.3**	Bridge (Maltaverne)
PK **11.2**	Bridge (Justices)
PK **10.3**	Bridge (Mathérat)
PK **9.2**	Lock 2 (Cornillon), bridge (château, l/b, 500m)
PK **8.6**	Bridge (Escroqué)
PK **7.3**	Bridge (Mably)
PK **6.1**	Bridges (Bonvert) and footbridge
PK **5.6**	Private quay serving Roanne arsenal, l/b
PK **5.3**	Pipeline crossing
PK **5.2**	Bridge (Aiguilly), D482
PK **4.6**	Bridge (Vadon)
PK **3.6**	Footbridge (Matel)
PK **3.1**	Bridge (Gardet)
PK **2.3**	Oudan aqueduct
PK **2.2**	**Oudan** basin, l/b, 800m long but silted up
PK **1.9**	Bridge (Côtes)
PK **1.8**	Bridge (N7, Roanne bypass)
PK **0.9**	Lock 1 (Roanne), bridges
PK **0.0**	**Roanne** *port de plaisance* in basin 850m long connected to the Loire (navigable for 1km, but not in use), *Capitainerie* Quai du Commandant de Fourcauld, 04 77 72 59 96, email *port.roanne@suez.com*, 130 berths, night €8.60, water (per person on board), electricity per amperage, wifi, shower, slipway, crane on request, good winter moorings, trip boats

Wintering is possible but has to be booked in advance. Montchanin Marine may be called for repairs 06 86 02 69 43. Diesel may be supplied by truck from several companies. The harbour captain will give details. Roanne has the unfortunate reputation of being a town of reserved and not particularly friendly people, but it obviously grows on you, because the port is one of the most popular on the system. The surrounding countryside is gorgeous, and includes the Côteaux Roannais vineyards. Good train service to Lyon, or coaches to the TGV station at Le Creusot-Montchanin-Montceau-les-Mines.

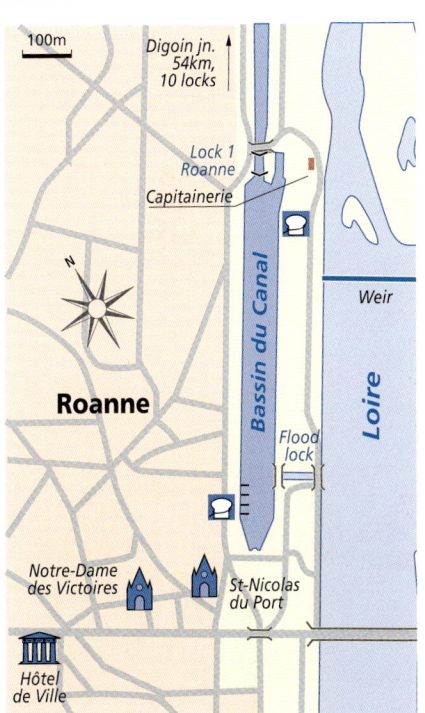

The last lock in Roanne opens into the enormous basin which has become a popular destination and wintering place for long-distance boaters. © PIERRE GLEIZES

189

III – Central France and routes to the Saône

35. Canal d'Orléans

The Canal d'Orléans was the third watershed canal to be built in France, after the Canal de Briare and the Canal du Midi. It was completed in 1692, to provide a link between the Loire valley near Orléans and the river Loing (hence the Seine) at Montargis. As originally built, it was 73 km long with 30 locks, joining the Loire at Combleux, short of Orléans. An extension to Orléans added 5.5 km to the length, hence the total distance of 78.5 km. Two sections of the canal have been restored, but are not yet open to navigation since they remain to be dredged. From the junction with the main system at Buges, three locks were restored in the 1990s up to the village of Le Mée, a distance of 14 km, while west of the summit level, locks were restored from Fay-aux-Loges to Combleux. The latter section has now been extended to the terminal basin in Orléans, making a total of 19 km with 4 locks. The eastern section is also now being extended to reach Grignon lower lock and its reservoir, 26 km and 14 locks from Buges. These sections are opened for unpowered craft only. The western restored section is also used by a passenger boat. The 'missing link' of 33 km with 10 locks remains to be restored, but the works were stopped in 2016 and the Loiret *département* wound up the Syndicat Mixte that was managing the project.

After the Canal de Briare was opened in 1642, traffic was limited by the poor conditions of navigation on the Loire above Orléans. A canal from this lower port on the Loire to the Briare at Montargis was an 'obvious' project, all the more so since Robert Mahieu had already started building a canal over part of the route from the Orléans forest to Grignon. Surveyors for the Duc d'Orléans found a route incorporating Mahieu's canal. Royal assent was given to the prince (Louis XIV's brother) in 1679, and the works were let to Lambert & Cie in 1682. The canal was completed in 1692. Unusually for a small-capacity canal, it was extended to the centre of Orléans, along the bank of the Loire, as late as 1921, while the locks west of the summit were upgraded to Freycinet dimensions. The canal was abandoned in 1954, but is being restored by the Loiret département, which took over the canal from the State in 1985. Loiret has invested €30 million, out of an estimated total of €80 million for complete restoration.

Navigation

The narrow canal is currently open to unpowered private boats only, as well as electric or horse-drawn passenger boats, which operate in the Orléans section and at Grignon.

Canal d'Orléans

Locks
There are 28 locks, of which 17 climb from the Loing to the summit level (originally 18 including Buges lock, now part of the Canal du Loing), and 11 drop down to the Loire (originally 12). Those on the Loing side offer navigable dimensions of 30.00m by 5.00m, while those on the Loire side are of Freycinet dimensions.

Draught
The maximum available draught is 1.20m. It was planned to dredge the canal to a depth of 1.40m, but as indicated above, all investments are currently suspended.

Headroom
Bridges originally offered a headroom of 3.50m, but this is restricted to 2.70m, especially where pipes have been placed under the bridge deck.

Towpath
The towpath is being developed as a cycling and hiking trail, and should be completed by 2023.

Authority
Conseil départemental du Loiret, Direction des Bâtiments, Canaux et Environnement
 – 15 rue Eugène Vignat, 45000 Orléans   02 38 25 45 45

Nestin Lock at Fay-aux-Loges, a unique heritage site, PK 59. © SMGCO

The restored lock at Chancy (PK 15.8). © WIKIPEDIA COMMONS

Route description

PK 0.0	*Junction with the Canal du Loing and Canal de Briare* at Buges lock, towpath bridge
PK 0.7	Bridge (D40)
PK 1.3	Lock (La Folie), bridge
PK 2.6	Railway bridge
PK 3.0	Bridge (D94)
PK 3.3	Lock (Sainte-Catherine)
PK 3.6	Overhead power lines
PK 4.4	Motorway bridge (Pannes), A77
PK 4.6	Bridge
PK 6.9	Lock (Machault), bridge
PK 7.8	Bridge (D950)
PK 8.4	Main road bridge (N60)
PK 10.0	Lock (Le Mée), bridge
PK 11.2	Bridge
PK 13.8	Lock (Marchais-Clair)

This lock has not yet been restored. Upstream limit of navigability.

PK 14.2	Bridge
PK 15.8	Lock (Chancy), bridge
PK 17.3	Lock (Chailly), bridge
PK 17.9	Bridge
PK 19.8	Lock (Rougemont)
PK 20.1	Bridge
PK 21.7	Lock (Vallée), bridge
PK 22.9	Lock (lower Hateau), reservoir upstream
PK 23.2	Lock (upper Hateau)
PK 24.0	Lock (de la Chaussée), bridge
PK 24.8	Bridge
PK 25.2	Lock (Choiseau)
PK 26.3	Lock (lower Grignon), bridge, basin u/s

The basin is partly for regulation of the water level in the short pound, and partly to give manœuvring space for the right-angle turn. The passenger boat *Belle de Grignon* is moored on the quayside in this basin.

The restored lower lock at Grignon © BINNENVAART IN BEELD

PK 26.4	Lock (middle Grignon), bridge
PK 26.5	Lock (upper Grignon, Gué des Cens)
PK 27.7	Lock (Grignon summit), bridge
PK 29.0	Reservoir (Noue-Mazone), west side
PK 30.6	Bridge (Verrerie)

III – Central France and routes to the Saône

PK 31.6	**Châtenoy** quay, west bank, village 800m
PK 33.3	Bridge
PK 38.8	New road bridge (N60)
PK 39.0	Bridge (Besniers, D114)
PK 39.7	Bridge
PK 41.0	Bridge
PK 42.7	**Sury-aux-Bois** bridge, village north bank
PK 45.6	**Combreux** bridge, village south bank
PK 46.5	Lock (Combreux), bridge
PK 48.2	Lock (Moulin-Rouge)
PK 49.5	Lock (Vitry-aux-Loges)
PK 49.7	**Vitry-aux-Loges** bridge, village r/b
PK 52.3	Turning basin
PK 52.7	Lock (Chennetière), bridge
PK 55.0	Lock (Gué-Girault), bridge
PK 57.0	Lock (Jonchère), bridge
PK 58.7	Lock (Nestin), bridge
PK 59.1	Turning basin
PK 60.0	**Fay-aux-Loges** bridge (D11), small town l/b
PK 63.2	Lock (**Donnery**), bridge, village r/b
PK 64.7	Main road bridge (N60)
PK 67.5	Basin (canal widens)
PK 67.7	Railway bridge
PK 67.9	Lock (Pont-aux-Moines), bridge, **Mardié** 800m l/b
PK 69.9	**Chécy** bridge, village r/b
PK 70.4	Footbridge
PK 71.8	Turning basin
PK 72.0	Swing bridge
PK 73.0	Footbridge
PK 73.1	Junction with lock (Combleux) to Loire, l/b
PK 73.2	Swing bridge (Combleux)

The canal lined by plane-trees, reminiscent of the Canal du Midi, at Chécy, PK 70 © CROQUANT

PK 73.4   Lock (Combleux), bridge

From this lock through to the end of the canal is an extraordinary sequence of structures and glorious river landscapes, the canal being perched on the bank of the mighty river Loire. Boats are seriously needed to complete the picture, and the canal owners and managers need all the encouragement they can get, to make the complete restoration a reality. The canal gets good exposure every two years at the River Loire Festival in September.

PK 75.0	**Saint-Jean-de-Braye** bridge
PK 76.7	Bridge, canal museum
PK 77.5	Bridge
PK 77.9	**Orléans** canal basin, town centre 1200m
PK 78.2	Railway bridge (Pont de Vierzon)
PK 78.3	Bridge (René Thinant), basin d/s, *port de plaisance*, tourist office and services
PK 78.5	Entrance lock from the Loire

The terminal length of the canal in Orléans was restored after severe floods had damaged this embankment wall. The wall was restored by the Loiret département with a €2.8 million subsidy from the State, financed as flood protection works. This enabled rewatering of the 5 km long pound in 2006. © LAURENT PITOT

36. River Cher and Canal du Berry

THE RIVER CHER WAS MADE NAVIGABLE in the 19th century over a distance of 130 km from the confluence with the Loire west of Tours to the market town of Vierzon. After restoration work carried out in the 1980s it formed an attractive cruising waterway, extending from Larçay (26 km above the confluence) to Selles-sur-Cher, a distance of 66 km including the first 12 km of the historic Canal du Berry.

Restoration and maintenance of the river navigation suffered a serious setback in the 2003-2005, when the *département* of Loir-et-Cher stopped all works on two new gated weirs, designed to replace the earlier needle weirs. These were dangerous and had deteriorated beyond repair. One new weir had been built then, at Saint-Aignan, and the lock here is in operation. However, with the weirs removed between Saint-Aignan and Montrichard, all development of navigation on the river ceased, the small hire fleet of narrow boats was moved and the passenger boat at Montrichard was sold by its operator and replaced by a shallow-draught vessel.

The Cher was canalised starting from 1830 from the Loire confluence to Vierzon, a distance of 130 km. The Canal du Berry was a 'narrow' canal, inspired by the economic model of the English canals, and opened in 1841. Starting in 1985, three 'Syndicats Mixtes', bodies set up by the local councils, actively restored the Cher navigation and the lower part of the canal, with the aim of eventually restoring navigation throughout the 130 km from Tours to Vierzon, but the project is facing opposition from State bodies defending the interests of migrating fish species. Sensible compromises have still to be made to complete the transfer of ownership from State to Region, and preserve the heritage value of this unique waterway.

Key dimensions (m)	
Length	35.00
[Canal du Berry	28.65]
Beam	5.20
[Canal du Berry	2.70]
Draught	0.80
Air draught	3.90
[Canal du Berry	2.60]

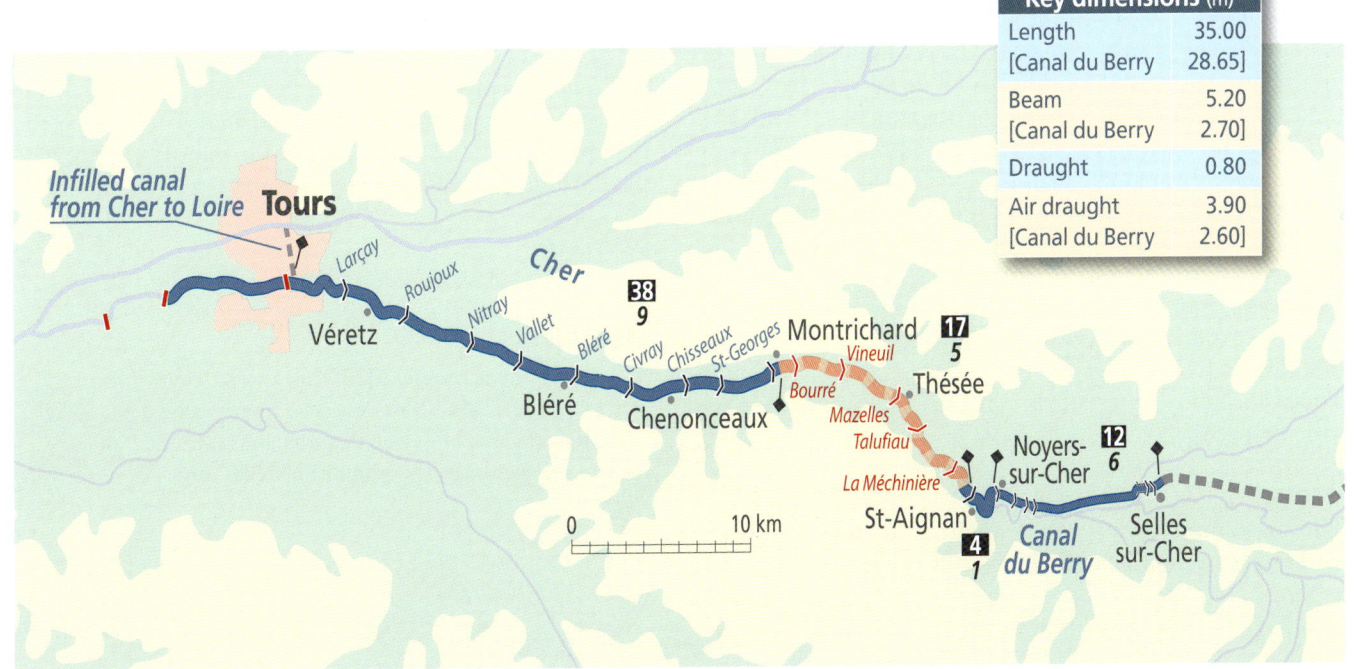

III – Central France and routes to the Saône

The State bodies which issue authorisations for works on rivers are insisting that weir gates, old or new, should not be raised until the end of the fish spawning season on 1st July each year, which naturally calls into question the feasibility of the weir rebuilding programme. The current situation is an unsatisfactory stalemate, while all parties involved are maintaining their positions. One prospect currently being discussed is handing over management to the public agency for the river Loire, which would run the waterway on behalf of the region.

The situation is as shown on the map. The Canal du Berry is navigable over the last 12km from Selles-sur-Cher to Noyers-sur-Cher, while the canalised river Cher is navigable from Noyers to just beyond Saint-Aignan lock, then again from Montrichard to Tours (PK 59.5).

The main obstacles are the two weirs to be completely rebuilt, and the following three to be restored without modernisation. A further obstacle is siltation in the lake created in the flood plain of the river immediately downstream of the last lock of the Canal du Berry.

A boat passes under the famous five-arched bridge of the château de Chenonceau. The owners were objectors to the restoration project; now it is non-existent migrating fish that are threatening the navigation. © MATTHIAS HARTUNG

Navigation

The river Cher flows gently through a broad valley bordered by low hills, making a most attractive landscape, with many sites of cultural and historic interest, including the spectacular château across the river at Chenonceaux. The principal difficulty is the lack of protection on the approach to the locks, which means that boats are exposed to the currents above and below the adjacent weir. The Canal de Berry is a narrow canal similar to the English canals, unsuitable for craft with powerful engines, because speed has to be kept very low to avoid damaging the banks. As indicated, for the time being there is no through navigability pending authorisation to rebuild the three weirs that are no longer operational, and dredging to restore the channel through to the canal at Noyers.

Locks

There are 14 locks on the reopened length of the river Cher, offering navigable dimensions of 35m by 5.20m (the fifteenth lock at Larçay remains to be restored), and 6 locks on the navigable section of the Canal de Berry. The first of these, at Noyers, is 35.30m long and 5.20m wide, while the others are for narrower boats only (28.65m long and 2.70m wide). Once through the manned entrance lock to the canal at Noyers, the locks are worked by boat crews using paddle gear installed on the gates, and a windlass supplied by the waterway staff. The 8 locks on the Cher in Loir-et-Cher are automatic, and remote-controlled with an electronic key available from the waterway authority. The charge for the key ranges from €6.20 for one day to €39 for a month. The 6 locks in Indre-et-Loire are manually operated by lock-keepers.

Draught

The maximum authorised draught is at present 0.80m (although the depth over the lock sills is between 1.20 and 1.30m).

This recent view of the château de Chenonceau shows a water level significantly drawn down by removal of the gates on the weir located 2 km downstream at Civray. The château administrators would like to see navigation permanently removed from the river. © ERIC DESPRENTES

Bridges

The lowest bridge on the Cher, at Saint-Aignan, offers a headroom of 3.90m above the normal water level; the other bridges offer a minimum headroom of 4.50m. The least air draught available on the canal is 2.60m.

Towpath

None on the Cher. Rough path on the Canal du Berry.

Authority

Syndicat du Cher canalisé, Mairie, 37270 Larçay
02 47 45 56 74, (PK 28-60, but also manages by default the length in the neighbouring département of Loir-et-Cher, where the Syndicat has been disbanded)

River Cher and Canal du Berry

Route description

Canal du Berry

PK 0.0	**Selles-sur-Cher** bridge (blocks navigation), turning basin and moorings d/s, village 1 km on l/b of Cher

Village with all services.

PK 0.4	Bridge (La Thizardière)
PK 0.7	Lock (La Thizardière), bridge
PK 1.5	Lock (Val de Sauldre), bridge
PK 2.4	Sauldre aqueduct

Fine aqueduct with five arches of 7m span.

PK 3.6	Pipeline crossing
PK 4.6	**Châtillon-sur-Cher** lift bridge, small village r/b
PK 4.9	Lift bridge (Trévety)
PK 7.0	Lift bridge (La Rue)
PK 8.5	Les Martinières lift bridge, small village r/b
PK 8.9	Lock (Les Roches), bridge
PK 10.2	Lock (Trompe-Souris), bridge
PK 10.4	Bridge (Noyers by-pass)
PK 10.7	Lock (La Hémonnière), bridge
PK 11.7	**Noyers-sur-Cher** lift bridge at u/s end of canal basin, village r/b
PK 12.1	Lock (Noyers), bridge, *junction with river Cher*

River Cher

PK 0.0	*Junction with Canal du Berry*, limit of navigation on the Cher
PK 0.2	Bridge (Noyers by-pass)
PK 0.3	Footbridge, narrow passage
PK 1.9	New weir r/b, beware of cross-current
PK 2.5	Lock (**Saint-Aignan**), bridge, small town l/b
PK 2.5	Current limit of navigation, insufficient depths in downstream reach following demolition of the following weir
PK 6.0	Lock (La Méchinière), bridge
PK 8.2	Motorway bridge (A85)
PK 9.3	Lock (Talufiau)
PK 11.1	Bridge (D976)
PK 11.6	Thésée bridge, moorings on quay d/s r/b
PK 12.9	Lock (Mazelles), gîte in lock cottage
PK 16.7	Lock (Vineuil)
PK 17.1	Bridge
PK 19.2	Lock (Bourré)
PK 21.3	**Montrichard** bridge
PK 22.1	Lock (Montrichard)
PK 23.9	Overhead power line
PK 25.6	Bridge
PK 25.8	Lock (Saint Georges)
PK 27.6	Limit of Indre-et-Loire département, r/b
PK 28.6	Limit of Indre-et-Loire département, l/b
PK 28.9	Lock (Chisseaux)
PK 29.5	Bridge
PK 30.5	**Chenonceau** château bridging the river
PK 32.6	Lock (Civray)
PK 33.0	Bridge (La Canardière), camp site r/b
PK 36.4	Lock (Bléré) r/b, weir
PK 36.7	**Bléré** bridge, small town l/b
PK 38.2	Bridge (D31 Bléré by-pass)
PK 40.3	Lock (Vallet) r/b, weir, (disused mill on l/b channel)
PK 43.3	Bridge, **Saint-Martin-le-Beau** 1800m r/b
PK 44.3	Lock (Nitray) l/b, weir, mill r/b
PK 47.8	**Azay-sur-Cher** bridge, village l/b
PK 49.4	Lock (Roujoux) r/b, weir
PK 51.6	**Véretz** bridge, village l/b
PK 52.6	Overhead power lines
PK 53.2	Railway bridge (TGV Atlantique)
PK 54.4	Lock (Larçay) r/b, weir
PK 55.3	Overhead power lines
PK 59.3	Bridge (Arcole)
PK 59.3	Motorway bridge (A10), former junction with link canal to Loire
PK 59.5	Tip of island (Honoré de Balzac park), footbridge
PK 59.6	Weir on right bank arm (lock projected long term)
PK 61.1	Bridge (Bordeaux), through route railway
PK 61.7	Bridge (Sanitas), D910 trunk road
PK 62.7	Footbridge (Passerelle du Cher)
PK 63.1	Tours bridge (Pont Saint-Sauveur), town centre 2 km r/b
PK 64.1	Bridge (D37, Tours bypass)
PK 68.8	U/s tip of island, mill stream l/b
PK 69.0	Mill (Le Grand Moulin), no through navigation
PK 75.1	Mill (Savonnières), no through navigation
PK 75.3	Bridge (Savonnières)
PK 80.6	*Confluence with river Loire* (Bec de Cher)

Civray lock and weir are the first below Chenonceaux on the canalised river Cher. The whole navigation is threatened by the change in status of the river, which would favour the migrating fish species at the expense of navigation. State bodies and anglers want the modern weirs to be raised on 1st July each year, but fish counts have revealed that no shad enter the river from the Loire. The local Association des Amis du Cher Canalisé is campaigning for the migrators to be accommodated by controlled sluicing through the locks. Their research has revealed that migrators used the locks in the days of commercial navigation. © THOMAS IGLER

Index

Waterway names in bold (excepting historic names and disused waterways)
Topics (historic or current, including personalities) in italics

Aa, river 29, 32, 39, 40-42
Abbécourt 110, 112
Abbeville 82
Ablancourt 137
Accolay 165
Aigny 136
Ailly-sur-Somme 82
d'Aire à La Bassée, Canal 30, 33-4, 36
Aire-sur-la-Lys 33, 43, 44
Aisne, river 64, 85, 113-14
l'Aisne, Canal latéral à 113-14, 115
l'Aisne, Canal de l'Oise à 111-12
l'Aisne à la Marne, Canal de 116-19
Aisy-sur-Armançon 153
Alfortville 124, 129
Allaines 60, 62, 63, 66, 67
Alluy 164
Amiens 82
Ancy-le-Franc 153
Ancy-le-Libre 153
Les Andelys 90
Andrésy 93
Anizy-le-Château 112
Annet-sur-Marne 130
Appilly 110
Appoigny 149
Ardennes, Canal des 4
Ardres branch (Canal de Calais) 39
Argentenay 153
Argenteuil 94
Argenvières 178
Arleux 59
Armentières 43, 45
Arques 32
Arras 55
l'Arsenal, Port de (Paris) 85, 101
Artaix 188
Asnières 95
Asnois 162
Assevent 78
Athies 55
Les Attaques 39
Attichy 114
Aubencheul-au-Bac 7, 62
Aubervilliers 101
Auby 34
Audruicq branch (Canal de Calais) 39
Aulne 6
authorities 23
  see also start of each waterway
Autigny-le-Grand 141
automated locks 16
Auxerre 146, 149, 156, 160

Aveyron 5
Avon 126
Avril-sur-Loire 179
Avrilly 188
Aÿ 135
Azay-sur-Cher 195
Azy-sur-Marne 132
Babœuf 110
Bac-Saint-Maur 45
Bagneaux-sur-Loing 168
Bailly 160
Bannay 177
The Barge Association (DBA) 4, 10, 21
La Bassée old canal 30, 33
Bassou 149
Bauvin 46, 47
Bayard-sur-Marne 141
Baye 164
Bazarnes 160
Bazolles 164
Beaulieu 177
Beaulon 179
Beaumont-sur-Oise 108
Beaumont-sur-Vesle 118
Beaurains-lès-Noyons 61
Beautor 71
Beffes 178
Bellenglise 70
Belleville-sur-Loire 177
Belley 7
Bennecourt 91
Bergues, Canal de 26, 28
Berlaimont 78
Berneuil-sur-Aisne 114
Berry, Canal du 121, 193-5
Berry-au-Bac 115, 117
Béthencourt-sur-Somme 61, 83
Béthune 33
Beurizot 155
Beuvry, Canal de 30, 36
Bezons 94
Biache-Saint-Vaast 56
Biaches 66
Biches 164
Bienville 141
Bierne 28
Bisseuil 136
Blagny-sur-Vingeanne 145
Blanzy 185
Blaringhem 33
Blavet 6
Bléré 195
blue flag rule 14
Blue Links project 5
boat hire 10, 11, 12-13
boat licences (péage plaisance) 10-11
boat transport 11
Boismont 82
Boissettes 125
Boissise-la-Bertrand 125
bollards at locks 16
Bonnand 188
Bonnard 149
Bonneuil 134

Bonneuil Arm (Marne) 134
Bonnières-sur-Seine 91
books 19-21
Boran-sur-Oise 108
Bouchain 74
Bougival 94
La Bouille 88
Bourbonnais 19
Bourbourg, Canal de 27, 29, 30, 32
Bourdon 82
Bourg-et-Comin 112, 115
Bourg-le-Comte 188
Bourgogne, Canal de 19, 150-57
Bourgogne, Canal entre Champagne et 19, 138-45
Bousbecque 45
Boussières-sur-Sambre 78
Boussois 78
Braux 155
Bray-sur-Seine 8, 127
Braye-en-Laonnais 112
Brazey-en-Plaine 157
Brébières 56
Brégnier-Cordon 7
Brest, Canal de Nantes à 6, 17
Brethenay 142
Breuil 61
Brèves 162
Briare 172-3, 176
Briare, Canal de 169-73, 190
bridge signs 15
Brienne 164
Briennon 189
Brienon-sur-Armançon 151
Brittany Canals 6
Bry-sur-Marne 130
Buffon 153
Buges 170
Bussière-sur-Ouche 156
Bussy 141
Butteaux 151
Buverchy 61
Buxières-lès-Froncles 142

Calais 19, 37-9
Calais, Canal de 37-9
Cambrai 19, 72, 73
Camon 83
Campagne 61
Canizy 83
Cannes-Écluses 147
Canteleu branch (Canal de la Deûle) 49
Cappy 83
Carrières-sous-Poissy 92
Catigny 61
Catillon-sur-Sambre 79
Caudebec-en-Caux 87, 88
Centre, Canal du 16, 182-6
Cepoy 168
Cercy-la-Tour 164
Cergy-Pontoise 108
Cerisy-Chipilly 83
certificates of competence 9-10

CEVNI rules 9, 10
Chagny 186
Chalifert, Canal de 129, 130-31
Challuy 179
Chalon-sur-Saône 182, 186
Châlons-en-Champagne 136-7
Chamarandes 143
Chambilly 188
Chamouilley 141
Champagne 85
Champagne et Bourgogne, Canal entre 19, 138-45
Champagne-sur-Seine 126
Champigney 144
Champs 112
Champs-sur-Yonne 160
Champvert 164
Chanaz 7
La Chapelle (Canal de Bourgogne) 152
La Chapelle-Montlinard 178
Charente 17
Charenton 124, 129
La Charité-sur-Loire 178
Charlieu 189
Charly 132
Chartrettes 125
Chassenard 188
Chassey 154
Chassignelles 153
Château-Thierry 132
Châteauneuf 156
Châtel-Censoir 161
Châtenoy 192
Châtillon Branch (Canal latéral à la Loire) 174, 180
Châtillon-en-Bazois 164
Châtillon-sur-Cher 195
Châtillon-Coligny 171
Châtillon-sur-Loire 176-7
Châtou (Rivière-Neuve) Arm (Paris) 94-5
Chaumont 19, 143
Chaumot 162
Chauny 71, 110
La Chaussée-sur-Marne 137
La Chaussée-Tirancourt 82
Chautagne 7
Chavignon 112
Chécy 192
Cheilly-lès-Maranges 185
Chelles 130
Chelles, Canal de 128
Chenonceaux 195
Chépy 137
Cher 6, 121, 193-5
Cheuge 145
Chevenon 179
Chevillon 141
Chevregny 112
Chevroches 162
Chiry 110
Chitry-les-Mines 162
Choisy-au-Bac 114
Choisy-le-Roi 124

197

Index

Ciry-le-Noble 184
Cité, Bras de la (Paris) 96
Clairoix 109
Clamecy 162
Claye-Souilly 104
Cléry-sur-Somme 67
Clignon, Canal du 105
Colmar 5
Colme Diversion Canal 30, 32
COLREGS 10
Combreux 192
Comines 45
La Commanderie 105
Commissey 152
Compiègne 7, 8, 62, 109
Concevreux 115
Condé, Canal de Pommerœul à 72, 74, 75
Condé-sur-Aisne, 114
Condé-sur-Marne 19, 118-19, 136
Condé-Sainte-Libiaire 131
Condé-sur-Suippe 115
Conflans-sur-Loing 171
Conflans-Saint-Honorine 85, 87, 93, 107
Congis-sur-Thérouanne 105
La Copine 164
Coppenaxfort 29
Corbehem 56
Corbeil-Essonnes 125
Corbie 83
Corbigny 162, 163
Cornillon, Canal de 128
Coucy-le-Château 112
Coulanges (Loire) 179
Coulanges-sur-Yonne 161
Coulogne 39
Coupvray 131
Courcelles (Canal de Bourgogne) 34, 154
Courcelles-sur-Seine 90
Courlon-sur-Yonne 148
Courmelois 118
Courrières 34, 36
Cours-les-Barres 178
Courtrai 45
COVID-19 3-4
Crancey 127
Cravant 160
Crégy-les-Meaux 104
Creil 109
Créteil 134
Crèvecœur-sur-l'Escaut 69
Croix Branch (Canal de Roubaix) 53
Crouy-sur-Ourcq 105
Crugey 156
cruise planning 1, 9-21, 23
Cruising Association 21
Cry 153
Cuffy 178
Cumières 133
Curel 141
Cusey 144

Damery 133
Dammarie-sur-Loing 171
Dampierre-et-Flée 145
Dannemoine 152

DBA (The Barge Association) 4, 10, 21
Decize 164, 165, 179, 181
Decize Branch (Canal latéral à la Loire) 165, 174, 181
Denain 74
Dennevy 185
depths 13
see also start of each waterway
Deûle, Canal de la 34, 43, 46-9
Deûlémont 49
Digoin 180, 182, 183, 187, 188
Digoin, Canal de Roanne à 187-9
Dijon 157
dimensions, navigable 13
see also start of each waterway
Diou 179
Dirol 162
DIY locks 17
Dizy 135
documentation 9-11
Dommarien 144
Dompierre Branch (Canal latéral à la Loire) 174, 181
Dompierre-sur-Besbre 181
Don 47
Donjeux 142
Donnery 192
Dordives 168
Dormans 133
Douai 6, 34-5
Douai bypass (Scarpe diversion canal) 34-5, 56
Dourges 34
draught 13
see also start of each waterway
Draveil 125
Dreuil 82
Duclair 88
Dunkirk (Dunkerque) 26-9, *see also Liaison Dunkerque-Escaut*

Éclusier-Vaux 83
Éditions du Breil 19, 20
Elbeuf 89
Épenancourt 83
Épernay 134
Épernay Arm (Marne) 134
Épinay 94
Épisy 167
Éragny 108
Ercheu 61
Esbly 131
Escaut 6, 35, 72-4, 75 *see also Liaison Dunkerque-Escaut*
Escommes 155
Esnon 151
Estaires 45
Estrun 73
Eswars 73
Éterpigny 66
Étigny 148
Étreux 79
Étricourt-Manacourt 60
EU 5, 6, 7-8, 9, 10
European Boating Association 10

Eurville 141
Évin-Malmaison 34
Évry 125
Fampoux 55
Fargniers 71
Fay-aux-Loges 192
La Fère 71, 79
La Fère branch (Canal de Saint-Quentin) 71
La Ferté-sous-Jouarre 132
La Ferté-Milon 105
Fesmy 79
Feuillères 83
flags 9, 14
Fleurey-sur-Ouche 156
Fleury-sur-Loire 179
Flez-Cuzy 162
Flogny 152
Fluviacarte 20-21
Fontaine 186
Fontenoy 114
formalities 9-11
Fort-Bâtard 39
Foulain 143
Fragnes 186
Frelinghien 45
Fresnes-sur-Marne 104
Fressies 35
La Frette-sur-Seine 93
Freycinet (standard) waterways 13, 16-17
Frignicourt 140
Frise 83
Froissy 83
Froncles 142
Fulvy 153
Fumel 4
Furnes, Canal de 26, 28

Gannay-sur-Loire 179
Gard 79
Gargenville 92
Garnat-sur-Engièvre 179
Garonne, Canal de 16
Génelard 184
La Genevraye 167
Gennevilliers 94, 95
Germancy 179
Germigny 151
Germigny-l'Évêque 131
Gernicourt 115
Ghyvelde 28
Gimouille 178
Gissey-sur-Ouche 156
Givet 4
Givry 180
Givry-Fourchambault Branch (Canal latéral à la Loire) 174, 178
Goncourt 140
La Gorgue 45
Gournay-sur-Marne 130
grand gabarit (high-capacity) waterways 13, 14, 16-17
Grande-Synthe 29
Les-Granges-sous-Grignon 154
Gravelines 40-42
Grenelle, Bras de (Paris) 96
Gressy 104
Guarbecque 33
Gudmont 142

Guerlédon 6
Guernes 91
Le Guétin 178
guides (publications) 19-21
Guignicourt 115
Guînes branch (Canal de Calais) 39
Guny 112
Gurgy 149

Halligincourt 141
Halluin 43, 45
Ham 7, 83
Hangest 82
Hannapes 79
Harfleur 98
Harnes 36
Hasnon 57
Haubordin 48
Le Haucourt 70
Haute-Colme, Canal de la 32
Haute-Saône, Canal de Montbeliard à la 8
Haute-Seine, Canal de la 122, 127
Hautmont 78
Haverskerque 45
Le Havre 85, 97-8
Havre à Tancarville, Canal du 85, 87, 97-8
Havrincourt-Hermies 60, 66
Hazebrouck canals 43
headroom & heights 13
see also start of each waterway
Hem-Lenglet 35
Hennuin 39
Herblay 93
Hergnies 74
Hermies 60
Herry 178
Heuilley-sur-Saône 138, 145
Heuilley-Cotton 144
Hinges 33
hire boats 10, 11, 12-13
Honfleur 85, 86, 88
Houlle river 42
hours of navigation 18
Humes 144

Iguerande 189
Imray publications 19, 20, 21
Inchy-en-Artois 60
Inland Waterways International 4
insurance 9
Isbergues 33
L'Isle-Adam 108
Isse 118
Ivry-sur-Seine 124

Janville 65, 109-110
Jaulgonne 133
Jaulzy 114
Jaux 109
Jeanty, Canal de l'Île 28, 29
Jeumont 76, 78
Joigny 148
Joinville 142
Joinville-le-Pont 128, 129
Jonction, Canal de (Dunkirk) 26, 28

198

Index

Jonction, Canal de (Scarpe) 57
Jorquenay 144
Jouy-le-Moutier 108
Juvigny 136
Juvisy-sur-Orge 125

La Bassée old canal 30, 33
La Bouille 88
La Chapelle (Canal de Bourgogne) 152
La Chapelle-Montlinard 178
La Charité-sur-Loire 178
La Chaussée-sur-Marne 137
La Chaussée-Tirancourt 82
La Commanderie 105
La Copine 164
La Fère 71, 79
La Fère branch (Canal de Saint-Quentin) 71
La Ferté-sous-Jouarre 132
La Ferté-Milon 105
La Frette-sur-Seine 93
La Genevraye 167
La Gorgue 45
La Mailleraye-sur-Seine 88
La Neuvillette 117
La Tombe 127
La Villeneuve-sur-Vingeanne 145
Lacroix-Saint-Ouen 109
Lagny-sur-Marne 130
Lallaing 6, 57
Lamotte-Brebière 83
Landrecies 76, 77, 78, 79
Langres 19, 144
Laroche-Migennes 150
Laroche-Saint-Cydroine 148
Le Haucourt 70
Le Havre 85, 97-8
Le Pecq 93
Le Pont d'Ardres 39
Lens 36
Lens, Canal de 30, 36
Léré 177
Les Andelys 90
Les Attaques 39
Les Mureaux 92
Les Pavillons-sous-Bois 104
Les Rues-des-Vignes 69
Les-Granges-sous-Grignon 154
Lesdins 70
Leval 78
Liaison Dunkerque-Escaut 8, 13, 19, 30-36, 62
Libermont 61
licences 9-11
Licey-sur-Vingeanne 145
Licourt 66
lights 15, 16
Lille 46, 47, 48
Limay 92
L'Isle-Adam 108
Lizy-sur-Ourcq 105
locks & lock-keepers 14-18
  see also start of each waterway
Loing, Canal du 166-8, 191
Loire, river 19, 165, 174
Loire, Canal latéral à la 165, 174-81
Long 82

Longecourt-en-Plaine 157
Longueil-Annel 110
Longvic 157
Lot, river 4-5, 17
Louette Valley Reservoir 64
Lourches 74
Louvroil 78
Lucy-sur-Yonne 161
Luzancy 132
Luzy-sur-Marne 143
Lyon 7, 19
Lys, river 43-5, 47, 49

Mailly-le-Château 161
Mailly-la-Ville 161
Maisons-Alfort 129
Maisons-Lafitte 93
Maizy 115
Manancourt 66
Manicamp 110
Mantes-la-Jolie 92
maps 19-21
Marchiennes 57
Marcigny 188
Marcilly (Canal du Nivernais) 163
Marcilly-sur-Seine (Petite Seine) 126, 127
Marcoing 69
Marcq-en-Barœul 50, 52
Mardié 192
Mardyck Diversion Canal 30, 31-2
Mareuil-sur-Ay 135
Mareuil-lès-Meaux 131
Mareuil-sur-Ourcq 105
Marigny (Canal du Nivernais) 162
Marigny-le-Carouët 154
Marly Arm (Seine, Paris) 94
Marnay 127
Marnay-sur-Marne 143
Marne, river 19, 128-34
Marne, Canal de l'Aisne à la 116-19
Marne, Canal latéral à la 135-7
Marne au Rhin, Canal de la 16, 19
Marne à la Saône, Canal de la see Canal entre Champagne et Bourgogne
Marolles (Canal de l'Ourcq) 105
Marolles-sur-Seine 126
Marpent 78
Marquette-lez-Lille 46, 48, 50, 52
Marquion 60, 66
Marseilles-lès-Aubigny 178
Mary-sur-Marne 131
Masnières 69
mast manoeuvres 11, 18, 85
Maubeuge 78
Maxilly 145
Meaux 104, 131
Meaux, Canal de 128
Médan 92
Melay-sur-Loire 188
Melun 125
Ménétréol-sous-Sancerre 177
Méricourt-sur-Somme 83

Mériel 108
Merry-sur-Yonne 161
Merville 45
Méry-Auvers 108
Méry-sur-Marne 132
Meulan 92
Meurchin 34
Mézières-sur-Oise 79
Mézy-Moulin 133
Midi, Canal du 18
Migennes 148, 151
Missy-sur-Aisne 114
Misy-sur-Yonne 147
Mœuvres 60, 66
Moislains 60, 66
Monceaux-le-Comte 162
Monéteau 149
Mont-Saint-Père 133
Montargis 170-71
Montbard 154
Montbéliard à la Haute-Saône, Canal de 8
Montbouy 171
Montceau-les-Mines 19, 184
Montchanin 185
Montcourt-Fromonville 167
Montcresson 171
Montereau-Fault-Yonne 126, 146, 147
Montmacq 63, 110
Montrichard 195
mooring 11, 17, 18
Morchain 66
Moret-sur-Loing 167
Morsang-sur-Seine 125
Mortagne-du-Nord 57, 72, 74
Moselle 8
Moÿ-de-l'Aisne 79
Muids 90
Mulhouse 8
Les Mureaux 92
Mussey-sur-Marne 142

Nanterre 94
Nantes à Brest, Canal de 6, 17
Nanteuil-sur-Marne, 132
Nargis, 168
navigable dimensions, 13
  see also start of each waterway
navigation, hours of 18
navigation signs & signals 14, 15
Nemours 168
Nesle 61, 66
Neufchâtel-sur-Aisne 115
Neufchelles 105
Neuffossé, Canal de 30
Neuilly (Paris) 95
Neuilly-sur-Marne 130
Neuville-Day 4
Neuville-sur-Escaut 74
Neuville-sur-Oise 108
La Neuvillette 117
Nevers 181
Nevers Branch (Canal latéral à la Loire) 174, 179-81
Nivelle 57
Nivernais, Canal du 13, 19, 158-65

Nogent (Canal de Bourgogne), 154
Nogent-l'Artaud 132
Nogent-sur-Marne 130
Nogent-sur-Seine 8, 127
Noisiel 130
Noisy-sur-Oise 108
Nord, Canal du 13, 19, 58-61, 66, 67, *see also Seine-Nord Europe Canal*
North Sea-Mediterranean link 8
Noyelles-sous-Lens 36
Noyen-sur-Seine 127
Noyers-sur-Cher 195
Noyon 61, 66, 110
Nuits-sur-Armançon 153

Œuilly 115
Offoy 83
Oignies 34
Oise, river 8, 13, 19, 64, 85, 106-9
l'Oise, Canal latéral à 62, 85, 106-7, 110
l'Oise, Canal de la Sambre à 4, 76-9
l'Oise à l'Aisne, Canal de 111-12
Oisilly 145
Oissel 89
Oisy 79
Omey 137
Orconte 140
Origny-Sainte-Benoîte 79
Orléans 192
d'Orléans, Canal 6, 121, 190-92
Oudan 189
l'Ourcq, Canal de 13, 85, 99-100, 102-5
Ourscamps 110
Ouzouër-sur-Trézée 171
overtaking 14, 17

Paillencourt 36
Palluel 59
Panneçot 164
Paray-le-Frésil 179
Paray-le-Monial 184
Pargny 61, 83
Pargny-Filain 112
Paris 85, 86, 96, 122-3
arms & branches 94-6
Paris canals 85, 99-105
routes from 19
Les Pavillons-sous-Bois 104
Le Pecq 93
Percey (Canal de Bourgogne) 151
Percey-sous-Montormentier 145
Péronne 19, 60, 66, 83
Petite-Seine, river 86, 121, 122, 123, 126-7
Picquigny 82
Pierrefitte-sur-Loire 179
Pignicourt 115
Pimprez 65, 110
Pinon 112
Plagny 179
planning a cruise 1, 9-21, 23

Index

Plombières-lès-Dijon 156
Pogny 137
Poincy 105, 131
Poissy 92
Pommerœul à Condé, Canal de 72, 75
Pommiers 114
Le Pont d'Ardres 39
Pont d'Ouche 156
Pont de la Tournelle 96, 122, 123, 124
Pont-Arcy 115
Pont-l'Eveque 61, 110
Pont-Remy 82
Pont-Royal 155
Pont-Saint-Mard 112
Pont-Saint-Maxence 109
Pont-sur-Seine 127
Pont-à-Vendin 34
Pont-sur-Yonne 146, 148
Pontoise 108
Port de l'Arsenal (Paris) 85, 101
Port-à-Binson 133
Port-Cergy 108
Port-aux-Perches 85, 105
Poses 87, 90
Pouillenay 154
Pouilly-en-Auxois 155
Pouilly-sur-Charlieu 189
Pouilly-sur-Vingeanne 145
Pousseaux 161
Précy-sur-Oise 109
Prégilbert 160
priority rules & etiquette 13-14
publications 19-21
Puy-l'Evêque 5

Quesnoy-sur-Deûle 49
Quierzy 110
Quillebœuf-sur-Seine 88

Raches 57
radio telephone ship licence 9
Ravières 153
Recquignies 78
Récy 136
registration documents 9
Reims 19, 117-18
Remigny 185
Rethondes 114
Reuil 133
Rhine 5-6, 16, 19, 85, 106
Rhine-Rhône waterway 7, 8
Rhône au Rhin, Canal du (northern branch) 5-6
Rhône à Sète, Canal du 8
Ribécourt 65, 110
Ribemont 79
Rieux 109
Ris-Orangis 125
Risle 86, 87
Rivière-Neuve (Châtou) Arm (Paris) 94-5
Roanne 187, 189
Roanne à Digoin, Canal de 187-9
Robecq 33
Rœux 56
Rogny-les-Sept-Écluses 171
Rolampont 143

Rolleboise 91
Roubaix 52
Roubaix, Canal de 5, 50-53
Rouen 85, 86-7, 88-9
routes (through routes) 19
Rouvroy 142
Rouy-le-Petit 61
Royal Yachting Association 9, 10, 11
Rueil-Malmaison 94
Les Rues-des-Vignes 69
rules & regulations 9-11
rules of the road 13-14, 17
Rully 186
Ruminghem 39
Ruyaulcourt 66

Saâcy-sur-Marne 132
Sailly-Laurette 83
Sailly-sur-la-Lys 45
Sailly-le-Sec 83
Sains-lès-Marquion 60
Saint-Aignan 195
Saint-Amand-les-Eaux 6, 57
Saint-Aubin-lès-Elbeuf 89
Saint-Aubin-sur-Yonne 148
Saint-Aybert 75
Saint-Bouize 177
Saint-Christ-Briost 61, 63, 66, 83
Saint-Denis (Seine) 101
Saint-Denis (Yonne) 148
Saint-Denis, Canal 94-5, 99, 101-2
Saint-Dizier 141
Saint-Fargeau-Ponthierry 125
Saint-Florentin 151
Saint-Floris 45
Saint-Folquin 42
Saint-Germain-la-Ville 137
Saint-Gilles 185
Saint-Jean-de-Braye 192
Saint-Jean-les-Deux-Jumeaux 131
Saint-Jean-de-Losne 150, 157
Saint-Julien-sur-Dheune 185
Saint-Laurent-Blangy 55
Saint-Léger-sur-Dheune 185
Saint-Léger le Petit 178
Saint-Léger-des-Vignes 164
Saint-Léonard 118
Saint-Leu-d'Esserent 109
Saint-Louis, Bras de (Paris) 96
Saint-Mammès 126, 167
Saint-Martin (Marne) 136
Saint-Martin, Canal 85, 99, 100-101
Saint-Martin-le-Beau 195
Saint-Martin-la-Garenne 91
Saint-Maur, Canal 128, 129
Saint-Maurice 145
Saint-Momelin 32, 42
Saint-Omer 42
Saint-Omer, Canal de dérivation de 30, 32-3
Saint-Pierre-du-Vauvray 90
Saint-Quentin 70
Saint-Quentin, Canal de 19, 68-71
Saint-Rémy 154
Saint-Satur 177, 180

Saint-Seine 145
Saint-Simon 71, 83
Saint-Thibault 155, 180
Saint-Thibault Branch (Canal latéral à la Loire) 174, 180
Saint-Usage 157
Saint-Valery-sur-Somme 80-82
Saint-Venant 45
Saint-Victor-sur-Ouche 156
Saint-Vinnemer 153
Sainte-Marie 156
Sainte-Pallaye 160
Saintry-sur-Seine 125
Sambre 76-8
Sambre à l'Oise, Canal de la 4, 76-8, 79
Samois-sur-Seine 125
Sancerre 177
Santenay 185
Saône, river 8, 16, 19, 138, 139, 145
Sapignicourt 140
Sardy-les-Épiry 163
Sarry 137
Sartrouville 93
Savières, Canal de 7
Scarpe, river 6, 34-5, 54-7, 72
Scarpe diversion canal (Douai bypass) 34-5, 56
Scarpe inférieure 6
Scheldt, river 43, 106, 122
seasons, 18
Sedan 4
Seille, river 17
Seine
 – Lower (Seine aval) 86-96
 – Upper (Seine amont/Haute Seine) 8, 96, 121, 122-7
see also Petite-Seine
Seine-Nord Europe Canal 7-8, 19, 62-7, 85, 106
Seine-Port 125
Seine-Scheldt Waterway 43, 72
Selles-sur-Cher 195
Sempigny 110
Sens 148
Sensée, Canal de la 30, 35, 36
Sept-Saulx 118
Seraucourt-le-Grand 70
Serbonnes 148
Sermaize 61
Sermoise-sur-Loire 178
Sery 160
Sète 6, 8
Sevran 104
ship's radio licence 9
signs & signals 14, 15
Sillery 118
Small Ships Register 9
Soissons 114
Somerville, Robert 17-18
Somme, Canal de la 7, 63-4, 80-83
Somme Branch (Seine-Nord Europe Canal) 66, 67
Sommette-Eaucourt 83
Soulanges 137
sound signals 14, 15
Souppes-sur-Loing 168

speed limits 14, 17
Spycker 29
Strasbourg 5, 19
Suresnes 95
Surgy 161
Sury-aux-Bois 192
Sury-près-Léré 177

Tancarville, Canal du Havre à 85, 87, 97-8
Tanlay 153
Tannay 162
taxes 9
Thiant 74
Thiennes 44
Thomery 126
Thonnance-lès-Joinville 142
Thorey 157
Thourotte 65, 110
time of day 18
time of year 18
tipping 17
La Tombe 127
Tonnerre 152
Tosny 90
Tourcoing Branch (Canal de Roubaix) 53
Tournedos-sur-Seine 90
Tours-sur-Marne 136
towpaths
 see start of each waterway
trailer-sailing 11
Travecy 79
Triel-sur-Seine 92
Trilbardou 104
Trilport 131
Trith-Saint-Léger 74
Tronchoy 152
Tupigny 79
turning 14, 17

Ussy-sur-Marne 132

Vadencourt 79
Vailly-sur-Aisne 114, 115
Vaires 130
Valenciennes 74
Vandenesse (Canal du Nivernais) 164
Vandenesse-en-Auxois 156
Varesnes 110
Variscourt 115
Varreddes 105
VAT documentation 9
Vaudemanches 118
Vaux (Canal du Nivernais) 160
Vaux-sur-Seine 92
Vauxaillon 112
Velars 156
Venables 90
Venarey-les-Laumes 154
Vendeuil 79
Vendhuile 70
Vénérolles 79
Venette 109
Vénizel 114
Verberie 109
Verbiesles 143
Véretz 195
Vermenton 165

**Vermenton Branch
 (Canal du Nivernais)** 165
Verneuil (Canal du Nivernais) 164
Verneuil (Marne) 133
Verneuil-en-Halatte 109
Verneuil-sur-Seine 92
Vernon 91
Vesaignes-sur-Marne 143
Vésigneul-sur-Marne 137
Vétheuil 91
Veuvey-sur-Ouche 156
Vic-sur-Aisne 114
Vieux-Condé 74
Viéville 142
vignettes 10-11
Vigneux 125
Villegusien-le-Lac 144
Villeneuve-la-Garenne 94
Villeneuve-Saint-Georges 125
La Villeneuve-sur-Vingeanne 145
Villeneuve-sur-Yonne 148
Villenoy 104
Villers-Carbonnel 66
Villers-en-Prayères 115
Villevallier 148
Villiers-sur-Marne 142
Villiers-sur-Yonne 162
Vincelles 160
Vincelottes 160
Viry-Noureuil 71
Vitry-en-Artois 56
Vitry-le-François 138, 140
Vitry-aux-Loges 192
Vitry-sur-Seine 124
VNF *(Voies Navigables de France)* 1, 3-11, 23
Voyennes 83
Vraux 136
Vred 57

Wambrechies 48
Warneton 45 50-53
waterway categories 13-17
Watten 32, 42
Wavrin 47
weather 18
websites 20-21
Wervicq 45

Yonne, river 13, 17, 126, 127, 146-9, 158
Ytres 66

Zuydcoote 28